LORETTE WILMOT LIBRARY
Nazareth College of Rochester

Rochester City Ballet

Makarova: A Dance Autobiography (editor)
Baryshnikov: From Russia to the West

THE GREAT RUSSIAN DANCERS

THE
GREAT
RUSSIAN
DANCERS

Gennady Smakov

ALFRED A. KNOPF NEW YORK 1984

THIS IS A BORZOI BOOK
PUBLISHED BY ALFRED A. KNOPF, INC.

Copyright © 1984 by Gennady Smakov
All rights reserved under International and Pan-American Copyright Conventions.
Published in the United States by Alfred A. Knopf, Inc., New York, and
simultaneously in Canada by Random House of Canada Limited, Toronto.
Distributed by Random House of Canada Limited, Toronto.
Distributed by Random House, Inc., New York.

LIBRARY OF CONGRESS CATALOGING IN PUBLICATION DATA
Smakov, Gennady.
The great Russian dancers.

Bibliography: p.
Includes index.
1. Ballet dancers—Soviet Union—Biography.
I. Title.
GV1785.A1S62 1984   792.8′2′0922 [B]   84-47772
ISBN 0-294-51074-7

Manufactured in the United States of America
First Edition

For my mother,
Olga Smakova,
and for
Tatiana and Alex Liberman

CONTENTS

Les Grandes Tragédiennes

"The Weeping Spirits"

The Ideal Soubrettes and Ingenues

The Decorative Ballerinas

DANSEURS

Dancers Without Category

Danseurs Nobles

The Dancer as "Superman"

ACKNOWLEDGMENTS

IN WRITING this book, I drew on many conversations I had with some of its subjects. I am greatly indebted to Mikhail Baryshnikov, Natalia Makarova, Maya Plisetskaya, Olga Spessivtseva, and Vladimir Vasiliev. My special thanks also to my friend Vera Krasovskaya, whose quotations adorn these pages and whose remarkably well-documented two-volume history of the Russian ballet at the beginning of the twentieth century, unfortunately not yet available in English, was a valuable source of information.

For specific help in working with parts of the manuscript I wish to thank my friends Elena Tchernichova, Helen Atlas, Evgeny Poliakov, and Alexander Minz, and my typist, Lois Abrams. I am also grateful to Helen Atlas and Valery Golovitser for the generosity with which they shared many very rare items from their collections of otherwise unobtainable photographs. In Russia, Evgeny Yanushevich and Vladislav Kostin, as well as many others whose names I prefer not to give for their own safety, provided me with photographic rarities, and I offer all of them my heartfelt thanks. My thanks also go to Catherine Ashmore, Mary Clarke, and Clement Crisp for the photographs they sent from England for inclusion in this book. For their support and care in a time of troubles, I would like to thank Sheldon Atlas, Sally Johnson, Henri and Eugenia Doll, Galina and Mikhail Klugge, Joseph Brodsky, Ludmila Shtern, and Emily Los.

The Great Russian Dancers is dedicated to Tatiana and Alexander Liberman. I wrote the book in their country house in Connecticut, and it was only the care and love of those special people that enabled me to finish it.

Finally, my special thanks to my editors—Robert Gottlieb, Susan Ralston, and Eva Resnikova—whose enthusiasm, professionalism, and unflagging attention to detail were truly exemplary. We worked like a perfect team under Bob's invigorating and inspiring guidance, which never ceases to impress me. His taste, knowledge of ballet, and perfectionism were essential contributions to the creation of this book.

PREFACE

UNLIKE THE drama, which was vitalized by the audacious experiments of Tairov and Meyerhold, classical ballet was never able to develop in Russia as an advanced form of theatrical art. A Russian synthesis of musical theatre and dancing flourished only outside the country, under the aegis of Serge Diaghilev, during the twenty-year life of his Ballets Russes.

In Russia itself, the greatness of ballet has lain in the achievements of those exceptionally gifted dancers whose abundance seems to compensate for the dearth of major choreographers. In nineteenth-century Russia, choreography was dominated by two remarkable Frenchmen, Charles Didelot and Marius Petipa, and the twentieth century has seen a similar paucity of native-born talent—with Mikhail Fokine and George Balanchine as dazzling exceptions. It may be that Russians are deficient in the visual instinct that makes for great stagecraft as well as great painting. But there is no doubt that they are brilliant performers and dancers; no wonder that Nijinsky and Pavlova, Nureyev and Baryshnikov, are household names.

The choice of dancers to include in this volume presented some difficulties. First I put a historical limit on my selection, which begins with the artists of the 1890s. For the previous sixty years, Russian ballet had been dominated by extraordinary foreign-born ballerinas: Taglioni, Elssler, Grisi, Cerrito, Rosatti, Granzow, Dor, Zucchi, Legnani. The local stars, no matter how talented, were eclipsed by the gigantic shadows of the foreigners. Even the most enlightened St. Petersburg balletomanes, who adored Avdotia Istomina, Elena Andreyanova, Martha Muravieva, and Ekaterina Vazem, would never have dared to measure them against Taglioni or Grisi; they remained local treasures, although Andreyanova and Muravieva were occasionally applauded in Paris. The truth is, these exceptionally good dancers were merely footnotes to dance history: for all her airiness and charm, Istomina (eulogized by Pushkin) was never a Russian Taglioni; Andreyanova, the first Russian Giselle, was a far cry from Grisi, the creator of this role; Muravieva and Vazem, for all their virtuosity and steely pointes, lacked artistry and personal projection. The first generation of really great Russian ballerinas came immediately after them—Kschessinskaya, Preobrajenskaya,

Egorova, Karsavina, and, of course, Anna Pavlova, the only one among them who can be considered a genius. It was they who profited by the invasion of the Italian ballerinas, absorbing their new technique and startling the world with a new intensity of projection.

As for male dancing, it was more neglected than nurtured throughout the nineteenth century: division of dancers into three categories—danseur noble, demi-caractère, and *comique*—was still valid, but only the danseurs nobles were developing technically. The Swedish dancer Christian Johanssen, a student of Bournonville, became the first Russian Prince Charmant: the majestic elegance of his movements, his impressive terre-à-terre technique and jumps, were the major Western influence in shaping the character of the Russian danseur noble from the 1840s to the 1860s. Later, the incomparable artistry of Pavel Gerdt and Vasily Tikhomirov enabled them to distinguish themselves amid the predominance of female dancers, and they are presented here as the glorious ancestors of all the classical princes in Russia.

A further limitation on my choice was my decision to exclude all those exceptional Russian-born dancers whose careers developed mainly in the West. Danilova, Toumanova, and Lifar were great performers but their art was shaped beyond the strictly classical Russian tradition, within a new European repertory, in a highly Westernized fashion.

Choosing among the multitude of extraordinary talents and selecting the greatest was difficult. "Greatness" is a disputable matter, and any choice is inevitably colored by the individual preferences of the author. To me, it connotes, first of all, technical mastery or uniqueness of projection, or the combination of both, within the classical repertory that is the heart and soul of Russian ballet. Thus a great dancer is one who excels in the classical repertory above all and whose unique portrayals, virtuosity, and power of projection have extended its range.

Among the host of great dancers there are differences of caliber. Happily, there are certain incontestable names: Pavlova, Nijinsky, Kschessinskaya, Preobrajenskaya, Spessivtseva, Ulanova, Plisetskaya, Makarova, Nureyev, Baryshnikov. These multifaceted artists are the pathfinders who have enriched the ballet lexicon, enhanced the possibilities of choreographic expressivity, and given new insights into the classical roles. Against them we measure the value of all other performers.

But there are exceptional dancers of lesser scope, the creators or interpreters of one or two roles on which they put their unique personal stamp and with which they are often identified. Yuri Soloviev's Blue Bird, Natalia Dudinskaya's Raymonda, Natalia Bessmertnova's Giselle, and Nikita Dolgushin's Albrecht were extraordinary achievements, and their artistic impact remains engraved on the memory of those who were lucky enough to see them. When I recall Bessmertnova's mad scene in *Giselle*, Alla Osipenko's death scene in Igor Chernyshev's *Cleopatra*, or Irina Kolpakova's entrance as Aurora, I re-experience the joy I felt many years ago.

Having made my final selection, I was distressed by the exclusions. Many wonderful dancers who have won international acclaim do not appear in these pages: Nina Timofeyeva, Mikhail Lavrovsky, Maris Liepa, Alexander Godunov. To justify these omissions, I can only point out that these artists excelled within the cumbersome framework of Bolshoi drama-ballet; in the classical repertory, their performances were bland or insignificant. And although I cherish the memory of Lavrovsky's buoyant Spartacus, Timofeyeva's intense Mekhmene-Banu, Liepa's ferocious Crassus, Godunov's wild Tybalt and high-strung Don José, nonetheless I feel these portrayals to be of lesser artistic value than, say, Vasiliev's Basil, Maximova's Kitri, or Osipenko's Lilac Fairy. I have also omitted current stars—Ludmila Semenyaka, Nadezhda Pavlova, and Vyacheslav Gordeyev—all of whom are quite remarkable dancers but not yet inimitable artists.

This book is meant to be something more than a standard ballet history. Besides its purely informative function, it was conceived as an initial attempt to define the major trends in the art of ballet as practiced in Russia and to classify the categories and the types of dancers as they took shape in the golden age of Marius Petipa and as they survived in the much less golden Soviet period.

The idea of organizing the book by stylistic categories was prompted by Giacomo Lauri-Volpi's remarkable book *Voci Parallele* (*Parallel Voices*), in which he scrutinized the vocal types that can be discerned throughout the history of opera. Each operatic voice—be it *hochdramatisch* soprano, *tenore di grazia*, or Verdi baritone—is expected to function within strictly defined vocal boundaries. Most efforts to transcend these limits sooner or later result in damaged

vocal cords and diminished technique. Ballet too has its restrictions, but they are less rigorous. A gifted ballerina, building on solid classical training, can succeed equally in Romantic and academic styles: Margot Fonteyn was glorious as both Giselle and Aurora; Plisetskaya was unforgettable as Myrtha and Raymonda.

Before my principles of classification can be made clear, it is necessary to delve into the rather vague subject of balletic *emploi*. *Emploi* refers to the area of the repertory suited to the individual dancer, within which he may fully realize his potential, both physical and artistic—that is to say, the range of roles suitable to his technique and projection. But this is still a very confusing matter, and even the most knowledgeable authorities, such as Fyodor Lopukhov and Vera Krasovskaya, have failed to clarify the question.

In the final analysis, the adherence to *emploi* in casting ballets maintains the purity of each work's style. Said Marius Petipa, the creator of Russian academicism: "Any style is based on the repetition of means, and the more limited the means, the purer, more evident, the style that is brought about." His motto, in fact, echoed Goethe's "In der Beschränkheit zeigt sich der Meister"—a master reveals himself through self-limitation. This is the hallmark of artistic classicism.

Petipa thought of ballerinas as synonymous with ballet itself. (Male dancers were never in the focus of his attention—they served merely as *porteurs*—supporters—and cavaliers.) It was the proper usage of the ballerina—in other words, the appropriateness of her *emploi*—that provided the purity of style and the true aesthetic bliss of *Giselle*, *Le Corsaire*, or *The Sleeping Beauty*. When the *emploi* is disrupted, Petipa felt, the audience is duped, forced to tolerate an aesthetic surrogate, a falsity that undermined his own efforts as a choreographer. For half a century Petipa worked arduously on the code of rules and restrictions that is so perfectly mirrored in the structure and style of *The Sleeping Beauty*, his most masterful composition. When he created *The Sleeping Beauty*, he also defined the ingredients of balletic *emploi*: physical qualifications, technical equipment or training, and artistic projection. Ideally, these should be maintained in perfect correspondence and harmony; in the balletic practice of Petipa's time, this happened rather seldom.

Petipa himself never wrote down his classifications of dancers, but his opinions and remarks—scattered through his interviews and articles in Russian periodicals—formed the springboard from which I established my own categories. Balletic *emploi* has always been related to the technical thesaurus of classical dance and evolved simultaneously with its development and the increase of choreographic means. In the eighteenth century, when classical technique was still developing, ballet competed with dramatic theatre and borrowed pantomime tricks from it. Not surprisingly, the categories of dancers, both male and female, preserved the theatrical labels that originated in the French dramatic tradition: *tragédienne, ingénue, soubrette, jeune premier, jeune comique*, and the like. The great, albeit drama-oriented, ballet innovator Jean-Georges Noverre, the creator of drama-ballet as a genre, only reinforced the ties of dance with theatre. This relationship prevailed throughout the early decades of the nineteenth century, when balletic *emplois* were still defined in dramatic terms. The decisive breakthrough occurred in the Romantic period, when the technique of soaring jumps and the increase in pointework caused critics and public to divide female dancers into two categories: the aerial ballerinas and the terre-à-terre. The great representatives of the Romantic ballet—Marie Taglioni, Carlotta Grisi, Fanny Elssler, Fanny Cerrito—overwhelmed Russian balletomanes from the 1830s to the 1850s. They differed among themselves, but all of them displayed the precious balance of physique, technical skill, and powerful projection. Taglioni was a master of the jump, a vision of elusive femininity, an aerial ingenue without a developed terre-à-terre technique. The first Giselle, Grisi, was also an aerial ingenue; although she displayed impressive pointework, she was at her best in Jules Perrot's Romantic dramas and comedies. Fanny Elssler was not endowed with a big jump; however, she excelled in *taqueté* variations with a strong demi-caractère flavor. No Russian ballerina in the mid–nineteenth century possessed such a well-balanced combination of artistic qualities: Maria Surovshchikova-Petipa, though an ideally built ingenue, was never a mistress of leaps or turns; Martha Muravieva, while an outstanding terre-à-terre technician, lacked artistry.

In the 1860s, classical technique progressed rapidly due to the evolution of the ballet slipper, which acquired a more solid point, providing ever-increasing stability for the ballerina. Dancers demanded far swifter tempos; gradually the adagio rhythm gave way to allegro, since dancing unsupported on pointe slowly, after the Romantic fashion, was almost impossible. Also in this decade, Saint-Léon and Petipa worked out terre-à-terre technique, and Ekaterina Vazem proved to be the first Russian virtuoso, reveling in various turns on pointe and displaying the power of her steely toes. Virtuosity became the hallmark of Russian style, and the differences between the aerial and the terre-à-terre dancer were less evident.

Petipa's choreography for *La Bayadère* was the manifesto of a new classical style in which the aerial and the terre-à-terre elements blended into an artistic unity. The earlier, Romantic style now only shaded the brilliance of technical tours de force. In the 1860s and 1870s, artistic projection was overshadowed: like an inspired conjuror, Petipa invented tricks that saturated his ballets with a heretofore unseen virtuosity, now the main value of a performance. This tendency became even more pronounced when, in the mid-1880s, the army of Italian virtuosos introduced their new technique, in response to which Petipa revamped and enriched the classical lexicon he had already established. Having absorbed the best of Italian virtuosity, Petipa's classical style took on the last touch of finish, and Russian academic ballet was born. In the 1880s, a generation of Russian ballerinas was formed and fostered that would outstrip the Italians and eventually reign supreme on the St. Petersburg stage. These dancers did not make much distinction between the two former types of ballerina.

The beginning of the twentieth century saw the appearance of the lyrical ballerina, one in whom aerial and terre-à-terre qualities blended; but, somehow, the poetic understatement the lyrical ballerina was supposed to convey only indirectly referred to the old Romantic style of Grisi and Elssler. This type of ballerina had an ideally proportioned body. In the early 1900s, Pavlova epitomized such perfection. She was the first, and possibly the most flawless, lyrical ballerina, excelling in the poetry of fleeting moods and feelings ranging from sadness and sorrow to a tragic intensity. The Romantic lineage manifested itself in her soaring jump, high extension, and expressive arms, their movements less rigid than the academic canon demanded. As a rule, the lyrical ballerina did not distinguish herself by her virtuosity or bravura technique: Pavlova, Egorova, and Ulanova never displayed stunning turns, fouettés, or special skill in allegro. Compared with them, Makarova seems a remarkably accomplished technician and also a multifaceted one: she has a gift for comedy (a rare quality among lyrical ballerinas) and a particular affinity for modernist expressiveness. But the true domain of the lyrical ballerina remains Giselle, Odette, the Sylphide, and the romantic heroines such as Juliet and Manon. She rarely succeeds as Aurora, Odile, or Raymonda.

The virtuoso ballerinas who appeared in the 1890s were

actually terre-à-terre dancers with good academic technique. In this group are found Olga Preobrajenskaya and Matilda Kschessinskaya; their descendant was Natalia Dudinskaya. Unlike the lyrical ballerinas, who were often moving or enchanting in their frail femininity, the virtuosos dazzle us with the perfection of their flamboyant technique and pyrotechnics. They are brilliantly equipped to dance for the sake of dancing, without expressing any message but their own joy in what they do. Virtuoso ballerinas are not necessarily well built—their legs are often short, which makes it easier for them to execute turns at breakneck speed. They often lack a big jump and fluidity of movements, so they can seldom excel in adagio; rather, they are the queens of allegro technique. They breathe freely in drama-ballets such as *Esmeralda* and *Laurencia* and in *The Sleeping Beauty* and *Raymonda*, which call for sheer virtuosity. The doomed romantic heroines of the Giselle-Odette type are not for them. Occasionally, as was the case with Preobrajenskaya and Kschessinskaya, they reveal a propensity for comedy and sparkle as Lise and Swanilda.

Some outstanding ballerinas have managed to combine happily the qualities of both these types, but it was not this hybrid conjunction that distinguished their artistic profile. It was Russian impetuosity, a regal manner, and emotional range that was central to the style of Ekaterina Geltzer, Marina Semyonova, and Lidia Ivanova. I have united them in a special group as ballerinas of a uniquely Russian style. Semyonova, both a lyrical and a virtuoso phenomenon, was a perfect blend, while Geltzer and Ivanova relied more on virtuoso tricks and bravura; but each of them was an impetuous and fiery performer of a species that seems to be extinct today. It is true that this utterly Russian verve and energy was not alien to Pavlova, for instance; but no one else poured forth these qualities, no one else struck the audience, with the impact of Geltzer, Semyonova, and Ivanova. In their steely pointework, whirling turns, and regal poses, they are sisters of the virtuosos. Geltzer and Semyonova had a good jump, but neither *Giselle* nor *La Sylphide* nor *Les Sylphides* was their realm. The lyricism of Semyonova and Geltzer was less nuanced and poignant than Ulanova's or Pavlova's. But both were magnificent as Aurora, Odile, and Raymonda.

In some respects, Sofia Fedorova, Alla Shelest, and Maya Plisetskaya were only distantly related to these exemplars of Russian flamboyance—Plisetskaya's impetuosity was of a different sort. At first, these ballerinas seem to have little in common: Fedorova was famous not for her pointework but for her expressivity; Shelest was the epit-

ome of Petersburg academicism; Plisetskaya displayed a highly individual technique which deviated from Petipa's standards. But what united these three was their tragic intensity; each was unique as a dancing *tragédienne*. Fedorova was the unrivaled interpreter of Gorsky's choreographic expressionism. Shelest was a consummate classicist, but whatever role she undertook was imbued with charged emotions, tragic theatricality, and high-voltage energy. The spectrum of Plisetskaya's dance gift was richer and broader than either of theirs. She colored her Odette and her Dying Swan with a tragic tonality, but she was also a master of bravura. The intensity of her tragic heroines was worlds away from the vivacity of her Kitri, the role to which she imparted all of her own untrammeled sense of joy.

Vera Trefilova, Irina Kolpakova, and Ekaterina Maximova represent the type of ballerina that I call "the ideal ingénue." Technically, they were very close to the virtuosos. Romantic ballets are not their element; all three danced *Giselle* and *Swan Lake*, but their characterizations were bland and characterless. Their domain is academic dance, which also allowed them to dazzle in classical ballets (Kolpakova could have been an ideal interpreter of Balanchine). Trefilova and Kolpakova were frequently accused of lacking a strong individual personality, although Maximova charmed the audience with the soubrette appeal that so mischievously tinged her characterizations of Kitri and Cinderella. All three ballerinas excelled as Aurora.

Olga Spessivtseva and Natalia Bessmertnova were of an entirely different mold. Although they too danced Aurora, it was not this role that brought them fame. By nature, they were both akin to the lyrical ballerinas—their physiques were utterly feminine and frail; their technique was best suited to Romantic roles. It was their spectral presence that made their stage images so special, invariably conveying a sense of piercing sorrow close to what the German Romantic poets implied by *Weltschmerz*. Talking of Spessivtseva, Akim Volynsky aptly called her "the weeping spirit." Spessivtseva and Bessmertnova were the most mournful and otherworldly Russian ballerinas, a far cry from the virtuosos, the flamboyant stars, the ingenues. Their one great role was Giselle, on which they each put a slightly pathological, supernatural stamp. While both failed in Petipa's academic canon, they were uniquely successful evoking the poetry of vague premonitions and ghostly, doomed femininity.

Tamara Karsavina and Alla Osipenko were ballerinas one might characterize as "decorative." Each of them could have been called "the one and only" had they not displayed a number of mutual qualities: their strength lay in the expressiveness of beautiful bodies with exquisite lines, their stylistic sensitivity, and their ability to subjugate themselves to the will of the choreographer. Their classical technique could not be compared: while Karsavina's technique is still disputable, Osipenko epitomized the Kirov's academic purity of style. Nevertheless, Karsavina became the emblem of Diaghilev's spectacular innovations, while Osipenko conveyed better than anyone else the appeal and essence of Jakobson's expressionism. Neither excelled in the Petipa repertory. They impressed their audiences with their reserved manner, eschewing native Russian spontaneity; both were highly Westernized, refined ballerinas whose dance images appealed to the senses and who teased the imagination with enigmatic power.

MALE DANCERS pose fewer problems for classification, because male dancing is less elaborate and diversified than the mature art of the ballerina. Moreover, the number of major classical male roles is limited: Siegfried, Albrecht, Desiré, and Jean de Brienne are quite conventional princes, and their collective image calls for a specific quality of nobility.

In his essay "On Balletic Emploi," Fyodor Lopukhov divided male dancers into two main categories. The danseurs nobles were tall and endowed with softly curving, longish "Apollonian" muscles. With their flexible plié they excelled in regal, flowing movements. This *emploi* traces its lineage to the childhood of classical ballet, the era of the *fêtes galantes* at Versailles. In Lopukhov's second category were the heroic dancers, distinguished by their "Herculean" muscles and a less soft plié. The heroic repertoire included the drama-ballet roles in Gorsky's choreodramas (e.g., Mato in *Salammbo*) and in the socialist-realist spectacles that became popular in the Soviet era. Lopukhov never elucidated the extent to which the technical qualifications of the male dancer might shape his *emploi*. The problem seems to be complicated by the fact that male technique and virtuosity, in particular, are a comparatively recent phenomenon.

Oddly enough, male dancers reigned supreme in ballet two hundred years ago. The eighteenth century saw the unparalleled virtuosity of Auguste Vestris, whose artistic essence was so imaginatively interpreted by Mikhail Baryshnikov in Leonid Jakobson's cameo ballet *Vestris*. But as female technique progressed swiftly, male dancing was relegated to the periphery, and for half a century—until the mid-1860s—the Western and Russian ballet worlds witnessed its decline. Pointe technique helped the ballerina to gain an impalpable lightness with which her male partners could not compete. The champion of the Romantic ballet, Théophile Gautier, remarked that seeing a male dancer turn in the air or perform beats was simply ludicrous. No wonder that in nineteenth-century France, there was only one great dancer of Vestris's caliber, Jules Perrot. By the mid-1860s, the casting of ballerinas in male parts en travesti was almost universal, although in Russia, perhaps because of the prevalent puritanical attitude toward sexual ambiguity, this practice never caught on.

Pavel Gerdt, who appeared in the mid-1860s, was the first Russian danseur noble. Thirty years later his pupil Vassily Tikhomirov followed his example and conquered Moscow with the elegance of his manners and exuberant technique. The abilities demanded of the danseur noble increased rather slowly until 1887, when the appearance of Enrico Cecchetti suddenly set new standards of virtuosity. Cecchetti himself looked nothing like the ideal danseur noble: squat, bowlegged, less than classically handsome, he nevertheless dumbfounded his Russian colleagues with his unprecedented feats: the grand pirouette, totally unknown to the Russians, and intricate combinations of tours en l'air with jetés or assemblés. The impact of Cecchetti's virtuosity is hard to overestimate; each of Gerdt's and Tikhomirov's followers—Nicolas Legat, Samuil Andrianov, and Mikhail Obukhov in St. Petersburg, Laurent Novikov in Moscow—either imitated Cecchetti or learned from him as a coach. Cecchetti's classes and performances (his stunning Blue Bird in particular) became the real source of knowledge and inspiration for many generations of male dancers. Danseurs nobles brought their new flamboyant technique to the old, choreographically thin roles of Siegfried and Albrecht and began to compete with the artistry of the leading ballerinas. This expansion of male technique evolved further (and quite rapidly) during the Soviet era, especially in the 1920s, when dancers, encouraged by the progress in sports, set new standards of skill and prowess for themselves.

From the 1930s to the 1970s, there were three noble dancers who, each in his own way, epitomized the image of Prince Charming: Konstantin Sergeyev, Nikita Dolgushin, and Yuri Soloviev. Physically, Sergeyev and Dolgushin were ideal; their technical potential was indisputable; their stage presence, though quite dissimilar, always suggested something bigger and nobler than life. Sergeyev's characterizations breathed the energy of Romanticism, bringing to the fore emotional intensity and passion. Dolgushin gave his protagonists an intellectual dimension; they seemed philosophers and men of great insight rather than passionate romantics. As for Yuri Soloviev, technically he definitely outdid both Sergeyev and Dolgushin, but his physique was of a less noble cut, and his projection never achieved emotional heights or piercing lyricism.

Many qualities of the danseurs nobles seem to be refracted through the performing art of Mikhail Mordkin, Pierre Vladimiroff, Alexei Yermolayev, Vakhtang Chabukiani, and Vladimir Vasiliev, whom I have called the "supermen." At first glance, their artistic profiles and technical qualifications seem quite different. Mordkin was a "dancing actor" rather than an impeccably trained classicist; like Sofia Fedorova, he excelled at bringing Gorsky's choreodramas to life and imbuing them with powerful dramatic vitality. Vladimiroff was an extraordinary product of Petersburg academicism, although his flamboyant and indomitable temperament often caused him to explode the rigid confines of the noble style. Chabukiani and Yermolayev were daring virtuosos, technical groundbreakers in the thirties and forties. More than anyone else, they must be credited for the development of a virtuosity, especially with jumps, and the creation of the choreographic vocabulary that was used by generations of Soviet dancers. These two invested classical dance with the dynamism and showiness that became emblematic of the Bolshoi style. Vladimir Vasiliev, Chabukiani's and Yermolayev's direct successor, was a far more finely trained virtuoso. During the sixties he extended their accomplishments with unprecedented feats. And, not unlike Dolgushin among danseurs nobles, Vasiliev was the intellectual among the "supermen," bringing mental energy and purpose to each part he performed. His charged interpretations always endowed the choreography with profound consistency. But it is the special dynamism, vitality, and buoyancy so characteristic of their stage images that unites all these artists. By their technical innovations, energy, and virility they greatly contributed to the creation of that special effervescent style that captivated the Western world during the 1950s and 60s.

Finally, there are three dancers who are united as "dancers without a category": Vaslav Nijinsky, Rudolf Nureyev, and Mikhail Baryshnikov. These three are unique luminaries in ballet annals; each is a legend, and possibly, as with any legend, each is beyond the customary definitions. To a certain degree, they combined certain qualities of the danseurs nobles and the "supermen." Possibly owing to this precious amalgamation, each became synonymous with male dance and, at the same time, bigger than classical ballet itself. Like Nijinsky, Baryshnikov is of short stature: though well-proportioned, he lacks that special regality of feature and line that gives a dancer a noble and imposing look. The unprepossessing appearances of these two dancers, which would seem to indicate a demi-caractère *emploi*, belie their limitless technical prowess, which put each of them ahead of the aesthetic criteria of his time. They set the standard for St. Petersburg-Leningrad classicism. Nureyev, on the other hand, looks much more the noble prince, but his technique is not "neat"; it is very unorthodox and is often subjugated to his fiery temperament—a trait he shares with the "supermen." It is not surprising that at the dawn of his career Nureyev was invariably likened to Chabukiani.

But there is another quality that distinguishes these rare dancers from both danseurs nobles and "supermen": the incomparable artistic sensitivity that allowed them to master many styles so triumphantly. Baryshnikov revels in the works of Balanchine, Robbins, and Tharp; Nureyev made himself into an exponent of both Ashton's neoclassicism and Graham's expressionism. As an extension of Nijinsky's plasticity, his own highly iconoclastic choreographic compositions were a foray into the modernistic lexicons central to the twentieth-century ballet. Sadly, Nijinsky's premature artistic demise prevented him from exploring the possibilities of his unique body and overwhelming the world with its revelations.

As with any system of artistic classification, mine cannot be imposed too strictly or rigidly. Nevertheless I hope these "choreographic parallels" will shed light on what has constituted the perpetual appeal of Russian ballet, its grandeur in the past, and its achievement—and decline—today.

THE
LYRICAL
BALLERINAS

Anna Pavlova · Lubov Egorova
Galina Ulanova · Natalia Makarova

Giselle, 1909

ANNA PAVLOVA

ALTHOUGH Pavlova's dancing was somehow resistant to the camera, an experienced eye can easily discern in her imperfect films the manifestation of her genius, despite the slipshod, amateurish corps de ballet framing her in the distorted *Les Sylphides*; despite the "campy" quality of *La Nuit* (set to Anton Rubinstein's schmaltzy music), with its unbearable swinging garlands, seemingly the last wreaths on the grave of the Belle Epoque; despite the odalisquelike tilt of her torso and the decadent mannerism of her arms in *The Dying Swan*. The "steel and élastique," as Isadora Duncan once characterized Pavlova's image, the power of her preparation and attack, the vertiginous buoyancy of her flight—all are there, as are her fabled arabesque, ethereal and sculpturesque; her face in *Dying Swan*, poignantly transfigured by the anticipation of death as a release from the torments of her existence; the dedication and total self-confidence in her larger-than-life projection.

Pavlova's uniqueness seems to be derived from the inseparability of her life and her art and from the sense of identity with which the balletic stage endowed her. Her colleagues and friends enjoyed love affairs, happily or haplessly arranged their family lives, regarded ballet as an exciting addition to life as a job, a craft, a means of survival. But for Pavlova, ballet was an obsession, as poetry was for Emily Dickinson or music was for Wagner. It was the only outlet for her inner life, her sexual fantasies and dreams; it was her second, yet true, identity. The pent-up energy of her unfulfilled emotional life and her subconscious resources poured forth with a devastating impact on her audiences, who wanted her to dance forever and never leave the stage. No wonder that many of those who were fortunate enough to see Pavlova "building up her fugitive yet enticing imaginary worlds on stage," as Sergei Khudekov once put it, were subsequently her artistic followers: Tamara Toumanova, Ruth Page, Robert Helpmann, Frederick Ashton, Margot Fonteyn, and hundreds of others.

Pavlova's life, which she herself illuminated with the colors of legend, resembled a kind of Cinderella fairy tale. In many books, including the spurious biography by Victor Dandré, we are presented with an idealized portrait. The actual contours of her life are bleached in the dazzling light of her universal glory; fiction prevails. The date of her birth

and the names of her parents are still uncertain, but apparently she was born on January 31, 1881, in Ligovo, a suburb of St. Petersburg. In 1909, when the ballerina sparkled as the brightest diamond in the Maryinsky crown, the *St. Petersburg Gazette* unscrupulously reported that she was the illegitimate offspring of Lubov Pavlova, an impoverished laundress, and a banker named Poliakov, and that she had been adopted by her mother's second husband, Matvey Pavlov.

According to Pavlova's own memoirs, her invincible passion for ballet was first aroused by her impressions of *The Sleeping Beauty* at the Maryinsky Theatre in the 1890s. Her first attempt to enter the famed Imperial School on Theatre Street failed miserably. Her ethereal yet sickly slightness, overdeveloped, high-arched feet, too-long arms, and frail, straight neck made her resemble "a puny giraffe," as she put it. By no means did she look like a budding ballerina in an era when the Maryinsky standard favored brawny, strongly shaped flesh.

She was finally accepted as a student in 1892. Her Cinderella tale continued within the walls of the school. A slightly stylized portrait of the young Niura (as she was then called) is drawn in several memoirs—an introverted, lonely *"petite sauvage"* whose fellow students nicknamed her "the Broom" for her gauntness and her ungregarious attitude. Apparently it was only Pavlova's early unsociability that impressed her instructors, for her lack of turnout, her weak knees, and her imperfect placement intimated mediocrity rather than a promising talent.

At the time of Pavlova's graduation her physique was still more than controversial. Her narrow feet, with their overly arched insteps, and her thin ankles lacked the strength for good pointe work. Bearing her long-limbed and flexible body, her insteps could not easily sustain the balance necessary for high-speed pirouettes or fouettés. Instead, endowed with high extension and enormous ballon, softly soaring in flight and soundless on landing, she perfectly embodied the "lyrical Romantic ballerina," with a modest potential in terre-à-terre technique. She could execute flawless développés, arabesques, and attitudes, as well as soft cabrioles, swift ronds de jambe, sissonnes, and jetés en tournant. Another quality that especially distinguished her from her colleagues was her flair for character dance. According to Sergei Khudekov, "she was a great master of character, genre and stylized folk dances," in particular excelling in the Spanish, Russian, and Greek forms. In Russian dances she was the only rival of Ekaterina Geltzer.

Pavlova's sundry debuts were both inspired and amateurish. She looked like a weakling in the throng of Italian and Russian virtuosi who overwhelmed the St. Petersburg balletomanes with their impeccable academic technique and circus tricks on stage. Pavlova's attempts to outdo them at times resulted in disaster: during one of her student performances she spun around so energetically that she finished up sitting on the prompter's box with her back to the audience. On another occasion, as a soloist at the Maryinsky, she struggled so desperately with the Fairy Candide's hops on pointe in *The Sleeping Beauty* that she rechoreographed Petipa's patterns, to the great astonishment of the old maestro.

Nevertheless, her graduation performance on April 11, 1899, in *The False Dryads*, Pavel Gerdt's cameo ballet set to Pugni's music, drew the attention of Nikolai Bezobrazov, a patriarch of St. Petersburg's ballet critics. He praised the debutante for her natural ballon, lingering arabesques, and frail femininity.

Her subsequent appearances in pas de deux and pas de trois from *La Fille mal gardée*, *Camargo*, and *Marco Bomba* and her variations in *Coppélia* and *Le Roi Candaule*, which she danced from 1899 to 1902, merely confirmed her reputation as a good soloist. To Pavlova's credit, she used these years to increase her technical means. As she strengthened her feet, increased her extension, and developed coordination under the tutelage of Christian Johannsen and Gerdt, and later with Catarina Beretta, an Italian teacher, Pavlova's special quality became more and more visible.

It may have struck some as atavistic that at the height of Petipa's canonized academicism, Pavlova's manner of dancing seemed to revert to the standards of Romantic ballet under Jules Perrot and Arthur Saint-Léon. Unlike Kschessinskaya, who wrote choreographic poems through her flawless technique and presented balletic drama as stylized action, Pavlova seemed to have restored the lost vitality of old Romantic ballets. The effect of her dancing on the audience was augmented by the expressiveness and ecstasy of her total emotional involvement. This old-fashioned dedication to the dance, characteristic of such legendary figures of the Romantic era as Carlotta Grisi and Fanny Elssler, in many ways precluded the virtuosity and

academic purity in performance that were then regarded at the Maryinsky as synonymous with real art.

Like the public at large, the enlightened balletomanes and critics were puzzled at first by the peculiar combination of Pavlova's enthusiasm and her obvious neglect of academic rules: she frequently danced with bent knees, disregarded the purity of balletic positions, and moved her arms in a fluid, Romantic style which did not conform to Petipa's rigid code of port de bras. Curiously enough, these particular qualities, belittled or disparaged by the critics at her debut in 1899, began to enthrall them three years later. In their rapture they went so far as to see in the curve of Pavlova's instep "all the yearnings of the Russian soul," as André Levinson once remarked.

But essentially Pavlova's style had not changed. Impelled by criticism and by her determination to excel, she worked day after day to improve her technique under the guidance of Pavel Gerdt and Nicolas Legat. Only a few at the Maryinsky realized that virtuosity per se ought never to be Pavlova's ambition. Her imitation of Pierina Legnani's thirty-two fouettés, which she attempted in class in 1903, only infuriated Gerdt. As Walford Hyden recollected, Gerdt almost shook her in his rage: "Leave acrobatics to others, Anna. . . . It is positively more than I can bear to see the pressure such steps put upon your delicate muscles and the arch of your foot. . . . I beg you never to try again to imitate those who are physically stronger than you. You must realize that your daintiness and fragility are your greatest assets. You should always do the kind of dancing which brings out your own rare qualities instead of trying to win praise by mere acrobatic tricks."

Petipa also was quite aware that Pavlova's unique appeal could not be separated from her technical limitations. He saw her as a dancing reincarnation of the Romantic era, a spectre from his own youth. Whether influenced by her admirer and future manager, Victor Dandré (Petipa's devoted friend), or guided by her own rare intuition, Pavlova would cling to the old maestro, listening to his advice.

Coaching her in *The Naiad and the Fisherman*, *La Bayadère*, and *Giselle*, Petipa strongly believed in Pavlova's ability to infuse these old masterpieces with new vitality. Moreover, in his view, her seemingly old-fashioned style, reminiscent of the 1840s, might eventually look very much up-to-date, with decisive consequences for the development of classical ballet in the twentieth century. Petipa's instinct did not err. The ballerina needed only the chance to demonstrate her unusual gift.

Pavlova's biographers somehow underestimate the fact that her debut as Nikiya in *La Bayadère* took place during her third season at the Maryinsky. This seems almost inconceivable in view of Kschessinskaya's total control over the repertory. Had luck not played into Pavlova's hands, she might have shared Lubov Egorova's fate, her talent unrevealed until the second decade of her career. As Egorova recalled: "In 1902, due to her pregnancy, Kschessinskaya had to find her replacement in *La Bayadère*, certainly one who would be unable to overshadow her in one of her illustrious parts. She fixed her choice on Pavlova, whom she had simply despised as a ballerina, saying, 'Poor thing, she can hardly stand on pointe.' . . . Moreover, [Kschessinskaya] herself undertook the coaching of Pavlova for her debut, and this gesture of dubious generosity caused a storm of approval from the critics. Kschessinskaya strongly believed Pavlova would fail; but, against her expectations, Pavlova scored an enormous success." In fact, her performance turned her into a Maryinsky star overnight. As Nikiya, she continually reaffirmed her lyrical and tragic gifts, from her debut in 1902 to her last *Bayadère* in 1913.

When, at the end of 1902, Kschessinskaya rejoined the Maryinsky, she found herself an unwilling witness to Pavlova's greatness. Possibly for the first time on the Maryinsky stage, the role of Nikiya was seen not as a skillful but impersonal stylization or as a combination of dance sequences and contrived mime scenes but as a dramatic unity, permeated with tragic intensity and consistency in terms of "various feelings and their intermingling transitions," as Pavlova herself put it. Pavlova's whole approach struck the viewer as breathtakingly new. She compensated for the shortcomings of her technique with her innate sense of stagecraft in the mime scenes and her keen sensitivity to Romantic style in the Kingdom of the Shades scene.

The dramatic impact and neo-Romantic mannerism that were to flourish during the Diaghilev era in European ballet seemed to be foretold by Pavlova's Nikiya. Her 1902 performance overwhelmed Diaghilev, who was still germinating his daring conquest of the European audience. The new qualities of her interpretation can be discerned in Akim Volynsky's inspired (if slightly florid) description:

> Covered with a veil, she made her appearance on top of the staircase leading to the vestibule of an Indian temple and froze there for a second. This moment alone conveyed her art, full of temperament and inspiration. She knew how to stand immobile to the accompaniment of murmuring string instruments, wailing violins, and the sighs of the entire orchestra. She descended slowly toward the footlights and after a few measures of music lifted her dark veil. The roaring applause shook the theatre, but this thunderous ecstasy quickly subsided at the first sounds of a captivating melody. How irresistible Pavlova was at this moment! Two thick black braids, interlaced with pearls, rested heavily on her shoulders; reddish gold discs, bound with wires, adorned her hair. Her head was beautiful, unique in the expressive features of her dark-skinned face, the fiery specks in her black, almond-shaped eyes blazing under arched brows. Golden bracelets and glittering cords hung along her body and twined around her arms. Her blue attire shimmered with sparkling sequins.
>
> The Fire Dance commenced as a choreographic ritual, channeling the beauty of lines and inspired poses into the flowing, measured andante. The dance did not abound in intricate patterns; it was compact, even limited, still corresponding to the style of Petipa's early masterpiece. The ballerina would nervously thrust her bent knees upward when circling around the stage on pointe. Among them one sequence was particularly striking: while she stretched her leg backward, the ballerina seemed to roll her torso up into a ball and then draw herself slowly up to her full height. This slow extension of the entire body, to the accompaniment of the languid violin music, seemed to resemble a young tree passing through the whole cycle of growth, accumulating strength to straighten itself in full bloom before the audience. Conveying so enticing and meaningful a theatricality requires the combination of impeccably classical feet, a supple waist, and a well-positioned head guiding the entire movement. In Pavlova's interpretation this moment was particularly impressive: the tension of her body, suggesting the inner strain, passionate impulses, and will, discharged slowly to subside and release her torso, arms, and feet for a graceful pose. The ballerina imbued the movement's snakelike character with the fire and strength of her Slavic temperament, calling to mind not so much the submissive character of a blooming or dying plant as animal exultation, equally ravishing on earth and in the air.

Another description by Volynsky, of Pavlova's dance with the snake in Act III, stresses the innovative qualities she brought to her characterization of Nikiya in 1902:

With broad gestures, she races onto the plaza, coming to a stop before the attentive and loving gaze of the warrior Solor. Her blue cloak is removed from her. Wringing her hands above her head, she rocks first to the right, then to the left, closes her eyes, and with a deep sigh springs to her toes and traces diagonals of arabesques. Then she weaves from side to side, freezing on pointe. Her figure is full of Oriental languor and the love that devours her like a disease. Now she throws herself toward those ranged about the throne of the maharajah—his subjects, his daughter Gamzatti. But her gaze, filled with alarm and love, is directed toward Solor. He cannot withstand the emotional onslaught and turns away, racked by pangs of conscience. After all, he traduced his own love for Nikiya by obeying the maharajah. As if by force, the bayadère is tossed into the air, her jeté entrelacé cutting the air, lands on her knee, sharply bends into a grand port de bras, again takes wing in a jeté, and freezes in arabesque.

The slave of Princess Gamzatti extends a basket of flowers to the bayadère, who, as if sensing her impending death, begins a cascade of tours. She slips the basket onto her head, plucks one flower, another . . . ready to toss it to Solor, when suddenly she reels, tearing away with her thin fingers the snake that has fastened itself to her shoulder.

The High Brahmin extends the antidote toward her. Nikiya shakes her head. Already weakened, she raises her hand to the heavens and looks at Solor, pale as a sheet. For the last time, she springs up on pointe; then, like a flower cut down with a scythe, she sprawls on the stage.

After *La Bayadère*, Pavlova asserted herself on the Maryinsky stage as a synthesis of inspired dance and stylized plastique, which was enhanced by her extreme frailty and lightness. More and more her dancing was likened to the dancing of 1840, when Romantic ballet reigned supreme in Europe and Marie Taglioni triumphed in Russia. "The old etching comes to life on stage, smooths out the tutu, and effortlessly enters the domain of abstract dancing. Pavlova is a dance of the Shade." These words are typical of Pavlova's reviews after *La Bayadère*.

In 1903 Pavlova essayed *Giselle*, interpreting it not as an old, elegiac poem but as a tragedy. The intensity of her portrayal grew out of her powerful projection, breaking through both mime and dance sequences, yet differently orchestrated in the two acts. The strength of Pavlova's Giselle derived mostly from the consistency of drama and extreme emotion that permeated both her dancing and her acting. André Levinson poetically described her mad scene, abounding in details that were the essence of Pavlova's early artistry:

> She stands right at the front of the stage. Her face is fixed in a look of estrangement, a blank expression. She is plucking the petals of a daisy, telling her fortune, seeming to know already that it will come out "He loves me not." Hastily tossing away the crumpled petals, almost in anger, she leans on the arm of an invisible lover and, oblivious, dances on her unsteady legs. Doing coupés and glissades, she tries to catch the rhythm of her recent dance with Albrecht. But the rhythm slips away. It is as if Giselle were gripped by despair over the fact that it is impossible to return to the past, that all is forever lost. And she races around in a circle past the villagers, who are speechless with fear.
>
> Abruptly, she stops short at Albrecht's discarded sword—a mocking reminder of the chivalrous nobility of her beloved, who turned out to be false. She shivers at the sound of metal, which breaks through to her confused consciousness and calls forth an association with death. Giselle circles feverishly, as if she were already doomed to the death symbolized by the sword. She instinctively strains to break out of the circle; but the sword, which she holds by the blade, describes loop after loop. And Giselle, in a panic, tries to flee from the serpentine weaving of the sword hilt and at the same time, as if enchanted, does not take her eyes off its shimmering cross. The cross . . . the grave . . . death . . . these merge in her weakening consciousness into a single fateful association. She will not escape death—she raises the sword high in her hands and flies forward onto its point, as if racing to her end. [Hilarion] tears the sword from Giselle's hands. She staggers, as if the blade had been pulled from her heart. She flings herself toward Albrecht and glances boldly into his eyes. Whatever it is that she sees there—repentance, compassion, or a reminder of their former love—causes her to hold herself upright, triumphantly—only to collapse in the same instant at his feet.

In Act II Pavlova was the first ballerina to emphasize the idea of forgiveness beyond the grave as a mystic basis for peace and transfiguration. And her contemporaries did not remain indifferent to her daring message. Her powerful

Top: (left) Kitri in *Don Quixote*, 1900; (right) Flora in *The Awakening of Flora* (Petipa and Ivanov), 1900
Right: Lise in *La Fille mal gardée*, 1909

OPPOSITE
Top: Flora, 1900
Bottom: (left) Vint-Anta in *Pharaoh's
Daughter*, 1906; (right) *Russian Dance*,
1910s

Above: (left) *Invitation to the Dance*, 1913;
(right) Lise in *The Magic Flute*, 1901
Right: The Panaderos in *Raymonda*, 1905

Chopiniana, 1908

The Dying Swan, 1910

Above: *Bacchanale*, with Laurent
Novikov, 1913
Right: *Dragonfly*, 1915

projection of this theme compelled André Levinson to remark: "Pavlova's dancing is beyond critical appraisal, which is unavoidably superficial and fragmentary. Its lofty poetry cannot be accounted for by psychological insights or pure technique. Nor does it refer bluntly to Taglioni's tradition, since Taglioni's charm was rumored to have stemmed mostly from the innocent, asexual appeal of her appearance. The Taglionism is but one of the innumerable facets of Pavlova's artistry, as intricate as the contemporary mind."

When he referred to the "intricacy" of Pavlova's artistry, Levinson meant those various meanings that her image suggested and that she saturated with her emotional energy. These poured forth lavishly, at times to the detriment of academic dance technique. In his unpublished memoirs her colleague Nikolai Soliannikov recalled: "Pavlova's dances never allowed one to distinguish what kind of arabesque she was performing or to be aware of which arm should be outstretched with which leg. She lived through her dancing, spoke through it, and each step was not abstract or meaningless but a precise manifestation of joy, love, anger, or coquetry, suitable to the action of the moment."

But there was something indefinable in her dancing, something more than the eye usually caught: within the confines of the classical technique, Pavlova knew how to imbue each element with so many emotional shadings that their unity resisted immediate perception. During the performance and after, the enticing yet inscrutable forms and meanings of her dances haunted and teased the imagination. And that was precisely Pavlova's miracle.

No wonder that Pavlova's many roles, particularly Giselle and Nikiya, revealed themselves to the critics and the audience like profound books, inexhaustible in their depth of meanings. In her first *Giselle* especially the twenty-three-year-old ballerina displayed a strikingly new approach—one that would become emblematic of the twentieth century, which was intent on revising the classical legacy.

Referring to Levinson's and Volynsky's prose poems on Pavlova, Vera Krasovskaya noted the way Pavlova transcended the rigid basics of dance principles—for instance, the en dehors and en dedans positions:

What Fokine subsequently took as a direct visual offspring for the Moor-Petrushka antithesis had manifested its essence through Pavlova's dance in terms of expressivity and musicality: the sparkling, explosive en dehors as opposed to the lusterless, warm, and opaque en dedans. She managed to unearth numberless shad-

ings within each of them by rendering them obvious in pirouettes and elusively fugitive in ronds de jambe. She rejected their one-colored monotony but blended them on her palette the way she orchestrated the juxtaposition of croisé and effacé. The closed, elusive croisés and the open, defiantly triumphant effacés played iridescently, enjoying their poetic license. In her variations these positions intermingled variously in succession, being subjected to the changing rhythms of flashing beats, soaring and lingering jetés, or the untrammeled exultation of pas de basque.

In this unparalleled variety of shadings lay the genius that made Pavlova unique among ballerinas at the turn of the twentieth century. She imprinted a special mark on each role, however small: the Naiad in *The Naiad and the Fisherman*, Medora in *Le Corsaire*, Aspicia in *The Pharaoh's Daughter* (first in Gorsky's version, then in Petipa's original), or Diane in *Le Roi Candaule*. In each of these roles Pavlova demonstrated the quality that the critic Yuri Beliayev so incisively described: "She dances with her soul. At one moment she throws herself at the audience and in the next she draws back. She blossoms at the footlight like some fabulous fern, and then she shrinks in the fashion of a *mimosa pudica*. She conducts an intimate conversation of the heart, plotting an uneven line on the chart of her artistic pulse." An apparent exception was her Aurora in *The Sleeping Beauty*. The terre-à-terre technique required for this role did not permit any of those Romantic liberties in which Pavlova excelled. She concentrated on mastering the academic patterns, which finally eluded her. She succeeded only in Act III, as Aurora's vision; curiously enough, she was also successful in the mime part of the Lilac Fairy.

She also shone in character parts. "Fire, zest, soaring enthusiasm, and temperament" equally distinguished her classical Spanish heroines in *The Fairy Doll*, *Paquita*, and *Don Quixote* and the purely character figures of *Raymonda's* panaderos, *Carmen's* fandango, and *The Nutcracker's* Chocolate variation.

In Spanish dance, supported by even a perfunctory plot, as in *Paquita* or *Don Quixote*, Pavlova was a prodigy of dance exuberance. As Kitri, she was equally brilliant in the romanticized style of Don Quixote's dream and in the demi-caractère sequences. Soliannikov recalled: "Pavlova's Kitri was incomparable, starting with her grand battement in the grand pas de basque of her entrance, set to the waltz music. Her Spanish-flavored classical dances aroused a storm in the audience by her dashing flights and her illustrious high jumps. In particular, she succeeded in the variation from the dream that started with sixteen entrechats six and ended with petits jetés en tournant around the stage."

By 1907, having mastered almost all of the Maryinsky repertory, Pavlova attained her artistic zenith. Like many of her colleagues, she might have suffered a crisis had unique alternatives not suddenly emerged—her first tours abroad and her brief yet fruitful collaboration with Fokine in 1907–08, and then in 1913, when he choreographed *Les Préludes* to Liszt and *The Seven Daughters of the Mountain King* for one of her Western tours.

In such ballets as *Eunice*, *Une Nuit d'Egypte*, *Le Pavillon d'Armide*, and *Les Sylphides*, Fokine intelligently capitalized on the keen sensitivity to any stylization that Pavlova had so strikingly manifested in *La Bayadère*. In 1907 this particular aspect of her artistry was reinforced by the influence of Isadora Duncan, whom Pavlova had observed in 1904–05, not only on the St. Petersburg stage but in Pavlova's own home.

Among Pavlova's choreographic miniatures, Fokine's *The Dying Swan* to Saint-Saëns is the only piece that has survived, thanks to the inspired interpretations of Galina Ulanova, Yvette Chauviré, and Maya Plisetskaya. Fokine's mini-ballet, or choreographic monologue, composed as a stylized improvisation, was in fact Duncanism on pointe. Arms, shoulders, and the tilt of the torso sustained the solo, while the legs, flowing in pas de bourrée, suggested the swan gliding on the surface of the water. In 1907 its choreographic audacity derived from the mimetic presentation of a swan image, so unlike the classically abstract Odette of *Swan Lake*.

The Duncanesque plastique pervading the structure of *The Dying Swan* provided Pavlova with a certain freedom to saturate the choreography with expressive shadings that changed over the years, depending on her mood or psychological condition. The emotional messages could range from transfiguration before death to tragic sorrow and submissiveness to fate. All of them were equally thrilling and rich in dramatic energy.

Pavlova made her first Western tour, to Finland, Sweden, and Germany, in the spring of 1908. The repertory consisted primarily of the Maryinsky warhorses, such as *Giselle*, *Paquita*, *The Magic Flute*, *The Cavalry Halt*, and Act II of *Swan Lake* (she never performed the full-length ballet in Russia). A year later, in the spring of 1909, she headed for Berlin, Prague, and Paris, where she arrived after the first Diaghilev season had already begun.

Her universal success and her ever-increasing independence were the main reasons for her rebellion against Diaghilev's artistic tyranny. Despite the fact that Valentin Serov's poster with her fleeting silhouette en arabesque hovered over Paris to become emblematic of Diaghilev's great experiment, Pavlova was determined not to put up with Nijinsky's inflated publicity or her own position as only one of several ornaments of the first season. Diaghilev's friend Walter Nouvel wrote to the poet Mikhail Kuzmin in St. Petersburg of "Pavlova's intractability, the outbursts and scandals, and the resounding clash of two wills." Diaghilev's policy mostly imitated that of the Maryinsky, with himself in the place of its inflexible directorate. But Pavlova was determined not to have left St. Petersburg only to lose her artistic freedom in another kind of servitude. Despite her enormous success in Paris, and under the influence of Victor Dandré as her artistic advisor, she was intent upon extending her prestige beyond Diaghilev's reach, first in America (her New York debut was in February 1910, and she proceeded to Boston, Philadelphia, and Baltimore) and then in England (April-May in London at the Palace Theatre).

Pavlova was not disconcerted by the taxing circumstances of her early tours, when she occasionally had to share her success with jugglers, conjurors, or "trained circus dogs of all nationalities," as the showbill announced in London in 1911. Nor was she intimidated in 1916 when she intrepidly accepted the challenge of performing her condensed *Sleeping Beauty* on a vaudeville bill at the New York Hippodrome. After 1910 she became resigned to touring as a modus vivendi, with a railroad car to substitute for a house, and hazardous provincial boards for the security of the Imperial stage.

Her explosive individualism and craving for artistic independence gradually involved Pavlova in a process of self-transformation. In St. Petersburg, Petipa's worn-out pas de deux invariably appealed to the Russian audience the way Shakespeare's plays did to the English public: a new interpretation could still provide aesthetic pleasure. In the West these pieces, torn out of the context of a full-length ballet, frequently aroused boredom. For all Pavlova's devotion to the Maryinsky standards, she ventured to replace these old pas de deux with more dramatic and vital one-act ballets such as *La Nuit*, which she had performed in St. Petersburg in 1909 and then in London.

After 1911 she was even more vehemently intent on breaking with her Russian past. She had ventured to reestablish her previously thwarted collaboration with the

Diaghilev company in London, in 1911 dancing (among other roles) Giselle with Nijinsky and the Slave in *Cléopâtre*. That same year, driven by rivalry, vindictiveness, and unrequited love, she scandalously ended her artistic union with her best partner, Mikhail Mordkin. Her strong bond with the British audience was formed at this time, and her dancing had an impact so powerful that "British high society, adults and children, all of them suddenly began to dance," as Moscow ballerina Elizaveta Charpentier recalled.

A FTER her London tour in 1910, Pavlova launched a balletic marathon that lasted for twenty strenuous years. At the dawn of her international fame, she seemed to be unaware of the price she would pay for her success: loneliness, cultural isolation, perpetual anxiety, and the never-ending struggle to maintain her status as the high priestess of dance. It required a tremendous effort from a dancer who was perfectly conscious of the limited technical means at her disposal. Nor was she unaware of her inner bond with the Maryinsky, with its polished corps de ballet and its solemn cult of lofty art. Her genuine element was the dance-drama fostered by Perrot and Petipa, the kind of large-scale production wherein she could reign supreme. No wonder that her parting with the Maryinsky was painful.

Driven by his vindictive feelings, Diaghilev wrote in the *St. Petersburg Gazette* in 1910 that "in the pursuit of money, Pavlova vilified the Russian ballet by performing at the London variété." The great impresario certainly was mistaken. Having begun her triumphant progress through the world, Pavlova could not bring it to a halt. From the outset she was least concerned with financial success: in 1910 she had paid twenty-one thousand rubles (an enormous amount of money in those days) to the directorate of the Maryinsky as a forfeit for breaking her contract. After the London tour, she was pulled involuntarily into the long process of self-transformation into the prima ballerina assoluta del mondo. Gradually her stage image became her true identity, as well as the only outlet for her dreams and sexuality. Ballet tempted her like a potent, irresistible drug. And the more Pavlova's cult and glory grew, the more she slavishly succumbed to it.

After 1910, Pavlova settled down at Ivy House on the outskirts of London, but she still returned to Russia periodically. Cutting her ties with the Maryinsky took several years. During the season of 1911–12, she performed two *Giselle*s and three *Bayadère*s; in 1912–13 she danced one *Bayadère*, five *Don Quixote*s, and four *Pharaoh's Daughter*s

and participated in a gala performance of Glinka's opera *A Life for the Tsar*. The *St. Petersburg Gazette* announced: "Yesterday in *La Bayadère* Anna Pavlova bid her farewell to the public.... She goes abroad again, to return to St. Petersburg for a while in September." In 1914 she visited the Maryinsky for the last time before political events cut her off from Russia forever. The first World War broke out while she was in Berlin; in South America she learned of the Russian Revolution.

The ransom for her success proved to be enormous. The financial problems of her company increased heavily, a leaden burden on her shoulders. Dandré, her manager and so-called husband (in fact they never married), contracted her for so many engagements that occasionally she had to dance fifty times a month—at times she danced afternoon and evening performances in different cities.

In fifteen years she traveled 350,000 miles with her company, gave over four thousand performances, and appeared in more towns around the world than any other artist of any kind before or since. This excruciating marathon required gigantic physical effort and fed her perpetual apprehension about her technique. In the 1910s Petipa's companion-in-arms Alexander Shiriayev coached her, witnessing the combat between Pavlova's willpower, her stamina, and her physical qualifications. Sergei Khudekov also maintained in the 1910s she began to lose her extension and her jump, which compelled her to arrange the programs with an emphasis on what had become an unflagging terre-à-terre technique. She no longer sought diversity in her performances but organized them in a sequence that would guarantee immediate success.

Apart from *The Dying Swan* and *Les Sylphides*, every single work in which Pavlova created a leading role has sunk into oblivion. Most of the ballets she preferred to dance during her Western period (1910–30) were artistically negligible: *The Romance of a Mummy*, set to Tcherepnin; *Gavotte*, to Paul Lincke's "Glowworm"; *California Poppy*, to the Tchaikovsky Melody in E-flat; *Amarilla*, a gypsy ballet, to music by Glazunov and Drigo. From year to year she danced *The Dragonfly* to Fritz Kreisler's "Schön Rosmarin," choreographed by herself. The piece stemmed from an image that she maintained had struck her childish mind in Ligovo: she saw a country urchin tear off a dragonfly's wings and break its iridescent flight. At that moment, she said, she realized the fragility of beauty and the price one must pay for being beautiful. Many of the ballets danced by her company (which existed from 1913 until her death in 1931) were sloppily choreographed by Ivan Clustine, a former Bolshoi ballet master, who concocted or patched up odds and ends in order to emphasize Pavlova's strong points.

A typical Pavlova program of the 1910s and 1920s consisted of three parts, each about fifty minutes long. The first two parts were one-act ballets starring Pavlova. As a rule, these were followed by adaptations of leftovers from Petipa's banquet: Amarilla mimicked the gypsy girl Esmeralda, dancing at the wedding of her truant lover; *Invitation to the Dance* echoed a routine Petipa divertissement. The latter, consisting of seven numbers, with Pavlova in two of them, crowned the evening. For years she indulged in this routine, concerned mostly with her appeal to mass audiences and her prestige as a star.

Under the pressure of her schedule she began to make compromises inconceivable during her Maryinsky period: she cut the intricate passages and mutilated the musical scores by adjusting the tempos (which infuriated her conductors). She strongly believed that to the ignorant public of Venezuela or Peru, her presence spoke more than any choreography. Her life ran at breakneck speed with no time for experiments; but then, regardless of her earlier work with Fokine, she was never fond of novelty. She had become a belligerent traditionalist (though less so than Dandré), believing that the greater the confines, the greater was the challenge, and the more striking the artistic result. As the years passed, her repertory, quite impressive at the beginning, shrank to a dozen worn-out, convenient pieces: she had to spare her stamina, survive financially, and sustain her still blossoming legend. Her real home was a train or a steamer; she spent more time in transit than Margot Fonteyn or Rudolf Nureyev in the era of the jetliner. She celebrated Christmas at the Equator, ate painted eggs for Russian Easter on a train to Barcelona; beyond the window flashed dappled landscapes and towns of which sometimes she could not even get a glimpse. All of her energy was concentrated on her technique and her endurance, which she was afraid to lose. Gradually she began to resort to cunning tricks to perpetuate her legend. She even designed special pointe shoes. Lydia Sokolova remembered in her memoirs:

Taking shoes which were made somewhat too large for her, she would insert an extra support of thin leather or cork in the forward part of the shoe, but some distance from the tip. Then, soaking them in water, she would tread down the padded pointes as far as the support. When they were dry, she cut a slit in the rear edge of the pointe and inserted a plait of tape. Finally, she would darn all over and round the pointe in the normal way. She thus contrived for herself solid platforms on which to balance. Her shoes, however, were only part of the method which enabled her to hold an arabesque for so long. She would keep this up for ages, then suddenly do a couple of pirouettes and go flitting away. . . . Pavlova, asked how she did that, told me that as soon as she took the position, either an attitude or an arabesque, she would start to concentrate. From the pointe of the toe which rested on the ground, she would think her way through the ankle—to the calf—to the knee—to the thigh—to the waist—to the breast—to the head— through the arm—to the tips of her fingers. And when she had finished the controlling thought process, it was time to move on.

According to Serge Lifar, this customized shoe enabled her to make a dashing appearance from the wings in the Prelude of the Fokine-Clustine *Les Sylphides*, freeze in her now legendary arabesque, and sustain herself on pointe as long as she could. This little trick enthralled the audience.

Her Dying Swan became the true emblem of her art; and, according to Pavlova's contemporaries, her interpretation gradually took on more tragic, poignant shadings: she imbued it with that particular energy which she, by nature frail, had accumulated in her Western pilgrimage to survive as a ballerina and a person. The stage lured her as the realm where she belonged without reserve and where she felt fulfilled as a woman and as a prima ballerina. With the years her offstage persona became an extension of her theatrical image; her curtain calls looked like a mini-performance within her larger one. In Lydia Lopokhova's words, "She was quite conscious of her special theatricality, which made itself felt even in her manner of taking curtain calls. It was a performance by itself." And Sokolova recalled:

Accepting them with a charm which is rarely seen on the stage, she would press the flowers to her body, moving first one hand and then the other as she almost cuddled them. She would bend deeply from the waist, bowing to various parts of the house, give a brilliant turn of the head and shoulders, then run off, with head thrown back to reveal the line of her neck, taking the longest possible route to the wings. . . . Before she had taken two curtain calls people had entirely forgotten her earlier performance in watching another important and exquisite aspect of Pavlova's art. She was the only one who was able to build up applause from nothing.

Nevertheless, despite her universal success, Pavlova suffered from what Sergei Khudekov in his unpublished memoirs called "loneliness and vulnerability, aggravated by her spurious marriage to Dandré, which slowly degenerated into a kind of business agreement." Dandré had been a fervent admirer of hers in St. Petersburg; he succeeded in melting the ice of her mistrust and attaching her to himself. But according to many reports, she never loved him, although she returned his devotion and friendship with affection. When he became a major force backstage, pulling her into the vortex of contracts and commitments, she began to blame him for all her compromises and to regard him as the main cause of her inner unfulfillment. Her inborn theatricality usually helped her hide the resentment that at times broke through her mask of reserve, unleashing outbursts of hysteria and inexplicable tears. As André Oliveroff recalled in his memoirs: "She had a habit, in such black moods, of biting her knuckle, or sucking a piece of amber which she used to wear about her neck; mile after mile, aboard a train, I have seen her thus, sitting alone, chewing on her hand or her amber pendant—staring out the window, with the vacant expression almost of one demented, tears streaming down her face. No one ever knew what she was thinking about, what it was that made her suffer so. . . ."

Pavlova the woman puzzled as many people as Pavlova the ballerina thrilled: she never let people penetrate her facade of indifference and slightly arrogant condescension. The ambiguity of her identity seemed to torture her, and the fear of revealing it apparently was stronger than her craving for love and fulfillment as a woman. Kathleen Crofton, who worked in Pavlova's company in the 1920s, told me:

> She communicated her tension to everybody. Indeed, she poured it forth, somehow discharging it on the stage. With us, her humble balletic subjects, she was harsh; but her severity had never been perceived as her natural quality. She seemed to be apprehensive about displaying her humanity, which might make her vulnerable, as though she were afraid that someone would take advantage of it and hurt her feelings. Therefore, she sort of played hard with us. Aware of it, we forgave her sudden

rudeness and the bizarre mood fluctuations—from aggression to tears and heightened sensibility. In my view, none of her successes could assuage her overwhelming homesickness, which she mentioned constantly in conversations, her solitude and excruciating anxiety.

Her ever-increasing fame and wealth contributed to the development of her typically Russian sense of guilt with respect to her Maryinsky colleagues who were suffering from hunger and various hardships during the postrevolutionary and Civil War years. In the 1920s she sent food and clothes to the Maryinsky dancers: her letters, preserved in the archives of Elizaveta Gerdt and other artists, are full of anxiety, bitterness, and resignation to her lot.

Her life turned into a kind of vicious circle. In the 1920s she accelerated her marathon, changing countries and towns like the gloves and shoes she loved to collect, until she found herself totally immersed in the web of engagements and ensuing compromises. At times she thought she had made an irretrievable step by giving way to Dandré's advice and machinations. The more she resented him and herself, the more carefully she hid her self-contempt and fear behind her ostentatious arrogance and intractability. Her infatuation with Mordkin, who brought her near to himself and then humiliated her, had reinforced her sexual insecurity and fear of men. To break away from Dandré, her administrative strength and right hand in business, was beyond her.

In 1920 Pavlova fell in love with the Russian artist Alexander Jakovlev. The affair engaged all the passion of an unfulfilled woman. According to Jakovlev's niece, Tatiana Jakovleva-Liberman, Jakovlev was a talented painter, a genuine product of the Russian intelligentsia, brilliant and highly educated—both tempting and unsuitable. Pavlova's slightly belated dreams about a real family and a child hardly fit the life style of a dedicated bohemian, traveler, and bachelor like Jakovlev. This love affair, both the happiest and the most frustrating of Pavlova's life, lasted until Jakovlev's expedition to Tibet—the so-called *croisière jaune* (yellow voyage)—in 1929, and Pavlova's death in 1931.

The last decade of her career proved to be sheer self-repetition and a kind of brilliant coda. She began to avoid taking chances the way she had with *The Sleeping Beauty* in New York in 1916. Everything new in ballet, emerging from the Diaghilev seasons (Balanchine's *Apollo* and *The Prodigal Son*, for instance), only aroused her anger and resentment, partly because of her inveterate dislike of Diaghilev and partly because she was no longer a participant. Her journey to India in 1924 released her from her ever-increasing fear of death and apprehension about her technique and the unavoidable end of her career. She was greatly interested in Gandhi and in Indian philosophy and dreamed of restaging the Kingdom of the Shades scene from *La Bayadère* in an Indian philosophical key.

But her health was drastically shaken. Earlier problems with her knee suddenly led to a serious injury. In December 1930, working in an unheated Parisian studio, she caught a chill that led to dangerous pleurisy. She lacked the inner strength to resist the illness. When asked to undergo a resection of two ribs necessary to save her life but fatal to her dancing, Pavlova forbade the operation and died. As Dandré recalled: "About midnight she opened her eyes and with difficulty raised her hand as though she wished to make the sign of the cross. A few minutes later . . . Pavlova said: 'Get my Swan costume ready.'"

On Sunday, January 25, 1931, the Apollo Theatre in London saw a performance of the Camargo Society. Dancers in the costumes of Cephalus and Procris from the ballet of the same name by Ninette de Valois were taking a bow in front of the curtain. The audience was waiting for the second number on the program. The conductor, Constant Lambert, turned and announced Saint-Saëns's *Death of the Swan*. The curtain rose to reveal an empty, darkened stage with gray backdrops. A spotlight seemed to grope for the figure of a dancer who was not there. While the music played, the stage became darker and darker, becoming one bluish-black spot, not unlike Pavlova's last train traveling off into eternity, shrinking to a dot. . . .

Even on her deathbed, Pavlova could not have imagined the scale of the revolution she sparked in the minds of her millions of admirers or the number of spiritual children to whom she, childless herself, had given birth. If Diaghilev unleashed the vitality of ballet as a colorful spectacle, aware of its own values as distinct from dramatic theatre, Pavlova revealed the spiritual impact of dance as a source of inner energy and hidden truth.

Pavlova's profound faith in herself imparted a special life to her dancing, rendering her technical flaws and limitations insignificant. This faith of a Russian ballerina who proclaimed herself a priestess of dance reverberated in the mind of an American dancer, Ted Shawn, who had studied for the ministry and strongly believed that "dance is the most perfect symbol of the activity of God and his angels" and that "dance is a way of life which will lead humanity into continually higher and greater dimensions of existence." Undoubtedly Pavlova would have lent her name to this creed.

The Blue Dahlia

LUBOV EGOROVA

THE ARTISTIC destiny of Lubov Nikolayevna Egorova (born July 28, 1880) evolved slowly and painfully on the Maryinsky stage. A pupil of Madame Cecchetti, Egorova graduated from the St. Petersburg Imperial Theatre School in the spring of 1898, along with Mikhail Fokine. She joined the illustrious company that same year, which was marked by the premiere of *Raymonda*, the last flash of Petipa's choreographic genius. At that time his masterpieces already seemed to fill the pages of Russian ballet history. The classicism he had fervently implanted and propagated was just beginning to petrify.

On the other hand, as if to compensate for its artistic stagnation, the Maryinsky of that era had become an arena of unremitting competition among many striking balletic personalities. Vying for command of the old Imperial stage at the turn of the century were such artists as Matilda Kschessinskaya, Olga Preobrajenskaya, Vera Trefilova, Anna Pavlova, Julia Sedova, and Agrippina Vaganova. Despite their differences of type and technical qualification, they were all challenged and restricted by the immutable, stale repertory, which clearly defined the contours of the battlefield. Each sought to put her rivals to shame before the balletomanes and connoisseurs who saw the same roles danced three times a week in the theatre of blue velvet and gilt.

In this furious combat Egorova failed at first. She had

the comely face of a soubrette rather than the reserved mien of a Romantic ballerina, and an ideal body endowed with highly arched insteps and admirably slender legs (which were often seen in the pages of St. Petersburg periodicals).

Nobody doubted her "Italian" technique, but her subdued, almost unprepossessing manner of dancing was difficult to categorize. She could easily execute the most daring pirouettes and dazzling renversés, but never with the dashing strength or hurricanelike energy that were held in such high regard at the Maryinsky. The lyricism she brought to her early parts was neither poignant nor piercing. One critic compared Egorova's image to "a candle, that gives light but does not warm you." At the dawn of her career many critics shared the opinion of Sergei Khudekov, who characterized Egorova rather severely in his *History of Dance*: "Lacking flamboyant temperament, she was unable to enthrall the audience in the major roles. Her lot was to remain a beautiful, elegant, and quite strong soloist—a lot with which she had to be content." Moreover, Khudekov unkindly likened Egorova's style to that of "a professional journalist, writing without mistakes his dry, impersonal articles, which only leave the impression of *déjà lu*."

Egorova was a quaint bird in the flock of striking virtuosos like Kschessinskaya and Preobrajenskaya and dramatic and lyrical ballerinas like Pavlova. She seemed not to have concerned herself with the virtuosity that had been fashionable since the time of Pierina Legnani. Unlike Pavlova, she never went to Milan to take classes from Catarina Beretta, the famous Italian teacher; she perfected her purely academic style under the aegis of Ekaterina Vazem, who had created the role of Nikiya in *La Bayadère*, and Christian Johannsen. These mentors improved her technique, although she had little chance to display it in the relatively minor roles she was given from 1900 to 1905, in Petipa's *The Cavalry Halt* and *The Blue Dahlia*, Ivanov's *The Enchanted Forest*, and the like. She rehearsed with Petipa himself in those rare moments when the old maestro, tired of his constant squabbles with the courtiers who supervised his theatre, relaxed by initiating the Maryinsky's youngsters into the secrets of the academic ballet. Petipa encouraged Egorova with praise; but, like many critics of the day, he considered her a good soloist rather than an inspired artist capable of infusing new vitality into his ballets. His attention was totally drawn to the young Pavlova, whose Romantic verve gave new life to his slightly desiccated masterpieces. In his *Diaries* he mentioned Egorova with disapproval more frequently than with praise. Her subdued lyricism seemed irrelevant to Petipa at a time when he was more concerned with re-establishing his own reputation as an unflappable and ageless maestro than with discovering new talent or providing a showcase for the virtuosity or personal projection of individual dancers.

Egorova's artistic creed was amazingly consistent at a time when two trends of interpretation so obviously clashed: the display of technical tricks and the desire for meaningful dramatic expression. She never subjugated herself to either. She tried to be herself, despite the rebukes of the critics and the tepid approval of the spoiled and moody St. Petersburg audience. She enjoyed her modest reputation and was constantly praised for the purity of her style, "without obvious choreographic blunders," as André Levinson once remarked. Even her primary classification as an ingenue-soubrette seemed somewhat blurry. As Teresa in *The Cavalry Halt* or Ilka in *The Enchanted Forest*, she never poured forth the gaiety or glee the audience expected from her. Always smiling, modest, charming, she shattered their expectations by performing the most intricate tricks almost too smoothly, without visible effort. Gradually even her technique began to be regarded as something customary, simply a part of her elegant, inconspicuous dancing. After a performance of *The Enchanted Forest*, the major critic of the day, Valerian Svetlov, wrote: "Miss Egorova is much more successful dancing elegant bagatelles or creating simple characters, as, for instance, in the variation in this unpretentious ballet. In the pas d'action she excelled in pirouettes and renversés, but the czardas was beyond her temperament and technical means."

Critical complaints about the lack of brio in Egorova's dancing gradually became accusations of a lack of individuality. She often was regarded as a dancer who, according to one anonymous critic, "dispatches her legs in a carriage to the theatre, while remaining herself at home and quietly enjoying her coffee." She diligently learned new soloist parts, performed them accurately, and enjoyed her modest position as an attractive and useful dancer, as if oblivious of any competition. In 1905 she captured the attention of the observant Mikhail Fokine, who willingly danced the *Swan Lake* pas de trois with her. Like her other frequent partners, Nicolas Legat and Mikhail Obukhov, Fokine found her to be submissive, benign, and reliable.

Also in 1905, she danced *The Blue Dahlia* and was praised for her "subtle coloring" and "delicately sketched movements." Thenceforth, she began to attract more attention. Critics came to appreciate her as a true personality,

Clockwise from top right: Princess Florine in *The Sleeping Beauty*, 1905; The Tsar Maiden in *The Little Humpbacked Horse*, 1911; *Les Sylphides*; *Eunice*

albeit a rather anachronistic one: the poetic understatement of her dancing, as Vera Krasovskaya pointed out in her essay on Egorova, harked back to the Romantic traditions of Russian style that had distinguished Elena Andreyanova, the first Russian Giselle, and Marta Muravieva, the virtuoso of the 1860s, with her unspectacular manner and "ostentatiously quiet femininity." "The charm of Egorova's dancing," wrote Krasovskaya, "lay in the serenely unwinding melody of flowing lines, unobtrusively tinged with joy or sorrow."

Nicolas Legat, who replaced the aged Petipa as chief choreographer in 1903, attempted to use Egorova's propensity for understatement by giving her the role of Myrtha in *Giselle*, which she performed for the first time in February 1907. Thereafter she danced the imperious and vindictive queen of the Wilis frequently, enjoying much more favorable reviews than for her other roles: "Physically and technically Egorova was captivating," wrote Svetlov in 1909; "this strictly classical role suits her appealing gift magnificently," remarked another critic in 1910. As Myrtha, Egorova was regularly praised for her impassivity, her cold brilliance, and her academic facility; but apparently she never felt any affinity for the role. In 1910 Alexander Pleschayev grudgingly remarked that "Miss Egorova danced her Myrtha accurately, without damaging the role, yet adding no luster to her dancing."

Nevertheless, as Myrtha, Egorova fascinated Diaghilev, who invited her to dance the role in London. Only her contractual obligations with the Imperial Ballet prevented Egorova from participating in the early Diaghilev seasons, for the great impresario obviously appreciated her individuality: her subtle ability to intimate rather than to designate; her reticence and restrained lyricism, which corresponded more to the modern, "impressionistic" style he advocated than to the old, affected theatricality.

When Egorova made her debut as Princess Florine in *The Sleeping Beauty* in 1909, Svetlov enthusiastically welcomed her portrayal: "Miss Egorova ideally fits Florine as much by her physical appearance as by her graceful approach." But, characteristically, he added: "She has only to polish a few details to turn her exemplary classical dancing into an achievement of virtuosity." As Krasovskaya pointed out, "The experienced, usually sensitive critic Svetlov did not understand in this particular case that classical dancing is not necessarily tantamount to virtuosity. In particular, it would be inappropriate to the role of Florine, which must embody the process of blossoming. [The name "Florine"

derives from "Flora."] The echoing voices of Florine and the Blue Bird are heard in the music, either overtly or in a subdued manner. . . . The juxtaposition of Egorova's flowing and stretching lines, the gentle chiaroscuro of her plasticity, utterly corresponded to the undulation of Petipa's seemingly repetitious movements."

Egorova confirmed her success as Florine later in 1909, when her partner was Vaslav Nijinsky. "On that evening we actually took the audience by storm," Egorova recalled in an interview in Paris in 1933: "Vaslav practically hovered over the stage, because at that time his elevation was especially stunning. I enjoyed his partnering, although sometimes he became so involved in his fluttering leaps and mercurial beats that he seemed not to pay much attention to his enchanted princess. But the princess did not complain. Vaslav gave her his magic and energy, and, as far as I recall, after our duet I did not feel tired and was not even in a sweat. It was such an invigorating experience to dance with Vaslav. He inspired me by urging me to catch up with his artistry."

Nijinsky, in a way, helped Egorova present herself in a new and more favorable light. After their appearance in the pas de deux from *Le Roi Candaule* on October 12, 1909, she became the talk of the St. Petersburg balletomanes. According to an anonymous critic, "Egorova and Nijinsky were simply amazing in the last act. In addition to their success as a couple, Nijinsky astounded the audience by his gigantic jumps across the whole stage."

In December 1910 Egorova made her debut in *Raymonda*. This virtually unattainable role had been considered the possession of Olga Preobrajenskaya, but the great ballerina coached the debutante. Compared with her instructor's, Egorova's Raymonda seemed more reserved and noble, lending the character a touch of medieval austerity. Hers was a less spectacular Raymonda as well. Her emphasis was not on the virtuoso passages but on the pensive, detached, slightly mysterious character of the heroine, revealing her essence through the serenely unwinding pas de bourrée and the string of softly drawn ballottés in the dream scene. Even in the growing exhilaration of the Grand Pas Hongrois Egorova kept her reserved mien, as if dancing for herself, immersed in her reverie. Volynsky ascribed this quality to an absence of temperament, but André Levinson was probably closer to the truth when he wrote: "Miss Egorova's profile is both frail and graphic; she danced with confidence, subtle grace, reserve, without emphasizing the choreographic intricacies. Her performance was marked by more propriety than inspiration; her style, which was not animated by her personal feelings, responded to that of the choreography. Her mime and gestures were impressive in terms of conventional dramatic expressiveness." But Raymonda was given to Egorova only once a year, when she replaced Preobrajenskaya. In fact, she never got a chance to polish the role.

The beginning of her second decade on the Maryinsky stage marked the real breakthrough in Egorova's career, in part because Anna Pavlova and Vera Trefilova virtually abandoned the theatre in the 1910s, and the prima ballerina assoluta, Matilda Kschessinskaya, became a guest artist. Free of comparisons with rival ballerinas, Egorova began to be perceived differently. She had been dancing various parts—Medora in *Le Corsaire*, the Tsar Maiden in *The Little Humpbacked Horse*, Kitri in *Don Quixote*, Paquita, and Aspicia in *Pharaoh's Daughter*—that did not necessarily suit her or required nothing but flamboyant virtuosity, never her forte. But at last, after ten years in the company, Egorova was given a chance to essay Aurora, Giselle, and Odette-Odile.

In December 1911 she made her debut as Aurora. "In Act I," wrote Krasovskaya, "she did not astound the audience with a frolicsome entrance, as did Kschessinskaya with her brilliant cabrioles and sudden renversés. Nor did Egorova excel in the serene quietness or austere proportions of the adagio, in which Trefilova was inimitable. The core of her portrayal was her variation in Act I: her graceful glissades shone with lyricism; the pas de bourrée softly unfolded its ornamental patterns; even double pirouettes en dehors, as Svetlov noted, 'were devoid of cheap spectacle but remained within the limits of grace.'" No one equated her lack of sheer bravura, which would be inappropriate for Aurora, with a dearth of imagination. In 1912 Svetlov even compared her favorably to Trefilova, noting that in Act III "Egorova was a real young bride, radiating happiness and subdued femininity."

Her Aurora was followed by her Odette-Odile in November 1913. *Swan Lake* was a far more serious challenge for her than *Raymonda* or *The Sleeping Beauty*, for the shadow of Pierina Legnani's Odette still haunted both the Maryinsky stage and the memories of the audience. Egorova's Odette bore only a remote resemblance to Legnani's Swan Queen; nor did she imitate Trefilova's classical perfection and impersonal brilliance. The originality of Egorova's Odette lay not so much in intensity of coloring or tragic interpretation as in the profundity of her subdued emo-

tional response to Tchaikovsky's music. The power of her portrayal was all the more moving in view of the economical means from which it grew. Her tremulous, aloof, grieved Odette was rendered with immobile face and quiet, seemingly spellbound movements, which seemed to envelop her in an aura of mystery. Krasovskaya wrote: "But what gave a special touch to her performance was the 'swan coloring' of the movements of her arms. They stretched out, bent, and threw themselves back like wings; her head tilted like a bird's from shoulder to shoulder. The anguished *sauvagerie* of Pavlova's *Dying Swan* was revealed in Egorova's Odette academically yet more poignantly than in Kschessinskaya's or Trefilova's interpretations, true to the principles of Imperial classicism." Egorova's understated lyricism, once criticized and disparaged, now thrilled both critics and audience. Even Sergei Khudekov, still classifying Egorova as a strong soloist, was "pleasantly surprised by her modest and utterly moving Odette, a manifestation of her increased artistry."

In her Odile, there was no such miracle. The demonic Black Swan was utterly alien to Egorova's own character, and after Trefilova's and Kschessinskaya's thirty-two fouettés, Egorova's jetés en tournant appeared insufficient. Instead of the usual infernal enchantress, her Odile had a quality of vulnerable femininity, even of weakness, which, as one critic remarked, "made her an unwitting weapon in the hands of Rothbart."

If Odette-Odile came to Egorova at the right moment, when her artistic maturity was reinforced by perfect technical equipment, the realization of her dream of dancing Giselle came a bit too late. Despite her personal triumph in *Giselle*, in which she made her debut in May 1914, her peasant girl looked too adult in Act I and too much a mournful spectre in Act II. The Romantic serenity Pavlova had brought to the role—a very important color in the symbolic palette of the ballet—was missing. The unavoidable comparison with Pavlova was not favorable to Egorova. Nevertheless, Egorova brought new colors to the hapless heroine: touching simplicity of mind, sacrificial commitment, and dramatic understatement. Egorova's acting, as the critic Konstantin Kudrin observed, "possibly is not so overwhelming as Pavlova's, but it is more natural, less dramatic, more simply orchestrated."

These words reveal the essence of Egorova's talent. Her understated expressiveness, enhanced by the natural, unaffected manner of her dancing, was never fully appreciated at the Maryinsky. Virtuosity prevailed among the academicians, while Fokine's innovations called for a spectacular theatricality and a slightly exaggerated manner of presentation foreign to Egorova's talent.

Nonetheless, after she established her reputation in *Swan Lake* and *Giselle*, Fokine took a revived interest in her as a dancer. Egorova, for her part, always admired his innovations. In the interview she gave after her promotion to the rank of ballerina, she welcomed Fokine's quest for expressiveness, thanks to which "the contemporary ballet is put on a more realistic basis, giving priority to content. For the sake of content, Fokine considerably simplifies the dances themselves: in his productions the beautiful poses reveal as much as the expressive, subtle pantomime, and all these means contribute to the dramatic impact of the choreography as art."

But the artistic marriage of Fokine and Egorova was not to be. While he responded to Egorova's unexpected recognition of his experiments by staging Tchaikovsky's *Francesca da Rimini* for her in 1915, the ballet was a failure. (Pierre Vladimiroff played her lover Paolo.) Unfortunately, Fokine had created a static and pedestrian tableau vivant enshrouded in a purple dusk, so dimly lit that Egorova was quite lost in the crowd, as were Cleopatra (Felia Doubrovska), Helen of Troy (Olga Spessivtseva), and the others. Volynsky called the ballet "a chaos of Fokine's odds and ends," overloaded with too-realistic pantomime, and complained that Egorova had virtually nothing to dance.

In 1916 Fokine restaged the famous Act III pas de deux from the Petipa-Gorsky *Don Quixote* for himself and Egorova, but once again he failed to use her successfully. Their artistic paths never crossed thereafter.

The revolutionary storms of 1917 shattered the cultural life of St. Petersburg, precipitating an exodus of Russian dancers that eventually transfigured European ballet. In January 1917 Egorova appeared in her last *Swan Lake*. In the fall of 1918, when she went on tour in Finland, a short notice appeared in the press: "The committee of the State Ballet decided to invite Miss Egorova as a guest artist to dance several old productions on the Maryinsky stage just to breathe new life into them. Such ballets as *La Bayadère*, *Giselle*, *The Talisman*, and others are to be revived mainly for her." This project was not realized; the ballerina never returned to Russia.

Egorova's life in the West was untroubled and satisfactory. She was happily married to Prince Troubetskoy, and her career continued in Paris under the guidance of Diaghilev for a span of five years. But if her subdued yet poign-

ant lyrical talent arrived at the Maryinsky too early, the thirty-eight-year-old Egorova joined Diaghilev's company too late. She gave classes and coached the young Olga Spessivtseva, but she danced infrequently.

At the London premiere of Diaghilev's *The Sleeping Princess*, Egorova performed the Canary Fairy. As Lydia Sokolova wrote in her memoirs: "I remember her in this, dressed in canary yellow with a long feather in her hair, running about the stage on her pointes faster than I could believe possible, fluttering her hands. Nobody did this variation nearly as well."

But her final artistic victory over age and failing strength was to be Aurora, which she shared with Olga Spessivtseva and Vera Trefilova, holding her own against the challenging competition. "When she danced Aurora," Sokolova recalled, "she displayed an amazing assurance and was very strong. She was always unusually calm and controlled, showing neither exhaustion, fluster, nor nerves. Egorova had not the glamour or suppleness of Spessivtseva nor the miniature charm of Trefilova, but I never had any fear that she might fail to bring off a step or give a satisfying performance."

Unlike Spessivtseva's rather aloof Aurora, Egorova shone with the radiance of youth, "reveling in the most intricate choreographic vignettes, as if reminding us of the dawn of her modest, yet so meaningful, glory on the Imperial stage," wrote André Levinson.

Sokolova provides a rather peculiar detail in her memoirs, referring to Egorova's technical equipment during her Diaghilev period:

She had one strange characteristic: she was never at any time right on the very top of her toes. We used to wonder how she could do such difficult steps just off the pointe. I was intrigued by this, and as I have always been fascinated by the different ways dancers "fiddle" their ballet shoes, I took the chance of examining a pair of Egorova's shoes which she put down in the wings. Most of us had Italian shoes with rather square papier-mâché toecaps, but I think Egorova's were French. At any rate, I found she strengthened them with cork heel-lifts stuck in back to front with the thick end towards the toe, but with quite a gap left at the very end, into which she would insert her toes. How her toes were not pinched I cannot imagine. I was impressed by the lightness of these shoes, lined with cork, and tried to imitate her method of fixing the shoe, but without success.

In 1923 Egorova opened her own school of ballet in Paris. Fourteen years later she organized a troupe called Ballets de la Jeunesse, whose members included Jean Veidt, George Skibine, and Yuri Algarov. She also taught at the Royal Danish Ballet, for which she mounted *Aurora's Wedding*. Egorova died in Paris in 1969.

Although Egorova's lyrical talent was not fully realized or appreciated by her contemporaries, a quarter of a century later it was reincarnated in another ballerina, Galina Ulanova, who was able to infuse the most unimpressive or even trite ballets with genuine lyricism and poetic value.

Studio portrait, early 1930s

Giselle, early 1950s

GALINA ULANOVA

FOR MILLIONS of ballet cognoscenti and fans, both in Russia and in the West, the name of Galina Ulanova connotes genuine lyricism and understated poetry. Her rare talent and the circumstances of her career caused her name to shine brighter than those of her no less gifted colleagues (Marina Semyonova, Alla Shelest), who remained unknown in the West or at best enjoyed limited recognition. Ulanova, in a way, won fame for all of them.

In Russia Ulanova is a symbol of so-called "balletic realism." She has been officially pronounced an unparalleled lyrical genius, lavishly honored with many State rewards, and canonized as one of the priceless icons of Soviet culture, the equal of Stanislavsky, Sholokhov, and Shosta-

kovich. Her art was eulogized in a dozen books and thousands of articles; the way she turned, or froze in arabesque, flitted, mimed, ran, strolled on pointe, or tilted her head, has been profusely described and scrutinized in detail.

I saw her first in 1954 as Maria in *The Fountain of Bakhchisarai*, but on that occasion the impact of Maya Plisetskaya's performance as Zarema literally transfixed me, and Ulanova was obscured in Plisetskaya's gigantic shadow. Later I was fortunate to see Ulanova in her performances of *Les Sylphides*, Lavrovsky's *Romeo and Juliet*, and *Giselle*. It was an exciting yet disturbing experience. Actually seeing a "legend" dance always shatters one's expectations, but Ulanova's stage image confirmed this principle in a very painful way. The problem was not that she was in her forties, although the flaws in her physique were indeed more obvious than before. Her short neck and arms, broad shoulders, and protruding knees, which she was rumored to have concealed so skillfully in her salad days, were somehow at odds with her famed lingering arabesques and birdlike flitting leaps, her simplicity of mime and emotional understatement. What is more, Ulanova's art seemed more puzzling than thrilling, suggesting something old-fashioned and almost forgotten. At the time I felt it was my own aesthetic immaturity that prevented me from appreciating Ulanova's genius.

These feelings resurfaced in New York in 1977 when, after watching the film of Ulanova's Giselle, Natalia Makarova said to me: "It's good but strangely *démodé*. Essentially it is a very Soviet interpretation." This statement was all the more surprising as it came from a ballerina viewed in Russia as Ulanova's direct successor. Makarova's strong opinion immediately recalled to me the gala performance in Ulanova's honor at the Bolshoi in 1974, when she was given the Soviet award of "heroine of Socialist labor." Her pupils, such as Ekaterina Maximova, Nina Timofeyeva, and Vladimir Vasiliev, along with the Bolshoi corps, were to dance a tribute to the living monument. Ulanova herself was sitting in the director's box, on the ledge of which the participants laid enormous bouquets of roses and gladiolus, so that eventually Ulanova's seat of honor took on a solemn, sepulchral appearance. Yuri Grigorovich's paean to the heroine of the evening preceded the performance, with its emphatic last sentence: "Galina Ulanova is dancing on the Bolshoi stage." On the screen above the Bolshoi boards appeared excerpts from Ulanova's films. She performed the Chinese dance from *The Red Poppy*, Giselle's first scene with Albrecht, Juliet's farewell to Romeo, and the Waltz from *Les Sylphides*. Ulanova's "solo performance" was followed by those of her pupils, which seemed to me to indicate not so much their greatness as the yawning gulf separating their artistic approach from their illustrious teacher's. What was most remarkable was that Ulanova hovered over her talented disciples as a figure from the past whose style had not the least affinity with contemporary Soviet ballet and precluded any imitation or transcendence. Her unique lyricism, compounded of subdued femininity and a striking economy of means, seemed to be such an elusive and even bizarre phenomenon that it could not be captured in a contemporary dance tribute.

As the years go by, Ulanova's artistic personality seems ever more enigmatic and intriguing. Nevertheless, the secret of her dance gift and her enormous popularity in Russia, as well as the hidden meaning of this canonized Soviet icon, become easier to explain and decipher.

I N 1907 ANNA PAVLOVA went to Moscow with a group of other dancers. Then at the peak of her career, she performed almost every day, while her less busy colleagues enjoyed the delights of the "Tartar city" and its picturesque environs. In these pleasant circumstances the dancer Sergei Ulanov fell in love with a member of the corps, Maria Romanova, and soon they were married. On January 8, 1910, Maria gave birth to a daughter, whom they called Galina.

According to Romanova, she and her husband began to take their daughter to the Maryinsky when Galina was six years old, to watch the performances in which they participated; gradually these forays became a habit, and the little Ulanova managed to see Karsavina, Preobrajenskaya, and Kschessinskaya on the Maryinsky stage. Nevertheless, the girl showed no desire to dance. But during the years of the Civil War, when the ever-growing hardship of everyday life and her complicated schedule prevented Romanova from taking care of her daughter, she decided to place Galina in the State Choreographic School (the former Imperial Theatre School), where she herself taught. Galina was her mother's pupil from 1919 to 1923 and then was accepted into Vaganova's intermediate class, where she remained for five years.

As a student, Ulanova revealed a certain musicality; and after each annual examination performance, professors and critics singled out her beautiful poses—"recalling good sculpture," as they put it. But that was all. At her graduation performance in May 1928 she danced as one of the corps in Fokine's *Chopiniana* and the Fairy Dragée (Sugar Plum Fairy) in the *Nutcracker* divertissement. In contrast to Semyonova, who had made an astonishing debut three years earlier, the young Ulanova amazed nobody. Rather, she surprised the audience by her shyness and by the utter simplicity of her manner.

Thanks to Romanova's insistence and Vaganova's influence, Ulanova joined the former Maryinsky company as a soloist and soon appeared in *Chopiniana* (as *Les Sylphides* is still known in the Soviet Union). Frail, with weak pointes, and small of stature, she was an awkward yet touching baby sprite. If anything distinctive marked her, it was her broad shoulders and lack of extension. She also displayed a peculiar lack of confidence. Ulanova's arabesques were not emphasized with aplomb like Semyonova's; they seemed rather vague. In one critic's words, they looked "slightly off balance, as if a beginner were trying to hide from the audience and avoid its scrutinizing stare. She seemed to be dancing for herself, concentrating on her emotions as if listening to herself." As Ulanova herself subsequently recalled, she was timid and insecure and had not yet penetrated Fokine's aesthetics. Like most of the debutantes, she tried as diligently as possible to express diverse emotions. "My teacher told me 'Here you have to rejoice,' and I did it, or 'There you must be sad,' and I mimicked sadness."

Nonetheless, judging by the reviews after her debut, Ulanova did reveal a certain style, stemming from her technical insufficiency. One critic defined it as introverted dance, performed at half-force; the vaguely etched arabesques and attitudes or slightly underpowered jetés seemed to imply that the ballerina had potential of which she did not want to make much use. "Ulanova brought to our stage a touching charm of diffidence and imperfect dancing," the critic Talnikov observed.

Ulanova's approach seemed to doom her to failure. At this time, Semyonova's virtuosity prevailed, and lyricism per se was rejected by the proletarian critics, who regarded any "debilitating sentimentality" as incompatible with the invigorating mission of the young Soviet arts. But from the outset Ulanova remained faithful to herself and the angular lyricism of her adolescence. That her technique was inferior even to Pavlova's, for instance, she managed somehow to conceal very skillfully. What is more, she turned her limitations to her undisputed advantage. Whether guided by her mother and Vaganova or by her own intuition, she learned to raise her shoulders in a slightly affected, chaste way and tilt her head (the characteristic feature of her Giselle, Odette, and Cinderella) to screen her too-short neck, and to stretch out her hand energetically, so that her fingers might elongate her short, unswanlike arms. She could adopt an expression of childish, almost disarming innocence, like that of a girl on a sugary Christmas card, to extract the maximum of expression out of the most economical pantomime. The young Ulanova's image recalled Lillian Gish's heroines, with their seemingly inborn vulnerability and frailty: delicate blossoms unable to resist destruction. Ulanova's persona and style seemed to illustrate Akim Volynsky's assertion that a woman's dancing is a metaphor for a flower in its blossoming and death.

During her first season (1928–29) Ulanova danced Florine in *The Sleeping Beauty* and a Slave in the Pas d'Esclave from *Le Corsaire*, which, in her own words, "eluded me completely." The complexity of Petipa's academic patterns was obviously beyond her technical abilities. According to the reviews, her debuts as Odette-Odile and Aurora were far from successful. Aurora especially defeated her poor academic training; her angular childishness was not potent enough to compensate for her sloppy chaînés and slack turns. Little wonder that she never returned to Aurora! Nor did she return to Odile, with her fouettés and devilishly intricate diagonal of pas de chat and attitudes. (In the thirties at the Kirov, Odette and Odile were often performed by different ballerinas.) The character of Odile was totally foreign to her; in Talnikov's words, "her Odile looked like a strange child whose frisky mood somehow drove her to ape infernal passions."

But Ulanova's first Odette bore her individual stamp: she was not a traditional queen of the swans but rather a young princess from an enchanted kingdom, who pined not so much for freedom as for a kindred spirit to alleviate the burden of her captivity. According to one critic, in the Act II adagio "her lingering sissonnes, ronds de jambe, and long pauses, full of contemplative concentration and reserve, added a touch of moving vulnerability to her Odette." Ulanova's Odette seemed to enjoy the peace of her childish dreams, equally detached from her sad reality and from the Prince, her potential rescuer.

In her third season at the Kirov (1931–32) Ulanova enjoyed continuing success as Masha in the old version of *The Nutcracker* and as the Tsar Maiden in *The Little Humpbacked Horse*. Although she never mastered the latter role technically, the appeal of Ulanova's subdued lyricism captivated the audience. But her total victory was won by her poignant interpretation of Giselle. Ulanova worked throughout her career on this role—it became the pinnacle of her art—and it was as Giselle that she enthralled Western audiences in the mid-fifties.

With utmost tact and common sense, Ulanova and her partner, Konstantin Sergeyev, responded to the infatuation of Soviet ballet theatre with Stanislavsky's dramatic realism. They were able to interpret *Giselle* as Romantic drama without blurring its contours with excessive social or psychological "insights." Moreover, ignoring the vulgar Marxist doctrine that obliged Soviet dancers to stigmatize Albrecht as a depraved product of the feudal system, Ulanova and Sergeyev humanized the old drama, investing it with sincerity and eschewing any social message.

In *Giselle* Ulanova revealed for the first time her stunning theatrical instincts. Like many Soviet ballerinas, she perceived ballet as a form of dramatic theatre, but her realization of this idea on stage was completely her own: she capitalized on her childish angularity, apprehensive style, and unglamorous face and figure. Her Giselle was a fair-haired, plain, bashful, Cinderella-like peasant girl. Instead of struggling to overcome what seemed to be her limitations and shortcomings, Ulanova boldly took advantage of them. The utmost economy of dramatic and dance means in the context of Gautier's artless legend intensified her poignant lyricism and revitalized the entire ballet.

Ulanova did not delve into the mystic depth or symbolic structure of the old Romantic drama. Her almost primitive approach was strongly motivated by her understanding of the circumstances of the plot, which she viewed as a chain of consequences of Albrecht's juvenile, irresponsible nature, fatal for a hypersensitive child. This Giselle was a new Gretchen who fell in love with total abandon, could not bear betrayal, died, and remained faithful to her love even after death. Essentially, Ulanova's approach marked a return to the pre-Pavlova attitude: simple, without any psychological or pathological insights. She managed to blend the poetry and the prose of *Giselle* as if it were a realistic drama. Her Giselle was at first ashamed of her feelings, avoiding Albrecht's too-avid eyes as she leaped up from the bench, simplemindedly seeking to learn her fortune by plucking daisy petals, refusing to acknowledge Albrecht's betrayal, and finally losing her sanity.

In Act II she emerged as the same Giselle but in the guise of a Wili. Ulanova did not underscore the transition from reality to the no-man's-land of the moonlit cemetery: she made one believe that in life Giselle would have protected her beloved from any danger, just as she saved him from Myrtha's mortal vengeance. With the same awesome trustfulness and love she would cling to Albrecht as she did in Act I; she would entrust herself to his arms in the romantic adagio with the same childish confidence she had in the Act I passages with him and her girl friends. Ulanova never acted like a spirit; she remained a loving child who had not yet learned to hate. She herself compelled Albrecht to undertake his dance duel with the Wilis, so that he might save his own life. She encouraged him with her loving, intent gaze. When, at daybreak, Giselle began to withdraw into the flowers of her sepulchre, her arms meekly crossed on her chest, her open eyes were fixed on Albrecht, and her seemingly unreal, almost transparent body breathed the same love that it had in Act I. It was the invincible strength of this love that compelled Albrecht to experience purifying repentance at the end of the ballet.

Ulanova did not change her interpretation with the years, but she orchestrated it in various ways. In the fifties, in my view, it was overtheatrical, but her early Giselle is reported to have displayed the absolute golden measure of artistry.

The theme of faith in love as an ultimate value was woven through Ulanova's Odette in Agrippina Vaganova's new version of *Swan Lake* (1933). In the spirit of Soviet socialist realism as propagated in the thirties, Vaganova mounted *Swan Lake* as the tale of an idle aristocrat and the personification of his daydream, the enchanted queen of the swans. Although realistically set on a German country estate of the nineteenth century, Vaganova's version in a way echoed the evocative atmosphere of Fokine's *Les Sylphides*, an ambience congenial to an innately Romantic ballerina like Ulanova. Ulanova sought to convey the mysterious character of Odette, introverted and detached from reality, without specifying her nature: enchanted girl or fairy-tale bird. In the context of Vaganova's version this ambiguity was irrelevant, because Odette was no more than a figment of Count Siegfried's imagination. Her image appeared to him in the ball scene, where he seemed to recognize her in one of the female guests, clad in the masquerade attire of Winter, adorned with scraps of swan's-down and a headdress resembling a swan's wing. She constantly emerged before him as a recollection of the dream-girl he had seen at the lake and even interrupted his pas de deux with Odile (here the daughter of a landowner), like Nikiya's shade in the last act of Petipa's original *La Bayadère*. "No one could flash so soundlessly or imbue the movement of her hand, covering her face, with such a poignant sorrow as Ulanova did," a critic observed. At the finale the Count came running to the lake, only to find his swan wounded by a shot from the rifle of a landowner(!!). Ulanova's death scene was unforgettable: her resignation to fate, reserved sorrow, and all-forgiving love for Siegfried were full of such grandeur that, to a certain extent, they justified the melodramatic suicide of the Count at the final curtain.

The *Swan Lake* of 1933 was a turning point in Ulanova's career, for her Odette made her a living legend in Russia. The appeal of her highly Romantic portrayal was potent enough to undermine the social message of the ballet, meant to discredit the unproductive daydreaming of the aristocracy. As a result, her image reverberated in an unparalleled way in the mental climate of the thirties, permeated with forebodings of Stalin's future purges and

Giselle, with M. Gabovich as Albrecht, 1948

Above: Odette, 1940s
Right: (top) Odile, early 1930s; (bottom) Odette, 1940s

Left: Juliet, with Alexander Lapauri as Paris, 1957
Below: Juliet, with Yuri Zhdanov as Romeo, mid-1950s

Top: Giselle, 1952
Above: *Les Sylphides*, 1950s

OPPOSITE
Clockwise from top right: Maria in *The Fountain of Bakhchisarai*, with Vladimir
Bakanov as Khan Giri, early 1950s; Tao-Hoa in *The Red Poppy*, 1950s;
Cinderella, mid-1940s; Maria, with Tatiana Vecheslova as Zarema, 1930s

massacres. The secret of Ulanova's irresistible appeal lay not only in the poetic value of her vulnerable femininity but in the fact that everyone could identify with her un-spectacular figure and ordinary, peasantlike face. During these years, when, in Osip Mandelstam's words, "bodily fear used a typewriter in each house," Ulanova's heroines, with their indestructible moral code of love and fidelity, were perceived by the collective mind as a symbol of inner strength and resistance, able to endure despite visible frailty. The cultural ambience that inspired Mikhail Bulgakov's *The Master and Margarita* responded keenly to the vitality of Ulanova's persona, because the universal problems of moral values and inner survival acquired existential power and validity through her dancing.

On the other hand, Ulanova's subdued, seemingly self-sacrificing placidity, devoid of any sexual overtones or emotional excess ("the eternal *valse triste*," as it was called by Ulanova's few detractors in the thirties), perfectly matched the ideological standard of emotional moderation and sugary female charm propagated by the official Soviet art.

Like any totalitarian society, Stalin's Russia never tolerated sensual excess or tempestuous emotionalism, which were considered socially dangerous and hard to control. Soviet movies and literature, streamlined by censorship, disseminated the image of the submissive female able to endure any kind of physical or emotional deprivation. Ulanova's image happily satisfied the needs of both the Russian collective mind and Soviet propaganda. What made her image all the more recognizable and appealing was the genuine Russian touch of timorous legato the ballerina brought to her characterizations.

As the thirties progressed, both the audience and the Party supervisors came to favor the heartfelt manner of dancing, lyricism, and simplicity of means that were Ulanova's forte, rather than bravura tricks. These qualities, reinforced by the appeal of her popular image, enhanced Ulanova's prestige, which grew even greater in the era of the Soviet drama-ballets. This dubious genre, a powerful vehicle for Communist propaganda, might have had to be introduced by force, as potatoes were in the reign of Catherine the Great, had Ulanova not facilitated the process of its cultural acceptance. The artistry of her interpretations seemed to justify the trend. In historical perspective, these drama-ballets were the descendants of Jules Perrot's works of the pre-Petipa period, with their minimal dance passages and inflated mime scenes. Ulanova's inspired portrayals made her emblematic of the so-called Soviet ballet realism.

She flourished within the confines of these works, because they allowed her to conceal her technical flaws and to capitalize on her mimetic abilities and on the rare expressivity of her poses. In this genre she perfected herself as a dancing actress, although beyond the boundaries of the ballet stage she hardly existed as an actress. (Eisenstein wanted to cast her as Anastasia in his *Ivan the Terrible*, but she failed the screen test.)

Ulanova's special qualifications were highly appreciated by the champions of drama-ballet, such as Rostislav Zakharov and Leonid Lavrovsky: after 1934 they never failed to cast her as the heroine in their cumbersome full-length productions. Ulanova was the only Soviet ballerina who enjoyed this privilege. Recognizing her special gift for the poetic transformation of mime-oriented choreography, Zakharov mounted *The Fountain of Bakhchisarai* (1934), *Lost Illusions* (1936), and *Cinderella* (1945) for her. Lavrovsky staged *Romeo and Juliet* (1940) and *The Stone Flower* (1954) and reshaped *The Red Poppy*. Except for *Fountain of Bakhchisarai* and *Romeo and Juliet*, even in Russia these productions have all sunk into oblivion.

Ulanova soon bade farewell to Petipa's classical oeuvre, although she danced Odette until 1948. It is noteworthy that the most iconoclastic and daring Soviet choreographers, such as Leonid Jakobson and Kasyan Goleizovsky, never worked with Ulanova (although in 1930, at the dawn of her career, she portrayed a rather abstract Komsomol girl in the Vainonen-Jakobson experimental, acrobatic ballet *Golden Age*). Both viewed her as a mistress of mime with a weak technique and a strictly defined Romantic manner. For her part, Ulanova never sought any opportunity to work with Goleizovsky or Jakobson, not only because such collaboration might jeopardize her career, which depended upon the approval of the Kremlin, but also because she was truly a committed Soviet traditionalist, a champion of realistic dance-drama. In her interviews she invariably declared her dislike for plotless ballet or any kind of modern dance.

Her roles, whether Maria in *Fountain of Bakhchisarai*, Masha in Vainonen's *The Nutcracker* (1934), or the dancer Coralie in *Lost Illusions*, were distinguished choreographically only by their insufficiency of dance. They were mostly based on a few steps and poses from the Romantic vocabulary (arabesque, glissade, attitude) which Ulanova was uniquely capable of animating with her poetic understatement and mobile facial expressions. The part of the Polish princess Maria, who is captured by the Tartar Khan Guirey and perishes by the dagger of Zarema, his jealous harem wife, was an apologia for the arabesque. The critics may have been sincerely inspired or simply politically obliged to praise Ulanova in the officially approved ballets; but they gave the ballerina her due by describing the role as a collection of poses rather than a sequence of movements, a skillful mimicry of sculpture, magically brought to life. Ulanova herself made her approach quite clear: "If choreography based on ordinary simple steps is performed perfectly, it is sufficient to make a hardly perceptible movement, suggest a pose, raise your head or glance differently in order to alter a characterization or create a special atmosphere on stage." And Ulanova was unique in her mastery of these glances, meaningful gestures, and demi-poses full of indefinable yet grippingly moving poetry. Fyodor Lopukhov likened Ulanova's demi-arabesques in *Fountain* to the mysterious charm of Leonardo's smiling Mona Lisa.

Eisenstein once said that ballerinas usually know how to captivate at the beginning of a dance sequence and at its end. Ulanova knew how to enthrall in the middle, because in every major role, no matter how static or choreographically meager, she made the audience feel the beauty and mystery of the most crucial moments in life—those of love and death. Vadim Gayevsky poignantly called her "the ballerina of the morning." Ulanova's smile, both bashful and radiant, and her body, high-strung, palpitating with anticipation and fright, could convey Giselle's or Juliet's morning of love as no one else. Her death scenes became legendary: no other ballerina could so potently express physical frailty in the face of death, and the spiritual victory over it. Maria's death scene was the epitome of Ulanova's spiritually charged art. Quietly, with serene determination, she seemed to direct her body toward Zarema's dagger. As she died, her body slowly glided down along a column, while her arm was softly thrust in the air and lingered there, subsiding softly like a clipped branch or flower.

All these qualities were visible in her portrayal of Juliet in Lavrovsky's balletic transcription of Shakespeare's tragedy, set to Prokofiev's music, which was mounted especially for her. Choreographically, the role of Juliet was also poor, consisting mainly of statuesque poses, turns, and arabesques. Ironically, when I recall Ulanova's Juliet, the most dynamic dance passage seems to be her cloak-fluttering headlong run to Friar Laurence or her luminous and sorrowful arabesques in the arms of her Romeo in the farewell scene. Clad in the tunic of Botticelli's Primavera, her hair modestly bound in a Florentine snood, her Juliet only re-

motely resembled Shakespeare's passionate heroine. She was never impetuous or ardent. In the most dramatic scenes, she invariably maintained a kind of poetic aura, conveying inner peace and self-sufficiency. Her Juliet was a composite of the qualities of her earlier Romantic heroines: the simplicity of Giselle, the vulnerability of Maria, and the childish awkwardness of Odette. But Juliet's character was elusive rather than precise, poetically indefinable; and that, in its turn, extended the rigid confines of Lavrovsky's drama-ballet. Only Ulanova could transform Lavrovsky's realistic Juliet, surrounded by a pompous production and a prolix, explicative libretto, into a legendary figure of chaste and tragic love. By all reports, Ulanova, partnered by Sergeyev, managed to sustain a kind of Romantic mini-ballet within the original Leningrad production of 1940.

In the fifties, when I saw her Juliet, she was different. As her technique waned, she became more a dancing actress than a ballerina. Inspired by Stanislavsky, she instilled into the part such an abundance of realistic accents and shadings that, in my view, she undermined and flattened the metaphorical fullness of Juliet's image. Nevertheless, the unique understated lyricism was still there, and Ulanova's special stamp on the part eluded those ballerinas who tried to imitate her in the 1960s.

Ulanova's roles of the 1940s and 1950s, following her Juliet—Cinderella in Zakharov's ballet of that name, Parasha in his *The Bronze Horseman*, Tao-Hoa in Lavrovsky's *The Red Poppy*, and Katerina in his *The Stone Flower*—were mostly based on mime; dance itself was peripheral. They only remotely echoed Ulanova's great Romantic achievements of the 1930s and 1940s; she seemed to have readapted them to the needs of realism, more concerned with the justification of a plot than with its poetic transfiguration. At times she indulged in pantomime, her undisputed forte, while sacrificing the steps themselves. This artistic approach gave rise to some strong, though unofficial, opinions. "As a ballerina she is no one. She is merely a mime of genius. When her Giselle dies, even her chin seems to sharpen and turns waxen," the great Russian poet Anna Akhmatova once remarked.

The more Ulanova's technique flagged in the 1950s, the more she relied upon her still impressive posing and miming to invest every step and gesture with her seemingly artless poetry of understatement. She put so much effort into it that by the end of the 1950s her dancing began to look mannered, even contrived. The times seemed to work against her. When Nikita Khrushchev's liberal reform indirectly contributed to the release of dance from the iron grip of drama-ballet, my generation began to consider Ulanova's famed artistry and legend as a product of the Stalin era's artificial aesthetic. As the Soviet audience gradually became acquainted with the innovations of contemporary Western ballet (Balanchine, Ashton, Robbins), Ulanova's artistry seemed to stand more and more for Soviet melodrama; it even appeared "campy."

However harsh and ungrateful this may seem, it contains a grain of truth. Ironically, when her Giselle comes to mind, I recall not so much her soaring jumps in Act II as her poignant accents in the mad scene. Without loosening her hair, she stared intensely at Albrecht's sword. She did not raise it high in her hands or rush forward onto its point. Rather, she sluggishly directed the sword into her heart and then dropped it with an indifferent, detached gesture. One recalls also the simplicity of her modest grace in the arabesques in *Chopiniana*, which she could sustain as no one else, and the peace and spiritual concentration that her image conveyed.

During her last decade at the Bolshoi, Ulanova did not create anything new. Curiously enough, Western acclaim came to her in the years of her gradual decline. In 1951 she first appeared in Florence. Her *Dying Swan* took the audience by storm with its tender resignation and oversimplicity of interpretation—with all those qualities that in Russia now made her seem old-fashioned and one-dimensional.

In 1956 Ulanova's portrayals of Maria, Juliet, and Giselle whipped London into a state of hysterical adoration; three years later she conquered New York. Only a few cognoscenti, Anton Dolin in particular, dared to disparage the ballerina for her earthbound, overly realistic Giselle, devoid of those mystical insights that had marked, for instance, her legendary predecessors like Spessivtseva and Markova. Most Western opinions bordered on naiveté or sheer nonsense. Arnold Haskell saluted her as a ballerina who won fame "not though the recognition of enlightened balletomanes but from the audience at large." The British ballet historian apparently was quite unaware of Ulanova's appeal to the totalitarian Soviet state machine which promoted her in every possible way. Nor did he know that Ulanova's transformation into a Soviet icon was related to her conformist, obedient behavior, her support of oppressive political actions of the Soviet government, and her intractability vis-à-vis any balletic experiment beyond the dictates of socialist realism.

This side of Ulanova's career certainly did not undermine her artistry, which was very special and more representative of the grandeur and misery of Soviet ballet in the Stalin era than anyone else's. Therein lies her unique contribution as a great lyrical talent, as well as her limitation.

Nikiya in *La Bayadère*, late 1970s

NATALIA MAKAROVA

MAKAROVA is the last avatar of the great lyrical balle-rina and the most iconoclastic of her sisterhood. In physique and technique she is akin to Pavlova and Ulanova, a genuine Romantic ballerina. It is no wonder that among her most refined achievements are Giselle, the Sylphide, and Odette. Like Pavlova, her fragile lines, thin, girlish neck, and long face with its finely chiseled features, as if drawn by some old Dutch painter, call forth an image of elusive femininity.

Her status as a Romantic ballerina was asserted at the outset: the elevation of her seemingly effortless leap, her light step, the innate fluidity of her movements, and her flexible torso constituted a rich potential and pointed the direction of her career. Had Makarova remained within the boundaries of Romantic technique, she would have been Ulanova's legitimate successor. But Makarova, like her frequent partner Baryshnikov, is driven by enormous artistic curiosity that constantly challenges her to extend the limits of this category in search of more perfect classical technique, heightened expressiveness, greater self-realization. Her restless spirit and her potent dramatic abilities make her unique among Romantic ballerinas.

Makarova's plasticity is marked by a contemporary tone—she is a changeable being whose body and face reflect mobility and conflict. Her broad smile is enticing and mocking in its unconcealed coquettishness; her Romantic, seemingly ethereal lines often give hint of a soubrette. She breathes easily in the doll realm of *Coppélia*, the music hall ambience of *Don Quixote*, and the jovial Gallic atmosphere of *La Fille mal gardée*.

The restlessness of Makarova's personality is constantly apparent during rehearsals and in everyday life. It may surface at any moment in the most unexpected circumstances: in the play of interchanging lines, which at one moment may be flowing and at another brittle; in her almost mercurial transitions from joy to sadness. When pondering her private affairs she may become detached, mysterious, inscrutable, and then suddenly burst into laughter over a trifle. It is difficult to predict her reactions, just as it is impossible to know in what sort of mood she will appear that evening on the stage. Churning inside is a constant labor of the soul, a never-ending process. It is this very labor of the soul that lavishly colors her dancing, transforming her body into a series of spiritually charged transfigurations. This is the origin of that "human humidity," to use Vladimir Nabokov's phrase, which permeates the art of Natalia Makarova in each of her roles. As Beliayev said of Pavlova, in each performance she plots "an uneven line on the chart of her artistic pulse."

NATALIA ROMANOVNA MAKAROVA was born into an educated Leningrad family on November 21, 1940, the eve of the great war that turned Russia upside-down. These circumstances implanted certain qualities in her character which were later reinforced by experience. The Makarova genes are a mixture of the intellectual and the peasant. Her paternal grandfather was an architect whose artistic fervor provided an unconscious stimulus to her early infatuation with painting and theatre. Her father, an engineer, left no trace in her memory; he was killed in the first months of the war. Her mother, a housewife, remarried, and her stepfather became the only father she ever knew.

By sheer chance, at the age of twelve Makarova became a member of an amateur ballet group at the Palace of Pioneers. From there, her first rather awkward experience on the stage inexplicably led the youngster to the doors of the Vaganova School in 1953. Vaganova was no longer alive, but had she presided over the selection committee, the angular, long-limbed, long-necked girl, reminiscent of the early Picasso *saltimbanques*, would probably not have captured her imagination. "I was like a little giraffe," recalls Makarova, unaware that Pavlova used a similar expression

to describe herself at that age. And like Pavlova, Makarova was not one of the best students, although she was put in an accelerated six-year program specially designed for talented teenagers. The consequences of her insufficient training made themselves felt throughout her entire Kirov period.

Makarova grew up in the special climate of the Khrushchev era. Her inner restlessness, total commitment to fantasy, disregard of reality, artistic curiosity—all were strongly encouraged by the invigorating spirit of the second half of the 1950s. She belonged to the generation known as "the children of the pause," a period marked by a loosening of controls as a result of Khrushchev's liberal reforms and the revelations concerning the cult of Stalin. The shadows of Stalin's countless colossal statues, which were now tumbling everywhere, had blanketed the aspirations of the young. Now it began to stir again, the hope of seeing a new life through the bleak web of socialist dogma that had been spun around them since childhood. The web was being pierced by a process of creative thinking, a desire to find nourishment in Western philosophy and religion as well as in the traditions of classical Russian literature.

These great expectations took deep root in Makarova's quick mind, always impelled by curiosity, open to any experiment, however risky or insane it might seem. This has made her the only ballerina of her generation who has managed to absorb into her bloodstream the spiritual essence of Russian culture, with its lofty concern for the moral and religious message of art. In *A Dance Autobiography* she constantly discusses the possibilities of expressing a "human soul" through formal balletic patterns and emotionality, which in her view constitute the essence of performance in ballet.

From her first steps on the stage, she has always sought to imbue her heroines with her own fantasies and the fluctuations of her mood. Each performance for her involves self-discovery and self-exploration. Makarova cannot dance simply for the sake of dancing, because she is invariably concerned with finding emotional truth in a performance, no matter how elusive that truth may be. Thus, her approaches to her roles alter quickly, resulting in a new shift of dramatic accents. Makarova is an unpredictable ballerina in the best sense. Her intense inner life and longing for self-knowledge are her most potent stimulant.

When Makarova joined the Kirov in 1958, she hardly resembled the consummate classicist of our day, equally radiant in Romantic adagio, crisp allegro, or the most intricate neoclassical patterns. The insufficiency of her six years of training made itself felt in her desperate struggle to master Petipa's academic vocabulary, which resisted her for many years.

On the other hand, the perpetual conflict between her quest for self-expression and her technical inadequacy lavishly colored each of the classical roles that she performed at the dawn of her Kirov career. In some respects, the originality of her dramatic approach, the intensity of her stage presence, and her unusual, at times iconoclastic, slant on traditional roles were more spontaneous and appealing than the polished maturity of the prima ballerina she has become in the West. To a certain degree, her shortcomings turned out to be her forte, an unmistakable stamp of individuality that distinguished her from her gifted Kirov colleagues.

Even when extending or distorting stylistic boundaries, the young Makarova was prodigiously talented, as she demonstrated in her debut in *Giselle* in December 1959. Although later on the Kirov forced Makarova to tame her unbridled imagination, the rebellious spirit of her early Giselle still reverberated through her more mature characterization. Makarova's Giselle put the viewer on guard because of its daring novelty, setting all the traditions and canons of Romantic ballet topsy-turvy. Not a trace of meekness, dreaminess, and distrustfulness were to be found in her peasant girl—traits that marked the interpretations of every Russian ballerina from Pavlova to Ulanova.

Makarova's Giselle was spirited and wily. She made eyes at Albrecht and responded to his courting with teasing coquetry; the features of a soubrette could be seen in her portrayal. An angular figure, concealing her essential vulnerability, she unexpectedly reflected the spirit of her own young generation of the 1960s. As she dolefully faced deceit for the first time, death became the price of her longing for happiness. In the second act, free of pantomime and impeccably faithful to the old Romantic style, she became an ethereal being, but her spirit did not shed its earthly vestments. It did not dissolve in a harmony overflowing with moonlit peace and the silence of the forest, as in the interpretation of Anna Pavlova. It did not waft like a spirit of goodness and forgiveness as had Ulanova's Giselle. Makarova radiated a sense of restlessness that clung to Giselle even in the world beyond. Her jumps, lifts, and arabesques emitted a special kind of nervous energy, infectious and disturbing. It seemed that even in her grave, Giselle was unable to achieve peace or tranquility; and,

tearing herself from her captive state, this Wili continued to be ravaged by disquiet. Hers was a search for self-expression, and her defense of Albrecht was merely an outlet for her energy.

In the beginning Makarova did not attempt to clip the wings of her own individuality. She was delighted by the fact that in dance she could express her distinct character, which she was not about to sacrifice to the demands of style, where limits and boundaries count for so much.

Her changeable moods, the capriciousness of her soul, marked all the roles Makarova performed at the Kirov, creating a kind of nervousness and dissonance that at times bordered on bad taste. Probably she herself did not know what to expect from the difficult child still within her or how it could affect any given scene or role. Every Makarova performance promised the viewer either a lavish surprise or a lamentable letdown. Even in the stylized domain of *Les Sylphides* Makarova, for all her physical and stylistic suitability, caused amazement with her sharp accents, as if purposefully repudiating the delicate contours of Fokine's Romantic pastiche. I was particularly overwhelmed by Makarova's performances in this ballet, so different from Ulanova's memorable ones. In the D-sharp Mazurka Makarova never floated across the stage in a smooth line, without any visible rupture between her upward surges and her landings. Instead, she tore the design to shreds as she flew from one end of the stage to the other. Her C-flat Waltz was danced with the same determination, as if a demon had taken possession of her, giving her spirit no rest.

Her artistic growth at the Kirov was hindered mostly by the frustrating discrepancy between her imperfect technique and her enormous aspirations and desire to express herself. At best, the young Makarova performed four times a month at the Kirov, hardly enough to enable her to increase her technical mastery. Apart from *Giselle*, *Les Sylphides*, and the virtuoso part (which she could not master) of the Tsar Maiden in *The Little Humpbacked Horse*, she was frequently cast in drama-ballets, performing Nina in *Masquerade*, Maria in *The Fountain of Bakhchisarai*, and Juliet in Lavrovsky's *Romeo and Juliet*.

In the mind of the Russian ballet-goer the roles of Juliet and Maria have been always associated with Ulanova. They were created for her unique talent, which could forge the essentially cheap melodrama into something approximating true poetry. In the 1960s, both *Fountain* and *Romeo* had become exhibits in a sad ballet museum. It was doubtful that they could ever elicit the proper response from Makarova's theatrical instinct. The choreographic inadequacy of the two roles bordered on poverty; one could hardly even call them "academic" or "professional."

The melodramatic story of *Fountain of Bakhchisarai*, that antediluvian though reworked *ballet oriental*, unfolded against the colorful bric-a-brac of an Eastern curio shop filled with water pipes, baggy trousers, and Oriental skullcaps; the heavy pantomime meandered through the poorly designed dances, in which there seemed to be no place for Makarova.

She tried to annihilate the accepted traditions of this ballet by misplacing all the accents. Her Maria even went so far as to reveal a certain interest in the wild Tartar who was experiencing his first love; and into the famous death scene she instilled a definite energetic impetus, unlike Ulanova's poignant submissiveness. Makarova's fragile body collapsed convulsively against the smooth surface of a column; her last pose, hand bent at the wrist and flung back, in no way expressed a sense of peaceful acceptance. Critics spoke of Makarova's uncalled-for tampering with Ulanova's masterpiece, but in truth there was no tampering. Makarova was "doing her own thing," probably spontaneously and unconsciously, without looking back at tradition—which, in any case, she did not know very well.

When she came to Lavrovsky's *Romeo and Juliet*, Makarova was also far from the Botticellian spirit-rather-than-flesh image so well conveyed by Ulanova. Looking like a fun-loving fourteen-year-old who couldn't sit still, whose breasts had barely begun to develop under her tight bodice, Makarova's Juliet was an angular child who enjoyed teasing her nurse and imitating the adults who surrounded her. All her behavior emphasized her reluctance to give up the cozy world of her childhood. Even her feelings for Romeo reflected the awkwardness of first love rather than Shakespeare's all-consuming passion. The wild desire and turbulent longing of youth that resounded in Prokofiev's music were not to be seen. The touching teenager was locked in her own essence and remained there. In the contours of the Renaissance heroine there appeared the image of a typical unruly young girl of today.

At the beginning of the 1960s, Natalia Makarova's fame as the Kirov's most lyrical ballerina was not only firmly fixed at home but reached far beyond the boundaries of Russia. In 1961, right after Rudolf Nureyev's flight to freedom, Makarova gave a triumphant performance of *Giselle* in London, recalling to the enthusiastic critics the days of Pavlova, Spessivtseva, and Markova. Makarova won the applause of the American public in 1964, and the following year she was awarded a gold medal at the ballet competition in Varna. In 1967 the Paris Academy of Dance presented her with the Anna Pavlova award.

But the greater her success, the more evident was the developing rift between her personality and the frozen repertoire of the Kirov. Vera Krasovskaya sounded the alarm, having carefully watched Makarova's artistic development and seen how her path was blocked: "Choreographers are frightened by Makarova's personal sense of drama. Is it possible that they are not aware of the fact that even if they do not elicit a response to their own creative input, they may reap a reward ten times greater? For in this case stubbornness goes hand in hand with creative curiosity and a professional talent that cannot go by without arousing interest." But hers was a voice in the wilderness.

Makarova's early attempts at *Swan Lake* revealed her immaturity and technical inadequacy, although she managed to put her unmistakable stamp on Odette as a frightened baby-swan in the grip of doom. Coming on stage, Makarova's Odette did not fold her arms over her head in the Kirov's traditional circular fashion. One arm was tucked under her body crosswise, like a wing, while the other was pressed against her shoulder, covering her breast, as her frightened face rested against her bent wrist. Stepping out of the lake onto the shore, her Odette did not enjoy the peaceful moonlit night: she was full of anxiety and pain. She spread her wings in a flying attitude for one brief moment, immediately folded them again, and, lowering her neck, peered from under her wing. At this moment she saw the Prince, froze, expanded her arms frontwards in a resisting motion and flapped them furtively, as if trapped, paying no heed to the Prince or to the magician who had now come on the stage, seemingly unable to differentiate between her savior and the evildoer.

The same anxiety pervaded her movements in the throng of swan-girls. She ran across the stage with determination, and when she paused, her head was turned away from the Prince. Even in the next sequence, when she flung her arms open to Siegfried, her gesture did not suggest that she recognized him as her long-awaited lover. Her overt terror subsided, but the feeling of estrangement persisted. This sense of alienation, laced with an intense and bitter passion, added some fresh inflections to the adagio. As she executed a series of turns, petits battements, and arabesques, her arms continued to relate the story of a captive spirit. They reached out feverishly, shuddered, fell listlessly, were delicately curled in their collapse.

In the variation the theme of Odette's longing for love

Left: (top) The Fair Maiden in *Wonderland*
(Jakobson), with Yuri Soloviev as Prince Charming,
1967; (bottom) *The Pearl*, with O. Sokolov as Kino,
1965
Above: Giselle, with Vladilen Semyonov as Albrecht,
1960s

Right: Odette, with Ivan Nagy as Siegfried, mid-1970s
Below: Odile, with Anthony Dowell as Siegfried, mid-1970s

Giselle, with Mikhail Baryshnikov as
Albrecht, late 1970s

La Sylphide, 1970s

Don Quixote pas de deux, 1970s

Top: *Bach Sonata* (Béjart), with Anthony Dowell, 1980

Above: (left) Manon, with Dowell as Des Grieux, late 1970s; (right) *Other Dances*, with Baryshnikov, late 1970s

and that of her poignant sense of isolation were both slightly subdued; they became more pronounced in the finale, through the nervous emphasis put on the changements de pieds and sissonnes. But essentially her Odette remained inscrutable. Perched on the Prince's knee, she did not protect him under the cover of her wings but spread them far apart as she gazed into the invisible distance. Floating away, she did not give her lover a farewell glance but continued to look into the distance with her eyes wide open.

The role of Odile eluded Makarova for years. Although she looked simply magnificent with her golden head wrapped in black feathers and her black tutu emphasizing the beauty of her chiseled legs, Odile remained the most difficult technical tour de force for her to master. Her fouettés did not work, and the turns of her last variation occasionally fell apart.

At the beginning of her Kirov career, to Makarova's credit, she sought an outlet for her modernist inclinations. In 1960 she began to work with the most liberal and unconventional of Soviet choreographers, Leonid Jakobson, performing in several of his ballets: his short *The Kiss*; *The Bedbug*, based on Mayakovsky's play; *La Valse* to Ravel; and *Country of Wonder*. Her association with Jakobson freed her body from its dependence on strict classical grammar, giving her the opportunity to experience a wild, expressionistic plasticity. Jakobson's style freely combined a pantomime that verged on caricature, sculptural gesture, elements of pure classicism, and neoclassicism. He favored turned-in positions, as Fokine did, and consciously ungraceful poses, throwing the classically trained body slightly askew and substituting the unexpected for the familiar.

In *The Bedbug* Makarova performed the part of Zoya Berezkina, a disoriented young woman who has lost the illusions of her forefathers and henceforth does not know which way to turn. Appearing on the stage in an old, faded dress, low heels, and boyish haircut, she cut a touching figure: a lost soul longing for love, trapped in an age of alienation. Finally, growing weary of it all, she thrust her neck into an invisible noose.

In *La Valse* Makarova created a stylized cameo of a mischievous beauty, both innocent and cruel; in *Country of Wonder* she was a touching, fairy-tale Russian maiden, strong in her fidelity to her beloved and resistance to violence. But Jakobson's choreography seriously jeopardized the purity of her still tenuous classical technique.

Makarova was longing for a part that was a happy fusion of classical and modernist elements, one that gave her more opportunity for emotional projection. She was happy to have Jakobson's creations as an emotional outlet, but classical and neoclassical ballet remained her primary interest, not his extreme post-Fokine innovations, which often bordered on parody of purely classical form. Therefore, when Konstantin Sergeyev revived *Cinderella* in 1964 and offered Makarova first the role of Cinderella's affected stepsister and then (a year later) Cinderella herself, everyone's expectations were aroused. But Sergeyev's *Cinderella* followed the highly traditional classical format. His leading characters were porcelain figurines rather than the real human beings so skillfully intimated by Prokofiev's music. Nevertheless, in performing the two contrasting roles, Makarova displayed not only her growing skill but also her ability to portray grotesque and comic characters in dance.

Makarova's affected stepsister did not at all resemble a typical fairy-tale character. The grotesque image of the nasty girl looked surprisingly contemporary. Vera Krasovskaya wrote: "If Makarova's affected stepsister were to take off her wig and bouffant sleeves you could find her sailing on her own yacht or sitting at an airport bar casually sipping a tasty cocktail as she awaited the arrival of her plane. . . . Her pose on pointe suddenly reminded the viewer of one of those girls on the cover of an American detective novel—in the way her hand was bent at the wrist, as if holding an invisible cigarette, while her eyes mocked." In the last act she did indeed appear without the wig and poufs, as she tiptoed across the stage in a nylon robe.

Makarova danced her first Cinderella in Chicago during the Kirov's 1964 engagement; the following year she danced the role in Leningrad. In her interpretation there was no hint of reverie or introspection; instead, the traits of a superactive, moody, slightly awkward child predominated. She could be hilariously funny cleaning, scrubbing, and polishing everything in sight, and then suddenly retreat into her shell, as if to reflect on what was happening around her. These transitions were subtly drawn, contributing to a vivid characterization.

The magic transformation, her crystal slippers and her crown, did not change her character. She looked around the ballroom with great interest; even her encounter with the Prince aroused her curiosity more than her feelings. Her happiness was self-sufficient. She did not even seem to be romantically involved with the Prince—her feelings did not depend on him at all but had an existence of their own. She was lonely; her emotions carried her along their own path.

Cinderella, incidentally, was Makarova's first and last encounter at the Kirov with contemporary music.

Mired in routine, Makarova longed for the chance to experiment, but from 1965 to 1970 she was not given any significant new roles. Still, her artistry grew, and in the Romantic realm of *Les Sylphides* and *Giselle* the elusive quality of her movements, her insecure balance, and her slightly tremulous arabesques irresistibly called to mind the legendary image of Pavlova.

Beyond the Kirov stage Makarova sought to appease her curiosity by performing short ballets by Georgy Alexidze (*The Syrinx*) and Leonid Jakobson (*A Passing Beauty*). In 1967 Igor Tchernichov began to choreograph for her his one-act *Romeo and Juliet*, set to excerpts from Berlioz's dramatic symphony. This was the only neoclassical role that was tailor-made for her potential and theatrical instincts; but, to her great distress, the ballet was banned on the spot after a preview for the Kirov management.

Later Makarova said that the action taken against Tchernichov's *Romeo and Juliet* was one of the causes of her defection. The bureaucratic veto was the last drop in a cup that finally ran over. Subconsciously, something gave way; her artistic discontent began to erode her inner being in a process that could no longer be stopped. She suddenly felt that the years were flying by senselessly. Her thirtieth birthday, a crucial point for any ballerina, was not far off, and a time of reckoning and maturity was about to begin. Her anxiety grew; a feeling of boredom followed, accompanied by a sense of exhaustion. Her last performances of *Swan Lake* in Russia were opaque and muted, as if all of her energy had been sapped. She herself was conscious of this and thought that perhaps she needed an external stimulus to activate her imagination.

In 1970, accompanied by these vague yet painful feelings, Makarova went to London with the Kirov, unaware that this journey would become a crucial point in her life and career. During the engagement she left the company and sought asylum with the British Home Office. Like Nureyev's defection in 1961 and Baryshnikov's in 1974, her leap to freedom was an impromptu flight, but her pent-up discontent and artistic maturity had long been leading her in this direction. Impulsively and spontaneously, she just "dove into it like into cold water," as she put it. Only years later did she fully realize that in 1970 her Kirov career had been over. "Russia could not offer me anything more than what was already given," she told me in 1977, when I was working with her on *A Dance Autobiography*, and she was faced for the first time with the task of evaluating her career and her feelings. "Although I felt I stood in heavy debt to the Kirov, nothing there could inspire me any

longer. My imagination was in a stupor; my technique did not progress; my intuition prompted me to run away from the void looming ahead."

Makarova's decade in the West has proved to be not only a period of experimentation with various balletic styles but also an endless *classe de perfection* during which she has become a consummate classicist, reveling in academic technique—"the most elusive thing in the world," in her own words. She came to the West "a dilettante of genius," as Baryshnikov once called her, but she has been unflaggingly persistent in making up for the shortcomings of her Russian training. She has strengthened and sharpened her allegro technique and mastered the intricate steps—fouettés, pirouettes en attitude, renversés—that previously eluded her. As her control increased, she has restrained her former wild impulsiveness.

At first she enjoyed her new freedom as a "citizen of the world," but since 1972 she has been affiliated mostly with American Ballet Theatre. She was universally acclaimed for her poignant lyricism in *Giselle*, *La Sylphide*, and *Les Sylphides* and for the wit and mischief she brought to her Lise in *La Fille mal gardée* and Swanilda in *Coppélia*. At the same time she eagerly gave rein to her modernist sympathies by tackling various styles (sometimes unsuitable to her), as in John Neumeier's *Epilogue*, Alvin Ailey's *The River*, and Ulf Gadd's *The Miraculous Mandarin*. Although subsequently she viewed these early experiments as useless, they certainly had a salutary effect on her body, hitherto trained exclusively in the Kirov style.

Her achievements were artistically uneven, owing to the constant conflict between her Russian schooling and the demands of Western choreographic styles. She had been trained to sweep through whole dance sequences with Russian fluency, accentuating the movement by lingering behind the musical measure, but Western styles required a sharpness of accent and a special knack for maneuvering the body swiftly. In one of our conversations Makarova aptly likened herself in those days to a "glittering limousine, forced to take uphill or downhill at the same speed, equally powerful on highway and swampy land." Small wonder that the demands of Balanchine's *Theme and Variations* overwhelmed her or that except for *Theme*, *Apollo*, and *Tchaikovsky Pas de Deux* she has never essayed Balanchine's choreography.

Even in *Pillar of Fire*, *Lilac Garden*, and *Dark Elegies*, whose plastique might seem to be suited to her, Makarova had to struggle with some of Tudor's expressive inversions and extensions of classical movements. Moreover, she had to substitute dramatic reticence for her Russian impetuosity, especially as Hagar in *Pillar of Fire*, where she finally found a reserved dramatic manner to convey emotional content implicitly, without flamboyant theatricality.

Her characterizations of Tudor's heroines were controversial. Makarova's detractors felt her interpretations lacked the physical and emotional intensity that marked Nora Kaye's portrayals. Nonetheless, Tudor himself seemed to prefer a more classical look in contemporary performances of his early masterpieces and welcomed Makarova's piercing lyrical note, which, in his view, refreshed his slightly old-fashioned choreography.

Makarova's collaboration with Tudor and other Western choreographers caused her to re-evaluate her approach to *Giselle* and *Swan Lake*. She has danced both ballets often in the West and has worked on them more than on anything else.

In *Giselle* she seemed to have found the golden mean. Her Giselle called to mind an unusual amalgam of Ulanova and Yvette Chauviré, though she never imitated either of them. In contrast to her Kirov Giselle, Makarova did not overact any dramatic moment, but she executed the combinations with so much natural abandon that she seemed to be inventing them on the stage at that very moment. Dramatically, from the beginning she made clear Giselle's predestination for an early death; in death she was to gain total happiness with Albrecht and demonstrate the power of her love beyond the grave, outside reality. Thus her Giselle suddenly echoed her Odette. In Act I of *Giselle* her muted dramatic accents recalled Ulanova's almost ascetic expressive means. In Act II her unearthly, spectral aspect perfectly matched her flawless sensitivity to the boundaries of Romantic style. But her uniqueness lay in the way the subtly stylized image of a simple-hearted peasant girl managed to suggest and prefigure the future Wili of all-forgiving wisdom and spiritual love.

In *Giselle* Makarova was much less unpredictable than in *Swan Lake*, in which she seemed never even to have sought the golden mean. Each performance of *Swan Lake* always meant for her a new and very personal experience. She took Plisetskaya's memorable portrayals as an inspiring model and blended the roles of Odette and Odile into a metaphor of femininity, vulnerable and touching, then aggressive and destructive. And like Plisetskaya, in *Swan Lake* Makarova manifested with spellbinding force her own unpredictable changes of mood. The fluctuations of her emotional life and her volatile feelings in fact turned each performance of this ballet into a kind of artistic impromptu.

When her Odette was self-sacrificing and serene, and the choreographic design was subjugated to the fluency of Russian legato, Act II was the focal point of her performance. But when she presented the Swan Queen as a grief-stricken, tragically anguished figure, her adagio sharply accented and her variation impulsively orchestrated, the melodramatic emphasis gave the fourth act a powerful intensity that made up for its choreographic weakness.

Her Odile underwent similar transformations, although Makarova's mind seemed to be more on technical survival than on anything else (the thirty-two fouettés still arouse the childish fears of her school days). Odile might emerge as a captivating stranger enveloped in a mysterious aura or perhaps as a mischievous child-woman, fascinating yet not overtly seductive. Makarova added a lyrical element to the portrayal of Odile, essentially shaping her as Odette's aggressive twin.

As a classicist Makarova grew swiftly, mastering both the legacy of Petipa and that of Fokine. Alone among the great lyrical ballerinas, she excelled in both styles. Some of Fokine's works (*The Firebird*, especially) struck her as irretrievably old-fashioned; at times she seemed emotionally out of touch, as in her adequate yet rather conventional *Dying Swan*. She performed *Les Sylphides* with impeccable Romantic technique yet in a low key compared with her unforgettable interpretation at the Kirov—partly because she never felt comfortable in Fokine's American version of the ballet, partly because, as she confessed, "I had outgrown Fokine's neoromanticism."

In 1974, for American Ballet Theatre, Makarova staged the Kingdom of the Shades scene from Petipa's *La Bayadère*, assigning herself one of the most taxing roles in Russian ballet. Nikiya was not one of Makarova's crowning achievements, but she undertook this tremendously challenging part despite her fear of the double pirouettes en attitude and the steellike pointe work. Nonetheless, as Nikiya she impressed one with the poignant Romantic aura through which she filtered Petipa's academic patterns; they took on the entire gamut of touching lyrical nuances so central to Makarova's art.

She portrayed Nikiya again in her own transcription of the full-length *Bayadère*, which she subjected to substantial revision when she staged it for American Ballet Theatre in 1979. To her credit, Makarova included the last act, never performed by the Kirov; she choreographed it from scratch. Although her design diverged drastically from Petipa's style, her portrayal of Nikiya was distinguished by remarkable dramatic integrity. Only a great Russian ballerina could bring to life this rather cardboard role, which usually looks like a collection of show stoppers. What particularly marked her characterization was the power with which she revealed Nikiya's evolution from a shy, chaste priestess to a woman smitten by passion, who dies and after spiritual transfiguration becomes an angel of revenge.

Makarova's individual stamp, which made her Nikiya so grippingly moving, somehow eluded her in *The Sleeping Beauty*. Aurora offered Makarova the ultimate challenge: at the Kirov she was deemed incapable of attaining this pinnacle of academic technique. Like Pavlova, though, Makarova proved to be miscast as Aurora. The role came a bit too late in her career; she looked mannered and contrived. Engrossed in the choreographic challenge, she failed to present a unified portrayal, although some passages were distinguished by her special polish and elegance: her entrance variation, the Danse Vertige in Act I, the Act III pas de deux. And, regardless of her problems with Aurora, she was an unsurpassed Florine.

In *A Dance Autobiography*, Makarova maintains that only in the West did she become fully conscious of her affinity for modern ballet, which she had striven to express in Russia, where occasionally its manifestations had been out of control. She felt that her theatrical instincts, her dependence on her mood at each performance, and her inner urge for self-expression were almost impossible to realize fully within the rigid bounds of classical structure. Makarova dreamed of finding a balance between her deep yearnings and modern ballet choreography.

She sought this coveted balance in Glen Tetley's *Voluntaries* and Kenneth MacMillan's *The Song of the Earth*. In these ballets Makarova created her most memorable modern roles, because both compositions are saturated with the metaphysics that immediately trigger her emotional responses. Such choreography compels her to perform "as if overcoming the utmost muscle strain, overcoming myself, through pain and torment." These ballets, with their strong spiritual implications, are Makarova's true element. In them her body becomes a powerful metaphor of religious ecstasy or the longing for spiritual fulfillment. She surpasses all her contemporaries in her ability to convey inner states of being, in implying a poetry of understatement or elusive femininity, which she expresses with unique artistry.

In Jerome Robbins's *Other Dances* Makarova found one of her best neoclassical roles. She lavishly orchestrated the image of alluring and mysterious femininity, throwing herself into a dance sequence with impetuous abandon and suddenly withdrawing with enigmatic reticence. In *Other Dances* her ability to hold poses on pointe (the essence of Romantic style) and alternate these lingering poses with sudden outbursts of bravura steps created an impression of "the lace of momentary feelings in the female soul," as she once defined it.

But no matter how insistently Makarova declares her affinity for plotless ballets, she has remained faithful to the concept of the dramatic ballet, in which, ideally, a consistent plot is projected by imaginative choreography. When in her numerous interviews Makarova has complained about the lack of new works of substance in her Western repertory, she means dramatic ballets—her tribute to her Soviet past. She is reluctant to abandon this aspect of her heritage; to be a dancing actress remains her major goal. She still dreams of Joan of Arc, of Nastasia Filippovna in Dostoyevsky's *The Idiot* and expresses her bewildered disappointment that no one except Kenneth MacMillan of the Royal Ballet has made much use of her dramatic talent. In MacMillan's *Romeo and Juliet* and his *Manon*, Makarova showed her unique gift for blending dancing and acting into a meaningful unity. Recently she added to the gallery of her most poignant characterizations Carmen and Esmeralda in Roland Petit's ballets. Despite the fact that she has already been on the stage for twenty-five years, Makarova is still curious about her own artistic potential, and one never knows where this curiosity will lead her and her public. One of these revelations occurred in the fall of 1982, when Makarova appeared on Broadway in the dramatic role of a cantankerous Russian prima ballerina in the revival of George Abbott's musical *On Your Toes*. In this production Makarova wrought a minor theatrical wonder—her half bitchy, half self-indulgent heroine was fun to watch and proved again what a perfect comedienne she is. The role brought her a Tony award which greatly added to her confidence as an actress and oriented her interests toward dramatic theatre and movies. Nevertheless, ballet still remains the focus of her attention, and, who knows, maybe one of the best of Makarova's roles still awaits her.

THE GREAT VIRTUOSOS

Matilda Kschessinskaya
Olga Preobrajenskaya
Natalia Dudinskaya

Кшесинская II.

ФОТОГР. Императорскихъ ТЕАТРОВЪ.

MATILDA KSCHESSINSKAYA

Perusing Matilda Kschessinskaya's memoirs, *Dancing in St. Petersburg* (published in 1961), a kind though naive reader might envision the author as a sort of charitable balletic bee, fluttering from one flower of success to another in order to share generously with everyone the honey of her art and goodness. Heartbroken in her love for the last Russian tsar, Nicholas II, yet fortunate in her long affairs with two grand dukes, Sergei and Andrei (the latter finally became her husband), she claims to have been a devoted friend of Diaghilev and Fokine, enjoyed the special favors of the old Maestro Petipa, and served as fairy godmother to the budding talents of Pavlova, Karsavina, and Nijinsky. That she sparkled and shone in every ballet on the Imperial stage goes without saying. As for the web of petty intrigues that were spun out of sheer envy around this embodiment of honesty, its filament was immediately broken at the behest of the tsar or through Providence, the outcome merited by Kschessinskaya's unquestioned high ethics. Kschessinskaya regarded as well-deserved rewards her luxurious palace on the Kronversky Prospect (from the balcony of which Lenin pronounced the victory of the Proletarian Revolution in 1917); her grandiose country house in the St. Petersburg suburb of Strelna, with its own small electric power station and winter garden; her special train, delivering guests to the *fêtes galantes* on her birthdays; the throng of servants; and the innumerable rubies, diamond rings, diadems, emeralds, amethyst brooches, and pendants—the list of which rivals only the number of enthusiastic reviews quoted by her in her own book. As fabricated myth, Kschessinskaya's memoirs certainly outdo those of Sarah Bernhardt (*Double Vie*) and George Sand (*Histoire de ma vie*).

But Kschessinskaya's book is interesting in one particular aspect: as an attempt at self-justification and the revenge of her imagination upon that formidable span of Russian history that made her the omnipotent hostess of the Maryinsky, then turned her life upside down and destroyed her as a ballerina. To understand this, one must decipher carefully all the omissions, deliberate misinter-

pretations, slips of memory and the pen, and spaces between the lines—all of which, in fact, constitute the real content of her life. These entertaining though mendacious memoirs are highly characteristic of her stunning personality, which stood out strikingly against the careless background of Russian impracticality and daydreaming. Kschessinskaya was an intelligent, dynamic, and strong-willed woman; she struggled for success and knew how to maintain it. For all that, her virtuosity and dance talent were glossed over in later years, for political reasons, in the books of Soviet ballet historians. Only Vera Krasovskaya has given the proper credit to Kschessinskaya's powerful dance gift.

It is rather hard to evoke Kschessinskaya's image from her reviews. Most of the critics flattered the awesome Matilda out of fear; independent opinions were rare. Possibly two specific, though biased, accounts pinpoint the essence of her technique, artistic projection, and physical qualifications. Fyodor Lopukhov wrote:

> Small, with legs far from ideal, with weak pointes and slightly swollen calf muscles, Kschessinskaya excelled mostly in lyrical-dramatic parts requiring good terre-à-terre technique. Her Daughter of the Air in *The Talisman* and her Esmeralda were unforgettable. Most of the classical steps she executed with a certain chic and exuberance, as if seasoning them with Polish brio [her father was Polish] and demonstrating her stamina and sharpness, as well as the sloppiness endemic to Italian training. But there was something in her movements that made her a genuine Russian ballerina as distinct from the generation of Italian virtuose: her boldness and swing, her swiftness and dynamism, which imparted a certain charm to her dancing and invariably excited the audience.

And Volynsky wrote: "When executing a virtuoso variation, she was able to astound the audience with her spectacular (though not high) jump, display her soft ballon and her remarkable beats that sparkled like pure diamonds, execute a circuit of movements on her impeccably pointed toes, and dumbfound with her pirouettes, with such fouettés and such a *contrapposto* of her head and torso that a storm of applause exploded in the theatre. . . ."

MATILDA KSCHESSINSKAYA was the daughter of the soloist Felix Kschessinsky, an outstanding character dancer whose arrival in St. Petersburg in 1851 had laid the groundwork for the development of this genre of dancing in Russia. She was born in St. Petersburg on August 19, 1872, and grew up in a well-to-do family with substantial ballet connections. Her sister Julia and her brother Joseph followed in their father's footsteps, and Matilda herself entered the Imperial School in 1880. On April 22, 1890, she made her debut in the pas de deux from *La Fille mal gardée*, with Nicolas Legat as her partner.

In her memoirs Matilda mentions the two Italian ballerinas she strove to emulate. Virginia Zucchi, who had appeared in St. Petersburg in 1885, when Matilda was a student, was the first swallow announcing the Italian invasion. By the end of the 1880s Zucchi and her colleagues had drastically changed many aspects of Russian acting, pointe work, and jump technique. But Zucchi astounded the young Kschessinskaya not so much by her virtuosity (which was rather modest) as by her mimetic expressiveness. This was Zucchi's unquestioned forte; according to many writers, it was a harbinger of the facial mime in the first silent movies. It was nothing like the conventional mime of Petipa's ballets. The spark of inspiration that enabled Zucchi to switch from the tragic Esmeralda to the hilarious romp of *La Fille mal gardée* ignited Kschessinskaya's imagination. It is no accident that the conniving Lise and the grief-stricken gypsy girl eventually became Kschessinskaya's most successful roles.

Matilda's other ideal was Pierina Legnani, who had arrived in St. Petersburg at the end of 1893. As Alexander Shiriayev said, Legnani "knew all the secrets of Italian dance art." First she astounded the St. Petersburg ballerinas with her dazzling fouettés, which they had never seen before. Shiriayev pointed out that "Legnani's forte was bravura steps performed at high speed. . . . For instance, in *Cinderella* she executed several consecutive tours en attitude."

Persistent and ambitious, Kschessinskaya made it her goal to combine Zucchi's theatricality and Legnani's virtuosity. She took classes from Johannsen and Cecchetti in an attempt to achieve flexibility of the torso and legato movements laced with swift pointe work and daring tours. Only jumps did not come to her easily, but for her lack of natural ballon Kschessinskaya skillfully substituted a lingering landing, creating the illusory effect of a soaring body.

During her first season, 1890–91, Kschessinskaya performed twenty-two times in ballets and twenty-one times in operas. In *The Harlem Tulip* she even dared to compete with Carlotta Brianza, the first Aurora. In the pas de deux from *Paquita*, according to Bezobrazov, "she astounded the cognoscenti with the audacity of her tours and her steellike pointes. We will soon have an accomplished ballerina, if the theatre administration doesn't obstruct her promotion."

Kschessinskaya herself knew how to ensure her promotion. After Brianza's failure in *Le Roi Candaule* early in 1891, St. Petersburg did not see any Italian ballet stars for a year. Shiriayev wrote: "Kschessinskaya never failed to take advantage of a situation. Using her influential connections at court, she got hold of Brianza's role in *Kalkabrino* and scored an enormous success. After her promotion to the rank of ballerina [in November 1896] she monopolized the most spectacular parts until her final days on the Imperial stage. Other ballerinas, however gifted they were, had to make do with the leftovers that Kschessinskaya generously discarded."

Shiriayev's account covers the glorious years up to 1904, when Kschessinskaya reigned supreme on the Imperial stage and even shaped the Maryinsky's artistic policy. She was mistress to the tsarevitch; as her brother Joseph stated in his unpublished memoirs, "She helped to establish his sexual identity by releasing him from unhealthy compromises with the flesh and his increasing fear of women." Kschessinskaya took full advantage of this special privilege. When Nicholas became tsar in 1896 and then married, she lost her lover but gained unlimited power over the Maryinsky. Nevertheless, she would hardly have been able to maintain her unrivaled position had she not possessed a rare dance gift. In *Kalkabrino* she surpassed Brianza with her rapid double pirouettes on pointe (the nemesis of many Russian ballerinas of the time) and energetic jetés en tournant. In 1891, when the critics were still more or less honest about the awesome Matilda, Bezobrazov noted that she "is in perfect command of the whole set of Italian choreographic means: her torso is powerful, her pointes are precise and firm: she executes impeccable glissades and even triple pirouettes on pointe"—a technical feat of which very few ballerinas could boast in those days.

In January 1893, during her third season at the Maryinsky, the twenty-one-year-old Matilda made her debut as Aurora in *The Sleeping Beauty*, a ballet she danced for the next twenty years with invariable success. Kschessinskaya's artistic growth in this most taxing role perfectly mirrored her special qualities as a dancer and clarified her approach to classical ballet in general.

Her Aurora was a dashing young princess, vivid, smartly dressed, sparkling with real diamonds—every inch the prima ballerina, reveling in her bravura, brio, and attack, sweeping through the ornamental patterns of academic design with untrammeled gusto and freedom. Each double pirouette on pointe, jeté en tournant, and attitude en effacé was exemplary in its precision, sharpness, and elegance. Judging by the reviews of her Aurora over a twenty-year span, Kschessinskaya never attempted a psychological characterization. She simply sought to master each pattern in Petipa's choreographic fabric and to demonstrate her prodigious attention to detail. It was through the perfection of detail, she thought, that the role revealed itself.

If in 1893 Kschessinskaya's technical imperfections were masked by unshakable aplomb and a cheerful temperament, in 1908 she was able to demonstrate "our most striking example of balletic coloratura." By using the operatic term, Svetlov made the point that like the mistresses of bel canto (Pasta, Malibran, Patti), Kschessinskaya made a careful study of balletic embellishments in order to adorn each of her roles lavishly—be it Lise in *La Fille mal gardée*, Aspicia in *Pharaoh's Daughter*, Esmeralda, or Odile.

Petipa revived several ballets for Kschessinskaya (*Pharaoh's Daughter* in 1898, *Esmeralda* in 1899, *La Bayadère* in 1900) by revamping the old choreography with an eye to her special qualities. The old maestro was less interested in catering to the favorite of the Imperial court than in keeping his early choreographic children from becoming petrified museum pieces. Pavlova tried to imbue Nikiya and Aspicia with a poignant Romantic spirit, but Kschessinskaya ensured their longevity by instilling them with a noble classicism.

In 1901 Kschessinskaya won her strenuous competition with Legnani, who left the Maryinsky shortly thereafter. Armed with her now unrivaled technique, Kschessinskaya was expected to go much further, but her more or less academic approach was in conflict with the new artistic trends developing in Russia at the beginning of the twentieth century. Personal projection, individual experience transfigured and expressed through dance, were becoming more highly valued than pure, unthinking academicism. This kind of personal involvement was totally beyond Kschessinskaya's range. Her status as prima ballerina assoluta, reinforced by the unflagging support of her influential benefactors, enabled her to maintain her prestige among the champions of traditionalism; but her art of balletic coloratura soon began to be perceived as a charming anachronism. Bronislava Nijinska in her memoirs passed a severe verdict on Kschessinskaya, referring to her style as "essentially that of the old classical acrobatic technique" and calling her "vulgar and brusque in all her movements."

Following Volynsky and Levinson, Krasovskaya is inclined to view Kschessinskaya's art as a final phenomenon of Russian classicism. "Her image in photographs does not change from role to role. Her head is slightly tilted, her hair is carefully curled; a string of large diamonds adorns her décolletage. Her waist is tightly corseted; the precise port de bras is perfect; the turnout of her feet impeccably demonstrates the fourth or fifth position. She conveys the aesthetic standards of her era as if frozen in its elaborate, immutable forms."

Kschessinskaya's problem seems to have been not so much her strict adherence to the rigid manner of presentation inherited from the masters of the French dramatic stage as her inability to color and diversify her roles emotionally. She put absolute trust in Zucchi's dramatic devices without realizing that in the twentieth century they had degenerated into lifeless, though visually pleasant, convention. Nevertheless, one of Kschessinskaya's famous roles—Esmeralda, which she shared with no one—captivated even the exacting André Levinson, the great champion of Pavlova's innovative art. Here is Kschessinskaya's Esmeralda in Levinson's incisive description: "In her portrayal the national coloration is hardly perceived. She dances with a straight, rigid torso; her abdomen does not reveal any Oriental undulation; her thighs never betray the bewitching quiver of the Spanish *gitanas*; her port de bras is entirely neutral. She depicts Esmeralda's demi-caractère role in the impersonal classical key. Her technical tricks seem exaggerated; but this spectacular display stirs our feelings deeply. . . . Moreover, it captivates the mind and teases the imagination."

Levinson acutely pinpointed the essence of Kschessinskaya's talent: whatever role she undertook—Kitri or Nikiya, Esmeralda or Aurora—she remained first and always the prima ballerina, whose main concern was to demonstrate her technical brilliance. In terms of this conventional

Esmeralda, early 1900s

КШЕСИНСКАЯ.(ДОЧЬ ФАРАОНА)

The Pas de Flèche in *Pharaoh's Daughter*, early 1900s

Top: (left) *Esmeralda*, early 1900s; (right) Armida in *Le Pavillon d'Armide*, 1910s
Above: (left & right) Armida, 1910s

presentation Kschessinskaya cannot be accused of a lack of imagination—for instance, in Nikiya's dance with the basket in *La Bayadère*, she used a real (though drugged) snake. For a great veristic charm of her Esmeralda, she kept a pet goat at home to use on stage as a companion of her vagabond gypsy girl. But such details merely diversified her old-fashioned style. Possibly most regrettable was the fact that with the years, these worn-out tricks began to accord poorly with the aggressiveness of her prima ballerina presence, degenerating into vulgarity.

According to one critic, Kschessinskaya as Esmeralda skillfully brought to the audience "the bouquet of sentimentality and idealism" encapsulated in this old Romantic role, but her main emphasis was on dancing. To make her brilliant pointe work more obvious, Kschessinskaya shortened her tutu; dancing among beggars, rogues, and courtiers, mimicking pain, jealousy, sorrow, and wounded pride, Kschessinskaya still kept a distance between herself and the corps de ballet. She, Matilda Kschessinskaya, not Esmeralda, was the real heroine of the performance, and she never allowed the public or her colleagues to forget that. Krasovskaya wrote that in *Esmeralda* Kschessinskaya embodied Petipa's ideal classical ballerina. Riccardo Drigo had responded keenly to Petipa's design for the Act II pas de six by shaping the music as a traditional classical adagio with a vaguely sketched motif of amorous languor. Kschessinskaya too showed remarkable sensitivity to Petipa's scheme, conveying the spirit of the music through flowing, solemnly mournful sequences interwoven with supported lifts and contrasting with swift pas de bourrée. The impact of the performance derived both from its technical complexity and from the special brio of her rendition. Levinson incisively characterized Kschessinskaya's artistry: "Her gesture and mime imply thoroughly and perfectly the universal feelings, their almost primitive integrity, revealed through dramatic and psychologically plausible forms."

According to Krasovskaya, Kschessinskaya's acting style harked back to the classicism that reigned supreme among the tragic actors of St. Petersburg in the last century. In a broader perspective this style of flowing, significant gestures and immobile, noble poses "was as inseparable from St. Petersburg's architectural ensembles, with their impeccable proportions of pseudoantique porticos and columns, as it was from the Petersburg military parades, with their precise rhythms of racing cavalry and sparkling swords."

Thus, Kschessinskaya's success in the mime role of Fenella in Auber's opera *The Dumb Girl of Portici* was not a surprise. She performed this role sporadically until 1917, the end of her career, when one critic reported, "The drama of a young girl seduced and abandoned by a duke, the confusion of her feelings, shifting from vengeance to compassion, and her despair over the note certifying the death of her brother—the entire gamut of human suffering—moved the audience to tears, thanks to the powerful dramatic talent of Miss Kschessinskaya, the impact of her gestures and the mime of her expressive face."

Another great characterization, on a par with her Esmeralda and Fenella, was Kschessinskaya's Aspicia in Petipa's first grand-scale ballet, *Pharaoh's Daughter*. She brought to this old warhorse the dazzle of her academic technique and the attack of her imperious personality. "Her Aspicia literally reigned on the stage, reigned and danced, and that was what made the old masterpiece vibrate with new colors," one critic observed. On the other hand, Krasovskaya wrote, "at the time of Fokine's *Eunice* and *Une Nuit d'Egypte*, Kschessinskaya's portrayal of Aspicia was no more than an audacious adaptation of the balletic style of 1862 to the academicism of the Imperial ballet."

Kschessinskaya's Egyptian princess was ostentatiously cosmopolitan, a peculiar extension of her public. "Evening gowns of all colors and shadings; shoulders adorned with sparkling diamonds; tailcoats and black ties; bits of English and French phrases; the inebriating aroma of fashionable perfumes—in short, the familiar picture of the *beau monde*": thus the reporter from the *St. Petersburg Gazette* depicted the audience at a performance of *Pharaoh's Daughter* in October 1907. He then described Kschessinskaya as the hostess of this soirée: "The public in the orchestra and the boxes, Russian in name only, adored the Egyptian princess clad in a ball gown from Paquin, loaded with diamonds from Parisian jewelers. They valued the astounding technique of the ballerina and her extraordinary mimetic abilities, delivered with such refinement."

Kschessinskaya's multifaceted personality was refracted differently through her Lise in *La Fille mal gardée*, her favorite role. As opposed to Preobrajenskaya's heartfelt sincerity, Kschessinskaya portrayed a shrewd, aggressive, conniving peasant girl whose feminine charm and intelligence fooled everyone. The critics correctly saw in her Lise the vivid projection of her offstage personality radiating in the frame of her dazzling virtuosity.

In addition to Esmeralda, Aspicia, Lise, and Aurora, in the 1910s Kschessinskaya frequently performed as a guest artist in Nicolas Legat's plagiaristic ballets (*The Fairy Doll,*

The Little Scarlet Flower, his version of Petipa's *Talisman*). Time did not seem to take its toll on her dazzling technique. She was especially good in *Le Talisman*, even in 1916, when she was forty-four years old. As Mikhail Mikhailov recalled in his memoirs, "Kschessinskaya encored the coda by repeating two fragments. In the first she executed the cabrioles en avant in effacé on the diagonal with such brio that her leg, thrown upward, effortlessly kicked her head. In the second, during a diagonal of bourrées she balanced on pointe in first arabesque several times. She invested the whole passage with such ebullience that her fans went berserk."

Kschessinskaya's impersonal manner of presentation, which sacrificed the individual traits of each character to the dazzle and charm of the ballerina, was utterly unacceptable to Fokine and Diaghilev, the standard-bearers of the new expressiveness. But despite her own hostility to Fokine's innovations, Kschessinskaya sought collaboration with him. Though she claimed in an interview that "dancing Fokine's ballet does not require any technique," her limitless ego and natural desire to keep up with the new trend drove her to undertake the title role in his *Eunice* (1907). Unable to assimilate Fokine's style, she was eclipsed by Pavlova in the smaller role of Actée. A born fighter, Kschessinskaya did not give up; she got involved in a rather intricate game with Fokine and Diaghilev that in her memoirs she described as a continuous triumph. In fact, the real account of their war of ambitions, in which all the participants tried to doublecross and defeat each other, might easily provide the plot for an amusing short story. But the sad truth is that Kschessinskaya lost this battle, which was detrimental to her prestige. Ironically, Anna Pavlova, whom Kschessinskaya had maliciously encouraged and coached in *La Bayadère* in 1902, now put her to shame in Fokine's ballets, and the Maryinsky's sovereign princess could not bear her rival's success.

The problem was not that Kschessinskaya, a perfect technician, was wasted in Fokine's tableaux vivants: *Le Pavillon d'Armide* and *Les Sylphides* were rich in imaginative choreography. But both were ensemble ballets with no prima donna turns. This may be why Kschessinskaya hesitated to tackle *Les Sylphides* until 1911, when (on February 13) the ballet was given at a gala performance celebrating her twenty years on the Imperial stage. She danced the Mazurka and the Waltz pas de deux with the affected brio with which she usually performed her bravura pieces.

Despite the rebuff from the critics, she renewed her cooperation with Fokine in 1912, when the choreographer strengthened his ties with the Maryinsky after a tiff with Diaghilev. In March 1912 Kschessinskaya appeared as Columbine in Fokine's *Carnaval* and in his *Papillons*, succeeding only in demonstrating Karsavina's superiority in these roles. Fokine's new ballet *Eros*, mounted on November 28, 1915, for Kschessinskaya and her young partner Pierre Vladimiroff proved to be a kind of deliberate failure: As Joseph Kschessinsky recalled in his memoirs, Fokine punished his "wolf in sheep's clothing" by satirizing the sentimental spirit of Kschessinskaya's Esmeralda. Not sensing the pitfall that Fokine had dug for her, the ballerina trotted out all of her conventional clichés and failed utterly.

As for Diaghilev, Kschessinskaya's artistic union with him was truly farcical. She could not endure the idea that she had no part in the glory of his first Paris season in 1909. She had enjoyed a succès d'estime on her first visit to Paris with Legat in 1908, appeared at the Paris Opéra again in 1909 hoping to tarnish Diaghilev's prestige, and attempted unsuccessfully to organize her own season in 1910. The loss of Nijinsky as a partner killed the project and hurt her ego.

In 1911 Diaghilev unexpectedly invited Kschessinskaya to dance with his small company in London, where, according to his speculations, "the relic of Imperial style" would thrill the British champions of traditional academicism. But her performances shattered his expectations. On November 14, 1911, she made her debut in the Grand Pas de Deux from the last act of *The Sleeping Beauty*, which Diaghilev called *Aurore et le Prince*. Kschessinskaya was so confident of her success that on the eve of her performance she was less concerned with rehearsals than with matching the blue of her costume to her large sapphires.

The London critics mercilessly noted that "she is a competent dancer of the stereotyped kind, extraordinarily skillful but often displaying quite unlovely gymnastics." Her Columbine in Fokine's *Carnaval*, which she danced the same evening, was considered "fat and passé, not on the same plane with either Karsavina or Pavlova." Pavlova's shadow seemed to loom over her constantly. When, on November 30, Kschessinskaya made her appearance in *Swan Lake* (condensed into two acts), the Londoners found not only "the music of little account and the choreography exceedingly dull . . . and full of padding" but also Kschessinskaya bereft of "that added touch of exquisite inspiration shown by Mme Pavlova." Her thirty-two fouettés, however, registered as "an extraordinary feat of precisely calculated design with finesse and mathematical exactness." Nevertheless, in February 1912, she went with Diaghilev to Vienna and Monte Carlo to dance *Le Spectre de la rose* with Nijinsky, a role that was definitely out of her artistic range.

The meager success of her later career somehow intensified her fervor: in 1914, she encored the extremely complex coda from *Talisman* four times—and one critic likened her to "an indestructible mausoleum." In April 1916 "the dancing mausoleum" boldly attempted Giselle—at the age of forty-four. Vera Krasovskaya has written: "Unfeigned lyricism and forthright theatricality without any affectation remained alien to Kschessinskaya throughout her long career. In Act I she executed the ronds de jambe on pointe correctly and swirled through her tours on the diagonal; but in the scenes with Albrecht, Giselle's mother, and Hilarion, Matilda looked pretentious and ridiculous. The reserved, crystalline dance of the young soloist Elizaveta Gerdt in the peasant pas de deux contrasted noticeably with the tense histrionics of the aging prima ballerina. In Act II her lack of soaring jumps, her rigid back, her earthbound, 'corseted' image seriously undermined the poetic aura of Giselle as a Wili."

In 1917 the February Revolution ended the career of the favorite of the tsarist regime. Twenty-five years of prima ballerina status and royal patronage left Kschessinskaya unable to reconcile herself to the total collapse of her way of life. After the October Revolution's ferocious reprisals against the family of the tsar, Kschessinskaya lived in constant fear, hoping only that the White Army, which many of her former admirers had joined, would crush "the rebelling rabble," to use her own words. Finally she lost heart; in February 1920 she left Russia on the Italian liner *Semiramis*, sailing to Constantinople. She lived on, as an émigrée, for over fifty years. Patching up her relationship with her enemy Diaghilev, she began to coach his dancers. In 1929 she opened a school in Paris; among her pupils were André Eglevsky, Tatiana Riabouchinska, Margot Fonteyn, and Yvette Chauviré. She died in Paris on December 5, 1971, at the age of ninety-nine, the longest-lived of all the great ballerinas.

In Soviet Russia her name was vilified or blanketed with silence. Her great achievements as a virtuoso ballerina were eclipsed by her fabricated reputation as the Russian Madame Du Barry. And yet her legacy of academic virtuosity did not perish in Russia. It lived on in Semyonova's balletic feats and was resurrected in the art of Natalia Dudinskaya, whose teachers at the former Imperial Theatre School never forgot "the awesome Matilda."

The White Cat in *The Sleeping Beauty*, mid-1890s

OLGA PREOBRAJENSKAYA

OLGA PREOBRAJENSKAYA was a ballerina with limited natural talent whose greatness emerged through hard work. In other words, the absence of natural gifts was compensated by ideal training, constantly reinforced and perfected. It was this that distinguished her brilliant virtuoso style among the ballerinas of her generation.

Squat, plain, yet charming, with swollen leg muscles and unremarkable feet, Preobrajenskaya seemed to fall naturally into the category of soubrette or *ingénue comique*, at best a soloist. Nevertheless, among her most successful, now legendary, roles, such as Lise in *La Fille mal gardée*

and Swanilda in *Coppélia*, her unrivaled Raymonda stood out as an example of Russian choreographic bel canto. This was all the more miraculous considering that Preobrajenskaya possessed an average extension, mediocre ballon, and weak toes. Nevertheless in her youth she was not inferior to Kschessinskaya in pointe work, pirouettes, and the academic finish of each step. Moreover, contemporary observers invariably praised the irresistible charm of her stage presence, a manifestation of her highly sympathetic offstage personality. Then, too, she was distinguished from other virtuosos by her extraordinary musicality. Many critics regarded her as the most musical ballerina on the Imperial stage. According to some, Preobrajenskaya danced not *to* the music but *in* the music, or beyond it, where her dancing deepened, complemented, or even rivaled it. Keenly sensitive to "the delicate balance between balletic algebra and musical harmony," as Volynsky put it, Preobrajenskaya's dance imagination enabled her to ornament or extend choreography, fascinating even Marius Petipa, who allowed her great latitude in performing his works. As Fyodor Lopukhov witnessed, Preobrajenskaya herself composed several of Raymonda's variations, in particular the famous one from Act III, in which classical steps were seasoned with elements of Hungarian folk dance.

The way Preobrajenskaya's career took shape in St. Petersburg was truly unprecedented, and the immense store of balletic knowledge that she accumulated during her thirty-year career at the Maryinsky enabled her in later life to become the most illustrious Russian teacher in the West.

O LGA YOSIFOVNA PREOBRAJENSKAYA was born on February 2, 1871, in St. Petersburg, into a family unknown to ballet circles. Her passion for dancing seemed to arise spontaneously.

At the age of seven, Olga began to take classes from the former Maryinsky ballerina Leopoldina Lozenskaya, but she was not accepted into the Imperial Theatre School until she was ten. Short, puny, somewhat "lopsided," as Nicolas Legat put it, with a slight spinal curvature and one hyperextended knee, she had been rejected at several entrance examinations. In fact, aside from her maniacal infatuation with ballet, the young Preobrajenskaya possessed no qualifications to be a dancer. In Lev Ivanov's intermediate classes, and later on in Johannsen's and Petipa's advanced classes, she impressed her instructors only with her fervor and indefatigable zeal and appeared destined to become a mediocre member of the corps de ballet. The acrimonious and caustic Johannsen called her "a hunchbacked devil," whose striving for perfection seemed to be doomed. In view of his prediction, the transformation of this ugly duckling into a great virtuoso seems all the more miraculous.

Preobrajenskaya's determination, in fact, is unparalleled in the history of Russian ballet. As a student, she struggled against her physical weakness. To strengthen her spine, she wore a steel corset for a whole winter, not even taking it off to sleep. As her devoted pupil and biographer Elvira Roné remembered: "Her spinal column and de-

formed knee kept her from developing strength in her legs, and her pointes were relatively feeble, but she was determined at all costs to achieve the goal she had set for herself—to become a technically impeccable dancer. . . . Unlike her colleagues, after rehearsals she did not leave the theatre but stayed on to perfect herself. Enrico Cecchetti could not help admiring her perseverance and devoted special attention to her. Preobrajenskaya truly penetrated the depths of his art and assimilated it as did no one else among her colleagues."

Interviewed by the *St. Petersburg Gazette* in 1900, Preobrajenskaya said: "I would like to see a ballet dancer able to rival me in terms of endurance and perseverance. . . . I worked on myself literally day and night. I became tempered, gradually turning my puny body into a steely mechanism. I can pride myself on saying that everything I achieved was a result of my willpower." Her artistic curiosity made her polish her musicality by playing the piano, taking vocal classes, and subjugating herself to various ballet teachers, from Johannsen and Cecchetti in Russia to Beretta and Mauri abroad. Her technique progressed slowly, but her career went steadily forward for thirty years.

Preobrajenskaya was truly obsessed with dance; but, unlike Pavlova, she never made it the outlet for her emotional life. Instead, she was driven to master classical technique in order to transform dance patterns into choreographic equivalents for music. She was mostly motivated by music and remained indifferent to theatrical projection; she was never stirred by a feeling of personal identification with her roles. As a mime she was mediocre; it was no wonder that the great dramatic parts—Odette, Giselle, Nikiya—did not add luster to her reputation. But always smiling, radiant, exuberant, she wonderfully conveyed the joy of dancing as the ultimate value.

After her graduation performance in March 1889, when she danced the character pas de deux from Act II of *Esmeralda* and the pas de trois from *The Pearl of Seville*, Preobrajenskaya could hardly even dream of becoming a soloist. For two years at the Maryinsky she was relegated to the last rows of the corps, dancing whatever was required. Then, in 1891, going on as a replacement in the Pas Chinois of the Perrot-Petipa *Catarina*, she attracted the attention of the famous critic Pleschayev, who praised her dancing— "without visible tricks"—and her consummate musicality.

Her career apparently would now have accelerated had it not been for the ever-growing influence of Kschessinskaya, who monopolized the Maryinsky repertory. With no support from important benefactors, and discouraged by her plainness and lack of theatrical projection, Preobrajenskaya had to make do with what came to her. For seven years, until 1898, she capitalized on her diligence, polishing her technique in various minor roles. More frequently than not she was entrusted only with replacing indisposed soloists. Her exceptional balletic memory was her greatest advantage: in 1891 she substituted for Kschessinskaya as the Fairy Candide in *The Sleeping Beauty*; in 1893 she replaced Maria Andersen as the White Cat. "The feline pas did not suffer from this replacement," wrote Bezobrazov. "Miss Preobrajenskaya gracefully conveyed the cat's movements and airs, for which she was rewarded by unanimous applause." She danced several variations in *Sylvia* and *Paquita*, portrayed Columbine in the Ivanov-Petipa *Nutcracker*, and appeared in character parts in *Carmen* and *Les Huguenots*. Merely being on the stage thrilled her, and she patiently waited for her moment of glory.

Her technique improved so much that in February 1895 she made her first tour abroad, with Matilda Kschessinskaya and her brother, Joseph Kschessinsky. She danced the Calabraise in Monte Carlo, with enormous success. Her reputation in the West began to grow, rivaling that of Virginia Zucchi, especially in Italy. Arturo Toscanini, a fervent admirer, invited her to participate in a South American tour with the company of Milan's Teatro alla Scala; she danced in Buenos Aires, years before Pavlova. Much later, in 1910, she brought London its first *Swan Lake*, though in a truncated version.

In Russia Preobrajenskaya's great opportunity came in 1898, when she was cast as the Butterfly in *Les Caprices du Papillon*, Teresa in *The Cavalry Halt*, Swanilda in *Coppélia*, and Galatea in *Acis and Galatea*. All these ballets belonged to the genre of lyrical comedy, marvelously suited to Preobrajenskaya's cheerful verve and frolicsome nature. Moreover, her straightforward presence, lack of affectation, and precision in every movement helped considerably to revive the simple choreography of these works. If the major comic roles, such as Lise in *La Fille mal gardée*, had not been monopolized by Kschessinskaya, Preobrajenskaya might have proved to be an ideal soubrette. But she danced in comedies only occasionally, and did not make her debut as Lise until early in 1906. Teliakovsky recalled: "Kschessinskaya took this assignment of the role as a personal insult and spared no possible means for causing trouble at the debut of her rival. It happened that the little door of the chicken cage was left open, and so during one of Preobrajenskaya's dances the chickens flew out over the stage, thus causing a certain commotion. But the truth is that nothing could

upset Preobrajenskaya; with imperturbable precision she performed her dance right to the end. As things turned out, this incident . . . served only to add a final touch of happiness to Preobrajenskaya's success."

After her triumph as Lise, Svetlov wrote that "with an easy, disengaged manner—roguish, gay, showing sparks of real humor in the comic situations and becoming naive and touching in the dramatic scenes—she created by everything she did a very colorful and graceful Lise, very different from the banal figure familiar in this role; and at the same time she settled her account with Kschessinskaya. It is unnecessary to speak of Preobrajenskaya's dancing, for it is beyond praise. Her technique is perfect, up to the highest standard of virtuosity, and this technical brilliance goes hand in hand with classicism and innate musicality."

Preobrajenskaya's success in *La Fille mal gardée* was a tribute to her sincerity and to the heartfelt lyricism she brought to even the most trivial or passé aspects of an old balletic vaudeville. Into the antediluvian ballet of Dauberval, which in the course of a hundred years had been transformed from a caustic comedy of manners into a pastoral entertainment, Preobrajenskaya instilled "the bashful simplicity and charm of a Russian peasant girl" (Lopukhov). She swept through the choreography (as revamped and enhanced by Petipa in the 1880s for Zucchi) with a rare freedom, embroidering its texture with the rich figures of her mature technique and artistic fantasy. The choreography as she danced it never looked like an amusing but independent addition to the plot—she knew how to blend the two elements to perfection. The role of Lise thus allowed Preobrajenskaya to display one of the major facets of her talent.

In the meantime, from 1898 to 1906 Preobrajenskaya had performed quite a number of shepherdesses, nymphs, dolls, and butterflies, portraying them with an elegant, humorous air, perfect vehicles for her own dance exuberance. Paraphrasing the motto of the great Russian actor Mikhail Tschepkin, she claimed that there are no small parts; there are only small dancers. Her painstaking attention to detail allowed every nuance of the choreography to be revealed. Leafing through the reviews of her Sylvia in Ivanov and Gerdt's *Sylvia* in 1901, or of her Javotte in Gerdt's *Javotte*, one is amazed at the seriousness with which she approached these bagatelles. Without excessive histrionics, she managed to build a ravishing balance between the naive plots and the choreographic tours de force. The critics called her a "queen of dances," a *"poetesse par la grâce de Dieu."*

Clockwise from top right: Ysaure in *Bluebeard*; The Street Dancer in *Don Quixote*; *Le Matelot*; Lise in *La Fille mal gardée*

Left: (top) *Nénuphar*; (bottom) Sylvia
Below: Giselle, with Nicolas Legat as Albrecht

Фотогр.
ИМПЕРАТОРСКИХЪ
ТЕАТРОВЪ.

ПРЕОБРАЖЕНСКАЯ.

306

"In *Sylvia*," wrote Elvira Roné,

she was admired very much for her brilliance and delicacy in little steps. Her combination of speed, grace, and precision in these steps was unparalleled, and it was said that her feet made patterns of fine lace. In spite of her great speed in these passages, she finished off each step perfectly before beginning the next one, and it was (among other things) for her unchallengeable virtuosity in such fast passages that she was admired by her colleagues in the company as well as by the public and the critics.

But it was not just in her fast patterns that she excelled. She was moving and perfectly controlled in her pauses, her unexpected halts in movements, and her slow patterns. She was marvelous in her slow waltzes; in *Sylvia* she performed some specially beautiful slow dances, notably the slow waltz of Act I and the pas de deux of the last act.

"A slice of real life, glittering with the vivid colors of reality," wrote Svetlov about her Javotte, "in many ways echoing her Lise from *La Fille mal gardée*. Her capricious, naive young girl in love is an enchanting characterization." Svetlov also mentioned "the precision of each step . . . the impeccable sense of timing . . . the filigree work of her attitudes and arabesques." *Javotte* was the ballet in which Preobrajenskaya captivated the Paris Opéra in 1909, a couple of months before the triumphs of the Diaghilev enterprise. A Russian observer commented on her performances, which were attended by Saint-Saëns, who had written the score for the original French production: "The Russian ballerina gave a good, memorable lesson to the Frenchman. She drew his attention to some serious shortcomings in the Parisian production of *Javotte* and a string of routine passages that were no longer acceptable in St. Petersburg. . . . The composer humbly sat down at the piano and went through the musical score with Miss Preobrajenskaya, attentive to her remarks."

Preobrajenskaya's charming stage presence was due mostly to her ability to convey the joy of dancing, seasoned with a dash of irony or mischief. It is not surprising that she shone in the ballet that Lev Ivanov set to Liszt's Second Hungarian Rhapsody in 1901. Although it was incorporated into the big divertissement in *The Little Humpbacked Horse*, it represented the first Russian foray into the domain of plotless ballet. In his review Svetlov described the intricate choreographic texture and swiftly alternating rhythms ("from the slowest and schmaltziest up to the fastest and most turbulent") and remarked: "Miss Preobrajenskaya dumbfounded the audience with her brio, her genuinely sincere involvement, and her flawless technical skill."

Preobrajenskaya's careful attitude toward worn-out conventional roles, such as Ysaure in Petipa's *Bluebeard*, seemed to erase the patina of old age that had appeared impossible to eradicate. She viewed Ysaure as a sheer dance exercise, meant to be performed without any dramatization. "She danced," Svetlov wrote, "gaily, animatedly, with perfect technique and an extremely supple grace, thus showing the distinctiveness of her lyrical talent. . . . The best of her mime scenes were those of her curiosity, of her separation from Bluebeard, of joy at her liberation—all portrayed by her with great sincerity and authentic feeling." Preobrajenskaya began her *Bluebeard* performance on September 3, 1900, as a soloist and completed it as a ballerina. From this point on, she constantly proved that classical and character dance were her true element, as she conveyed the joy of dancing regardless of any incongruities of plot.

Preobrajenskaya's control and emphasis on dance continuity could not make up for her one-dimensional portrayals in *Giselle* and *Swan Lake*. Of her first Giselle (a matinee in December 1899) a critic in the *St. Petersburg Gazette* remarked with reserve: "Miss Preobrajenskaya revealed her own design of Giselle and interpreted the role by herself, with her own sensitivity and her own feelings." But Preobrajenskaya realized that this dramatic role "was beyond her talent and its limits," as Svetlov noted in his monograph on her. Moreover, her purely "technical attitude" to the part reinforced the established reputation of this ballet as a chamber piece and a poor vehicle for a prima ballerina. Giselle as a Wili seemed especially irrelevant to Preobrajenskaya's gifts.

She was also unsuccessful as Odette-Odile in *Swan Lake*, which she first performed in November 1904. The critics approved of her confidence, choreographic aplomb, and virtuoso precision and tolerated her substitution of piqués en tournant for the traditional thirty-two fouettés, which she considered vulgar. But they all lamented her lack of swanlike arms, legato, and the contrasts that constitute the dramatic essence of the Odette-Odile juxtaposition. Curiously enough, Petipa approved of Preobrajenskaya's interpretation with a note—"Great!"—in his diary of 1904: he found her Odette "stylistically irreproachable."

Preobrajenskaya's career at the Maryinsky reached its peak in 1904. She performed an astonishingly wide range of roles, including most of the Maryinsky repertory: in addition to *Coppélia, Bluebeard, Camargo,* and *La Source,* she shone in *The Nutcracker, Raymonda,* and *The Sleeping Beauty.* After eight years of dancing Columbine in Act I of *Nutcracker,* in 1900 she performed the Sugar Plum Fairy, with her constant partner and collaborator Nicolas Legat. She reveled in this part for the next two decades and was always praised as "exemplary, graceful, feminine." As the charming Isabelle in *The Trials of Damis* and then as Summer in Petipa's *The Four Seasons,* "Her dances breathed *caresse,* grace, and musicality," wrote Svetlov. "She truly evokes the spirit of summer, with its fragrant roses, its soft sunshine, and the spellbinding serenades of the nightingale."

Preobrajenskaya made her debut as Raymonda in September 1903 and as Aurora in April 1904. In spite of the conspicuous difference in their choreographic styles, Preobrajenskaya's interpretations revealed the symphonic structure of each role. Elvira Roné wrote: "She was radiant in the pizzicato in the solo in Act I [of *Sleeping Beauty*], giving it a delightfully subtle flirtatiousness while marking the beats very clearly in a measured way. In slow passages she was marvelously languorous, while in the adagio at the beginning of the final pas de deux in Act III she was majestic." But according to André Levinson, Aurora was not Preobrajenskaya's most glorious achievement; her gift was not sufficiently refined for the part.

The entire spectrum of her rich, multicolored plasticity was visible in her Raymonda; her musicality and technique blended into a striking, inimitable unity. Ignoring the incongruities of the absurd plot, and not encumbering herself with psychological insights, she danced her five variations in total accordance with Glazunov's musical instructions and Petipa's choreographic design. The Raymonda that she danced for the next two decades was highly praised as a kind of "choreographic recitation to music." Svetlov saw in her dancing "pure music in movements, absorbing all rhythm and melodies." About her Raymonda he wrote: "The unique sense of rhythm in the variations on pointe, the dashing pirouettes, the nimble renversés, the irresistible and spectacular attitudes—all contributed to evoking the atmosphere of refined and subdued lyricism." These last words unerringly illuminate the core of Preobrajenskaya's artistic projection, which enabled her to produce on the stage "throngs of poetic metaphors," as Levinson observed. Preobrajenskaya's Raymonda was hailed by the critics as the embodiment of Russian choreographic purity and elegance, to which for many years the champions of Petipa's classicism vowed fidelity.

Her performances were all the more impressive in that they displayed her stunning talent for improvisation. As her contemporaries witnessed, she had a striking ability in her encores to ornament Petipa's variations or to improvise on stage. (It was normal practice at the time for dancers to repeat a variation at the audience's request.) Petipa himself valued her propensity for "artistic and imaginative fantasies." By reveling in his classicism, she seemed to explore its limits and possibilities. In 1910 a critic noted that "Preobrajenskaya turned Raymonda's five variations into ten," but in 1912 Konstantin Kudrin wrote: "Yesterday Preobrajenskaya was at her best, not merely performing, but choreographing on the stage. She diversified Raymonda's animated pizzicato. First she ended with dynamic fouettés en diagonal, demonstrating her beautifully shaped attitudes. Then, in her encore, she ornamented the same pizzicato with fleeting arabesques. In the variation from Act II she supplied its coda with the most intricate pirouettes sur le coup de pied and then with delicate and refined sissonnes sur les pointes. But her most perfect artistry was shown in a marvelous piece of choreography to piano accompaniment."

The critic was referring to Petipa's classical transcription of the czardas in the Grand Pas Hongrois from Act III. André Levinson noted that "Preobrajenskaya's single movement of the arm encircling her neck sufficed to imbue the abstract, sweeping patterns of her dancing with passionate Hungarian audacity. It is hard to imagine national coloration of style projected more strongly. Her ability to husband her means for the sake of artistry is, in a nutshell, the essence of Preobrajenskaya's style."

She was, in fact, a determined traditionalist, the champion of Petipa's and his imitators' styles. When confronted with Fokine's new plastique, Preobrajenskaya was inevitably vanquished. Only in *Les Sylphides* did she manage to subjugate her virtuosity to Fokine's stylistic restrictions. He composed the Prelude with an eye to her exceptional balance; in his words, "in a dance virtually devoid of jumps she gave the impression of being ethereal." Krasovskaya incisively wrote that in the Prelude in her runs and in her lingering balances on pointe "she flew like wind-borne pollen. . . . The ballerinas who came after her have lost this special weightless fluency of dance: they began to emphasize transitions and to split whole passages into fragmentary movements. The almost imperceptible small soarings in pas de chat and assemblé, which Fokine placed in the middle of dance sequences as linking steps, turned into climaxes. They split the dance phrase, designed as an integrated, flowing entity, into two parts."

The artistic union of Preobrajenskaya and Fokine was only temporary. Preobrajenskaya's total lack of decorative appeal, so fundamental for Fokine's picturesque tableaux vivants, made her unsuitable for a slave in *Une Nuit d'Egypte*. She was especially miscast as Armide in *Le Pavillon d'Armide*, a soubrette awkwardly portraying a cruel, sensual enchantress. Moreover, the static choreography of this role undermined Preobrajenskaya's virtuosity. What was more disturbing to her was that in Fokine's ballets she was no more than one member of an ensemble, which undercut her status as a prima ballerina.

To Fokine's whimsical and passionate heroines, Preobrajenskaya preferred the conventional dolls and little princesses of Nicolas Legat's imitative ballets, like *The Fairy Doll* or *Puss in Boots*, in which she continued to "weave the lace of her choreographic artistry" that always thrilled the St. Petersburg audience. And she frequently performed a short genre piece, *Le Matelot*, which she choreographed herself. When she danced it for the first time, at a benefit performance for Kschessinskaya, the audience demanded three encores, unprecedented in the history of the Maryinsky. *Le Matelot* was "a sailor's hornpipe for a little French cabin boy . . . who aroused roars of laughter when 'he' cocked his flat sailor's hat at a rakish angle and pulled up his trousers—above all when he spat over the imaginary rail into the imaginary sea."

In 1909, after twenty years of service at the Maryinsky, Preobrajenskaya became a guest artist there and began several years of extensive touring in the West. Her flawless technique and impish charm brought her international acclaim, especially in Italy, where she put the local virtuose to shame.

In 1918 Preobrajenskaya began her thirtieth season at the Maryinsky. Though her last years were uninspired, her technique, strangely enough, had not deteriorated. With unfailing abandon and gusto she continued to perform her enormous repertory and to encore and improvise her variations from *Paquita* and *Le Talisman*. She also taught at the Petrograd Choreographic School and at the School of Russian Ballet, guided by Akim Volynsky. As a teacher, Preobrajenskaya deserves a special study: according to Lopukhov, Vaganova reworked Preobrajenskaya's method extensively to make it a major part of her own system.

In 1921 Preobrajenskaya went on tour to Finland. She never returned to Russia: she could not abandon the great love of her life, the Russian pianist Alexandre Labinski, who was determined to escape from the Bolsheviks. During her first two years in the West she roamed from one place to another, like her memorable Street Dancer in *Don Quixote*. To support herself and Labinski, who worked as her accompanist, she even danced in the Russian Cabaret in Berlin. After a short contract with La Scala in 1922, she settled in Paris in 1923. For the next forty years, at the Studios Wacker, she trained many extraordinary dancers, including Tamara Toumanova, Irina Baronova, Nina Vyroubova, Nadia Nerina, and Igor Youskevitch. To the classes of "Madame Préo" came Margot Fonteyn, Rosella Hightower, Marjorie Tallchief, Mia Slavenska. Preobrajenskaya died in Paris in 1962, one of the last relics of the glory of the Imperial Ballet.

In 1913 André Levinson, Preobrajenskaya's ardent champion, gave a splendid summary of her career:

> This little woman, deprived of the enchanting fascination of a Pavlova, incapable of the tempestuous achievements of a Kschessinskaya, not gifted by nature with exceptional means of expression, with a small and slight body, lacking plastic beauty and sometimes dancing in the most mediocre ballets, is able to create the purest models of the dance, imbued with a rhythmic and dynamic beauty. The charm of Preobrajenskaya is without parallel; her humor is full of musicality and psychological perceptiveness, her renversés in the arms of her partner are full of passionate languor, the movements of her adagios are drawn out with melancholy, her humor is caressing in her pizzicato. . . . The dances of Preobrajenskaya are like an unforgettable vision.

And Tamara Karsavina in her memoirs, *Theatre Street*, paid a heartfelt tribute to the personality of Preobrajenskaya: "Whether péris, naiads, or nymphs, our leading ballerinas, in all but their short skirts, were like the fashionable women of the audience. Preobrajenskaya alone, aided by her uncommon intelligence, knew how to be distinct from the stereotype. So small as to appear undersized, she had a domain of her own: impish, graceful, and humorous— the irresistible Puck of our stage."

Raymonda, early 1950s

NATALIA DUDINSKAYA

IN THE HISTORY OF SOVIET BALLET Natalia Dudinskaya represents the embodiment of unlimited virtuosity.
In the 1960s and 1970s many of her pupils excelled their
instructor in artistic projection, beauty of line, or poetic
understatement, but none could equal the absolute precision with which Dudinskaya performed the most intricate
steps. Her impeccable timing, the exemplary purity of each
pose, and the academic perfection of every movement lent
an icy brilliance to her dancing.

Dudinskaya was endowed with a huge, soaring jump,
fabulous extension, natural coordination, and the aplomb
of a true ballerina. At the height of her career she could
easily whip off five pirouettes on pointe, laced with any
number of swift tours chaînés, piqués en tournant, or pirouettes en attitude. In a sense, she was a reincarnation of
Legnani and Kschessinskaya, occasionally surpassing both
in technique.

Throughout her long career the critics frequently described Dudinskaya's technique as so flawless that it became real art. In the Grand Pas from *Paquita*, the Kingdom
of the Shades Scene from *La Bayadère*, and the Vision
Scene of *The Sleeping Beauty*, Dudinskaya seemed to absorb the intellectual energy of Petipa's geometric configurations to the point of transcending plot. In this regard

Yuzovsky's critical comments are highly revealing: "'I'm showing you a classical dance in its pure essence,' she seems to say, 'released from any dramatic implications. . . .' It is as if Dudinskaya were scornfully snubbing self-important Duncanesque impressionism, with its neglect of technique and its improvisational license. . . . Dudinskaya's dance style reveals itself as a triumph of rationality and calculation after all."

Dudinskaya's power lay in her ability to subjugate her technique to the demands of the music and the will of the choreographer. She tamed her theatrical instincts, performing Petipa's patterns without emotional coloring. The more Petipa's choreography challenged her virtuosity, the more it acquired an intellectual dimension.

NATALIA MIKHAILOVNA DUDINSKAYA was born on August 21, 1912, in the Ukrainian city of Kharkov. Like Kschessinskaya and Karsavina, she grew up in a family affiliated with the ballet. Her mother, Natalia Tagliori (once a pupil of Cecchetti), ran a private ballet school that the young Talia attended from the age of seven, participating in school productions of *La Fille mal gardée*, and Ivanov's *The Enchanted Forest* and *The Magic Flute*. At the 1923 entrance exams for the former Imperial School, the eleven-year-old Talia's vast repertoire astonished Agrippina Vaganova: she knew the ribbon dance from *La Fille mal gardée* and the Sugar Plum Fairy's variation from *Nutcracker* and could even diligently reproduce the mime of Giselle's mad scene.

At the Leningrad Choreographic School, Dudinskaya was immediately placed in the second-year class. Only the age restrictions prevented her from entering the intermediate division.

Dudinskaya's potential and her physical qualifications were akin in many ways to Vaganova's: the ballon and extension that had made Vaganova famous at the Maryinsky in the 1900s also enlivened the young Dudinskaya's painstaking yet impersonal performances. Like her teacher, she was musical, impetuous in bravura pieces, and totally devoid of lyricism. With the years, Dudinskaya's brawny legs and imperious attack would even further enhance this resemblance to Vaganova.

As an advanced student, Dudinskaya enthralled the Leningrad audience with her flawless technical mastery in Vaganova's choreographic miniature set to the music of a Johann Strauss waltz. Yuzovsky recalls her etching the di-

agonal of swirling tours chaînés, freezing in arabesque for a moment, and then retracing the same diagonal with jetés entrelacés. At her graduation performance Dudinskaya sparkled in the *Le Corsaire* pas de deux, reshaped by Vaganova especially for her and the young Konstantin Sergeyev.

In 1931 Dudinskaya joined the former Maryinsky company as a soloist, making her debut in the *Swan Lake* pas de trois. She was soon entrusted with Odette-Odile, regarded as the perfect vehicle for her technical brilliance.

Nevertheless, despite Vaganova's powerful support and her own exuberant virtuosity, Dudinskaya's career did not progress as rapidly as had been expected. Drama was not Dudinskaya's forte, and when cast in Ulanova's parts, she invariably came to grief. As the doomed, pensive Princess Maria in *The Fountain of Bakhchisarai* and the frail, vulnerable ballerina Coralli in Zakharov's *Lost Illusions*, Dudinskaya looked one-dimensional, however hard she tried to justify every step or encapsulate the dramatic sentiment. "An accomplished virtuoso, Dudinskaya is incapable of getting under the skin of the role; she displays the specific brio of a traditional balletic prima donna rather than responding to dramatic essences," wrote the prominent music critic Ivan Sollertinsky.

In the early 1930s Dudinskaya was frequently deprecated for her emotional blandness, ostentatious control, and misapplication of awkward histrionics. Soviet drama-ballets, in fact, suited neither her inexpressive theatricality nor her technical exuberance. In lyrical classical parts such as Odette or Masha (in *The Nutcracker*) she often went on as a replacement for Ulanova, appearing quite subdued or even contrived in comparison with the latter's forthright lyricism. Had it not been Ulanova who provided the standard against which the young Dudinskaya was measured, she might have been less disparaged for "her pure, flawlessly academic, yet lifeless dances." Only two roles in Dudinskaya's repertory of the early thirties were of exceptional brilliance and classical finish: Odile and Aurora.

In Vaganova's 1933 recension of *Swan Lake*, Dudinskaya performed Odile as a straight bravura exhibition number: as her biographer Galina Krymshevskaya wrote: "In the famous pas de deux Dudinskaya's Odile did not even bother to seduce the Prince. She regally allowed him to become infatuated with her brilliance." She was an aloof stranger, selfishly enjoying her own confidence and the attack with which she swept through the most intricate steps. Most important to her were her irresistible brilliance and her joyous sense of physical victory over Petipa's cho-

Top: *Don Quixote* pas de deux, with Konstantin Sergeyev, early 1950s
Above: (left) Odile, mid-1950s; *Waltz* (Jacobson), with Sergeyev, early 1960s

Top: (left) Giselle, with Sergeyev as Albrecht, late 1950s; (right) Suimbike in *Shuraleh*, mid-1950s
Above: (left) Laurencia, early 1950s; (right) Giselle, mid-1950s

Giselle, with Sergeyev as Albrecht, mid-1950s

reographic scheme. Even in the mid-fifties, when I saw her as Odile, the forty-year-old Dudinskaya made one share her almost sensual delight when, executing tours en attitude, she thrust her leg high in the air as a challenge to everyone. For a few seconds she lingered on pointe; then she burst into an avalanche of tiny steps of almost inconceivable velocity.

Her Aurora was physically less attractive and delicate than Ulanova's or Semyonova's, but in virtuosity Dudinskaya was at least equal to the latter. "In Act I her balance in the Rose Adagio seemed almost improbable," a contemporary recalled. "The swiftness of her Danse Vertige, the blossoming arabesques in the variation, and her astounding precision and musicality—especially in the romantic duet in Act II, where Dudinskaya managed to maintain the spellbound aura of a sleeping princess—were amazing. The charm of her Aurora in Act III was not so devastating as Semyonova's. Instead, what regal manners she displayed, what coquettish arrogance, and what a triumph of academicism."

Ulanova's ever-growing success was enhanced by her unique partnership with Konstantin Sergeyev. Dudinskaya attempted to rival its greatness through an artistic marriage with Vakhtang Chabukiani. And they were, in fact, a perfect match, a union of kindred spirits. Thanks to this partnership Dudinskaya continued to develop her "sharp, impetuous, and persistent virtuosity," especially in *Don Quixote*, in which they scored their first enormous success, establishing canons of partnering that became a major feature of Soviet ballet.

In her book on Vakhtang Chabukiani, Vera Krasovskaya described this famous partnership: "In the final duet from *Don Quixote* both dancers were utterly expressive in revealing their innovative approach to this classical pas de deux: they imbued it with the joy of a dance competition on equal grounds. After crossing the stage with large jetés, Dudinskaya and Chabukiani took different directions in the middle of a musical phrase, reuniting to complete it with a rush of rapid, sharp pirouettes. The dynamic tension of their dancing gradually increased; the movements became more intricate and concentrated within the confines of a musical sequence, but the ballerina never tried to eclipse her partner. While Dudinskaya spun out the most taxing pirouettes à la seconde, Chabukiani maintained one of his sculpturesque poses which he would break in a split second to catch the ballerina and reorient the swirl of her pirouettes. . . . Especially noteworthy was the end of the adagio. In former

versions it had usually ended with a kind of ballerina's triumph, while she held the lift or pose in her partner's arms. The entire composition connoted the admiration of a cavalier for his lady, symbolically implying the union of loving hearts. At the final major chord, Dudinskaya and Chabukiani darted toward the edge of the stage to challenge the audience with their ultimate virtuoso tricks, like two rivals enjoying equal rights."

The exuberance of her Odile and Kitri undoubtedly prompted Chabukiani to choreograph *Laurencia* for Dudinskaya in 1939, a role that marked an important phase of her career. Chabukiani recalled: "Each variation of Laurencia's served a particular visual purpose. In Act I it was meant to evoke the flight of a sharp-winged, nimble dragonfly. Long-legged Dudinskaya, with her graphically etched manner of dancing, responded keenly to my idea and realized it perfectly. She was sensitive to the heroic ebullience pervading her wedding dance as well as to the evolution of a stage character developing throughout the ballet."

Dudinskaya's Laurencia was her most potent characterization of the 1930s, revealing the perfect balance between the concentrated choreography and the ballerina's bravura. She poured forth cascades of intricate turns and swirling, powerful split jetés, in the midst of which she seemed to hover in the air to heighten her portrayal of a heroic Spanish character, equally indomitable in passion and in hate. Her sharp, rocketing jumps seemed to assert her victory over the stage space; the fiery temperament she displayed caused many critics to proclaim her a heroic Soviet ballerina. In fact, Laurencia stood apart in her gallery of stage characters; her abundance of force and stunning virtuosity reappeared in her Street Dancer in *Don Quixote* but, oddly enough, not at all in her strong-willed yet abrasive Kitri, more a shrew than a scamp.

Far more significant was a role Dudinskaya added to her large repertory in 1941—Nikiya in the Chabukiani–Vladimir Ponomarev staging of *La Bayadère*. Unlike her glorious predecessors from Pavlova to Semyonova, Dudinskaya lacked the convincing theatricality to do full justice to the role's dramatic substance, especially in the mime duel with Gamzatti and the dance with the basket. But in the Kingdom of the Shades her academic finesse and cool persona conferred on her shade a mysterious remoteness and isolation. The fragment of her performance that has been preserved on film reveals that she and Chabukiani shared a profound stylistic understanding of Petipa's choreographic poetry. In the duet with the veil and in Nikiya's solo (studded with impeccably executed, slowly unwinding double tours en attitude and airy splits alternating with lingering arabesques penchées) Dudinskaya's dancing is unsurpassable in its precise match of effortless endeavor and total detachment. Without blurring a single detail of the most intricate steps, Dudinskaya subordinates them to rhythmical inflections so flawlessly that their expressive significance emerges as a brilliantly composed reflection of the music.

Dudinskaya's career was disrupted by the Second World War. From August 1941 to July 1944 she shared the hardships of the Kirov's evacuation to the Urals. At this time her partnership with Konstantin Sergeyev took shape. Since their student performance in 1930, Dudinskaya had been waiting for this moment, which proved crucial and inspiring to her later career. Sergeyev's natural lyricism and softness of manner somehow melted the ice of her dancing. In the postwar years she was criticized less and less for the angularity of her Odette, her overacting in *Giselle*, and the brittleness of her Aurora. She stopped thrusting her virtuoso tricks at the audience and developed her control to a phenomenal degree.

Her mature personal style was displayed in two ballets choreographed by Sergeyev especially for her: *Cinderella* in 1946 and a recension of Petipa's *Raymonda* in 1950. Though Sergeyev's choreography for *Cinderella* was a sentimental miscellany of quotations from Petipa, frequently at odds with Prokofiev's music, Dudinskaya's sustained floating quality, her calm completion of each pose and movement, somehow made it all work. Although one was not captivated by her correct yet still amateurish acting, one was held by her stylized, doll-like delicacy and frail femininity and by the unusual blend of modesty and impishness in her characterization.

But Dudinskaya's artistic greatness in the 1950s was most brilliantly manifested in her Raymonda, the role in which she reigned supreme. She was not concerned with bringing Petipa's medieval lady to life. She employed her extraordinary technical gift only to do full justice to Petipa's patterns; in her view, when flawlessly performed, they themselves would portray Raymonda. From Dudinskaya's musicality and sensitive adherence to Petipa's style emerged the most impressive Raymonda on the Soviet stage. With incomparable ease she switched from the swift pas de bourrée, tours, and emboîtés of the entrée to the Romantic serenity of Raymonda's variation with a scarf and the ballottés in the dream adagio with Jean de Brienne. In the pas d'action with Abdul-Rakhman in Act II she gave rein to her bravura in the entrechâts quatre and chaînés of the variation; she infused the pas de bourrée suivie in the wedding variation (Act III) with the inimitable flavor of Hungarian folk dance. Raymonda's five variations displayed the whole gamut of subtle emotional inflections, bewitching in their diversity and ephemeral feminine charm.

In the 1950s her artistry was diminished only when it was constrained by the rigid structure of Soviet dramaballet. Her Parasha in Zakharov's *The Bronze Horseman*, Pannochka in Lopukhov's *Taras Bulba*, and Baronne Strahl in Fenster's *Masquerade* were cardboard heroines cut from a single pattern. Attempting to become a dancer-actress, she undertook the role of Sari in Sergeyev's ballet *The Path of Thunder*, the melodramatic socialist-realist love story of a poor black man and a rich white girl. She performed the choreographic clichés with professionalism, but without going beyond illustration to art.

Her true element was, in fact, the plotless ballet, which did not appear in Russia until the 1960s, when Dudinskaya had left the stage. An admirer of Balanchine, she staged *Symphony in C* at the Vaganova School, where she continued to fortify the traditions of Russian academic dance as a teacher, possibly the most qualified replacement for Vaganova herself. Among her many pupils was Natalia Makarova, who paid heartfelt tribute to Dudinskaya's exceptional pedagogical gifts in *A Dance Autobiography*: "She was frequently accused of stifling the individuality of young ballerinas and making them copies (more often pale copies) of herself. Strangely enough, with me nothing of the kind happened. She did not interfere with my interpretations, never cut off my unrestrained flights of fancy, but concentrated only on my technique, driving and urging me on unmercifully in the classroom. She possessed such will and such uncontradictable authority. . . . Her military dictates were a salvation for me then."

THE UNIQUELY RUSSIAN STYLISTS

Ekaterina Geltzer · Lidia Ivanova
Marina Semyonova

фотогр.
Императорскихъ
ТЕАТРОВЪ.

Гельцеръ

EKATERINA GELTZER

EKATERINA GELTZER belonged to the ballet of Moscow as much as Pavlova did to that of St. Petersburg. She was both a great classical ballerina, surpassing Pavlova in technique, and a great actress. But if Pavlova's art harked back to the old Romantic tradition, through which the refined and Westernized facets of St. Petersburg's artistic life were refracted, Geltzer's genius seemed to reflect the grand style of Moscow, which manifested itself both in life and in the theatre.

Geltzer's dancing was larger than life, a tempestuous presentation from which all sense of measure and stylistic reserve was absent. Even had she been given the opportunity, Geltzer would hardly have been able to conquer the Western world the way Pavlova did. Her art was too regional; it was a product of Moscow and therefore less accessible to European perception. Fiery, unrestrained, even frantic, she was too unrefined and unpolished for St. Petersburg. Her artistic home was Moscow's Bolshoi Theatre; her choreographer was neither Fokine nor Petipa but the talented, eccentric Alexander Gorsky.

Akim Volynsky, the champion of St. Petersburg classicism, was responding to the genuinely Russian elements in Geltzer's art when he wrote: "This is a person who epitomizes in her astonishing dancing the spirit of Moscow, which seems to reverberate in the chimes of its innumerable steeples, the whirlwind sweep of its troikas and noisy festivities. . . . Geltzer's classicism asserts itself by joining the whole of age-old Russia to it and through it." The exaggeration of her port de bras, her facial expressions, her incredible terre-à-terre technique, the tremendous thrust of every gesture, led Volynsky to view Geltzer as "the most perfect dance calligrapher in the lofty Russian key."

She was by no means flawless. In Fyodor Lopukhov's words,

Geltzer was a vehement ballerina. Whatever she did, her dancing and miming, even in her lyrical roles, blazed and dazzled like flame. Her domain was roles demanding heroic projection, and I would define her as a heroic ballerina-actress. Her physical equipment was far from ideal. Her torso and arms bore a sculpturesque similarity to those of the huntress Diana. As for her legs, from

the aesthetic standpoint they left something to be desired—they had exaggeratedly swollen muscles at the calves and overrounded thighs. But nobody was able to conceal these shortcomings in dancing as Geltzer did. Her pirouettes fascinated with their swiftness; tours chaînés and other terre-à-terre steps she executed with such brio that they seemed to bring out the essence of her personality. She avoided first arabesque and other Romantic poses, realizing that they were unsuitable to her. She never possessed a soaring jump, but she knew tricks that in performance persuaded the audience of the opposite.

Geltzer was frequently called "the dancing Brünnhilde" by critics, who also likened her artistry to that of Sarah Bernhardt. Even her colorful costumes reminded people of the divine Sarah: in *Le Corsaire* Geltzer appeared in a golden-orange tunic under a deep blue cloak; her Salammbô was clad in a pinkish-purple dress; as Kitri she wore a bright red wig with a large scarlet ribbon on her brow.

Nevertheless, as Vera Krasovskaya incisively pointed out: "Geltzer always remained not simply a Russian ballerina but a genuine Muscovite, whose Russian 'enunciation' of the balletic grammar was worth emulating." Her sweeping, energetic style was epitomized by her portrayal of the Tsar Maiden in Saint-Léon's *The Little Humpbacked Horse*. She seasoned any variation, be it French, Italian, or Russian, with a dash of skillful stylization, giving the noble classical steps a touch of Russian folk dance. She knew as no one among her colleagues how to glide around like a sweet Russian fairy-tale swan, bowing low or gently undulating her shoulders. According to many critics, she was unforgettable in genuine Russian folk dance. Volynsky recalled: "A Russian woman would sail majestically out of the wings. Her dark golden shoes flashed softly on the stage, back and forth; her small heels beat nimbly against the floor. Lifting and coquettishly dipping her ravishing shoulders, she swayed her large sleeves with irresistible grace. Her dancing feet, emerging from beneath her long and lavishly embroidered Russian peasant dress, seemed to fly in the abundance of its changing motley colors."

EKATERINA GELTZER, born on November 2, 1876, was the daughter of an outstanding mime, Vasily Geltzer, and grew up in Moscow's artistic milieu. According to Geltzer, her interest in ballet was first aroused by Eleonora Duse's Moscow appearances in 1891–92: "Duse astounded me not by the way she wept on stage or stood in silence as the grief-stricken Marguerite Gautier while the ushers ran around the theatre whispering in French: 'Silence, silence, Madame pleure!' I was struck by her movements—it was a real ballet, with each gesture conveying drama. As a little girl I said to myself, If I become a ballerina, I'll try to dance the way Duse acts."

In 1889 Geltzer enrolled in the class of the uninspired Bolshoi choreographer José Mendez at the Moscow Choreographic School. Terre-à-terre technique came easily to her; her strong pointes resembled those of Marta Muravieva, the Russian virtuoso of the 1860s. In 1894 Geltzer was admitted as a coryphée to the Bolshoi company, whose repertory capitalized on the remnants from Saint-Léon's choreographic luxury. She was Aspasia in *Walpurgis Night* and danced a virtuoso variation in Perrot's *Catarina*. Two seasons later she was promoted to second ballerina, sharing the limelight with Adelina Djuri and Lubov Roslavleva; unfortunately, the Bolshoi could offer her only a few interesting roles.

In 1896, at her own request, Geltzer was transferred to the Maryinsky, where she began to take classes from Johannsen and to rehearse with Petipa himself. Johannsen refined her port de bras and strengthened her back and torso, singling her out as a promising young talent. For the next two years the young ballerina performed everything and anything, without discrimination; she danced fifty-six times during the 1897–98 season. Among her solos were one of the Fresques Réanimés in *The Little Humpbacked Horse*, the Spinner's variation in *Coppélia*, the variation in the Dream Scene and the Grand Pas Hongrois in *Raymonda*, and one of the four Jewel Fairies in *The Sleeping Beauty*.

Geltzer learned the Diamond Fairy under Petipa's supervision, and the great maestro's lessons remained with her for life. As she recalled in the 1930s:

> I planted my pointe firmly on the floor, which made the tempo twice as slow. After finishing the variation, I approached Petipa and said, "Marius Ivanovich, I know the dance." "You knows," he replied in his funny way of talking, "you not knows nothing. You knows what is a *bijou*? Ruby, emerald, topaz . . . You seen these stones in natural states? How afterwards they cut and polished in the factory?" I stood all in a sweat, trembling like a leaf. "And you knows how they break the granite in workshop? That's what you did. You breakened the *bijoux*." But I, who had a lot of guts in those days, dared to ask the maestro: "And what about my diamond?" Petipa said: "Diamond is many many sparkles—red, green, blue. It's twice as quicker."
>
> Before my departure for Moscow I asked Petipa how to dance Aurora. He replied: "You can do your *cruizy* things, but you should be the princess." "Your daughter is totally *cruizy*," Petipa used to say to my father, "but with *beaucoup de talent*." When asked how I danced the Cat in *Sleeping Beauty*, Petipa answered: "You is a little panther, but you should be a *chat*."

The St. Petersburg audience immediately appreciated Geltzer's regal carriage, her imperious attack, and her virtuosity, which equaled that of the Maryinsky stars. Her strong toes permitted her to cross the stage in pas ballonné hopping on pointe and "to circle the stage on pointe, arousing a storm of rapture and applause in the audience" (Khudekov).

She was frequently criticized for exaggerated and overly spectacular performances, which thrilled the balcony but not the blasé balletomanes in the boxes. She gained a reputation as the most "democratic" of ballerinas. "I dance for the balcony. Although I am constantly blamed for exaggerated gestures or steps, I am not going to change my style. I want to make every movement of my fingers visible from everywhere." Geltzer defended herself with a certain pride, but she herself was aware that St. Petersburg classicism never flowed in her veins.

In 1898 she returned to the Bolshoi in Moscow. Until the arrival of Alexander Gorsky in 1901, she had to make do with small roles. She made her debut in *The Naiad and the Fisherman* in 1899, dancing for the first time with Vasily Tikhomirov, who became her constant partner and her husband. The Naiad was followed by Teresa in *The Cavalry Halt* and Clairemond in Ivan Clustine's *Stars*; the verve of her performance seemed inversely proportional to the shallowness of the roles. In *Stars* Geltzer performed a Spanish dance with such exaggerated pertness that a Moscow critic requested that she "reduce the nimbleness owing to which [she] seems to jump out of her skin." At times her bravura solos outshone the ballerina's: in Julius Reisinger's *Little*

Magic Slipper her feminine, defiant, soaring Fairy God-mother pushed Roslavleva's Cinderella to the sidelines. Critics raved over her thirty-two fouettés, which she performed "almost frozen on the spot."

In January 1899, at the Bolshoi première of *The Sleeping Beauty*, Geltzer fascinated the Moscow audience as the White Cat, living up to Petipa's description of her as "a little panther." In the fourth performance of the ballet she made her debut as Aurora. It was an undisputed success, but, in her own words, "I did not find myself in this taxing role." An anonymous critic noted that her Aurora "was like a summer thunderstorm with its lightning in the overcast sky." Geltzer liberally imparted her Russian stamp to Aurora, but the "native" accents, quite appropriate in her final variation, were too richly orchestrated in the earlier scenes. The elegant French manner somehow eluded Geltzer, though she excelled technically. The role of Nikiya in *La Bayadère*, with its emphasis on reserved bearing, Oriental plasticity of arms, and subdued dramatic impact, was also a problem for her (she performed it as a substitute for Pavlova in St. Petersburg in 1902). But her Raymonda, suddenly brought to life by her impeccable technique and fiery temperament, was extraordinary as was her Myrtha in *Giselle*. When she confronted Enriquetta Grimaldi as Giselle, Geltzer put the illustrious Italian virtuoso to shame.

During her sporadic forays into St. Petersburg, even the severest critics now began to compare Geltzer to her idol Pierina Legnani, praising her steely pointes, whirlwind pirouettes, and exciting tours. She danced with her husband, Tikhomirov, whose exemplary correctness and noble manner served as the perfect background for the slightly eccentric virtuosity and license of his spouse.

After her St. Petersburg debut as Raymonda in 1901, Valerian Svetlov gave her an enthusiastic review:

> Her pizzicato on pointe and her pirouettes, both double and triple, are impeccable, performed boldly, with no apparent preparation and with astonishing precision. Her pirouettes are very clean, and the same is true of her renversés, which are executed with brio and bravura. Her jetés en tournant are generous and full of grace, as are her attitudes and développés. She knows how to hold herself, and her ports de bras deserve the highest praise. In fact, her true strength lies in her technique, which is adorned by the most florid touches of contemporary virtuosity. This determines the character of all her dancing. Mlle Geltzer is hardly less talented than Le-gnani, and that coming from a St. Petersburg balletomane is no mean compliment. Mlle Geltzer also has a very charming characteristic: the softness, the curve, the elegance of her movements.

However, when Geltzer essayed Odette-Odile for her first benefit performance, she failed utterly, and afterward she undertook the role only very rarely. Her rather short legs and arms, easily concealed when she danced Kitri and Raymonda, were all too visible in choreography based on the legato movements of the swan. Moreover, she never was a mistress of nuance, out of which the role of Odette is woven. Her Odile, in spite of her impeccably executed fouettés, romped onto the stage like "an Italian ingenue from Goldoni's comedies," in Sergei Khudekov's words.

In St. Petersburg Geltzer was allowed to perform only as a guest artist, for her virtuosity threatened the prima ballerina status of the omnipotent Kschessinskaya. In Moscow, however, Geltzer reigned supreme, once her rivals Djuri and Roslavleva left the stage in 1904.

It is hard to guess what would have become of Geltzer's career had Alexander Gorsky not made his appearance at the Bolshoi in 1901. A pupil of Petipa, Gorsky was as talented as he was quick-tempered in his attempt to "clear away all the litter left by Petipa." His innovations (realistic stage effects; a wider, less academic use of the corps de ballet; magnificent decors in a new style by Konstantin Korovine and Alexander Golovine) are not to be belittled. In the light of the new theatricality propagated first by Stanislavsky and later by Meyerhold, Petipa's enchanting but archaic balletic theatre seemed compromised and obsolete. When Gorsky transformed Petipa's old-fashioned *Don Quixote* into a colorful, zesty *españolada*, its pure-dance elements and theatrical devices perfectly matched in the context of a choreodrama, Geltzer, as a dancer-actress, welcomed his audacity. His reforms suited her flamboyant style: when she danced Kitri in September 1901, her theatrical instincts and virtuosity happily blended to bring this conventional operetta character to life. But when Gorsky, advocating the resurrection of Perrot's dramatic emphasis, declared war on virtuosity, Geltzer and Tikhomirov rebelled against this excess of zeal.

The choreographer and his leading ballerina gradually involved themselves in an intricate game—two powerful egos and striking personalities who, in fact, needed each other. Their collaboration actually turned out to be fruitful, a mutually favorable influence. For her part, Geltzer tamed

Left: (top) Gulnare in *Le Corsaire*, early 1910s; (bottom) *Bacchanalia*, 1911
Above: Publicity photograph with Vasily Tikhomirov, 1911

Е. В. Гельцеръ „Геній Бельгіи," (военный маршъ.) К. офицеръ 1914 г.

Above: Gulnare, with Tikhomirov as Conrad, 1912
Right: (top) The War March in *The Spirit of Belgium*, 1915; (bottom) Medora in *Le Corsaire*, 1912

Above: Tao-Hoa in *The Red Poppy*, 1927
Right: (top) The Panaderos in *Raymonda*, early 1910s;
(bottom) *Russian Dance*, c.1900

Gorsky's innovative but immoderate zest and defended the priority of classical dance. And when Gorsky's pictorial choreodramas did not fatally encumber Geltzer's dancing, she produced her best portrayals, such as Medora (*Le Corsaire*) and Salammbô, satisfying both Gorsky's champions and Petipa's. As Nikiya in *Bayadère* or the Egyptian Queen Bint-Anta (Petipa's Aspicia) in Gorsky's new version of *Pharaoh's Daughter*, Geltzer shone both as a technician and as a dramatic actress. But at times the impact of the choreodrama on her was so powerful that she seemed to lose perspective. Into her portrayal of Nikiya she introduced Isadora Duncan's "mute speech," for which an anonymous critic took her to task: "In an attempt to convey her feelings as realistically as she could, Madame Geltzer resorted to a device that, in my view, is absolutely inadmissible in ballet. She moved her lips, as if whispering words."

The imaginative, though at times incongruous, tricks with which Geltzer ornamented her roles in Gorsky's versions of Petipa's ballets were profusely displayed in her most illustrious role, Salammbô. According to Fyodor Lopukhov, Gorsky designed the part primarily as a series of sequences in the style of Isadora Duncan's free plasticity, which Geltzer orchestrated in her personal way by incorporating into it many classical elements. Despite her serious efforts at diversifying Gorsky's choreography, it retained its original qualities, stemming from the emphasis on the poses with the leg slightly bent in a kind of low attitude, on hops and runs, on curves of the torso, and on the mannered play of her arms.

Geltzer's Salammbô became her gem, her greatest artistic achievement, like Spessivtseva's Giselle and Pavlova's Nikiya. As Lopukhov recalled:

Her expressivity attained its summit in Salammbô. Through her mime and steps, her Salammbô convinced the public that she was both a proud servant of the goddess Tanit and profoundly female. She was consumed by passion for the leader of the insurgents, Mato, and torn by the conflict between her sensual nature and her priestly duty. Both sides of Salammbô's character were fully revealed in her variation with the dove. The scenes with Mato in the tent were imbued with the ambivalence of Salammbô's intentions: her powerful attraction to Mato warred with her determination to retrieve the goddess's veil from him at any price. And Geltzer's every movement was suggestive of this poignant duality.

During the decade that followed *Salammbô* Geltzer performed various roles in Gorsky's ballets, becoming deeply involved in his eclectic and intoxicating theatrical experiments. The gallery of her stage characters is extraordinary for its diversity and range: Medora in *Le Corsaire* (1912), which she enthusiastically saluted as "a choreodrama expressed by means of properly modernized classical dance"; the Doll in the style of Louis XVI in *Carnaval* and Ondine in *Schubertiana* (1913); Eunice in *Eunice and Petronius* (1915). Despite their questionable choreographic value, Geltzer reveled in these roles, generously sharing her enthusiasm with the responsive audience. But apart from her turned-in, weatherbeaten, stern fisherwoman in *Love Is Nimble*, depicted with full-blooded realistic strokes, Geltzer did not create any three-dimensional balletic character to rival her Salammbô. Her performances began to acquire a circus air, despite their obvious charm and irresistible impact on her large public. She was no longer disturbed by Gorsky's audacious but garish amalgamation of Petipa's academic patterns with Duncan's plasticity.

Here are a few descriptions of Geltzer's theatricality in Gorsky's repertory of the 1910s. In *Bacchanalia*, set to music from Saint-Saëns's *Samson et Dalila*, Geltzer "conveys the languid delicacy of a Jewish maiden still shy about revealing her feelings. But passion gradually envelops her, and she starts to spin around the stage in the grip of an ever-mounting fever, her hands, with open palms, stretched toward the sky" (Volynsky). In the divertissement *Genius of Belgium*, choreographed by Gorsky to the music of a Belgian march in the heat of patriotic anti-German fervor (1914), she "appeared in a light cape, spotted with green and red, and a glittering helmet with white plumage, holding a trumpet above her head, embodying heroic little Belgium. The audience exploded in applause that never ceased throughout her entire dance" (Ilya Schneider). As Eunice, clad in a tunic, she "shot arabesques and spun out double fouettés with inimitable gusto, not in the least embarrassed by her entourage of bacchantes hopping around in Roman sandals" (Alexander Tcherepnin). In Gorsky's pastorale set to Beethoven's Fifth Symphony, Geltzer danced barefoot, clad in a short tunic, portraying a coy Greek shepherdess who arouses two shepherds to amorous competition.

Around 1914 Gorsky's choreographic fervor subsided. After the Revolution of 1917, Geltzer performed only three new roles: Esmeralda, the Sylph in *La Sylphide*, and Tao-Hoa in *The Red Poppy*. *La Sylphide*, mounted in 1925, came to her too late, although even in her prime she had never excelled in Romantic technique. Her sprite looked heavy, earthbound, and contrived, and the lack of drama in Bournonville's fairy-tale plot gave her no chance to deploy her extraordinary histrionics.

As for *Esmeralda*, the dramatic and dance resources of this gem of the Romantic era offered a challenge to Geltzer. Unfortunately, Tikhomirov attempted to restore the slightly dated Perrot-Petipa choreography, because his advisor Volynsky maintained that "as in a Pushkin poem, there was nothing to be altered." But in order to keep up with the Marxist doctrine of the 1920s, Tikhomirov interpreted the naive, archaic *Esmeralda* as a social drama, emphasizing the conflict of the depraved feudal world and the tormented heart of a gypsy street dancer. Gone were the picturesque, multicolored crowd at the Cours des Miracles, the subtle balance between pure classical dance and primitive but poignant mime, and the unobtrusive accents of old-fashioned Romantic drama, which constituted the charm of the original choreographic design.

Nevertheless, by all accounts Geltzer "magically illuminated the performance." Volynsky gave a colorful description of her acting:

> At the sight of the gallows in front of the door leading to the chamber of tortures, Esmeralda loses her normal gait. . . . She suddenly shuffles her feet, in a state of mind bordering on paralysis. . . . Her simple glances at the gibbet give you an impression of her genuine, visceral fear. You suddenly start to feel in your own stomach the terror of this girl—so realistically, so physiologically, yet so enticingly is it expressed by Geltzer. The act ends with Esmeralda's triumph. The crowd raises up her body, ravaged by torture, and carries it above them like a precious trophy. . . . The curtain comes down, crowning the hysterical frenzy both on the stage and in the audience. You leave your seat depressed and almost sick.

The Red Poppy, set to music of Glière, was created in 1927 by Tikhomirov and Geltzer herself, who became the champions of the academic trend in Soviet ballet. It is not surprising that *The Red Poppy*'s structure harked back to the devices of the early Petipa ballets, although his enchanted nymph and her noble admirer were replaced by Tao-Hoa, a wretched Chinese bar dancer, and her beloved, the captain of a Soviet ship. Tao-Hoa sacrifices her life defending him from hired capitalist assassins. The melodrama was developed in pantomime, with classical dance in the worn-out guise of an exotic divertissement, "Tao-Hoa's Dream," thrown in for purposes of entertainment. The role of Tao-Hoa did not require much actual dancing of the aging ballerina, but she could display her marvelous acting technique, nurtured and polished in Gorsky's choreodramas. According to Geltzer's contemporaries, it was Romantic verve that made her Tao-Hoa so distinctive. Acting the hoary melodrama in a lofty Romantic key, Geltzer miraculously elevated it to the level of serious theatre, giving an inspired example to the whole generation of Russian ballerinas who were obliged to perform Soviet drama-ballets in the 1930s and 1940s.

Geltzer's career was unusually long. In the 1930s she toured throughout Russia, until the beginning of the Second World War, and even in the 1940s she was still dancing the Polonaise and Mazurka in Glinka's opera *Ivan Susanin* (*A Life for the Tsar*). Anecdotes of Geltzer's indomitable willpower are still told in Russia—once, already past the age of sixty, she reputedly told her colleagues in the wings: "Help me put myself up on pointe; after that I know what to do." Geltzer died in Moscow in 1962. A unique Russian stylist and flamboyant spirit, she remains unsurpassed in the annals of ballet.

Studio portrait, early 1920s

LIDIA IVANOVA

IT IS DIFFICULT to make a debut and immediately become part of ballet history. Lidia Ivanova did just that," wrote Akim Volynsky in 1924. But Ivanova's curriculum vitae is tragically short. She was born on October 4, 1903, into an old Petersburg family of the intelligentsia. In 1914 she entered the Maryinsky School, where she studied in the class of Olga Preobrajenskaya. She made her first appearance at the Maryinsky Theatre in 1921; she died on June 16, 1924.

But it was not her sinister and still unexplained death that prompted the finest ballet critics and writers of the 1920s to devote an entire issue of *Life of Art*, as well as a small monograph, to her memory. During her three years at the Maryinsky, Ivanova, who became a soloist immediately, never had the chance to perform the famous roles—Aurora, Giselle, Odette—for which she had been born. Nevertheless, even her smallest roles were profusely described by her contemporaries, something accorded to only one other ballerina: Anna Pavlova.

Ivanova was endowed with a huge extension and a rare soaring jump that, in Volynsky's words, constituted "the essence of her young art." Unlike Pavlova, whose jump was Romantic, light, airy, Ivanova "rose to the heights with a great rush like no other artist in the world before her."

Moreover, she possessed strong toes which allowed her to perform various kinds of runs and hops on pointe without apparent effort; her terre-à-terre movements and her landings were soft and soundless. But it was her expressiveness and dynamism, a certain exaggeration in the execution of each movement, that were the main features of Ivanova's style.

"An elemental Russian nature was manifested in her dancing," wrote Alexander Gvozdev. "She strained toward open space and was imbued with a stormy will to freedom. She astonished us with the beauty of free flight as she reveled in the unbridled scope of her movements."

As Preobrajenskaya's pupil, Ivanova sought from the first to breathe life and energy into her quickly attained virtuosity. In this she was not alone: at the beginning of the 1920s dynamism and flamboyance were the universal ideal of Soviet ballet. This vitality was so strong in her that occasionally she broke the boundaries of the academic canon. But her presence was so appealing that even Volynsky, that ardent opponent of modernity, troubador of Pavlova's and Spessivtseva's classical art, forgave Ivanova her willfulness. As he recalled in his eulogy: "In *The Little Humpbacked Horse* she executed . . . a movement that was almost monstrous from an academic standpoint—there was great strength in this. I turned to Lidia's mother, who was sitting next to me, and said: 'Tell Lidia that this is intolerable, but that I worship her art.'"

The exaggeration and concentration that later appeared to be especially significant in Maya Plisetskaya's performances were Ivanova's contributions to the new performing manner that was developing in the twenties. With her enormous jump and her special thrust, she easily transformed a conventional jeté into an aerial split, while her pas de chat, a step that normally calls for feline lightness and femininity, became sharp, distinct and lightning fast.

Her first student role was Lise in *The Magic Flute*; Alexander Shiriayev, Petipa's comrade-in-arms and Pavlova's coach, resurrected this simple peasant ballet, whose plot recalls *La Fille mal gardée*, for Lidia and her regular partner George Balanchine (then Georgi Balanchivadze). As their classmate Mikhail Mikhailov wrote in his memoirs, "In age, appearance, and character the young couple were so appropriate for their roles that it was as if the choreographer had had their particular external and internal attributes in mind when he composed the work. This was especially true of Lidia—expansiveness in all things was in general the distinctive feature of her nature. Her open,

purely Russian oval face with light brown eyes, her figure which avoided an unhealthy thinness—everything spoke to the truth that Lidia was not created to play illusory sprites or nymphs or balletic shades but to embody real living characters."

In the unassuming role of Lise, even as a student Ivanova was able to display all the tricks of her future mastery. Her huge extension and regal balance lent to her poses a ballerina's aplomb. The audience was excited by the daring with which she rose to pointe from demi-plié and by the swirling rush that energized her small runs about the stage and her manèges of jumps.

In the spring of 1919, for an examination performance in the former Mikhailovsky Theatre (now the Maly), Victor Semyonov staged a classical duet, *Adagio and Waltz*, for Ivanova and Mikhail Dudko, set to music from Tchaikovsky's *The Four Seasons*. "Lidia Ivanova," said one reviewer, "demonstrated vital, full-blooded poetry in complete accordance with the academic standard."

For Lidia's graduation performance in the spring of 1921, Olga Preobrajenskaya asked Alexander Chekrygin to revive *Graziella*, a one-act ballet to the music of Saint-Saëns, which Pavel Gerdt had choreographed for Preobrajenskaya herself. The role of a capricious young lady naively in love fit Lidia's physical and technical qualifications marvelously, and Preobrajenskaya felt that the youngster would surpass her teacher's own performance; but a sudden lung inflammation prevented Ivanova from dancing. Nevertheless, she was admitted to the Maryinsky company as a second principal soloist, bypassing the corps de ballet.

By the end of the 1921–22 season there was not a ballet in the repertory in which Ivanova had not participated. She danced the Fée de la Farine and the Silver Fairy in *The Sleeping Beauty*, one of the Fresques Réanimées in *The Little Humpbacked Horse*, the Wili Moyna in *Giselle*, and the Street Dancer in *Petrushka*. Later she performed the classical trio and the Pas d'Esclave in *Le Corsaire*, the pas de trois in Act I of *Swan Lake*, and the variation and pas d'action in *Pharaoh's Daughter*.

In each role a special facet of Lidia's talent sparkled. In the Feé de la Farine's variation from the Prologue to *Sleeping Beauty*, she displayed her amazingly strong pointe work. No one since Egorova had excelled in the part as Ivanova did. The variation, consisting of five small sequences, is built on sharp little hops, barely grazing the floor, and swift pas de bourrée. The melody unfolds in a staccato rhythm with a steady underlying accompaniment. Throughout the variation the last note of a four-beat measure is continuously stressed.

"In this variation," Mikhailov recalled,

Ivanova, cutting across the stage diagonally, seemed to thread her way along a path, playfully hopping from stone to stone. The accents were marked by movements of the hands. Raising first one hand, then the other, over her head on the fourth beat, Ivanova slyly shaded her eyes, looking over the noble ladies and cavaliers around her as if inviting them to see what she was going to present to the newborn princess. The eyes of the fairy glowed with goodness. Convinced that everyone was watching her, the fairy then displayed her magic: with a generous flourish of the hand, she seemed to scatter precious stones on the life-path lying before her godchild, strewing them in every direction and playfully tossing the remainder upward; then she unexpectedly rose to pointe in croisé en avant. With her whole being she said: "Now I have done all that I can for my favorite." Before and since Lidia, I have seen various soloists in this part, but no one else showed any attempt to interpret the meaning of Petipa's variation. Usually the dancer executed the steps diligently, accompanied by a smile that said nothing. But Lidia was expressive in every step. It would have been impossible to render more convincingly in dance image a young enchantress sowing good in the world.

Ivanova's jumps immediately became part of Russian dance history: they were so high and powerful, so masculine in their attack. One critic recalled: "Ivanova did not jump—she soared upward like an arrow and lingered there, at the same time covering a large part of the stage. She demonstrated her fabulous jump for the first time in the Fresques Réanimées from *The Little Humpbacked Horse*. Having executed several ronds de jambe, she then pushed herself from the floor with her legs held together. At the top of her leap, she split her legs and seemed to hover in the air in some incomprehensible fashion, doing two circular movements with her front leg. Having done this feat with astonishing daring, she returned to earth without breaking the legato line and then boldly rose on her toes in arabesque, followed by an attitude effacé. She repeated this sequence six times. This was stunning; it did not look at all like trickery but rather recalled the flight of a bird struggling against a hurricane."

When she danced the *Swan Lake* pas de trois, Ivanova's elevation drove the audience into a frenzy, especially in the whirlwind sauts de basque around the stage. Mikhailov wrote:

One leg was thrown high, then the other was pulled up, the body followed to the same level, and another turn was executed. Ivanova managed to freeze in the air for a moment, then land forcefully and leap up again. The jumps were stunning in their height and explosive force. Repeating them endlessly, she would circle the stage, dumbfounding both the public and her colleagues. No less impressive was the turn that followed, done on the diagonal. With a swift battement Lidia would fly into pas assemblé, followed by several sissonnes. The leg thrown high would be joined by the other and, held firmly together, they would carry the dancer, now without turning, across several meters.

In the second half of her first season (1921–22), Ivanova's repertory included Papillon in Fokine's *Carnaval*, a variation in the last act of *Don Quixote*, and one of the variations of the classical trio in *Le Corsaire*. During the 1922–23 season, she appeared in the Pas d'Esclave, proving herself to be a mature actress. This duet, in which Trefilova and Preobrajenskaya had both excelled by flaunting their academic technique, was transformed by Ivanova into a genre scene. Her slave girl was obstinate; she taunted the merchant who had decided to sell her to the old pasha. "Lidia's appearance turned the lazy atmosphere of the slave market into a whirlwind," one critic wrote. In Petipa's choreography the entrée consisted of three sections, in each of which the merchant, moving along the diagonal toward the audience, would toss the slave into various poses, displaying her to the pasha seated in the foreground. After each leap she either strained to break out of his hands, jumping a step back into first arabesque, or turned capriciously away from the pasha, adopting a pose with a leg extended forward in croisé. Ivanova put so much expression into these movements that, said one reporter, "behind the whole series of lifts alternating with forceful hops on pointe, the retort could be heard: 'Just dare to sell me to that old goat! I'll run away in any case!'"

In the flowing adagio that followed the stormy entrée, the turbulent emotions of the slave girl subsided. The merchant removed the veil from her face, revealing cunning eyes that looked askance at the buyer, and a mischievous,

Right: Moyna in *Giselle*, early 1920s
Far right and below: studio portraits, early 1920s

OPPOSITE
Studio portraits with Nicolai Efimov, early 1920s

fearless smile. In the picturesque poses of the duet Ivanova, with the bearing of a true ballerina, executed a multitude of pirouettes from various positions and exhibited her brilliant elevation, hops on pointe, and dynamic turns around the stage. Especially stunning, according to one eyewitness, were her cabrioles en avant, which were extraordinarily sweeping and high. "One of Lidia's legs, striking the other in the air in an elegant manner, would rise above her head."

Each role, no matter how small, even those of the Nymph in Fokine's *Eros* or Dawn in the Act III divertissement of *Coppélia*, was transformed by Ivanova into a miniature masterpiece. "From her first appearance as Dawn," wrote Mikhailov,

Ivanova, clad in the usual pale pink tunic, riveted the audience's attention. Her impact was the result not of spectacular posing, such as dancers usually adopt before the start of this variation, but by her portrayal of a state of melancholy. The lowered head trembled, the shoulders involuntarily stooped, and her arms were folded on her chest. Only the feet crossed in fifth position on pointe suggested the dance to come. It began with little pas de bourrée that floated in a straight line toward the audience. Gradually, the head was raised, the back straightened; the arms began to reach upward. Little by little the ballerina's gaze brightened, and she seemed to grow physically on the stage. It was a miraculous act of internal reincarnation. The human creature was transfigured into a beautiful phenomenon of nature—sunrise. Thanks to the animation of the artist and the expressiveness of her face, an image of the day being born was created with a seemingly unaffected visual device. It evoked the moment when the sun is only a glimmer, beginning to gild the horizon, pushing back the darkness that so recently covered everything.

In her three years at the Maryinsky, "the participation of this young dancer-actress, even in a small solo, constituted serious competition for the ballerina in the main role. The noisy applause that accompanied Ivanova's variations in *Le Corsaire* and *The Sleeping Beauty* more than once disconcerted Spessivtseva and [Elena] Lukom as Medora or Elizaveta Gerdt as Aurora" (Mikhailov). This was especially true of Ivanova as the Diamond Fairy in *Sleeping Beauty*, where, writes Yuri Slonimsky, "her boldly sweeping Russian style was particularly apparent." In this role the

soaring quality of her jumps in the entrée and the brilliant facets of her terre-à-terre steps stunned the audience.

Petipa had envisioned the dancer in this variation as a diamond, a chandelier in shining flame. The entrée, performed to a majestic, bravura waltz, was built on large jetés along the diagonal, alternating with pauses on pointe in attitude. Out of a brief glissade Ivanova rushed forward and, imperceptibly pushing off from the floor, propelled her body upward. Smoothly extending her legs in the air and soaring like a bird on a huge flap of its wings, she flew across the great stage space in two gigantic, regal jumps. In the presto, which consisted of tiny terre-à-terre steps and quickly alternating sculpturesque poses, Ivanova introduced a rare combination of swift movement and purity. She sharply joined the beats with short runs about the stage: from pas emboîté she progressed just as forcefully to nimble turns accompanied by fluttering wrists. "Ivanova's Diamond Fairy possessed a truly fabled majesty and blinded one with the multitude of sparkling rays playing on faceted surfaces" (Slonimsky).

After her second season at the Maryinsky, Lidia Ivanova was a household name in Petrograd. She was worshipped not only by the ballet critics such as Volynsky, Gvozdev, and Slonimsky but by many poets, writers, and actors. Among her friends and admirers were such famous dramatic actors as Mikhail Chekhov and Nikolai Monakhov, the writer Mikhail Zotchenko, and such outstanding poets as Mikhail Kuzmin and Nikolai Aseyev. For all of them she seemed not so much to embody the grandeur of the former Imperial ballet as to presage the future of classical dance in Russia, the birth of a new dynamic style. They saw in her dancing the condensed energy and invigorating vitality that made the harmony and precision of classical forms reverberate with a new power. "After Ivanova's jumps and airy turns, her dashing attack and inebriating brio," wrote Kuzmin in his diary, "it was impossible for ballet to continue in the old manner. Her brief career was like a cyclone or hurricane that stirred up the morass of the old ballet and swept away its debris. Possibly she was simply the catalyst that accelerated the development of a new style in the twenties, close to the pure forms of German expressionism. And possibly also her premature death was a kind of retaliation for her audacity. A rare talent, she was doomed to disappear at her bloom, as Emma Livry did in the 1860s, the most delicate spirit of fading Romanticism."

Like her classmate George Balanchine, Ivanova saw

the future of ballet in plotless dancing that would express abstract concepts rather than compete with dramatic theatre. She was open to experiment: in 1921 she participated in the evenings of the small Youth Ballet company organized by Balanchine. Together with him and Alexandra Danilova she took part in the experimental *Dance Symphony: Grandeur of the Universe*, which Fyodor Lopukhov set to Beethoven's Fourth Symphony. Its daring choreography combined neoclassical and character dance elements with sheer acrobatics, the stream of dance developing in accordance with the music, creating its visual equivalents.

The mournful Sibelius *Valse Triste* that Balanchine staged for Ivanova is interesting as an example of his early expressionist style. The choreography revealed a merging of Isadora Duncan's free plasticity with purely classical movements. Although Lidia wore toe shoes, there was little pointe work, and turnout was neglected. Mikhailov recalled:

> With the first notes of the gloomy music, the figure of a girl in a diaphanous dark-red tunic emerged on the darkened stage, lit by a single spotlight, from the rear left wing. She moved with her back to the audience, tense with fear before some threatening thing that was closing in on her, the body recoiling, the hands extended defensively, the head thrown back, the hair flying over the shoulders. . . . Moving forward diagonally, cringing helplessly, she stood stooped, as if listening for something; then, as if realizing the hopelessness of the situation, she raised her head. The dancer's face was revealed to the audience, expressing defenselessness and an appeal for help. With this the prelude was over, and the dance began. It developed along dynamic lines from piano to fortissimo. Jumps that barely managed to take her off the floor were intensified under the onslaught of feelings and finally overcame space in a grand fashion; then she soared upward in crisp turns. She swept over the stage, seeking a way out of the circle closing in on her. Squeezed into the center, she quivered like a wounded bird and froze with her back to the audience. With her arms flung up before her, she seemed to be trying to ward off a wave rolling toward her. She gave way toward the front of the stage, collapsed there, then fell, no longer able to resist.

Ivanova first performed *Valse Triste* on the former Maryinsky stage in the spring of 1924. Although the dance was only a small part of a large program, it overshadowed everything else that was done that evening. Her success was immense. But no one present could possibly have suspected that the tragedy played out by Ivanova in the dance would turn out to be a bitter prophecy of what awaited her.

O N JUNE 18, 1924, the following brief notice appeared on page 4 of the morning edition of the Petrograd daily *Krasnaya Gazeta*, under the headline "The Death of a Dancer."

> On Monday, June 16, around five p.m., a motorboat belonging to the second labor collective had an accident. In the boat were engineer Klement, A. Iazykov, E. Goldshtein, I. Rodionov, and Lidia Ivanova, a dancer of the Academic Theatre of Opera and Ballet [the former Maryinsky]. The passengers, who had set off from the Anichkov Bridge, were going downriver when they noticed that the motor had become seriously overheated. They began trying to cool it off, and, engrossed in this task, they failed to notice that the passenger ship *Chaika*, bound for Kronstadt, was moving toward them. The ship collided with the boat and knocked all the passengers into the water. A tugboat of the State Baltic Steamship Line arrived on the scene and managed to save three of the passengers, but engineer Klement and the dancer Lidia Ivanova were lost. The bodies of the victims have not yet been found.

Ivanova's death provoked a great flurry in the Soviet press and created many false rumors. Ivanova's own words "I would like to disappear like the sounds of my beloved Tchaikovsky" were constantly repeated. Most of the established critics and writers, many of them Ivanova's friends and admirers, commented on the accident: Lidia's sudden death seemed to them as sinister as it was tragic. There was, indeed, an element of mystery. The special department of the GPU (as the KGB was called at that time) was ordered to conduct an investigation, but no serious effort was made even to find the body, no matter how Ivanova's parents pleaded with the authorities to undertake the search. Lidia's grief-stricken mother ran along the shore literally tearing her hair. The suspicion of foul play was aggravated by the fact that on the evening after the accident Ivanova's fellow passengers were seen in a restaurant where they were obviously enjoying themselves as if nothing had happened. (I was given this information by Ivanova's niece,

Elena Gratcheva, in Leningrad in 1966.) In his article on Ivanova's mysterious death the writer Nicolai Nikitin blamed her fellow passengers and demanded that their suspicious conduct be investigated.

Ivanova's relatives were inclined to regard Olga Spessivtseva as the instigator of the murder of her "awesome rival," as Lidia was frequently called by her admirers. They even viewed Spessivtseva's mental illness in the 1930s as a kind of Dostoevskian punishment for her crime. Despite the persistence of this version in contemporary Russia, it is absurd. Spessivtseva left Petrograd in the spring of 1924, at the peak of her success, as a prima ballerina assoluta, whereas Ivanova, although much admired and with a promising career before her, had hardly begun.

In Leningrad in the mid-1960s my study of the work of Mikhail Kuzmin led me to the office of Ivanova's close friend Mikhail Schwarz, then the director of the Leningrad Theatre Museum. His information appalled me.

"Spessivtseva had nothing to do with this 'accident' that was really a murder," he told me. "As I remember Spessivtseva, she was a very decent person, shy, reserved, far from being capable of doing anything illegal. Her admirer Boris Kaplun, with whom she was rumored to have had an affair, worked in Grigori Zinoviev's office, but it is inconceivable for him to have been involved in an action that might have jeopardized his political career.

"Lidia's popularity was, in a sense, her own undoing. She was constantly invited to parties and receptions after performances. In this respect she was indiscriminate: she would even attend receptions arranged by certain members of the GPU. Among them Lidia had some fans, a fact that by itself flattered her ego. I used to warn her: 'Don't play with fire. You won't notice how they'll trap you.' But she only laughed at my admonitions.

"Incidentally, in those days the GPU was not as sinister as it became under Stalin in the 1930s. Even such poets as Osip Mandelstam didn't shun the chance of enjoying some cakes or sweets at the GPU parties. It's understandable: at the beginning of the twenties, when the whole country was starving, one had to have real courage to resist such temptations.

"Lidia got trapped. The consequences are obvious: through her new connections she might have learned something that no one outside the GPU could safely afford to know. Under certain circumstances she might become a source of trouble to her benefactors in leather jackets. Possibly they, or some one of them, decided to get rid of her."

In 1968, in Leningrad, I told Ivanova's story to Professor John Malmstad of Columbia University, who later interviewed George Balanchine as a witness to those events. Balanchine confirmed and in a sense enlarged my "Mikhail Schwarz report." In 1924 Balanchine formed a small company, Soviet State Dancers, consisting of Nikolai Efimov, Tamara Gevergeyeva (Geva), Danilova, and Ivanova. The troupe planned a short tour during the Maryinsky's summer vacation. Professor Malmsted writes:

> They learned of Ivanova's death only the day before their exit visas arrived. Balanchine well remembers his shock on hearing the news, as well as the apprehension of the group that their visas would not be granted. Too many Soviet cultural figures had left the country on temporary visas and had never returned, and the government was increasingly wary of granting such visas. The group did, however, leave in late June 1924, only to be summarily called back a few weeks later. . . . But the dancers decided to remain in the West. . . . Balanchine firmly believes . . . that when Ivanova applied for her visa with other members of the company, she in effect signed her death warrant.

Obviously Balanchine's decision not to return to Russia was influenced by Ivanova's death.

In her memoirs, *Split Seconds*, Tamara Geva writes of Ivanova's association with "questionable characters" and quotes Efimov saying that Ivanova was "close to all the Communist biggies. . . . She is in the know about everything. I sometimes think she knows too much. It isn't healthy."

According to Geva, on the night of the accident she, Balanchine, Efimov, Danilova, and Ivanova were to perform in the Izmailovsky Park in Leningrad. When Ivanova did not appear they grew apprehensive and decided to find her. They were stopped by a man who came to tell them about the accident. He warned them not to ask any questions and to stay out of the whole business. The man was obviously from the secret police.

The young dancers were not discouraged, however. They went to the harbor and found the captain of the ship that had run into the boat carrying Ivanova. They questioned the extremely agitated seaman. Evasive and suspicious at first, he blurted out the story under their persistent questioning, insisting that the accident was not his fault, that the small boat had been steered deliberately at his ship despite repeated warnings, and that as soon as the boat was struck someone had let ropes down for three of the men. And Ivanova? "'She fell into the water and was sucked under the boat into the propellers.' Suddenly, his eyes glimpsed something beyond us and deadened into a stare. His tone changed. . . . He pushed us away and slammed his door."

When they left, they noticed that the mysterious man who had brought them the news of Ivanova's death was outside watching them intently. Geva adds:

> The mystery of Ivanova's death was never unraveled. Every attempt to investigate it was promptly squelched, with a warning to lay off the subject. Although it was

officially ruled an accident, remembering the ropes ready for the three men, reason insisted that it was a premeditated crime. It was whispered that she had been in possession of some secret that represented a threat to the three men. Yet why was it necessary to simulate an accident in such a dangerous manner? One was forced to assume that the three men were afraid of being caught at it—afraid of someone higher up.

The small discrepancies between the different accounts are of no importance. Each of them, in its own way, only contributes to one of the most sinister pages in the history of Russian ballet.

From left to right: Tamara Geva (seated), Alexandra Danilova, unidentified, Lidia Ivanova, unidentified, George Balanchine; Petrograd, 1924

Odette, 1930s

MARINA SEMYONOVA

HER NAME is known only among a limited circle of Western cognoscenti, but in Russia Marina Semyonova is a legend, synonymous with the glory of Russian ballet. In 1972, when she was finally awarded the honorary title Artist of the Russian People, her pupil Maya Plisetskaya gave this concise summary of Semyonova's art:

> Her name connotes the beauty, grandeur, and regal carriage of Russian ballet. Throughout my professional life I would watch Semyonova on the stage in awe and amazement. As a budding ballerina, I would sneak into the Bolshoi to watch her, and I suffered if I missed one of her performances. When I think of classical ballet, Semyonova's beauty and the perfection of her dancing arise in my memory. Her appearance on stage was a visual feast, a permanent gala performance. . . . It is hard to believe that a ballerina can be applauded for one pose or a graceful tilt of her head. Semyonova enjoyed such applause frequently. She was the first purely virtuoso ballerina to add new dimensions to the idea of virtuosity. She opened a new era in the performing of classical ballets. What she demonstrated in her time was unusual, brand new, breathtaking. Now it is widely believed that it has always been this way.

As the foremost and favorite pupil of the great Agrippina Vaganova, Semyonova asserted the new approach to old ballets. She was the first who stood on pointe in arabesque with her back fully arched, dazzled with her regal port de bras, showed the new type of pirouettes. Her mere presence on stage made the audience take notice; she possessed the gift of a hypnotic presence.

Elegance and regal bearing marked her image. Chaliapin once said: "If you act a beggar, act him as a king." Semyonova always was the queen.

Her appearance in the Russian ballet world forced certain ballerinas to quit, for no one could compete with Semyonova. A throng of imitators arose, but nobody was able to outstrip or even approach her.

She was truly the greatest ballerina of her generation, unique, without peer even today. I always was, am, and will be her most biased admirer. I worship her gigantic talent.

Had Semyonova never been born, in Russia they might still be content with *La Bayadère*, *Swan Lake*, and *Sleeping Beauty* as they were performed in the era of Petipa. But the ballerina roles in those works were reconstructed and revised by Agrippina Vaganova with an eye to Semyonova's unprecedented physical equipment and artistic grandeur. Without Semyonova's breakthrough, the achievements of Ulanova and Plisetskaya, and their impact on Western dance, would have been far less striking. Semyonova truly stood at the threshold of the new performing style that began to take shape in the mid-1920s.

M ARINA TIMOFEYEVNA SEMYONOVA was born in St. Petersburg on May 17 (May 30, according to the new Soviet calendar), 1908. Like Pavlova, she grew up in a nonballet family; like Spessivtseva and Makarova, she lost her father in early childhood; and again like Makarova, she began to study ballet by sheer chance: she was encouraged by a friend of her mother's to enroll at the age of nine in a small amateur dance company. In 1918, small for her age, a pale, puny, and sickly survivor of the civil war and famine that ravaged and debilitated postrevolutionary Russia, the ten-year-old Marina appeared before the examining board at the Choreographic School, presided over by Agrippina Vaganova, who together with her colleagues decided to reject her. If Spessivtseva's partner Victor Semyonov, a good danseur noble and an exacting teacher, had not playfully

suggested that they accept the starveling in order to "perpetuate the Semyonov name on the Russian stage," Marina's destiny might have been very different. . . . But ten years later Vaganova would call Marina her most gifted pupil, and Victor Semyonov would become her partner and her husband.

At the Choreographic School, Semyonova found herself under the vigilant tutelage of the crème de la crème of Petersburg ballet, the confederates of Petipa: Leonid Leontiev, Alexander Shiriayev, Vladimir Ponomarev, and the great Vaganova herself nurtured the youngster's extraordinary talent. She spent eight years at the school on Rossi Street, absorbing the best of its heritage. She also shared the excruciating aftermath of the civil war and the ensuing economic dislocation. Marina was starving; in the unheated classrooms where icy winds blew through broken windowpanes, she studied in a winter coat and felt boots; at the barre she exercised in thick woolen pants.

Semyonova's development was swift and breathtaking from the outset. After only one year in the junior class of Maria Romanova (Ulanova's mother), the prodigy was transferred to the intermediate group under the guidance of Vaganova. The experience was truly fruitful for both. At that time the former "queen of variations" was developing her teaching method. She exercised alone for hours in front of the mirror, driven by the urge to find both the essential shape of each step and its physiological basis. Keeping this kinesthetic sensation in her mind, Vaganova would reproduce the same movement solely by virtue of muscular memory. She would then check its correctness in the mirror, scrutinize the muscular reactions, and note them down in order to refer to them the following day in class. The method was the result of years of such solitary experiments. It was based on mental control over the muscles and on the gradual development of every muscle involved. The main advantage of the Vaganova method was its emphasis on the dancer's ability to execute each step by muscular memory, reinforced by meticulous analysis.

Instead of the vague instructions ("Do it better" or "Watch your arms") standard in Petipa's era, Vaganova established precise formulae to overcome each shortcoming. For instance, "Pull up on your right side; hold the left thigh strongly turned out and abruptly move it backwards." Such precepts would be repeated over and over until a movement was executed with a sense of control over the working muscles. Olga Spessivtseva and Marina Semyonova were the first proofs of the validity of the Vaganova method.

After their fifth year at the school, Vaganova's pupils demonstrated their artistic growth in the pregraduation performances. Vaganova cast her fledglings as flowers in her unassuming miniatures *The Murmur of Flowers* and *Flowers and Butterflies*. Vaganova later recalled: "I deployed the girls like blossoms in a flowerbed. Marina, a fluttering butterfly, seemed to awaken them while barely touching them." The thirteen-year-old Marina so convincingly evoked the elusive flight of a butterfly that the audience cheered.

After this mini-debut Marina was regarded as a wunderkind. Her mastery grew: in 1921 she performed the leading role of Lise in the one-act ballet *The Magic Flute*, choreographed by Lev Ivanov to the music of Drigo. "Marina's movements were a marvel," recalled Tatiana Vecheslova, an outstanding ballerina of the 1930s and 1940s and later the coach of Natalia Makarova. "Marina's grace, a necessary quality in a ballerina, was God-given. Her jetés entrelacés, pas de bourrée, pirouettes—the stops on pointe, when she froze in a sculpturesque pose—everything looked so uncontrived, so effortless, that it seemed not to be learned; it was as if Marina had already possessed it in the cradle."

In *La Fille mal gardée* at another pregraduation performance Marina displayed her comic side. Then, in March 1925, she undertook her first solo part at the Kirov as the Queen of the Dryads in *Don Quixote*. Her biographer Svetlana Ivanova writes:

Semyonova began her variation, set to the slow waltz, with a soaring jeté à la seconde along the front of the stage toward the left wing. Her legs stretched, she seemed to hang for a second in the air; on landing, she bent her right leg in a coupé to open it swiftly in a broad écarté. She flew, circling the stage, as if catching up with her pointe. Embellished with grands fouettés in fourth and fifth arabesque, the combination was repeated ten times. The sweep of each movement was unparalleled; she literally covered half the stage with one jump, immediately followed after her soft landing by the highest écarté. . . . The variation ended with a traveling combination that included sharp entrechâts-six and double pirouettes en dedans.

This performance was the prelude to Semyonova's stunning success at her graduation performance in April 1925, when she danced the fairy Naïla in an old ballet, *La Source*, rechoreographed by Vladimir Ponomaryev. In her memoirs Tamara Karsavina called *La Source* "a parody of charades played by children," claiming that no balletic artistry "could redeem the absurdity of the plot or save it from ridicule." In choosing this nonsensical ballet for Semyonova, Vaganova was motivated not by the fact that *La Source* had been her own farewell to the Petersburg audience but rather by her sense of timing. She felt that in this showpiece Semyonova's dancing would dispel both the antiballet propaganda of the commissars and popular rumors about the flagging vitality of classical dance. And she was right: in her three variations Semyonova made the audience forget the incongruities of the insipid plot, magically transforming them into the jubilant exhibit of Petipa's legacy. In her first variation, the diagonal of jumps in arabesque on pointe, covering the whole stage, astounded by their unusual height, more common in male dancing than in female. In the second variation, consisting of swift pas de bourrée, Semyonova crossed the stage in all directions with amazing zest, accompanying the runs on pointe with the wistful play of her wrists (the so-called "Russian sprays"). The sequence flowed in an uninterrupted line, evoking the image of a perky murmuring stream. In the coda the young ballerina performed jetés entrelacés combined with sustained écartés à la seconde and a perfectly poised first arabesque.

The old-timers at the Maryinsky had not seen such aplomb since the legendary days of Kschessinskaya and Preobrajenskaya. The sixteen-year-old Semyonova put on display every feat of classical technique that had ever been recorded: steellike pointes, impeccably precise beats, enormous jumps, whirlwind turns, rock-steady balances even in abrupt stops on pointe, rare legato, and innate coordination. It was all the more astonishing because it was so effortless, as if the student had been born knowing these tricks.

The leading critic Alexander Gvozdev emphasized her youth by headlining his enthusiastic review "Ballerina Semyonova Is a Student": "A modest, simple-featured, reserved girl with large, theatrical gestures, she danced with inspiration and involvement, her musicality enthralling the audience. The impact derived not from the refined, temperamental artistry of a Pavlova, not from the enchanting appearance of a Karsavina, not from the impetuous verve that distinguished the late Lidia Ivanova. . . . It came from the lyricism of technically flawless dancing."

Semyonova was so phenomenal that despite the hundred-year-old tradition, the Maryinsky accepted her immediately as a leading ballerina. Although her career progressed rapidly, Semyonova was the subject of considerable discussion after her debut. That she was a flower of the old balletic art, whose appearance was at odds with the experimental spirit of the 1920s, no one could deny; but her theatrical instincts, the dramatic gift indispensable to the creation of Petipa's characters, seemed questionable. Some critics maintained that her talent was better suited to concert performances. Vaganova and her pupil perceived this judgment as a challenge.

In May 1925 Semyonova danced Florine, partnered by Victor Semyonov as the Blue Bird. Vaganova, the perfect Florine of the past, helped her to find the significant expressiveness of each step. Keeping in mind that the duet represents an exchange of amorous messages between the enchanted princess and her winged companion, Semyonova emphasized their affinity by imbuing her runs on pointe and arabesques with a birdlike lightness and timidity. Her Florine was both regal and touching in her innocence. Elegant and alert, she seemed to prepare herself for a flight toward the Blue Bird, but some mysterious charm prevented her from soaring. Her softly stretched arabesques ("like sighs of disappointment," one critic remarked) flowed gently into deep fondu. They were followed by double pirouettes on pointe, energetically spun and softly subsiding. Plunged into her dreams, Florine landed on her knee and smiled as if to salute her approaching Blue Bird. The whole sequence conveyed the spellbound creature's subtle transitions from languid reverie to amorous impatience.

During her four years in Leningrad, from 1925 to 1929, she performed an impressive number of leading roles, including Odette-Odile, Nikiya, Aurora, The Tsar Maiden in *The Little Humpbacked Horse*, Aspicia in *Pharaoh's Daughter*, Raymonda, Dushenka in *The Serf Actress*, and all the ballerina roles in *Les Sylphides*. She also danced four prominent soloist roles: Florine, one of Raymonda's confidantes, the Pas d'Esclave in *Le Corsaire*, and the Queen of the Dryads in *Don Quixote*.

Semyonova performed her first Odette-Odile in February 1926. This was a part she was to dance for twenty-seven years, until the end of her career in 1953; it became her greatest achievement and the pinnacle of her art.

The sense of a Wagnerian *Liebestod* in Tchaikovsky's music was alien both to Semyonova's personality and to the ebullience of the 1920s. Vaganova coached the seventeen-year-old ballerina to evoke the majestic image of the sweet, proud swan, so popular in Russian folklore. Semyonova's physique and looks conveyed this idea perfectly: her im-

passive oval face, her regal bearing, the imperious force of each movement, the soft, drooping lines of her shoulders and arms perpetuating the legato of the movements. Moreover, her dancing was marked by a special amplitude of gesture and pose, suggesting the passion that has long been attributed to the Russian national character.

Visually her Odette was far from traditional: while the position of her arms and torso varied, the line of her intrepidly curved chest held everything together, creating the profile of a great bird rending the air with enormous wings, striving to escape captivity. The symbolic meaning of her enchanted Swan Queen came through clearly: the captive yet unvanquished human spirit longing for freedom. Her Odette appeared with a majestically quiet pas de bourrée, her torso bent slightly forward, her rounded arms with drooping hands above her tilted head. As if testing the ground, she took several cautious steps, accompanied by strong strokes of her winged arms; then soundlessly she soared in small pas de chat, her arms imperiously conquering the air. Instead of emphasizing the quiver of the wrists as others had done, Semyonova accentuated the powerful movements of the whole arm—they seemed to flow out of her back and pass through her body to reveal its strength. After a soft glissade she froze in a statuesque first arabesque, then folded her hands on her chest and immediately stretched them downward as if to shed both the water that clung to her and Rothbart's spell.

At the sight of the Prince she cast a direct, almost challenging glance at him, seeming to disregard the arrow he aimed at her. Death did not frighten her, but she was curious about the intruder, as if asking him with her gaze, "What are you bringing to me, death or salvation?" Semyonova marvelously conveyed Odette's confusion through the different colorations of the circuit of arabesques that followed. She froze sharply on pointe, her head down and torso protruding, like "a hovering bird attentively examining the earth," as one critic remarked; or she bent her head so low and raised her leg so high that they formed a straight line in arabesque penchée. She seemed to avoid not so much the Prince himself as the spectre of suddenly aroused hope that he represented. When Siegfried caught her, Odette did not quiver—she stopped, staring at him very intently, as if saying: "Do you really want to know who I am? Then listen to me."

She began the adagio as a quiet confession, unwinding its choreographic texture in an uninterrupted stream of flowing arabesques, soft battements, sissonnes ouvertes and

Top: (left) Giselle, 1935; (right) Aurora in *The Sleeping Beauty*, 1930s
Bottom: (left) Odette, 1932; (right) Odette, 1930s

Top: (left) Naïla in *La Source*, 1925; (right) Mireille de Poitiers in *The Flames of Paris*, 1933
Bottom: (left) Nikiya in *La Bayadère*, 1930; (right) Esmeralda, 1934

fermées, fleeting ronds de jambe, and pirouettes. In the Russian tradition, Semyonova danced not so much on the beat as on its lingering echo. The adagio seemed to be Odette's first opportunity to express the pain that hitherto she had silently endured.

By all reports, the entire second act in Semyonova's interpretation was extremely well paced and consistent. Her variation unfolded as the conclusion of Odette's narration to the Prince, the epitome of her tragic lot. Unlike earlier ballerinas, Semyonova suggested neither perturbation nor despair at being earthbound. She began with a deep preparation that seemed like a painful sigh before her last words. After the soft ronds de jambe and the imperious flap of her winglike arms, Semyonova froze in a high écarté. The intensity of her desire to soar or fly away seemed to match the power that kept her bound to earth; her struggle for freedom was as powerful as Rothbart's charms. Semyonova keenly illuminated Odette's sorrowful plight in the second part of the variation: with her torso thrown backward, she did a sharp, upward-thrusting sissonne which suddenly broke as if gravity pulled her down, in order to freeze in her specific arabesque, with her graphically arched torso and strongly outstretched arms. Her figure called to mind the motionless flight of the Nike of Samothrace, while manifesting Odette's indestructible hope and spiritual superiority. Her reaction to her fate, the diagonal of piqués en tournant en dehors with each fourth turn doubled, was saturated with despair. Only in the coda, with its cascading fouettés into first arabesque, beats, and sharp relevés, did Odette reveal her suddenly aroused love for Siegfried. The circuits of tours chaînés seemed to crown the disarray of her feelings. But the tragic crescendo came to its climax at the moment when Rothbart's spell recalled her to her captivity. Without even looking at Siegfried, retaining her regal bearing and impassive mien, Odette slid away in pas de bourrée, proudly moving her arms, engrossed in her grief and perseverance.

Unlike her Odette, Semyonova's Odile seemed somewhat conventional, possibly because by nature this ballerina was hardly a femme fatale. But she took advantage of her virtuosity, all the more impressive because Vaganova had made the choreography more intricate. At the beginning of the variation, the double pirouettes were followed by tours à la seconde without coming off pointe, which established the contemporary standard. Vaganova increased the number of the turns and substituted triple pirouettes for the doubles. As Odile, Semyonova demonstrated

for the first time that the festivities of the ball were her true element. She behaved like a real queen, particularly in the performances that she gave in the 1930s. One noticeable detail was that her Odile did not imitate the quiver of Odette's winged arms. Reveling in the high spirits of the ball, this Odile seemed to dispel Siegfried's memory of Odette by her brio and the thrust of her victorious femininity. Believing that the thirty-two fouettés of the coda were an insufficient demonstration of Odile's evil charm, Semyonova swept around the stage in two whirlwind manèges of turns performed at dizzying speed. The first consisted of piqués en tournant en dedans, with each fourth turn doubled; in the second, performed twice as quickly, turns on one leg alternated with tours chaînés. In Odile's famous diagonal, Mikhail Mikhailov recalled, "she flew like an arrow at breakneck speed to freeze suddenly like a pillar in first arabesque, maintaining her balance endlessly. Nobody has been able to perform so stunning a trick since Matilda Kschessinskaya and Pierina Legnani."

By contrast, Act IV was impressive for its heartfelt lyricism, as Semyonova's Odette lost her regal aloofness and became a suffering woman. The tragic facet of her artistry gleamed with an irresistible radiance. She traced her swift pas de bourrée across the stage with her head tilted sorrowfully. In her turbulent monologue she seemed to bid farewell to her hopes, which revived again at the entrance of the repentant Siegfried. Her Odette never castigated him with reproachful looks—she forgave his weakness, she was jubilant at the reunion that gave her the strength to shatter Rothbart's evil spell. Although her highly optimistic interpretation was at odds with Tchaikovsky's mournful music, Semyonova's pathos was too convincing to resist.

In December 1926 Semyonova made her debut as Nikiya in *La Bayadère*, a role that became one of her greatest artistic achievements. Technically Nikiya fitted her like a glove; but with the great shade of Pavlova still persisting in the memory of the Maryinsky old-timers, the role entailed a special challenge for her.

Severe, inscrutable, her Nikiya appeared on the threshold of the temple, two black braids framing her long, regal neck, and clad in a short, lotuslike skirt and tight bodice that outlined her flexible torso. Semyonova's Nikiya was a devoted priestess in the grip of an unaccountable passion for the warrior Solor. Knowing that Semyonova's forte was pure dance, Vaganova deliberately reduced the explicative pantomime to a minimum, especially in Act I, thus enhancing the mysterious aura of her majestic bayadère.

Semyonova's artistry revealed itself in all its magnitude in the dance with the basket, one of Pavlova's undisputed masterpieces. According to Fyodor Lopukhov, in this variation Semyonova surpassed her predecessor; he considered it on a par with Pavlova's Dying Swan, Mordkin's Mato in *Salammbô*, Chaliapin's Boris Godunov, and Geltzer's Esmeralda. Petipa's variation, reshaped by Vaganova, pinpointed two choreographic leitmotifs. One was the vertical axis stretching through Nikiya's body from her closed feet to her wrists rounded above her head, a line that Petipa meant to underscore Nikiya's religious striving. The other was horizontal, in the guise of the recurrent third arabesque, implying the force of passion and sensuality bending Nikiya down to earth. The struggle of these two leitmotifs in Semyonova's dance seemed to motivate the development of the variation, ornamented with soaring jetés entrelacés and sauts de basque. The symbolic confrontation of conflicting feelings was brought out here more obviously than in her Odette. Her transitions from pious concentration in the vertical poses to passion in the horizontal ones were amazing. As Ivanova noted: "Semyonova extended her arms to Solor and after a high jeté entrelacé landed on one knee in despair. Her grief-stricken figure seemed nailed to the earth by her passion; her outstretched arms revealed the essence of Nikiya's tragedy." This enchaînement was repeated three times, alternating with a swift diagonal of tours chînés and a sudden assemblé soutenu, which was followed by the slowly developing vertical pose, addressed to the gods, and the recurrent motif of the third arabesque, which she lingered on longer and longer as if unable to resist her ever-growing passion. The fatal snake in Gamzatti's flower basket seemed to release Nikiya from perpetual anxiety and pain; she welcomed her death as a delivery from her torment.

In the Kingdom of the Shades scene, the Hindu concept of death prevailed: Semyonova's Nikiya enjoyed her new state, detached from the pain of life and her excruciating passion for her truant lover. As a shade, Semyonova echoed the theme of Act II of *Giselle*: forgiveness beyond the grave.

Semyonova's Aurora and Raymonda, two roles that were free of any tragic implications, revealed the instrumental facet of her dance gift. Both were products of Petipa's choreographic maturity, concerned with pure classical dance as an expressive visualization of music. If Semyonova's majestic and feminine Raymonda displayed the entire vocabulary of her academic virtuosity, her Aurora was distinguished by her genuinely Russian pronunciation. As if seeking to overcome Aurora's characteristic passivity, Semyonova imbued the choreography with a broad Russian sweep. Act I bore her unique stamp—it is entirely understandable that during the performance of *Sleeping Beauty* on May 22, 1947, at the Kirov, commemorating the one hundred twenty-fifth anniversary of Petipa's birth Semyonova performed Act I, while Ulanova and Dudinskaya danced Acts II and III, respectively.

Semyonova's Aurora was pronouncedly Russian and attractive but was perhaps at variance with Petipa's refined rococo mannerism. Nevertheless, her interpretation established the standard against which generations of Russian Auroras have been measured: it prescribed the dynamic verve of the first variation, in which the sauts de chat were transformed into energetic aerial splits; the slow développé into attitude, taking shape behind the beat; the "blossoming attitudes" (as Semyonova put it) of the Rose Adagio, and the Russian folk-dance accents and flowing legato in the final variation in Act III.

As judged by the numerous enthusiastic reviews, Semyonova's Aurora was truly second to none. But apparently her interpretation of Act II came to the audience as a revelation indeed. Romantic and academic elements were fused in Petipa's pas d'action, and Semyonova shone equally in both, "beating sparks of meaning out of a confrontation of two perfectly matched yet opposed styles," as one critic remarked. Here her sensitivity to Petipa's style and purpose served to highlight one of the main themes of *The Sleeping Beauty*: the juxtaposition of dream and reality.

But dreamy characters were difficult for Semyonova; her personality was too flamboyant and effervescent. Thus she brought too much vehemence to *Chopiniana*, conceived as a refined pastiche of the Romantic era. Possibly she followed her teacher Vaganova, whose swift, hovering flights across the Maryinsky stage in the Mazurka invariably aroused a storm of applause. Be that as it may, among four pieces in *Les Sylphides* (the Prelude, Nocturne, Mazurka, and Waltz), Semyonova excelled only in the Mazurka. But Fokine's poetry of understatement remained alien to her.

By 1930 the twenty-two-year-old Marina had attained the summit of her artistry and glory. The former Maryinsky with its stale repertory seemed to possess nothing that could challenge her creativity. She was determined to conquer the Bolshoi. Moscow offered more tempting opportunities for growth; there Gorsky's spectacular choreodramas flourished, and Kasyan Goleizovsky, who had been a major influence on the young Balanchine, continued his experiments. At the Bolshoi Marina could reign unrivaled: Geltzer was old, and Semyonova's future successor and pupil Plisetskaya had not yet even entered the Moscow Choreographic School.

In Moscow Semyonova looked like a rare Petersburg bird. The exuberance and purity of her classical training was less valued than the ability to convey the potent though exaggerated theatricality of Gorsky's condensed balletic dramas, which possessed neither the shadings nor the subtlety that had long been the hallmark of the Maryinsky. Nevertheless, Semyonova's sweeping, majestic attack, her broad and encompassing gestures, and her ability to dominate the stage were perceived in Moscow as the reincarnation of Russian theatrical Romanticism, the traditions of which were much stronger in Moscow than in the cosmopolitan, Europe-oriented Petersburg.

For her debut Semyonova chose Gorsky's spectacular, gaudy version of *La Bayadère*. It was a triumph. Vadim Gayevsky wrote: "The whole audience rose to its feet when Semyonova, her arms stretched backward in gypsy fashion, soared into an airy split and landed on one knee, then thrust her body upward in one dynamic movement like a flame of a bonfire. Sparks seemed to fly from the stage into the mesmerized audience—one of those magic contacts that only the legendary artists of the past could create and for which the present generation of spectators was longing."

During her first Bolshoi season, 1930–31, Semyonova danced Florine and Aurora, Odette-Odile, Raymonda, and even the Danse Manu—the dance with a pitcher in *La Bayadère*, Act II. As Asaf Messerer wrote in his memoirs: "Semyonova sparkled and dazzled in these ballets, asserting the value of classical dance. . . . She knew how to dominate both the stage and the audience, how to dumbfound or spellbind them by the speed of her tours, her aplomb, her chic, her attack. She threw herself into dancing as one might into a raging sea—reckless, blind, yet full of indestructible confidence in reaching the crest of the wave." Her Odette, in Gayevsky's words, "called to mind a majestic sculpture of a swan, carved not so much by the chisel as by a swan wing: the power of a monument and the tenderness of a bird were blended there; the image conveyed the precision of a bas-relief and the flowing melody of a violin solo."

Nevertheless, in Moscow the great Semyonova was also bitterly criticized for the first time in her career. The critical verdict was that "her dancing is emotionless; she seems to be more concerned with *how* to perform than *what* to perform. This is dancing for its own sake." And so the ballerina who was treasured in Leningrad had to prove her value as a dancer-actress and meet the standard established by Geltzer. It was not easy.

Her situation at the Bolshoi was aggravated by the fact that the company could offer her new opportunities only in drama-ballets. She essayed the part of Tao-Hoa in *The Red Poppy*, one of Geltzer's famous roles, but the wretched bar dancer eluded Semyonova completely: she was at a loss in pantomime, and her projection lacked dramatic power. To build her reputation as an actress she undertook the character part of the street dancer Concitta in a trifle called *The Comedians*, but it was another disappointing experience for her.

In April 1931 she performed Kitri in Gorsky's *Don Quixote*. Her entrance was fiery: clad in a black embroidered bolero, with her hair smoothly combed back, she turned the initial saut de chat into a kind of aerial lightning split. But her assemblés en tournant, her way of lingering on pointe after jumps and turns, were too academic. The sweep of her attitudes en croisé and effacée and her grands fouettés allongés, effortlessly executed, were more rewarding than her diligent but awkward acting.

Semyonova was conscious of this. Her uneasiness grew, since in Moscow even her virtuosity was at stake: she was pining for Vaganova's tutelage and vigilant eye. She went to Leningrad frequently, but these sporadic returns to her alma mater could not compensate for the lack of ongoing, systematic training. Moreover, she obviously trusted Vaganova's taste more than her own. Although her Moscow admirers pronounced her "the queen of the Bolshoi," their enthusiasm was unable to alleviate her discontent and anxiety. Semyonova did not participate in the Soviet new drama-ballets of the thirties, but she was unwilling to maintain her prima ballerina status only by repeating the classical roles for which she had already won acclaim. She challenged the Bolshoi by attempting to become a dancer-actress in hitherto unessayed classics: in February 1934 she performed her first Esmeralda, and two months later she made her debut in *Giselle*.

As Esmeralda, Semyonova made every effort to eclipse Geltzer's memorable portrayal. Her lack of confidence in her own theatrical instincts led her to Nikolai Podgorny of the Moscow Art Theatre, who began to rehearse Esmeralda and Giselle with her in the Stanislavsky manner. Podgorny illuminated the devices of the famous method, but they did not work for *Esmeralda*'s melodramatic plot, which could be brought to life only by the most straightforward pantomime. In the 1920s only Geltzer still knew how to imbue the role with vitality and sincere dramatic pathos. As for Semyonova, she diligently obeyed Podgorny's instructions, only to underscore the embarrassing incompatibility of the obsolete Romantic attributes and her amateurish overacting. Moreover, in *Esmeralda* she had only one variation, with turns in arabesque flowing into double pirouettes on pointe. With nothing more to dance than that, she could hardly amaze the Moscow public. During one of Semyonova's short visits to Leningrad, Vaganova restaged Esmeralda's out-of-date variation for her, but the new version was nearly identical to Nikiya's dance with the basket.

Semyonova also attempted to refashion her Kitri in the mold of Stanislavskian realism: she sat cross-legged on a chair, hugged Basil sensuously, drank from his mug . . . irrelevant strokes in the colorful picture of a stylized *españolada*.

In 1932 she applied the "method" to *Giselle*, in which Ulanova now shone in Leningrad. Between them they laid the foundation of the Soviet interpretation of this character. In both her dancing and her mime, Semyonova sought a psychological justification for every step and gesture. But her view of a Romantic fairy tale as a heavy-set realistic drama led to an undermining of the poetry of overtones and mystical insights that provide *Giselle*'s undying freshness. Moreover, judging by photographs of Semyonova as Giselle, it is hard to believe that this robust milkmaid could die of a heart attack caused by a perfidious lover. As a Wili, she seems even more improbable.

Nonetheless, in the 1930s Semyonova's Odette-Odile, Nikiya, and Giselle consolidated her glory in Moscow. She became Stalin's favorite ballerina; to amuse him, she often performed the lezghinca, a dance of his native Georgia, in male attire. And she charmed the Moscow audience as Queen of the Ball in various operas and drama-ballets. As Gayevsky recalled: "Just her appearance, her presence on the stage, evoked the atmosphere of the *grand bal* that haunted the imagination of choreographers, composers, and poets from Pushkin and Glinka to Tchaikovsky, Berlioz, and Ravel. Semyonova conveyed the spirit of a Romantic ball, dazzling, mysterious, infernal."

Despite her unparalleled success and unique star status at the Bolshoi, Stalin did not spare Semyonova: her second husband, the diplomat Karakhan, was arrested in 1936, one of the first victims of the great purge, and soon afterward perished in the Gulag. For a while Semyonova herself was under house arrest. From this harsh blow, aggravated by her artistic insecurity and unfulfillment, Semyonova could never recover. Ballet suddenly seemed to lose its appeal for her and turned into a tedious routine. She began to neglect classes and rehearsals, counting on her rare stamina to get her through performances; she would even take a hot shower before a performance instead of doing a regular warm-up. She grew stout and became indifferent and lazy. Photographs of her from the end of the 1930s and the postwar period are simply embarrassing and shocking. A love affair with a dramatic actor named Aksenov apparently drained her as a person and as a ballerina. She gave birth to a daughter and never got back into shape. In the fifties her new roles in the Soviet drama-ballets, such as the title role in Vainonen's *Mirandolina* or Liza in *The Noble Peasant Girl*, obviously demanded the minimum from her. In 1953 Semyonova danced her last *Swan Lake*.

Unfortunately, there is no record on film of Semyonova at the exuberant peak of her artistry. In Soviet movies like *The Big Concert* or *Stars of Soviet Ballets* we see the Semyonova of the late forties and early fifties—plump, heavy, ungraceful, but still irresistible in her regal carriage and musicality.

Since 1956 Marina Semyonova has been a coach at the Bolshoi. Among her pupils are such contemporary stars as Maya Plisetskaya, Nina Timofeyeva, Natalia Bessmertnova, and Nadezhda Pavlova. Plisetskaya once said: "A good ballerina is not necessarily a good teacher. As a teacher and coach, Semyonova is equally stunning. She glitters in both fields. She is aware of all the secrets in the art of ballet. She knows everything."

LES GRANDES TRAGÉDIENNES

Sofia Fedorova · Alla Shelest
Maya Plisetskaya

SOFIA FEDOROVA

SOFIA FEDOROVA was one of many ballerinas who greatly contributed to Diaghilev's Parisian triumph, although even in Russia her name is known today only to a few ballet historians. Nevertheless, in the illuminating memoirs of such a severe and exacting analyst as Fyodor Lopukhov, Sofia Fedorova is described as exemplifying

the omnipotence of talent. . . . Squat, plain, seemingly utterly unsuitable to the stage, she knew the secret of transforming herself through dancing in moments of tremendous tension. In the grip of emotional outburst her body generated an inexplicable trembling; her face radiated an inner light; in a state of ecstasy she simply dazzled. . . .

She was awkwardly built, slightly bow-legged, and unattractive; she possessed an ordinary jump with no ballon and quite modest terre-à-terre technique, precluding virtuosity. Still, the public was infatuated with Fedorova at first glance, overlooking her obvious shortcomings. Her fiery temperament and theatrical ability to make every step or gesture convincing and thrilling produced an irresistible impact on the audience. When she danced the last act of Gudule's Daughter her admirers sobbed openly or secretly brushed away tears. In *La Fille mal gardée*, on the other hand, she made them cheer and laugh by her moving portrayal of the simple, loving Lise. She was an actress who knew how to transform herself totally into a pure theatrical illusion. In the ballet world of my time such artists were few.

Fedorova's career was tragically short. Born in Moscow on September 16, 1879, the daughter of a copper founder, she joined the corps of the Bolshoi company directly after her graduation from the Moscow Theatre School on September 1, 1899, under the name Fedorova II. In 1917, when she was at the peak of her artistry, her career, like Spessivtseva's and Nijinsky's, was interrupted by mental breakdown.

In December 1900 Fedorova went on for the ailing Ekaterina Geltzer as Mercedes in Gorsky's *Don Quixote*, scoring such an enormous success that she repeated her variation. Her swarthy, sullen Mercedes, overflowing with nervous energy, was followed by the Street Dancer in *Don Quixote*, Anitra in *Etudes*, and the Khan's Wife in *The Little Humpbacked Horse*—an Oriental enchantress, "perfidious and shrewd," in the words of Sergei Grigorov, her biographer.

Grigorov called her performance of Anitra's dance "a poem written by the crimson Northern autumn." Fedorova made her swift entrance clad in a Greek tunic and golden sandals, her orange cloak and unbound hair fluttering behind her. Gorsky's choreography, with its emphasis on free plasticity, boldly anticipated the artistic innovations of Duncan and Fokine, and Fedorova reveled in it.

She integrated herself wondrously well into Gorsky's picturesque dance-drama, with which he attempted to duplicate in ballet Stanislavsky's realistic innovations in the Russian theatre. Gorsky valued the expressiveness of Fedorova's arms, eyes, and torso and overlooked her weak pointe work, unclassical port de bras, and sloppy turnout. Fedorova became one of the most important colors in his palette; she saturated his canvas with her visceral, disturbing vitality. Her talent fed on the nervous energy that poured out in her poses, in her sullen, feverish glances, in the explosion of her Bacchic temperament. Her body, endowed with unusual flexibility, extended the limits of the characters she portrayed, adding a new dimension to Gorsky's choreography. This was Fedorova's genius. Grigorov's biography provides minimal information about Fedorova's technique; apparently her powerful projection merged so overwhelmingly with her dancing, subordinating it to her emotional impact, that these elements were impossible to differentiate.

Fedorova seldom essayed the big roles, except for Giselle and Lise. To disguise the weakness of her pointes, Gorsky reshaped Petipa's staging of *La Fille mal gardée* in the realistic style, harking back to the original choreographer, Dauberval, emphasizing pantomime and skillfully mingling lyric and comic episodes as prescribed by Noverre. Fedorova portrayed Lise as a simple but stubborn peasant girl with a dash of impetuosity, spontaneously reacting to the joys and sorrows of life. Her angular manners evoked an image of awkward adolescence. The critics compared her to what they had read of Fanny Elssler. Like her glorious predecessor, Fedorova shone in the chicken-feeding scene, making the audience roar with laughter.

Vera Krasovskaya's description of Fedorova as Mercedes and as the Street Dancer in Gorsky's *Don Quixote* illustrates the ballerina's unusual talent:

> Fedorova's heroines challenged the motley crowd with arrogant detachment and self-destructive passion. In both roles she produced the effect of a sudden thunderstorm on a beautiful day, disturbing the gleeful Spanish throng. At the dashing appearance of Fedorova's Street Dancer the crowd froze. . . . Surrounded by two semicircles of idle spectators and toreros, she stood alone, casting her sullen glances toward some distant point in the audience. Sparkling in the air, the daggers were thrust into the floor, and she slid between them drawing a whimsical pattern. An impetuous jump carried her beyond the shafts, but some force drew her back, inclined her lithe body, and propelled it through the air. A dance of pleasure was transmuted into a dance of ritual and seemed to ignite the toreros' scarlet capes into a blaze around the black-clad figure. Finally, on the verge of collapse, she fell into Espada's arms as if discharging all her latent violence. . . .
>
> The bustling crowd in the tavern became quiet at Mercedes's sudden appearance. Her entrée and dance were subdued: ecstasy could overwhelm on the plaza, but not among tables, benches, and bottles of wine. Mercedes performed for the throng, but kept the same lonely distance that protected the Street Dancer from the crowd. Her slow promenade of flowing, undulating movements was like an unpretentious tune she hummed to herself. She seemed to collect her energy as the crackling castanets and quivering fans spurred her on. Then someone in the crowd suddenly grabbed her and threw her onto the table. She seemed to explode in a cascade of ebullient movements, as if scattering sparks. Jumping off the table, she began to spin like a fiery top as the onlookers scattered in every direction. Her dance ended abruptly, and her sullen look again seemed to mark the distance between her and the crowd.

But Fedorova's great success cannot be ascribed only to the temperament of her willful heroines. Her balletic images reverberated in the cultural atmosphere of the early twentieth century, permeated with the cult of suffering, self-destruction, and fatal female beauty which the sym-

bolists borrowed from the novels of Dostoevsky. The concept of the freedom-loving gypsy girl, not exactly a femme fatale but a woman who brings destruction to her male partners and herself, often emerged in Russian poetry (e.g., Carmen in the poems of Alexander Blok).

Some of Fedorova's most impressive stage characters were gypsy girls. Krasovskaya has reconstructed the portrait of one of them, from *The Little Humpbacked Horse*:

> a gypsy girl who has exchanged her nomadic wanderings for nightly debauchery, although the love of freedom still runs in her blood. Her eyes cast wild watchful glances from beneath a furrowed brow; her lips were pursed bitterly; locks of hair came out from under her kerchief; with one hand she pressed a tambourine firmly to her chest, as if protecting her indomitable soul. Her attire was far from the conventional gypsy costume, having neither a flowered flared skirt nor large sleeves. Her dark dress falling in straight pleats revealed a natural grace, as the clothing of a real gypsy woman is the extension of her flexible body. The poetic authenticity of Fedorova's appearance promised a dance full of passion and rebellious impetus—a tragic dance.

Fedorova was first seen as a dancing *tragédienne* in 1902, in Gorsky's "mimodrama" *Gudule's Daughter*, set to Simon's mediocre music. Gorsky's choreography and dramatic design descended more from Victor Hugo's *Notre Dame de Paris* than from the naive Romantic style of the Perrot-Petipa *Esmeralda*. It was obviously influenced by the young Stanislavsky's naturalistic productions. *Gudule's Daughter* unfolded through a series of picturesque pantomime scenes depicting, like some grim medieval chronicle, a boiling stream of frenzied emotions and unleashed instincts against a background of Parisian beggars and vagabonds. Fedorova's Esmeralda, a bewildered young gypsy girl, sullen and impulsive, was the victim of fate, destroyed by her ineradicable passion for the dashing and merciless officer Phoebus (Mikhail Mordkin). Her natural frailty and morbid passion stood out marvelously against Mordkin's macho sex appeal. She compensated for the intentional paucity of the choreography with a richly veristic portrayal that infuriated and perplexed as many viewers as it thrilled and inspired. Yuri Beliayev, insulted by Gorsky's encroachment upon the forbidden ground of naturalistic theatre, described Fedorova's acting in detail:

Esmeralda was carried in on a huge cart. Dressed in rags and tatters, she rolled herself up into a ball, her arms bound and her hair undone. Her face expressed dull horror. Her cheeks, forehead, and hands were smeared with blood mixed with mud. . . . The executioner rudely pulled her off the cart, unwound her bonds, and stuck a huge penitential candle into her hand. The little hands did not obey her. The candle flickered, bending lower and lower until it fell to the ground. Then Esmeralda fell also . . . Quasimodo picked her up and ran with her toward the cathedral. The poor girl hung helplessly from his shoulders. Her head, with disheveled hair, seemingly dead eyes, and outstretched neck revealing swollen veins, bounced sporadically, while one arm trailed to the floor.

The range of her characters in Gorsky's ballets was vast: a Spanish girl in the panaderos from *Raymonda*, a Bacchant in *The Four Seasons*, the slave Hita in *Pharaoh's Daughter*, the Hindu Dancer in *La Bayadère*, the Old Hag in *The Goldfish*. Krasovskaya points out that many of Fedorova's balletic portrayals evoked the spirit of Baudelaire's *Les Fleurs du mal*. The poet's satanism, his instinctual frenzy and extremes of morbid sensuality, represented only one of the aspects of Russian symbolism, concerned with the struggle of God and the Devil within the human being and also with the duality of Apollo and Dionysus. This struggle was manifested in artistic creation achieved in a state of ecstasy, when the artist abandons control over powerful instincts. In this respect Fedorova's dancing was like a sacred trance in which she poured forth waves of energy that overwhelmed the audience.

An anonymous critic described her Hindu Dance in *La Bayadère* as "the dance of a primitive human being," suggesting both "the naive and wild coquetry of a savage and the impetuosity of a frolicking beast."

Fedorova's fame as an ecstatic dancer led to her engagement by Diaghilev in 1909. During her first Paris season she appeared in *Polovetsian Dances*, the bacchanale in *Cléopâtre*, and a czardas in *Le Festin* with Mikhail Mordkin. "Fedorova displays the ecstasy of the mysterious Russian soul," wrote a Parisian critic. The following year she danced one of the Odalisques in *Schéhérazade*. She felt at home in Diaghilev's troupe, enjoying the affinity of his artistic innovations with those of her teacher Gorsky.

In 1913 she undertook the part of the slave Ta-Hor in Fokine's *Cléopâtre*. Her acting had an overwhelming impact on the young Cyril Beaumont, who described in detail how Fedorova's Ta-Hor transfixed everyone by her expression of horror and tense anxiety when she crossed glances with Amoun. She clasped and unclasped her hands unceasingly, in the grip of fear, overwhelmed by her morbid compassion for her lover. She seemed almost unnoticed on the deserted stage, so imperceptibly did she merge with the shadow of the gigantic statues. Fedorova made her steps slowly and with effort, as if her feet refused to obey. Her face hardened. She pressed one arm to her side and the other to her chest. She lifted the veil from Amoun's face, and bending slowly over him she kissed his forehead, tore away a string binding his hair, and began to beat her chest in a fit of extreme despair.

Diaghilev, spellbound by Nijinsky and Karsavina, somehow overlooked Fedorova's potential for tragedy; one can only imagine what she could have done as Cleopatra. Possibly her technical weaknesses caused Diaghilev to lose interest in her.

Fedorova never thought of herself as a classical ballerina. The only classical part that she dreamed of performing was Giselle, which took her five years to master. She made her debut in this role in April 1913 in Gorsky's unorthodox staging. He presented the old gem of Romantic ballet as a psychological mimodrama. The choreography of Perrot, Coralli, and Petipa was revised and abbreviated— Gorsky's contemporaries later compared Act II, with its Wilis dressed in shroudlike tunics, to a horror movie. But what was truly effective in this production was the iron consistency of Fedorova's portrayal. Her Giselle perished from the touch of evil, but its contagion transformed her into a carrier. This Giselle challenged the ideology of Romantic ballet and cancelled its message of love and redemption. Giselle's optimistic though naive Romanticism was refracted in Fedorova's mind through the symbolist prose of d'Annunzio, Huysmans, and Fyodor Sollogub, with its vampires, basilisks, and mystical horror of the beyond. In Act I she depicted Giselle most naturalistically, emphasizing "the paleness of her face, the roving look, the twisted mouth, her awkward attempts to dance—everything was so shockingly real that it overwhelmed one and made one shudder," one critic remarked. And in Act II, another reviewer noted, "her Giselle was too bound to earth; her dances revealed a passion that destroyed the poetic aura enshrouding the Wilis." Her colleagues have said that Fedorova dreamed of appearing in Act II as a real corpse with a chalk-whitened face (which she was not al-

Esmeralda in *Gudule's Daughter*, 1902

Above: The Khan's Wife in *The Little Humpbacked Horse*, 1909
Right: Ta-Hor in *Cléopâtre*, 1913

Hita in *Pharaoh's Daughter*, 1909

lowed to do) and attired in a shroud (which she indeed wore). At the sight of this Giselle, an image that bordered on parody, "the audience froze with fear and some people ran from the theatre"—such was the impact of Fedorova's tragic intensity. Her controversial portrayal provoked violent arguments. Some likened her tragic tension to Sarah Bernhardt's acting in the finale of *La Dame aux camélias*; others claimed that in *Giselle* Fedorova had demonstrated a clinical case of brain disease.

As if anticipating the sad tale of Spessivtseva, Fedorova now began to exhibit symptoms of mental illness. In October 1913 a theatre physician certified that the ballerina suffered from insomnia, dizziness, and fatigue, as well as "irritability, impressionability, easy fatigue, and abrupt changes of mood, alternating from total inertia and apathy to hysterical tears or an exaggeratedly vivid and pert state of mind."

From 1914 on, as her vitality ebbed, more and more she danced only character parts. In September 1917 her last contract with the Bolshoi expired; in 1919 she submitted a petition for a pension "due to total incapacity as the result of serious disease."

Fedorova moved to Petrograd in 1919 to join her husband and went abroad in 1922, after his death. In 1923, in Berlin, she played Pierrette in the Schnitzler pantomime *Pierrette's Veil*, partnered by a mime of genius, Chabrov. Nina Berberova recalled in her illuminating memoirs, *The Italics Are Mine*: "Even now I remember every detail of this striking performance. Nothing has ever so struck me as this *Veil*—not Mikhail Chekhov in Strindberg, not Anna Pavlova as the Dying Swan. . . . When Chabrov and Fedorova danced the polka in the second act, and the dead Pierrot appeared on the little balcony . . . I understood for the first time and forever what is real theatre, and even now a shudder goes up my spine as I remember the Schnitzler pantomime performed by these actors."

After 1925 Fedorova made Paris her home. In 1925 and 1926 she appeared with the Pavlova company, performing Russian folk dances. She walked onto the stage for the last time in 1928, during Diaghilev's season. "She enthralled Paris again in the *Polovetsian Dances* as she had nineteen years ago," Sergei Grigoriev reported. Then her illness took over. She endured her ordeal courageously, drifting from one mental institution to another, and dying at last in her small apartment in Neuilly, a suburb of Paris. "She lived quietly between outbursts of consciousness and delirium," said an obituary that appeared in a Russian newspaper six months after she passed away on January 3, 1963, at the age of eighty-three. But her spiritual death had occurred long before. Like Nijinsky and Pavlova, she lived her real life on stage. Dance was the only outlet for her complex personality and her tormented reaction to the reality of Russian life in the early twentieth century, whose troubled spirit Fedorova expressed in her own way.

Zarema in *The Fountain of Bakhchisarai*, early 1950s

ALLA SHELEST

ONLY BY AN IRONIC TWIST OF FATE has Alla Shelest's reputation been less illustrious in the West than Ulanova's or Plisetskaya's. In Russia and beyond its borders, her name is blanketed in silence; nevertheless, in Romantic style, dramatic gift, and statuesque expressiveness, Shelest was at least Ulanova's equal, and she undoubtedly excelled Plisetskaya in technique. Both Ulanova and Plisetskaya, usually sparing of praise, worshiped Alla Shelest as a unique artist. Such outstanding choreographers as Fyodor Lopukhov, Kasyan Goleizovsky, and Leonid Jakobson considered her the ideal *tragédienne* of Russian ballet, as did thousands of her devoted admirers. This essay, by a witness to Shelest's artistic triumphs of the 1950s, is an unjustifiably belated tribute to her genius.

The tragic stunting of her career is perceived today as an unmerited consequence of her dazzling but iconoclastic uniqueness. Even during her best years Shelest was misunderstood and disparaged. She retired from the stage in 1963, and thus she did not share the Western triumphs of the Kirov in the 1960s. During her single Western tour (1953) she was allowed to display her art only in two cameo parts, in Jakobson's *The Blind One* and *The Eternal Idol*—both campy and melodramatic. Preserved on film, they suggest Shelest's artistry as the shadow of a shade, indeed.

In his memoirs, *Sixty Years in Ballet*, Fyodor Lopukhov lamented the Kirov's unforgivable neglect of Shelest: "I don't know any other ballerina whose career was as ill fated as Shelest's. For sixteen years [1937–53] she was condemned to make do with the second cast of every role; no ballets were created for her; she never enjoyed the prestige of an opening night. What talent she had to possess in order to retain her striking personality under such circumstances! Through two decades Shelest never ceased to polish her art, without any hope of being rewarded by a role custom made for her. Such was her lot. She was mostly granted roles inferior to her remarkable potential."

Shelest's uniqueness lay in the fact that she was both an accomplished virtuoso, excelling equally in Romantic and academic technique, and a tragic actress. Had she been only a pure technician and stylist, it would have been more than enough for the fussy, exacting Leningrad balletomanes who savored the perfection of her academic training. In *Chopiniana* she soared over the stage, her sinuous, flexible arms, bending at the wrists, the epitome of Romantic port de bras; the elongated lines of her torso and her well-shaped legs incarnated the poetry of understatement. In Petipa ballets the precision of her pointe work, the fluidity of each movement, her regal épaulement, and the special scale of every statuesque pose amazed the audience.

This precious combination of qualities was complemented by Shelest's unparalleled expressiveness. Plain offstage, she was nonetheless one of the most beautiful ballerinas on the Kirov boards. Of medium height, on stage she seemed tall and regal; her eyes blazed and captivated the audience. Her versatility was unprecedented and unmatched: she was the ballerina of Petipa and Fokine, Goleizovsky and Gorsky, Grigorovich and Jakobson. In the West she would have been equally successful in the works of Robbins and Tudor, Ashton and Cranko. Within the bounds of any style she managed to emphasize the steps in the strangest but most attractive way, thanks to her unorthodox dramatic gift.

In the 1930s and 1940s, when the Stanislavsky method was the officially recognized technique of socialist realism in the performing arts, Shelest appeared to be a champion of symbolist or expressionist theatre. She never consciously shaped her roles as a dramatic actress would; with great economy of means she somehow achieved the maximum effect with a minimum of effort. Besides her perfect dancing, three things come to mind when one summons up a mental image of Shelest: her eyes, her hands, and her stage presence, which in my view conveyed more than Ulanova's most inspired emulation of dramatic theatre. Shelest did not need to borrow anything from another medium—her image was both self-sufficient and compelling.

Remembering Shelest, one recalls the beauty of the attitudes or chassés croisés of her Lilac Fairy, stretching upward, holding beyond the beat, and her whirlwind promenade in Act II of *Giselle*. Even more vivid were her fiery, tormented, enigmatic glances cast at her partner; her arms in Nikiya's dance with the basket; and the crossed hands of her Giselle in the mad scene. This croisé position of the hands with the palms turned inward, symbolizing a dead person's leaving the natural world and turning to God, had a special meaning in the symbolic texture of *Giselle*. By this simple gesture Shelest implied that at the moment of Giselle's death she comprehended her transfiguration into a Wili, a pure spirit released from an earthly guise. In Act II she sustained this placement of her arms as a leitmotif emphasizing the main theme of the ballet, the triumph of spiritual love over death.

Such remarkable details were the hallmark of Shelest's art, thrilling the connoisseurs but infuriating critics, who thought them mannered and farfetched. She was the accomplished mistress of such symbolic, suggestive effects, controversial or unconventional in terms of style but irresistible in their expressive power. For instance, in *Les Sylphides* she did not simply hold a statuesque arabesque on pointe: leaning forward, on the brink of movement, she seemed to be listening to her inner voice, imbuing the pose with anxiety. The image of an "intellectual sprite" that she evoked was possibly not what Fokine had in mind, but the pose fascinated and teased the imagination. In portraying Giselle she eschewed realism—every gesture and step was carefully stylized, even in the mad scene. Remembering her dance with Albrecht, she repeated it beyond the music, off the beat. This is a manifestation of her artistry that many ballerinas, including Natalia Makarova, have reproduced.

In the Wedding Scene of *The Sleeping Beauty*, Shelest executed her variation impeccably, but in her eyes was the spellbound expression of a somnambulist. It was not that "after enjoying her centennial slumber, Aurora was not yet totally awake," as one critic jeered; she was simply dazed by her happiness.

Shelest's Odette in Act II of *Swan Lake* was not frightened by the appearance of Siegfried. Rather, she searched his face intently and turned her head away in despair: a wise, enchanted creature, she knew that the Prince would shatter her last hopes. Thus, she indirectly presaged the last act, when, unlike Semyonova, who swept around in pas de bourrée, she glided across the stage in a torpor. Her winged arms stretched down; then one arm suddenly waved as if brushing away unexpected tears.

Even in the virtuoso though inane role of Raymonda, Shelest made of her variations a sequence of interior monologues, illustrating Raymonda's changing states of mind. At times her interpretation might have seemed at odds with the cardboard character of Petipa's heroine, but Shelest's intensity was so convincing that one could not resist it.

In most of her roles—especially Giselle, Cleopatra in *Egyptian Nights*, Odette, Aegina in Jakobson's *Spartacus*, and

the cameos she created in his choreographic miniatures—Shelest revealed one very effective quality which I never noticed in other Russian ballerinas: the marvelous ability to alternate tension and relaxation in her movements. She never seemed to be carried away by her roles; rather, she seemed to employ her control to send tension to every muscle of her body—a tension of the mind transformed into a kind of muscular energy that traveled to every limb, to her fingers, toes, face . . . and then there followed a sudden relaxation. In *Giselle* this alternation was, in fact, highly convincing: the aloof peasant girl seemed to live between life and death. As Myrtha (and she was the best Queen of the Wilis I have ever seen) her effect was extraordinary: the tension of her jumps and arabesques conveyed an all-consuming desire for revenge, but when she confronted Giselle and Albrecht, she suddenly broke down.

In each of her roles Shelest produced enough expressive, unforgettable details to suffice a dozen first-rate ballerinas. Today one is eager to remember not only how she achieved this but also what she failed to achieve because of the paucity of the Kirov repertory and the unfavorable circumstances that attended her career. Like Plisetskaya, she was born to portray Medea, Phaedra, Electra, Mary Stuart, Lady Macbeth. One can only imagine her as the Siren in Balanchine's *Prodigal Son* or in his *La Sonnambula*; what new life she would have brought to Tudor's *Pillar of Fire* or *Jardin aux lilas*.

ALLA YAKOVLEVNA SHELEST, the daughter of an engineer, was born on February 26, 1919, in Smolensk. A sensitive, talented child, she drew, modeled, wrote poetry, played the piano, and danced. In 1928 she entered the Leningrad Choreographic School, where she studied under Pavel Gerdt's daughter Elizaveta, whose technique, said George Balanchine, "was distinguished by its crystalline purity, bordering on perfection." Gerdt inculcated in Shelest the essence of St. Petersburg classicism, eschewing any exaggeration or overstatement in placement, port de bras, or the shaping of steps. After six years of study the fifteen-year-old Shelest possessed the entire classical vocabulary, as she fully demonstrated by performing an old and intricate variation that Petipa had set to the music of Drigo. But in 1933 Elizaveta Gerdt had gone to Moscow to coach at the Bolshoi, and Shelest found herself in the stern hands of Agrippina Vaganova.

Gerdt had formed Shelest as a classical technician;

Vaganova tried to mold her into an actress in the mode of Soviet theatricality. Although Vaganova later referred to Shelest as "a gifted ballet actress," the reserved manners of her pupil annoyed her; she didn't fit into the general artistic trend of the day. Also, Shelest's technique obviously challenged the supremacy of Vaganova's favorite pupil, Natalia Dudinskaya, who was on her way to becoming the uncrowned prima ballerina of the Kirov. To safeguard Dudinskaya's prestige, Vaganova cast Shelest in Lavrovsky's *Katerina* for her graduation performance rather than in a classical piece. Her dancing was limited to "Amadée and Drias," a pre-Romantic vignette inserted into the drama-ballet. One writer recalled: "It was disheartening to watch a balletic gem framed in such nonsense. Shelest was at a loss—she overacted in an attempt to compensate for the dearth of choreography."

Shelest was engaged by the Kirov as a soloist in 1937 and saddled with small roles: Jacinta in *Laurencia*, Florine in *The Sleeping Beauty*, the Second Shade in *La Bayadère*, Natella in Chabukiani's *The Heart of the Hills*, Diane in *Esmeralda*. Even in these secondary parts her dramatic gift was so noticeable that she was constantly criticized for neglecting the sense of ensemble. The situation at the Kirov was most unfavorable to her. The repertory was strictly divided among the virtuosos (Dudinskaya, Feya Balabina, Olga Jordan), the lyrical ballerinas (Ulanova), and the "dancing actresses" like Tatiana Vecheslova. Shelest, who could fit all these categories, was forced to make do with cameo roles and second-cast assignments. Worse, she was frequently cast in drama-ballets—as a Russian partisan fighting the fascists in Burmeyster's *Tatiana*, or as the downtrodden Parasha in Zakharov's *The Bronze Horseman*, pseudo-roles in which she looked awkward and miscast.

In 1943, during the Kirov's wartime sojourn in Perm, Shelest was given two major roles: Zarema in *The Fountain of Bakhchisarai* and the Lilac Fairy in *The Sleeping Beauty*. In the Lilac Fairy's Prologue variation (composed by Fyodor Lopukhov for Egorova in 1915), based on chassés en croisé, soft attitudes, and first arabesque, alternating with pirouettes en dedans, she imbued the choreography with the regal fluidity of Russian legato, reminding one critic of "the lilac bush, stretching out its leaves and blossoms after the rain." Shelest enhanced this image with her flexible épaulement and the singing movements of her long arms. She was the true bearer of the symbolic theme of *Sleeping Beauty*—the blossoming of nature, spring triumphantly dispersing the gloom of winter. Her rare combination of

reserved and regal gestures, revealing the classicism of the true ballerina; her long, prepossessing promenades on pointe; her quiet, significant glances—each effect was paced, measured, stylized. In her mime duel with Carabosse, Shelest never stooped to involvement in a mute squabble; one glance, one imperious wave of her hand, and her rival shrank away in retreat.

Shelest danced Aurora at the end of the 1940s, marking this role, too, with her individual stamp. She attempted to convey the workings of a young girl's soul, childish at first, then submerged in reverie, and finally jubilant in her anticipation of womanhood. She was strikingly different in each act, and at the same time she was the most Romantic and enigmatic of all Russian Auroras I have seen. In her entrée, instead of the small pas de chat opening the variation, Shelest did a split in the air, and so energetically did she vary her sculptured poses in effacé and croisé that she appeared to be more a sprite than a human being. Every movement was significant, even the écarté pose repeated four times in the pas d'action: she would stretch into it slowly or swiftly, making the movement the image of Aurora's different feelings for each of her four cavaliers. Shelest thus added a new dimension to the most "passive" role in Russian ballet, a dramatic overtone that she also instilled into the Danse Vertige.

Shelest's rendition of Act II demonstrated the epitome of her genius, blending the classical steps and Romantic spirit of the traditional Vision Scene so marvelously that Aurora seemed to represent a spectral ideal of femininity that enchanted the Prince. In her Act III variation she embodied Petipa and Vsevolozhsky's concept of Aurora as a French princess dancing in the style of Russian folk dance. She flicked her wrist as if she were twitching the handkerchief that is an integral part of the khorovod, or round dance. Her refined Russian port de bras was complemented by the French design of her pointe work—the fleeting attitudes and especially the whirlwind circuit of chaînés and double tours alternating with arabesques that ended the coda.

Shelest danced her first Zarema in Zakharov's *The Fountain of Bakhchisarai* in 1943. "The most intelligent of all Zaremas," Nikolai Volkov, the ballet's scenarist, called her. She was truly comparable to Vecheslova and Plisetskaya, the other great interpreters of this role. The choreography was quite unusual for Russia in the thirties, but it suited Shelest perfectly. Unlike other Soviet drama-ballets, *Fountain* contained neither a pas de deux, nor a traditional

Below: Zarema, late 1940s
Right: (top) Odile, early 1950s; (bottom) The Queen of the Ball in *The Bronze Horseman*, early 1950s

Above: The Street Dancer in *Don Quixote*
Right: (top) Nikiya in *La Bayadère*, 1948; (bottom) Suimbike
in *Shuraleh*, mid- 1950s

Above: Aurora in *The Sleeping Beauty*, 1952
Left: (top) Katerina in *The Stone Flower*, 1957; The Street Dancer in
Don Quixote, early 1950s

OPPOSITE
Clockwise from top right: Parasha in *The Bronze Horseman*, late 1940s;
Giselle, early 1950s; Aegina in *Spartacus*, 1956; *The Native Fields*, 1950s

Nikiya, 1948

variation, nor a mime scene. The character of Zarema was portrayed mostly through dramatic solos that conveyed her thoughts and emotions.

Shelest's deepest responses were often triggered by choreography that expressed the basic emotions. Her Zarema was a woman engulfed by passion. Her entrée was unforgettable: the way she ran toward the fountain, avidly breathed its fine refreshing drops, and stretched herself in amorous languor, suggested that here was a sensual woman, feeding on love and consumed by it. Shelest's extraordinary ability to encapsulate an emotion in one step, gesture, or glance made her Zarema significant and distinctive. She knew instinctively how to draw the attention of the audience by her mere presence, as when she sat plunged in reverie among the harem wives and eunuchs, casting an occasional glance at their boisterous romping. No other dancer could charge these tedious passages with such electrifying tension.

Shelest's Zarema seemed to live as a stranger in the vain, stifling world of the harem, always awaiting her next encounter with her beloved master, Guirey. She paid no attention to the frail, fair Princess Maria, regarding the new captive as the Khan's transitory whim. Her first "monologue" was the tempestuous manifestation of her faith in love; even when Guirey turned away from her, her confidence was unshaken. She only seemed to become more thoughtful, lingering during the long stops on pointe, knitting her brows in perplexity, as if mentally examining the validity of her own code of love. Shelest deliberately eliminated the Oriental coloring of the arm movements; indeed, Ulanova called her "the most classical Zarema." In her four Act II solos she imbued the recurrent steps—split jetés, sissonnes, pirouettes, tours chaînés—with different emotional shadings: her womanly soul *en chagrin d'amour* seemed to pour forth all its poignant feelings, as the female psyche was revealed in all its complexity and vulnerability.

The scene in Maria's bedroom was strikingly original: Zarema contemptuously contemplated Maria, savoring the girl's fright. Suddenly she noticed Guirey's embroidered skull-cap. Shelest did not jump, as Plisetskaya did, in an uncontrollable fit of jealousy; rather, she looked long and hard at the captive, as if suddenly realizing the girl's mysterious power over Guirey, and then quietly and slowly stabbed her, seemingly aware that this act was her own death warrant. As her world collapsed, Zarema seemed to take leave of her life and her dreams; debilitated, crushed, with empty, dead eyes, she gazed at her beloved at the moment of her execution. Shelest's tragic intensity

elevated her Zarema to the level of Racine's heroines.

She was born to portray strong women in the grip of fate, such as Cleopatra in Fokine's *Une Nuit d'Egypte*, revived by Fyodor Lopukhov in the 1950s. One might think this mime role ill suited to Shelest, the incomparable technician; but as Cleopatra she revealed intimate facets of her own personality. Her comments on this role are noteworthy: "In Egypt, it was the desert that struck my imagination. The dead sands seemed to be living a distant, bizarre life. Immobile, seemingly frozen in space, they shifted constantly; drab and monotonous at first glance, they changed color imperceptibly, depending on the position of the sun and the elusive shadows. The light from the sharp blue sky imparted merciless distinctiveness to the desert. Cleopatra seemed to me akin to it: immutable in the dazzling light of her glory, royal, impenetrable, and, at the same time, constantly changing, incomprehensible in her elusiveness."

Shelest's appearance as Cleopatra was both unusual and strangely compelling: a small, slim woman, her frail wrists and ankles loaded with heavy bracelets, her mysterious eyes staring into the distance. This Cleopatra was no priestess of love; her amorous triumphs seemed to provide only intellectual delight. She resembled one of Marlene Dietrich's indolent femmes fatales, her impassive sexuality nourished by hatred for men: a woman more seductive in that it was impossible to fully possess her. The slave Amoun, ready to pay with his life for a night of love, only stirred her curiosity. Passing the cup of poison to him, she smiled at him ironically, as if to say: "This fool still believes in passion and love, but I know that all is dust in this world." She stepped indifferently over his corpse and froze in the pose of the idol Isis, a grimace of bitter irony and frustration distorting her features as she gazed past the messenger bringing her the news of the Roman victory. Inscrutable, compelling, she stood as if foreseeing the aftermath of her love for Marc Antony, the asp that would cling to her breast, her posthumous glory.

I N THE EARLY 1950s the situation at the Kirov changed dramatically, to Shelest's advantage. The once indefatigable Dudinskaya could no longer perform every night, and Vecheslova, Shelest's rival in drama-ballets, retired. Konstantin Sergeyev had recently renovated the old classical masterpieces: *Raymonda* and *La Bayadère* in 1948, *Swan Lake* in 1950, and *The Sleeping Beauty* in 1952. Shelest danced them all, though never in the first cast.

In *La Bayadère* she was striking and unforgettable—the

most unusual Nikiya on the Kirov stage. In the dance with the basket, like Pavlova and Semyonova, Shelest worked a minor theatrical miracle. The slow passage was like a conversation with a god; her stylized Indian arms suggested a ritual dance. She lingered endlessly in the recurrent third arabesque, as if marshalling her powers to survive Solor's betrayal. In the Kingdom of the Shades, her flowing, evanescent tours en attitude were absolutely unique, as were her soft battements à la seconde. Every movement was measured, peaceful, a sign of spiritual transfiguration. Shelest transformed Petipa's famous choreography into a metaphysical poem about death, eternity, and the immortality of love.

Her psychological approach, with its powerful, tragic overstatement, did not work for every role. In Lavrovsky's *Romeo and Juliet* she was exaggeratedly intellectual, more like Lady Macbeth than a fourteen-year-old girl; and in Jakobson's *Shuraleh* she turned the unpretentious fairy-tale bird-maiden into a sophisticated Firebird. But there were very few such obvious failures in her enormous repertory.

Shelest worked frequently in the 1950s with the controversial Jakobson, who designed for her the role of Aegina in *Spartacus* in 1956. Aegina was the centerpiece of his monumental "operatic" production, which harked back to Fokine's grand pictorial style. As a depraved but cerebral courtesan, blasé and impassive, Shelest was the human embodiment of decadent Imperial Rome. The choreography was a picturesque amalgam of the highly stylized dance patterns of ancient Greek black-figured vases, the frescoes of Pompeii, and Duncanesque free movement. Only Shelest, the mistress of refined stylization, could bring Jakobson's choreographic whimsy to life; her Aegina was the kindred spirit of her Cleopatra, drowning her frustration in joyless debauchery. She used to remarkable effect her hands, pressed flat to her body, and her turned-in feet on demi-pointe. As Aegina, Shelest sacrificed her instrumental classical gift for the sake of purely pictorial expressionism.

Shelest's participation in the ballets of Yuri Grigorovich, to whom she was married during the 1950s—such as *The Stone Flower* (1957) and *The Legend of Love* (1961)—was the last phase of her career. The choreography was tailor-made for her, and her contribution to the success of these works is hard to overestimate. During the Bolshoi's most recent American tour (1979), these Grigorovich ballets looked hopelessly corny, only distantly resembling the performances Shelest had appeared in twenty years before.

In *The Stone Flower* she danced both Katerina and the Mistress of the Copper Mountain. She lavishly introduced into her portrayal of Katerina the large stride of the Russian khorovod and other stylized elements of folk dance, but the role as a whole seemed to be an extension of her Oksana in Lopukhov's *Taras Bulba* (1954). The mature talent of the thirty-five-year-old ballerina was pinched by the narrow role of Katerina, but as the Mistress of the Copper Mountain she demonstrated both her dance gift and her acute sense of drama. If the choreography harked back to the acrobatic vocabulary of Lopukhov and Goleizovsky as well as to Petipa's pure classical lexicon, Shelest's performance was also a composite of her previous characters: the Mistress shared Zarema's passionate nature and vulnerability, Nikiya's pride and spirit of sacrifice, Aegina's mysterious evil charm. Shelest was all the more exciting in that she achieved these effects while portraying a creature who was part woman, part lizard.

Another of Shelest's fascinating characters was Queen Mekhmene-Banu in *Legend of Love*. This role was created on her, but because of her complex relationship with Grigorovich and his well-known hostility to aging ballerinas, she rehearsed it by herself and performed it only once. In this one performance her Queen was a truly Racinian heroine, torn between love and duty, passionate sensuality and sober intellect.

The last time I saw Shelest, in *Chopiniana* in 1962, she was even more overwhelming and convincing than when I had seen her for the first time in the early fifties; her grands jetés across the stage in the Mazurka were as dazzling as the perfection of her style. A short time later I learned that she had been advised to retire because she was "out of shape." The Kirov management, as destructive as ever, was in a hurry to dispose of its most striking, unusual talent.

Shelest's gala concert in Moscow in the spring of 1963, when she took the audience by storm in a solo and a duet from *Legend of Love*, constituted the finale of her anguished but magnificent career. She later taught at the Vaganova school and choreographed and coached in the provinces, but this kind of activity was definitely not her element. A mistress of detail, she imposed her own style on her pupils, working for hours on the position of the fingers or the technique of renversé while disregarding the overall design of the role under study. At times her instructions, quite intelligible and clear to herself, baffled and confused her pupils, for the revelations through which her tragic dance gift manifested itself were unique and could not be reproduced or mimicked, even with Shelest herself as instructor.

The Dying Swan

MAYA PLISETSKAYA

I N 1959, WHEN MAYA PLISETSKAYA first appeared in New York with the Bolshoi company as the Mistress of the Copper Mountain in Grigorovich's *The Stone Flower* and as a bacchante in *Walpurgis Night*, the *New York Herald Tribune* reported that she "compels one to forget everything but the wonders of her body, soaring in the air, spinning around with electrifying dazzle, balancing on pointe or suddenly freezing in lingering pauses amidst the swift movements. . . . The great ballerina, the great performer." Diana Vreeland, a member of the opening-night audience, recalled that unforgettable moment when the unknown and unpublicized Plisetskaya "came out on her pointes, and this

face, just the face, *traveled* right across the stage . . . and, in one breath, the entire audience stood up and shouted! Shouted! From that moment on, she's just been the only dancer in the world for me. She commands the earth!"

I, too, remember vividly the mesmerizing effect that I first experienced in 1954, of Plisetskaya's entrance as Zarema in *The Fountain of Bakhchisarai*: a vivid, auburn-haired Caucasian beauty who burst onto the stage and froze, absorbing the whole Bolshoi with her enormous, blazing eyes. At those performances Ulanova danced Maria, but she was like a plaintive violin solo in the symphony of sensuality and passion that Plisetskaya made of the ballet. Her inimitable defiance of classical grammar, which she subjected to her own code of limitless eloquence, still haunts my memory. She was a devastating firestorm of emotion, scorching the stage with her passion and zest for life. She was dance's visible manifestation of exultation, grief, joy, and sorrow. A unique phenomenon in Soviet ballet, she never sought to become a dramatic artist in the Stanislavsky mode. She epitomized artistic freedom in ballet; for my generation she was Ballet itself.

Plisetskaya was richly endowed by nature with a unique combination of chiseled arms, torso, shoulders, and swan-like neck. She is only slightly taller than average, but on the stage her body appears elongated, vibrating with all her melodious lines, which are repeated in a beautiful face whose features breathe mobility and expressiveness. The lines of Plisetskaya's body are her greatest treasure. They convey an extreme dramatic intensity: one pose, one movement of her arms is enough to evoke grief and sorrow. This made her the most accomplished, most charged trage-dienne on the Soviet stage. On the other hand, she reveled equally in the sheer bravura and triumphant vitality of bacchanalian dance, to which she brought her enormous soaring jump and the extraordinary ballon more usual to male technique. In the forties and fifties Plisetskaya literally hovered and soared over the Bolshoi stage. Like Nureyev, she was not an exponent of St. Petersburg classicism. Throughout her long career she continued to work on her technique, which deviated in many ways from academic standards; but however diligently she sought to become a "correct" dancer, she remained the most exemplary product of the flamboyant Bolshoi style.

Thanks to the multiplicity of Plisetskaya's gifts, her larger-than-life portrayals, and her highly individual technique, choosing her most revealing role is like selecting a representative novel by Dostoyevsky: so many of her achievements immediately spring to mind—her Odette-Odile and her Kitri, her Dying Swan and her Zarema, her Laurencia and her Raymonda, her Carmen and her Firebird. . . .

MAYA MIKHAILOVNA PLISETSKAYA was born on November 20, 1925, into a family strongly affiliated with the theatre and ballet worlds. In the 1930s her aunt Sulamith Messerer and her uncle Asaf Messerer were two of the most talented dancers at the Bolshoi; her mother, Rachel Messerer, was a star in silent movies. Maya was a born ballerina; from earliest childhood she not only dreamed

of dancing but actually did dance at every opportunity. The stories of the three-year-old Maya performing a Delibes waltz in the street before a startled crowd and whirling in a Chopin waltz in her kindergarten were not fabricated with hindsight. Like Pavlova, Plisetskaya was obsessed by dance.

In 1934 Maya enrolled in the Moscow Choreographic School. She spent six years in the class of Elizaveta Gerdt, who also taught Alla Shelest and Ekaterina Maximova. As a sixth- and seventh-year student, Maya was pronounced a wunderkind after her performances of such roles as the Canary Fairy in *The Sleeping Beauty*, the Cat in Alexander Radunsky's *The Little Stork*, and a soloist in the *Paquita* Grand Pas Classique.

Plisetskaya was a quick learner. Her keen sensitivity matched the natural spontaneity of her reactions. Marina Semyonova, whom Plisetskaya revered, once said, "Maya is able to absorb within a month what some other dancers cannot do in a decade." Even at her student debut she revealed one major facet of her gift: her capricious dependence on her mood at the moment, the impulsiveness and zest that compelled her to throw herself into the dance with total abandon. She bit into a choreographic sequence with more vitality and brio than anyone else; she infused a superhuman energy into the most ordinary combinations, to the point of disrupting their classical harmony. Unlike Shelest, Plisetskaya was becoming a dancer more intuitive than intellectual, more prone to unexpected emotional outbursts than to submission to the established choreographic design. "I was a little devil whom Gerdt was unable to tame," Plisetskaya maintained in one of our conversations several years ago. "Besides, our personalities did not match. I could get from Gerdt nothing but poor classical training. That's why after graduation I was a real dilettante—the gifted one, but without an ounce of training. I did everything by intuition. And the 1940s were the years of my wild dancing."

In 1943 Elizaveta Gerdt, proud of her exceptional pupil, showed the prodigy to Agrippina Vaganova, who had escaped to Moscow from besieged Leningrad. Vaganova, impressed by Plisetskaya's musicality and her other abilities, agreed to teach her for four months, until she returned to Leningrad. "She was an absolute genius," Plisetskaya told me. "Of her three thousand students, twenty-five hundred would never have become dancers were it not for Vaganova. Like a first-rate surgeon, she knew every muscle and knew how to manipulate each one. During my lessons with her I learned much more than in my ten years at the Bolshoi school. The difference between Gerdt and Vaganova can be illustrated by an example: Gerdt used to say to me: 'You are hanging onto the barre.' I knew that. But it was Vaganova who said: 'Change the position of your arm and stand closer to the barre.' And everything fell into place. She invited me to study in Leningrad. 'You need it,' she said. 'You are using only ten percent of your potential. We'll prepare such a *Swan Lake* that all the devils in hell will sweat.'"

Because of the insistence of Leonid Lavrovsky, who was afraid Plisetskaya would remain in Leningrad, she refused the offer "and never ceased to regret it all my life." What she called the years of her "wild dancing" was the time of her early triumphs. "What the critics labeled my 'revolutionary approach' to classical steps was essentially dancing by intuition. Without a strong training flowing in my blood, I danced the way I felt, without any reference to standards I never knew. That was the time of 'reinventing bicycles,' as I call it."

Nevertheless, as a pregraduate student in September 1941, Plisetskaya performed a variation from the *Paquita* Grand Pas and delighted the audience not so much by the height of her leaps as by her dynamic attack and her special way of minimizing preparations: she blended the linking steps and the major movements into one stream of dance, ebullient and sizzling. What was to become Plisetskaya's style was already hinted at in many of the roles she undertook upon joining the Bolshoi in 1941: the *Dying Swan* (1942), the Mazurka in *Les Sylphides* (1943), Masha in *The Nutcracker* (1944), the Lilac Fairy and Fairy Violente in *The Sleeping Beauty* (1944), the Queen of the Dryads in *Don Quixote* (1944). In 1945 she added to this already impressive list the title role in *Raymonda* and the Autumn Fairy in Zakharov's *Cinderella*.

Curiously enough, when one leafs through the early appraisals of Plisetskaya, one is amazed at the extent to which her captivating impact emanated from her physical exuberance and sheer kinetic power. Vaganova herself, who mounted the Mazurka in *Les Sylphides* for her, was astounded by the combination of space-cleaving dynamism and fluidity in her grands jetés. As Gerdt recalled: "Vaganova saw in Maya's Mazurka the reincarnation of her own brilliance in the role." Her tiny pas de chat, employed as a preparation for attitude, also mesmerized the audience. When she danced Myrtha in *Giselle*, her soubresauts were likened to Alexei Yermolayev's. Plisetskaya even managed to turn fourth arabesque into a dramatic moment when, in Vadim Gayevsky's words, "even the contours of her back brought to mind the image of a flying Firebird or the intricate figures

in an Oriental carpet." At times her brief variations stole the show: her solo as the Queen of the Dryads eclipsed the work of Chabukiani as Basil. Gayevsky recalled: "Plisetskaya's diagonal, consisting of three gigantic grands jetés crossing the entire stage, constituted the only value of the performance, overshadowing the theatricality of Act I and the brilliance of the classical pas de deux in Act III. Those three leaps reverberated in the audience like three shots."

At the outset of her career Plisetskaya both puzzled and captivated the audience with her unusual manner of executing large dance sequences "at one gulp." Each unit of time seemed to contain an extraordinarily high concentration of movement. Her overcharged style was innovative and compelling, but it was also at odds with the poetry of understatement and pure classical proportions fostered by Petersburg-Leningrad training. Little wonder that in Leningrad Plisetskaya was unpopular, the target of critical barbs, while in Moscow she enjoyed the prestige of an iconoclastic star and was worshipped at the Bolshoi.

Her reputation took on a hint of legend after her first *Swan Lake*, when she presented an Odette-Odile with an unusually long and slim figure; an austere, mournful face; and a way of moving that was both flowing and intense. Since 1947 she has danced this ballet more than five hundred times. Out of her enormous repertory, it is *Swan Lake* with which Plisetskaya is most identified and for which she is most likely to be remembered in Russia.

Odette-Odile proved to be her greatest classical role. As Odette she demonstrated a unique combination of nobility, expressiveness, and searing tragic intensity. As Odile she laced her virtuosity with fiery temperament and challenging bravado. Her performance was so devastating that Ulanova, unable to compete, ceased dancing *Swan Lake* in 1948. Western audiences never had a chance to see this magical interpretation at its peak, but for those who were overwhelmed by her artistry in the mid-fifties, she has always remained peerless.

Guided by her rare intuition, Plisetskaya revealed a strong affinity for the "Wagnerian" aspect of *Swan Lake*, the ballet as a tragedy of thwarted love triumphing in death— a *Liebestod*. Only a ballerina as sensitive as Plisetskaya could respond to all the shades of Tchaikovsky's musical spectrum and bring out the richness of meanings that both the music and the choreography suggest: doom and hope, the torment and doubt of the captive spirit striving for freedom and love. Plisetskaya's Odette was the most beautiful, vibrant, and compelling I ever saw. Her appeal was twofold: while her uniquely expressive arms and plaintive épaulement, and the tremulous, furtive birdlike movements of her head and swanlike neck, evoked the image of an enchanted bird, the movements of her flexible torso and legs exuded an irresistible human femininity. This duality of swan and woman gave her portrayal a rare poetic power that blended fairy tale and reality. Possibly the most conspicuous characteristic of her Odette was the impetuosity with which she imbued Ivanov's choreography. Unlike many of her predecessors, in Act II Plisetskaya never "sang the swan song of sorrow," as the choreographer had suggested. By infusing an utter intensity into each movement, she made one aware of Odette's tremendous inner resources, the latent power that was doomed to wither away in her passive captivity. The series of attitudes that represent Odette's flight from Siegfried was unforgettable: instead of growing into them, she exploded: arms thrown backward like large wings, head thrusting into the air, she would jump onto pointe to the ever-accelerating rhythm and finally freeze, as if on the brink of total collapse. Those five attitudes were also symbolic of the Swan Queen's flight from herself and her illusion of hope.

Plisetskaya never presented the adagio as a narrative; rather, she made the symphony of arabesques and sissonnes fermées and ouvertes an interior monologue suggesting her inner turmoil, her pain and sorrow. Sometimes she disrupted her legato movements by an overly accentuated wave of her arm or an abrupt dive into arabesque penchée. Even in the arms of Siegfried she seemed aloof and inscrutable, as if her true feelings were not to be revealed to anyone, and to Siegfried least of all. When at the finale of the adagio she timorously clung to the enraptured Siegfried, she seemed to submit to an irresistible hope stronger even than death.

Plisetskaya's individuality was especially noticeable in her Act II variation. Bursting energetically into small leaps, her Odette seemed to test her ability to tear herself away from the ground and fly away from Rothbart's dominion. Her goal was freedom, and Siegfried's love and pledge of fidelity were merely the means to attain it. Inimitable were the anguished, distrustful glances she cast upon Siegfried as he gave her his solemn oath: she seemed to foresee that her hopes would come to nought. In Plisetskaya's portrayal, lyricism was somewhat secondary. Unlike Ulanova's and Makarova's, her Odette did not affect one's emotions; rather, she overwhelmed, perplexed, and crushed one with the power of her pride and the wisdom of disillusion. Submitting to Rothbart's spell, as unknowable and majestic as ever,

she would withdraw into her swan state, moving her arms like long white snakes. "Through them I attempted to suggest the lake ripples, Odette's anticipation of whiling away the night on the water's surface," Plisetskaya told me.

Her tempestuous Odette in Act IV was so much an extension of her previous image that her total performance achieved a rare integrity. Unlike every other Odette I have seen, Plisetskaya in Act IV did not openly grieve. Desperately waving her winged arms, she encompassed the stage in the allegro agitato of her short solo as if reproaching herself for being deceived by the tempting lure of happiness. It was a tragic passage of remorse and embitterment; but when the penitent Siegfried arrived, she could not help forgiving him, as the strong person does the weakling. The optimism of the Soviet version of *Swan Lake* prescribed a blissful union of Odette and Siegfried. The consistency of Plisetskaya's interpretation made this farfetched finale look even more absurd.

The versatility of Plisetskaya's plastique was striking. As Odile, clad in a scarlet tutu with a black bodice, crowned with a panache of black feathers, she burst onto the stage like an explosion. The spiritual power of her Odette was fascinating, but her Odile, soulless and hollow, was sexually irresistible. Moreover, she seemed to be perfectly aware of her female charms and to enjoy herself immensely. Plisetskaya did not make much of Odile's evil bond with Rothbart—she seemed to emerge from nowhere to seduce Siegfried in cold blood, with the style of a professional. In her mien and manners there was something of the operatic diva. Confidence, challenge, ardor—all were there when she threw herself into the Act III pas de deux. She did not seem to be a symbol of evil; her seduction of Siegfried was merely an erotic adventure, and she reveled in her total victory over this new victim. Her famous diagonal of arabesques in the variation was unique: she seemed to dive through a tiny pas de chat as preparation for each arabesque. Just as breathtaking was her whirlwind of piqués en tournant (in place of the thirty-two fouettés), which devoured the stage in the coda.

PLISETSKAYA'S special gift was her ability to tinge the old masterpieces with disquiet, anguish, or electrifying power. When the choreography lent itself naturally to such artistic transformation, her dancing was capable of rising to the utmost heights of philosophical thought. This is what happened when she performed *The Dying Swan*.

In our conversations Plisetskaya often expressed her admiration for Pavlova's immortal interpretation, but her own was anything but an echo. The leitmotif of Pavlova's Swan—the enlightened peace before death—served Plisetskaya merely as a starting point from which to elaborate her own design. She sailed out from the left wings, her back to the audience, on a tiny, beadlike pas de bourrée. Following the languid cello inflections, her arms fluttered, evoking a powerful image; the blood had not yet chilled in the veins, the arm-wings beat the air and water, yet it was clear that life was irretrievably flowing out of them. Her movements were animated by the desire to halt this departing stream. The flapping of the arms and hands became more furious and frantic; one sensed in them her pain and despair as she lost the ability to fly. There was no hint of the submissiveness that had been so evident in Ulanova's memorable interpretation. The body was rebelling, resisting death. Plisetskaya's Swan was a metaphor of life and death, a tragic and cathartic experience for the audience.

The 1950s were Plisetskaya's heyday as a dancer. She participated in almost every Bolshoi production, undertaking the most diverse roles: Zarema (1948); Kitri (1950); Aurora (1952); the Mistress of the Copper Mountain in *The Stone Flower*, first in Lavrovsky's version (1954), then in Grigorovich's (1959); Suimbike, the bird-maiden in Yakobson's *Shuraleh* (1955); Laurencia (1956); Aegina in Igor Moiseyev's *Spartacus* (1958). The artistic results were uneven. Plisetskaya's Aurora proved merely an excursion into an alien aesthetic, a princess who lacked both refinement and radiance, but as the Lilac Fairy she captivated the audience with her flowing développés à la seconde, her regal mien, and the alluring charm of her épaulement.

Nor did she shun cameo roles in operas: she danced the Persian captive in *Khovantschina*, and a Bacchante in the *Walpurgis Night* scene of *Faust*. She knew the secret of transforming these insignificant roles into little gems, for example, the solo in *Khovantschina*, which was designed for her by the outstanding Bolshoi dancer Sergei Koren. As a languorous, sensuous Oriental beauty, Plisetskaya wrought a small theatrical miracle through the interplay of her expressive "Persian" arms. She was both compelling and vulnerable, suggesting ingratiating sensuality and at the same time pleading for her release from captivity. Another minor masterpiece, her *Walpurgis Night*, aroused the audience by the sheer exultation of her space-cleaving jumps, mischievous bravado, and lightning turns.

Besides Odette-Odile, in the immense gallery of her portrayals in the fifties three major roles—Kitri, Zarema, and Laurencia—stood out as Plisetskaya's most accomplished and influential characterizations. Her flamboyantly flirtatious Kitri was more than a music-hall character, although she resembled one with her gold hoop earrings, the flower in her hair, and the ringlet on her forehead. Plisetskaya played Kitri as a mischievous scamp enjoying to the full every ounce of attention she extracted from Basil, the crowd, and the Bolshoi audience—from her first entrance, every turn and kick-jeté was accompanied by a roar of enthusiasm from her fans. Her Kitri was larger than life, rather like the Spanish street dancer described by Rilke in his poem "Spanische Tänzerin." But at the same time Plisetskaya had a vitality that turned the set into a real Spanish square, hot and dusty, the sweet-smelling air filled with the sounds of merrymaking and heavy with passion. From the outset she appeared as the true mistress of this world, in which everything was familiar and obedient to her will and fancy. In the variation with castanets a frenzied whirl of pirouettes turned into a tornado of seething energy that made one dizzy. The impact of this superhuman vitality, so wonderfully caught in Vasily Katanian's documentary film on Plisetskaya, was so intense that some people in the audience began to cry—one of them was the young Nureyev, who told me that he had been devastated by Plisetskaya's portrayal. She never burdened her heroine with psychology; she simply reveled in dancing, pouring forth an incendiary joie de vivre and captivating the audience with her own boundless enthusiasm. Gorsky's choreography included many kick-jetés, which Plisetskaya executed in a way that became a paradigm not only in Russia but even in New York. Gelsey Kirkland's Kitri in Baryshnikov's *Don Quixote* mimicked Plisetskaya's kick-jeté. Performing sissonnes in the first variation, she arched her back so that her outstretched leg almost touched her thrown-back head. None of Plisetskaya's predecessors or colleagues could sustain such high, lingering, dynamic flights complemented by a spectacularly arched torso. She never ceased to embellish her dancing in *Don Quixote* with technical fireworks, and every performance contained a surprise that the public awaited avidly.

Her Zarema was another masterpiece. She seemed to be an avatar of ancient Eros whom fate had clothed in the flesh of a Georgian woman. Zarema's passion for Guirey was a sickness, an obsession that overcame thought and feelings. The wide, feline jetés and the tornado of tours

Top: (left) Odette, early 1950s; (right) Masha in *The Nutcracker*, mid-1940s
Above: (left) Zarema in *The Fountain of Bakhchisarai*, mid-1950s; (right) Aurora in *The Sleeping Beauty*,
with Yuri Kondratov as Prince Désiré, 1953

OPPOSITE
Top: The Queen of the Dryads in *Don Quixote*, 1951
Bottom: Zarema, mid-1950s

Top: (left) *The Dying Swan*, mid-1950s;
(middle) Raymonda, early 1960s; (right)
Odile, early 1960s
Above: Odette, late 1940s
Right: Myrtha in *Giselle*, early 1950s

OPPOSITE
Top: (left) *Anna Karenina*, early 1970s;
(right) *Isadora*, mid-1970s
Bottom: Nina Zarechnaya in *The Seagull*,
early 1980s

Above: The Mistress of the Copper Mountain in *The Stone Flower*,
with Vladimir Levashev as Severyan, 1959
Right: (top) Carmen, early 1970s; (bottom) Carmen, with Alexander
Godunov as Don José, 1974

chaînés and pirouettes in the dances of Act II breathed doomed but not defeated passion. Plisetskaya's technical miracles were a physical extension of Zarema's superhuman grief and despair; almost every step took on a tragic dimension. Thus, as she tried to rekindle Guirey's dying love for her, she flew into a very high saut de chat and in a split second stretched out her legs, her back arched so radically that her thrown-back leg hovered over her head and arms.

Her third great role in the 1950s was the heroine of Chabukiani's *Laurencia*, which she frequently performed with the choreographer as Frondoso. Their partnership was a phenomenon of matchless artistry. To Chabukiani's choreography, which he revised to exploit Plisetskaya's potential, she brought both the fiery Spanish temperament of her Kitri and the intense emotion of her Zarema. Moreover, she gave her heroine a strong heroic dimension corresponding to the spirit of Lope de Vega's drama. Plisetskaya's virtuosity in this role was truly limitless. One can never forget the bravura and concentration of her wedding variation, in which she performed a series of her kick-jetés taken without preparation. Her characteristic Spanish arms complemented this tour de force; her back leg was thrown so high, it almost touched her head. Plisetskaya performed this jump several times, alternating it with a cascade of swift pirouettes.

IN THE MID-FIFTIES PLISETSKAYA established herself as the Bolshoi's prima ballerina assoluta, but despite her success, her career was not officially promoted. Instead, it evolved painfully, with even more complications than that of Alla Shelest (the only ballerina among her colleagues Plisetskaya calls "a genius"). "It was like a smooth wall over which I was trying to scramble, getting my hands bloody," she once said. Plisetskaya's dancing was too tempestuous and iconoclastic to escape bitter criticism from all sides. Her audacious approach to the academic tradition and ostentatious negligence of the academic canons bordered on sheer blasphemy. In Leningrad she was invariably disparaged for her "vulgarity" and "circus tricks." Her stage-devouring jumps and her snaking arms in *Swan Lake* (which many ballerinas, including Dudinskaya, attempted to imitate) were jeered at and considered an example of Bolshoi sloppiness. To the Party supervisors, whose favors, unlike many of her colleagues, she never sought, her florid style seemed too energetic, perhaps untamable. Her early inde-

pendence, almost abrasive candor, and artistic nonconformity conflicted with the passive and obedient spirit of the 1950s.

Plisetskaya's family background made her position at the Bolshoi especially vulnerable. The daughter of a Jewish engineer who perished in one of the nameless icy tombs of the Gulag, and of a Jewish actress who was sentenced to a labor camp in the 1930s, Plisetskaya was viewed by the KGB as politically unreliable. Unlike Ulanova, Plisetskaya never had the support of the powers-that-be. The first ballet to be mounted for her, *Carmen Suite*, was created only in 1967, when her greatest days were over. Nor did she enjoy the personal advantages due a prima ballerina: although she excelled in the entire repertory, and her name was on everyone's lips, she lived in a huge communal apartment housing twenty families sharing two baths.

She had only one weapon—her dancing. With that she fought "like a general without an army. If I could have saved all the energy I wasted on my struggle, it would have sufficed me to cover a dozen ballets," she told me. Until 1959 she was forbidden to dance in the West. This was the KGB's punishment for an imaginary crime: because of her meetings with an admirer who happened to be a British diplomat, she was accused of working for British intelligence. Spied upon and hounded in the 1950s, Plisetskaya lived in constant fear. Moreover, the KGB harassed her admirers, accusing them of being bribed by their idol and demanding defamatory information about her. Disguised KGB agents came to her performances at the Bolshoi and physically prevented her fans from applauding. In Moscow she was a living legend, but she was left behind when the Bolshoi went to London in 1953 and to Paris in 1956. Her serious knee injury in 1960 caused the doctors to predict an early end to her career, but she survived, though the Western public never got to witness the wonders of her elevation. "I jumped around a little bit in New York, when Khrushchev 'liberated' me in 1959 after I sent him a penitent letter," she recalled with bitterness. In fact, Nikita Khrushchev assumed personal responsibility for her behavior in America during the Bolshoi's engagement. At last Plisetskaya's Western fame began to grow and flourish.

Plisetskaya was born to dance Shakespearean heroines. Today we may ask why we never saw her Cleopatra or her Lady Macbeth, but this is the type of role she danced least of all. She did dance Juliet, but this role came to her too late, in a choreographic style that was alien to her. Her attempts to revive Lavrovsky's choreography merely emphasized its incompatibility with Prokofiev's music and her own expressive gifts. Her strong-willed, ginger-haired Juliet was reminiscent of the Venetian beauties of Titian and Veronese. But the ballerina born for dancing was hemmed in by a sparse choreographic vocabulary, pantomime, and a mass of props. Responding to Prokofiev's music, Plisetskaya gave the poorly designed dance patterns a strong impulse of will and a change of emphasis, relegating the lyricism to the background and stressing Juliet's passionate revolt against parental authority. But for the first time her amplitude of dance and dramatic prowess were restricted everywhere by chains of balletic conventionality from which they could not break free.

Plisetskaya consummated the unrealized tragedy of her Juliet in her portrayals of Carmen, Anna Karenina, and Mekhmene-Banu in *The Legend of Love*. Her Mekhmene-Banu in particular was a character of Shakespearean dimensions, a heroine like those of the classic tragedies, torn between conscience and the longings of the flesh. Plisetskaya brought to the role the features of her earlier heroines, amalgamated naturally to give her psychological justification: the rebellious impetuosity of Juliet, the excessive passion of Zarema, the imperiousness and vulnerability of the Mistress of the Copper Mountain were combined in a single complex character, regally self-willed yet susceptible, cruel yet self-sacrificing, strong yet weak.

The ballerina herself described Mekhmene: "Desperate in the extreme, imperious in the extreme, resolute in the extreme, generous in the extreme, confused in the extreme, and finally submissive in the extreme. Mekhmene is fated to experience all feelings to the full—except joy." The intensity with which Plisetskaya saturated every step and her powerful stage presence showed her heroine to be larger than life. Through her overcharged characterization Plisetskaya seemed to demonstrate that tragedy differs from mere drama by virtue of the moral grandeur of the protagonist, who asserts his worth in combat with fate and a cruel world. *Legend of Love* is a tragedy of sacrificial altruism (Mekhmene gives up her beauty to save her sister's life) and passion (her blind and violent love for Ferhad, her sister's beloved). Plisetskaya's Mekhmene remained morally firm, inducing Ferhad to accomplish great things, to be spiritually regenerated as he embarked on the path of heroic self-abnegation.

Her Carmen was of a different mold. Alberto Alonso choreographed his *Carmen Suite* for her, using Bizet's music as strikingly rearranged by her husband, Rodion Shchedrin. The choreographer interpreted the music in the tradition of Spanish folk culture and imbued his ballet with the quintessentially Spanish metaphor of the bullring, the yellow arena in which Carmen's own drama is played out. Alonso's Carmen image is a duality: on the one hand, she seems to be a puppet in the closed world of Spanish metaphysics, whose inhabitants obediently play the roles allotted to them by fate; on the other hand, she is the only full-blooded character, who has turned her life into entertainment for others—Lorca's "idle spectators under a tent," glued to the railings around the ring. The charged inflections Plisetskaya brought to her resilient, strong grand battement on pointe (Carmen's recurrent choreographic motif), the provocative thrust with which she touched and brushed against "the marionette of fate" Don José, were designed to overcome her own enforced role as a puppet and to affirm her true personality, which recognized only one law: the freedom of choice, unhesitating and ruthless.

Carmen's craving for freedom seemed to constitute the only sense of her life, although she knew that her death would be the price of the luxury of disobedience. The sense of inevitable doom added a special acuity to each moment of her existence, which she enjoyed breathlessly, at the height of emotional intensity. Plisetskaya graphically etched this intensity on each movement, dragging the audience into the world of her willfulness and courage. She indulged in sheer vulgarity, seemingly daring fate to bring the corrida of her life to its fatal dénouement. The way she watched the toreador who had caught her fancy epitomized her art: she was full of tension, fraught with the explosiveness—indeed, almost the bestiality—that was to bring about her own death.

To some extent, Carmen's challenge to convention and her courage to face the most crucial problems of existence are echoes of Plisetskaya's own artistic boldness. However trite or provincial Alonso's choreography might seem in the perspective of contemporary dance, its appearance on the prim Bolshoi stage in 1967 insulted the Party supervisors, who criticized its "overt eroticism." The ballet was nearly canceled. Plisetskaya did battle for it in the office of the minister of culture, the late Ekaterina Furtseva, saying: "If Carmen dies, I die too." Plisetskaya won, a victory that caused her to be regarded as the most rebellious and controversial figure in Soviet ballet.

As if to reinforce this reputation, Plisetskaya embarked on another challenging project, a ballet based on Tolstoy's *Anna Karenina*, set to a score by Shchedrin. Despite Yuri

Grigorovich's strong opposition to the idea of translating Tolstoy's philosophical novel into the language of dance, and despite the unfriendly atmosphere at the Bolshoi, Plisetskaya was so determined to achieve her goal that she assumed the unusual role of stage director and choreographed the role of Anna herself. Unfortunately, her lack of choreographic experience was all too evident in the diffuse, sprawling design of the ballet. Nor was Plisetskaya provided with encouraging support by her co-directors, Natalia Ryzhenko and Victor Smirnov-Golovanov.

Not surprisingly, *Anna Karenina* emerged as a one-ballerina show, Plisetskaya's rich effort to create theatre through the potent expressiveness of her mere presence on the stage. The dramatic impact stemmed from her emotionally charged poses and the unique poetry of her arms. Her own lifelong dramatic theme of rebellious and oppressed femininity was implicit in her portrayal. Her Anna was a multifaceted woman, the victim equally of her self-destructive passion for Vronsky, her maternal and conjugal feelings, and the retribution of society.

Tolstoy's famous epigraph, "Vengeance is mine; I will repay," resounded with unexpected strength in Plisetskaya's characterization. Tolstoy was thinking of the family sanctified by religion and the church. Anna, who defiles the sanctity of family ties by adultery, challenges God ("I am avenged"), who punishes her for it ("I will repay"). Plisetskaya gave a broader interpretation to the epigraph: the rebel's challenge to society and the latter's retribution.

Plisetskaya always empathized with wronged, heartbroken, yet still tempestuous characters, and naturally her Anna's high-strung emotions prevailed in the duets with Vronsky, colored with almost neon vividness. Nowhere else did the electrifying impact of Plisetskaya's arabesques and jetés have such a cathartic effect as in these duets filled with love-hate, passionate obsession, and the sense of doom. Her flight across the stage in the scene of her Italian idyll with Vronsky was charged with such high-voltage intensity that it took on a larger-than-life dimension.

When engrossed in the dramatic action of a scene, Plisetskaya conveyed unerringly the spirit and fatality of Tolstoy's most tormented heroine. In the episode at the opera, Anna simply moved calmly toward the audience, her wide-open, blazing eyes staring ahead as the noiseless whisper of high-society gossip arose around her in the boxes. Plisetskaya made one feel almost as stunned as Anna was by forebodings of her downfall and death.

Anna Karenina was Plisetskaya's last tragic heroine at the Bolshoi; even now the role remains closely identified with her. But the decade after this controversial production was not, as one might have expected, the glowing sunset of a thirty-year career. The 1970s was a turbulent decade for Plisetskaya, filled with experiments and contacts with Western choreographers. Fortunately, the opportunity (rare for a Soviet ballerina) to travel extensively abroad and work with Western masters of dance was granted to Plisetskaya by the Kremlin as a delayed reward for her great achievements.

Early in the decade she developed stable artistic unions with Maurice Béjart and Roland Petit. Apparently she has a special affinity for these choreographers. Petit has said, "Plisetskaya's appearance on the stage is an event in itself. She can merely cross the stage with her legendary pas de bourrée or with her sculpturesque and charged attitude, and it's already great art."

Their collaboration has served their reciprocal interests perfectly. During the 1970s Plisetskaya began to shift from the domain of classical dance to the multifarious forms of contemporary art. This transition does not disconcert her: after thirty years of "classical drudgery," as she put it, "I am eager to experiment with any modern style in ballet, without discriminating." In Petit's *La Rose malade*, created for her in 1973, her arms, undulating like an aquatic plant, were the epitome of balletic expressivity. Guided by Mahler's melody, they sustained a solo while the body, unfolding like the petals of a flower or contracting with invisible pain, accompanied the lyricism of the arms—a song of dissolution and death. In Béjart's *Isadora*, however ridiculous its awkward blend of Duncanesque vocabulary and pedestrian realism may seem, Plisetskaya displayed the ever-magnetic power of her stage presence: her breathtaking appearance as the dying Isadora was an unforgettable image. She burst into the soaring jetés of Isadora's revolutionary dance, her free plastique vibrant and compelling. In Béjart's *Bolero* she inimitably undercut the impassive sex appeal of an idol with a slight touch of human mischief.

Thanks to her persistence and her exceptional star status in Russia, she managed to show these "avant-garde" pieces at the Bolshoi as an imaginative antithesis to Grigorovich's style of socialist realism. There is a certain irony in the fact that Plisetskaya, kept for years from being seen by the Western public, now became a fervent champion of Western dance in the Soviet Union.

Her experience with Béjart's theatrical extravaganzas influenced her own second ballet, a version of Chekhov's *The Sea Gull*, set to the music of Shchedrin, in 1980. As if repeating the history of Chekhov's play, blasted at the time of its premiere in St. Petersburg, Plisetskaya's *Sea Gull* aroused a storm of controversy in Soviet periodicals. Some critics raved over her experiment in the field of "psychological drama" in ballet, created through a lexicon similar to that of Antony Tudor in *Jardin aux lilas*. Others disparaged Plisetskaya's straightforward realistic design for its effort to cover every aspect of Chekhov's first existential play. Still, *The Sea Gull* is an imaginative choreographic composition. Plisetskaya treated the work in a very personal key, focusing the drama on Nina Zarechnaya's conflicting feelings about her passion for Trigorin, her dreams of female fulfillment, and her all-absorbing passion for the new forms of expression she sought as an actress. Plisetskaya's performance as Nina was so moving and dramatic that one critic observed, "She takes us beyond dancing, beyond theatre, to a plane of symbolism all too rarely encountered in ballet."

As she ended her fortieth Bolshoi season, Plisetskaya was not even thinking of retiring. The Rome Opera had begun negotiations with the Soviet government over her appointment as artistic director of the Opera's ballet company. She regularly performs *Carmen*, *Anna Karenina*, and *The Sea Gull* at the Bolshoi and continues to tour in Japan, Italy, Greece, France, and Spain. On stage she seems almost alarmingly frail, and the lines of her neck and arms have taken on a swanlike vulnerability. Her former fortifying aggressiveness has mellowed; her tragic intensity has given way to pure lyricism tinged with doom—understandably so, since every performance could be her last. But her awesome personality has not changed: she is still the same indomitable, intractable Maya, with all her strong opinions, stormy affections, and faith in her destiny. She is still the ballerina whom we worshipped in Russia in the 1950s, sixties, and seventies, who never betrayed our expectations; the only ballerina whom all the great Russian dancers revere as "a precious phenomenon of balletic theatricality," as Baryshnikov once described her to me. In 1959, during the first Bolshoi engagement in New York, she was called "the Maria Callas of the ballet."

Indeed, she is another La Divina, the most powerful spirit in dance since Anna Pavlova, and, to date, the greatest of all the Russian ballerinas.

"THE WEEPING SPIRITS"

Olga Spessivtseva
Natalia Bessmertnova

OLGA SPESSIVTSEVA

HOWEVER TECHNICALLY imperfect Olga Spessivtseva's dancing may seem on film (the variation and mad scene from Act I of *Giselle* and a snippet of the Act II pas de deux have been preserved), she makes an indelible impression. With her small head, frail torso, and incredibly long legs she seems as vulnerable as a doe. The touching fearfulness in her movements, her delicacy and fragility—all that is so marvelously suggested by the Italian word *morbidezza*—were absolutely unique. Also inimitable were the sculpturesque shape of her legs, her extraordinary turnout and extension in développé, and her high-arched instep. The tender turn of her ankle would usually preclude soaring jumps, but Spessivtseva's dancing was graced by a rare ballon. Her toes do not seem to have been strong, but her light relevés on pointe and ballonnés were effortlessly executed. Her supple arms swayed like broken blossoms on long stalks; the expression of her "Persian" face and large black eyes was aloof and enigmatic. And all these qualities were somehow part of an utterly strange manner of dancing—painful and tormented, as if the ballerina performed under stress.

André Levinson wrote: "Genius would find a worthy habitation in the body of Spessivtseva. In her dwells a spirit which is strange, mournful, exhausted, resigned, sometimes even withdrawn.... Spessivtseva—dreaming and wounded, her head bent, her shoulders drooping a little—is she not rather the melancholy weeping willow dear to Musset? ... This woman—if I may be permitted to change a celebrated phrase—is a dancing reed."

When she danced, Spessivtseva seemed to express a foreboding of her fate: in 1937, at the age of forty-two, she left the stage, the victim of schizophrenia. She lives now on the Tolstoy Farm in a suburb of New York City, where I visited her in the summer of 1976. I was anxious to see a legend but afraid of meeting a ghost.

Contrary to my pessimistic expectations, Mme Spessivtseva, a gaunt, grey-haired, amiable lady of eighty, immediately began a spontaneous and animated conversation. Contemporary Russia seemed to interest her not at all, but she reacted vividly to ballet talk: "Diaghilev? What a charming man he was! Incidentally, he still owes me money.... Nijinsky? In *Spectre* when I was the slumbering demoiselle in the armchair, Vatsa was flitting above the stage, and through my eyelashes I merely had a glimpse of his gigantic shadow, swaying up and down, up and down. We danced in New York, by the way.... Egorova? She was an extraordinary lyrical ballerina, a lovely person, and gave remarkable yet very complicated lessons.... No, unfortunately I don't remember Vaganova well. She was very severe and screamed like a parrot during lessons.... Have you also danced in Petrograd? You do certainly remember how at the beginning of the 1930s ... "

Her Russian, distinguished and adorably old-fashioned, was entrancing to my ears. Her faded eyes were still striking, though they stared somewhere into the distance. I was eager to look into them, to catch a glimpse of the mystery enshrouding Spessivtseva's life and legend. I did not succeed in catching it, yet the mystery is still there.

OLGA ALEXANDROVNA SPESSIVTSEVA was born on July 5, 1895, at Rostov-on-the-Don, a provincial town in the south of Russia. Her father was a government official of some importance. Commanding a good bass-baritone voice, he sang in the church choir and in third-rate opera companies. At the age of thirty-two, he died of tuberculosis, leaving his wife with five children and no means of support. Olga, with her brother Anatole and sister Zinaïda—both of whom danced at the Maryinsky in the 1910s and 1920s—grew up in an orphanage affiliated with the Stage Veterans House in St. Petersburg.

In 1906 Spessivtseva was enrolled in the Imperial School, where she studied until 1913. At first she attended the classes of Julia Rykhliakova and Vera Zhukova; in later years her teachers were Mikhail Fokine and Klavdia Kulichevskaya, Petipa's assistant. Bronislava Nijinska, five years older than Olga, recalled her as an intelligent, sociable little girl, talkative and responsive.

Spessivtseva's career developed rather smoothly in Russia, despite the turmoil of the Revolution and the hardships and economic dislocation of civil war. She frequently toured abroad, but until 1924 she faithfully returned to her alma mater. Like Pavlova, during her brief forays into the West she desperately missed the grand-scale ensemble productions and the festive ritual atmosphere of the Mary-insky. Promotion came more easily to her than, for instance, to Pavlova or Karsavina. Spessivtseva had no rivals: Pavlova gave her last Russian performance in 1914; Karsavina left Russia forever in 1918, at the dawn of Olga's career. The once omnipotent Kschessinskaya had retired to her villa in the south of France.

At the pregraduate performances in 1913, Spessivtseva was noticed by the most eminent ballet critics, Valerian Svetlov and Akim Volynsky, and even by Vladimir Teliakovsky, the director of the Imperial Theatres. Volynsky, whose florid prose poems might form a nice tribute-album for Spessivtseva, wrote after her first appearance on stage: "Slender and frail, she danced in the old dreamy and finicky manner of Taglioni. . . . In the pas de deux with Anatole Oboukhoff she was as charming as a picture suddenly brought to life."

At her graduation performance in April 1913, Spessivtseva danced the Queen of the White Night in Kulichevskaya's one-act ballet *Le Conte d'une nuit blanche.* (Also in the cast were Felia Doubrovska, Alexandra Danilova, and Anatole Oboukhoff, Olga's partner.) The following September, as a member of the corps de ballet, she made her debut in Act II of *Raymonda.* Petipa's colleague Sergei Khudekov took note of the aloofness that from the outset marked Spessivtseva's style: "She has acquired a special approach to performing both classical variations and character dances, somewhere between mannerism and sloppiness. At times in her solos she neglects the music and disregards stylistic boundaries in a way that borders on sheer ignorance."

The young Spessivtseva was measured against Pavlova and did not benefit by the comparison. She was considered too subdued—perhaps indifferent, but perhaps prevented by some invisible force from becoming involved in her dancing.

In October 1913 Spessivtseva danced the Snow variation in *The Seasons.* Volynsky reacted immediately: "Her little Snow was pure and fluffy, but owing to the sorrowful expression on her face it seemed to be dimmed, as if shadowed by a floating cloud." Moreover, Spessivtseva's technique still left something to be desired: her dancing was either slipshod or exaggeratedly erratic. When she appeared in the *Swan Lake* pas de trois, Volynsky scolded her for her untidy performance. This tendency also marred her appearances in *Don Quixote* and Saint-Léon's *Fiammetta,* so that when, in the autumn of 1915, she made her debut as

Diamond Fairy in *The Sleeping Beauty,* the audience was totally surprised by the precision of her grands jetés and sculptural attitudes. This technical breakthrough is usually credited to her classes with Vaganova, who wrought a real miracle of discipline with Spessivtseva's body. But, to tell the truth, Spessivtseva was never to become a flawless "academic" ballerina. Her technique was uneven, capriciously vacillating between perfection and sheer sloppiness.

Spessivtseva's first real success occurred in May 1916, when she danced both the adagio from the Kingdom of the Shades with Oboukhoff and Pierrette in Petipa's *Les Millions d'Arlequin.* Her Pierrette was adorable, full of graceful mischief; but it was her Nikiya that struck the audience as a revelation. Volynsky wrote:

The duet suggested an art of formal purity rarely attained by experienced ballerinas. It is a long while since I have seen such perfect pirouettes on the Maryinsky stage. The little girl turned easily and freely without any support from her partner, executing exemplary pirouettes with total control over her muscles. The beauty of her arabesques rivaled Pavlova's. Her leg, outstretched in the air, was straight and strong as steel. Each pose was measured and firm. Although she does not fully possess the technique of elevation, her jumps were aesthetically flawless. But an outstanding quality of Spessivtseva's art is her serious, almost ritually solemn approach to dancing. Everything is paced in her delivery, down to the tiniest detail.

The same year, Nicholas Sergeyev recommended that Spessivtseva be promoted to première danseuse. She was the toast of Petrograd, and Diaghilev, who was organizing an American tour and having problems with Karsavina, made several attempts to engage Spessivtseva as prima ballerina. Influenced by Volynsky, who disapproved of Diaghilev's "extravaganza," she first rejected the offer, preferring "to serve the temple of classical dance as a priestess instead of entertaining the public at the Vanity Fair of Europe," as she said in one of her interviews. Nonetheless, Diaghilev's personal secretary, Walter Nouvel, privately obtained from her a commitment to make her debut at the Manhattan Opera House in October 1916.

The American tour disappointed her. Unsure of Spessivtseva's availability, Diaghilev had also engaged Lydia Lopokhova, with whom she had to share the repertory: Fokine's

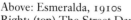

Above: Esmeralda, 1910s
Right: (top) The Street Dancer in *Don Quixote*, 1910s;
(bottom) Esmeralda, 1910s

Above: Odette, 1930s
Right: Giselle, 1930s

Above: Odette, with Anatole Vilzak as Siegfried, 1930s
Left: Odette, with Serge Lifar as Siegfried, late 1920s

Giselle, 1920s

OPPOSITE
The Creatures of Prometheus, 1930

Les Sylphides, La Princesse enchantée (the Blue Bird pas de deux from *The Sleeping Beauty*), which she danced with Nijinsky at the Brooklyn Academy of Music, and *Le Spectre de la rose*. Nijinsky's androgynous apparition and Spessivtseva's dreamy maiden evoked a Hoffmannesque vision of two spectres, the embodiment of desire, and the chastity of Romantic ballet. Nevertheless, Spessivtseva as a ballerina somehow got lost in Nijinsky's gigantic flitting shadow.

At the beginning of 1917, Spessivtseva returned to Petrograd, where she became the brightest star of the former Maryinsky. In 1918 she was given many new roles: the Sugar Plum Fairy in *The Nutcracker*, with Pierre Vladimiroff; the prelude in *Chopiniana*, in which she seemed oddly unable to grasp Fokine's style; and the Grand Pas Classique from *Paquita*, which demanded a technical virtuosity she never possessed. But she had her greatest success in the role for which she seemed least suited—Esmeralda in the old Perrot ballet that Petipa had restaged for Kschessinskaya. Spessivtseva performed it for the first time in November 1918. Technically, the role, reshaped for Kschessinskaya's virtuosity, was beyond her—it required powerful toes, terre-à-terre brilliance, the strength of an arched instep. Nevertheless, she put Kschessinskaya to shame in her most famous role, forcing the critics at last to recognize Spessivtseva's outstanding theatrical instincts. She portrayed Esmeralda as a vulnerable, innocent gypsy girl, consumed by her passion for the brilliant but shallow officer. Perhaps the sufferings she experienced in her love affair with Zinoviev's secretary, Boris Kaplun (with whom, several years later, Lidia Ivanova was also unhappily involved), imparted its poignancy to her interpretation; in any case, her personal involvement was so intense that she ended the performance in tears.

Despite her success Spessivtseva was aware of her technical deficiences, and in 1919 she began to study again with Vaganova. After spending several months strengthening her toes and torso and developing various turns, she decided to attempt Giselle, although she was profoundly apprehensive of the role. Pavlova's and Karsavina's extraordinary interpretations still lingered in the minds of the public; moreover, Spessivtseva mistrusted her own theatrical instincts. To sharpen the details of her characterization, she visited a mental institution, studying the patients' gait, gestures, and facial expressions.

Spessivtseva made her debut in *Giselle* in March 1919, partnered by Pierre Vladimiroff. Detachment, unwillingness to dance—these particular traits of Spessivtseva's the-atrical manner helped her create a Giselle whose mind seemed to vacillate between reality and her dream life. When she first emerged from her hut to meet Albrecht, the audience was almost appalled at the sight of her emaciated body, her angularity, the lack of coordination in her movements, her distant, confused eyes. Her Giselle breathed genuine insanity, not a theatrical illusion. It was as if this role pulled loose some hidden personal spring in the artist's psychological mechanism which, unwinding, unleashed its latent destructive force. Spessivtseva's biographer André Shaikevitch noted that the wonder of her Giselle stemmed from the flawless balance of her Romantic style and her inner pathology. The slightest exaggeration might have turned the performance into parody, but this did not happen: Giselle seemed to be an extension of Spessivtseva's own existence. As Petrushka had done for Nijinsky, Giselle served Spessivtseva as a psychological catalyst.

The energy of latent insanity held the audience spellbound. Spessivtseva executed her variation not as a peasant girl but as a woman who was already a Wili. In the mad scene she conveyed the poignancy of her twilight existence in a profusion of naturalistic details. "The gait grew weak, the feet turned numb. Her thin body seemed to shrink like a little white cloud. What tear-stained childlike eyes with a fiery gleam of fright, framed by her unbound, swaying hair!" Thus Volynsky depicted Spessivtseva in his typical hyperbolic style. Elsewhere he called her Giselle "a weeping spirit, bemoaning the boundaries of its being."

In Act II she truly seemed not a human being but an unearthly creature in the grip of death. The critic Valerian Bogdanov-Berezovsky wrote: "The lightness of her elevation was almost inconceivable; her profile and en face poses on stage seemed ghostlike and transparent. When she slowly emerged from the grave and timidly approached Myrtha . . . she seemed to be a figment of our imaginations, alluring and mysterious. Her gestures were demonic and sharp; her exultation powerfully disturbed our sensitivity, at times extending beyond the limits of art."

According to many cognoscenti, Spessivtseva's Giselle was even more perfect and supernatural than Pavlova's. Her diagonals of soaring jetés were breathtaking; her duet with Albrecht, with the spectacular lifts of the original choreography deleted, suggested the communion of a human being and a spirit.

In the spring of 1920 Spessivtseva was promoted to the rank of prima ballerina. In February she appeared as Medora in *Le Corsaire* and in November as Nikiya in *La Baya-*

dère. Her artistry was evident in the Kingdom of the Shades, but the role as a whole eluded her. She was awkward in the mime scenes, and her attempt at an Oriental style was unconvincing. Moreover, after years of hunger and deprivation during the civil war, Spessivtseva's health had deteriorated, and she was simply unable to cope with this technically exhausting role. She contracted tuberculosis during the 1920–21 season and left Petrograd for the Caucasus. It was rumored that she would be unable to continue her career, but she recovered; what is more, ignoring Volynsky's admonitions, she accepted Diaghilev's invitation to dance in his new London production of *The Sleeping Princess*, as he had rechristened *The Sleeping Beauty*.

Despite the fact that Diaghilev had collected the crème de la crème of Russian dance in exile—Vladimiroff, Anatole Vilzak, Doubrovska, Ludmilla Schollar—and notwithstanding the refined extravagance of Bakst's scenery and costumes, Spessivtseva was uncomfortable in this elegant and whimsical production and felt no affinity for the character of Aurora. In November 1921 she appeared as Aurora at London's Alhambra Theatre; for this occasion Diaghilev shortened her name to Olga Spessiva. The production was a succès d'estime, and in the words of one critic, "Mlle Spessiva's dancing was the ballet's chief attraction." But another writer recalled: "The stage machinery was inoperative, so the forest failed to grow. Moreover, as Aurora, Spessivtseva was frequently at a loss. Balance eluded her in the Rose Adagio; instead of smiling at her cavaliers, she frowned; in the Danse Vertige she overacted. She gave the impression that she was asleep during the whole performance and never awoke."

The only advantage of London, where Spessivtseva felt lonely and out of place, lay in Cecchetti's classes, which she took every day. The old maestro revealed to her his unique recipes for virtuosity, the benefit of which she displayed in her performance of Aurora at the former Maryinsky in October 1922. The critics praised her unanimously, but Spessivtseva soon dropped the role. During the next two seasons she added Aspicia in *Pharaoh's Daughter*, Kitri, and Odette-Odile to her repertory.

It was expected that her unique flowing lines would make her Odette very special, but the miracle did not happen. Her "weeping spirit" was muted. Even her devoted Volynsky criticized the ballerina for "inner emptiness, though she danced with impeccable technique." "Everything was flawless," he complained. "Only one thing was missing—the Swan, who was invisible from the outset. . . . One could

enjoy any kind of formal, physical beauty except that of the Swan." It seemed that Odette's drama, the torment of her captive spirit, failed to register in Spessivtseva's mind. Rather, she emphasized the Swan Queen's detached passivity, her nonparticipation and alienation. Her Odette was often described as a bird with clipped or wounded wings. The Prince and Rothbart seemed to exist beyond her; she was involved in their struggle by sheer chance. And as Odile, on the other hand, she indulged in mannered histrionics.

In *Swan Lake* Spessivtseva's utterly personal approach came into irreconcilable conflict with the choreographic design. For the first time she failed utterly in a major role. Her despondency grew. In 1924 she accepted an invitation to perform *Giselle* at the Paris Opéra, hoping to escape both the Maryinsky routine and her unhappy love affair with Boris Kaplun. She arrived in Paris in a state of psychological disarray which intensified her poignant projection even at rehearsals. Colette Salamon, who danced at the Opéra then, remembered: "We had arrived towards the end of the first act and for the first time Olga Spessivtseva mimed and danced before the entire corps the famous *scène de la folie*, in a silence so profound that the rehearsal room seemed more like a church in its solemn and holy atmosphere of religion. At the end of this wonderful scene . . . no one moved; a deathly quiet prevailed. The agony and sorrow of the lost love that she had so terrifyingly recalled in her mime and action kept us all transfixed, motionless, except for the tears in our eyes."

She danced her first Giselle at the Opéra in November, and had Paris at her feet. André Levinson wrote: "She is unique and singular; hers is the type of beauty created by Taglioni. The elongated and vibrant line, the human form idealized even to the point of exaggeration, has the contour of an angelic sprite. The delicacy, the touching fragility of this new Giselle seems even a little unhealthy. . . . There is none of that turbulence of soul that whirls through Pavlova." Spessivtseva continued to dance *Giselle* in Paris until the end of December, always deepening the pathological aspect of her role.

Giselle was followed by various ephemera: Clustine's *Suite de Danses*, Leo Staats's *Soir de fête* and Bronislava Nijinska's *Les Rencontres*. Spessivtseva did not shine in any of them. Nijinska's syncopated rhythm and turned-in style did not stir her imagination. She asked Nicholas Sergeyev to revive Saint-Léon's antediluvian *The Little Humpbacked Horse* for her. Sir Oswald Stoll, anxious to get her to dance in London, resisted this peculiar project; but the ballerina demanded full-length ballets with dramatic plots. She suggested that he remount Perrot's *Esmeralda*, but no one remembered it in London (where, incidentally, the ballet had been created in 1844).

Spessivtseva loathed one-act ballets, although she had little choice at the Paris Opéra. At the request of the Opéra's director, Jacques Rouché, Leo Staats mounted *La Péri* for her, to the music of Paul Dukas—a trivial post-Romantic vignette; it was followed by *Les Abeilles*, another short piece by Staats, in the same contrived style. Spessivtseva's frail, aloof beauty ravished the audience, but she danced perfunctorily, and the ballet soon sank into oblivion.

Now began the tragedy that Spessivtseva shared with many Russian emigrés who had regarded the West as a paradise where all their dreams would easily come true. Disappointed, lacking realistic advice, Spessivtseva started to make her way at random. To Russia and her painful past she did not want to return; in 1926 the Bolsheviks made repatriation impossible. As Roman Jasinsky recalled: "Olga was an overgrown child—naive, impatient, and tormented. In addition, she was an incorrigible perfectionist and wanted the best without delay."

Her path once again crossed that of Diaghilev. In December 1926 and January 1927 she performed with the Ballets Russes in Turin and at La Scala in Milan. The mixed bill could not satisfy her lofty aspirations: Massine's *Firebird*, *Swan Lake* Act II with Serge Lifar as her partner, the Act III divertissement of *The Sleeping Beauty* (now called *Aurora's Wedding* by Diaghilev). Her frustration increased, goaded by her total incomprehension of Massine's choreography. Once again she took class from Cecchetti, who had settled in Milan; she made amazing progress, learning to do triple pirouettes and double tours en attitude flawlessly and effortlessly.

Later in 1927 Spessivtseva danced with the Diaghilev troupe in Monte Carlo, Cannes, and Marseilles. In April she appeared in the premiere of Balanchine's *La Chatte*. "Olga's dancing was a revelation," remarked her biographer and frequent partner, Anton Dolin. "She had, in some uncanny way, with no exaggeration of body or face, transformed herself into a cat, feline and seductive."

After Spessivtseva's tremendous success in *La Chatte*, Diaghilev, eager to keep her as a prima ballerina and box-office draw, published this paean to her in *Le Figaro*:

I have always believed that in the life of a man there is a limit to joys; that to one generation it was permitted to admire only one Taglioni or to hear only one Patti.

Having seen Pavlova in her youth and in mine, I was sure that this was the Taglioni of my life. My astonishment was then unbounded when I met Spessivtseva, a creature finer and even purer than Pavlova. There is this to be said. Our great master of the dance, Cecchetti, who created Nijinsky, Karsavina, and so many others, said during the course of one of his lessons at La Scala in Milan: "An apple has come into the world; when one cuts it in two, one half becomes Anna Pavlova, the other Spessivtseva." I should add that for me Spessivtseva is the side that has been exposed to the sun.

If the great impresario intended to say, in his noble attempt to cheer up his despondent ballerina, that Spessivtseva's talent was riper or more lively than Pavlova's, he was definitely wrong. Spessivtseva's genius had much narrower confines than Pavlova's, who excelled equally in Romantic, neoclassical, and character dance. This is why Pavlova, with her multifaceted personality, her verve and straightforward emotionality, created a public for ballet around the world. Spessivtseva's "weeping spirit" stirred the imagination of the highbrows, the aesthetes and intellectuals, but her scope was much more limited.

Spessivtseva again broke off her relationship with Diaghilev, thus depriving herself of further opportunity to work with Balanchine—one can only lament the fact that she never danced his *Apollo* or *Prodigal Son*. Instead she returned to the Opéra to perform *La Péri* and *Giselle* and to appear quite successfully in Nicholas Guerra's *La Tragédie de Salomé* (music by Florent Schmitt), although she could not surpass Ida Rubinstein, for whom *Salomé* had been designed.

Despite his resentment of her defection, Diaghilev planned to produce *Giselle* for Spessivtseva in a new version by Kasyan Goleizovsky, who was supposed to come to Paris from Moscow. Spessivtseva had great hopes for this production, but Diaghilev's death in 1929 put an abrupt end to her expectations.

Again she returned to the Opéra, where Balanchine began to mount *The Creatures of Prometheus* for her; but he suddenly fell ill, and Serge Lifar completed the ballet. This led to another battle, this time with Lifar, who composed his ballets primarily for himself, relegating the ballerina to a secondary place. He infuriated Spessivtseva, a true disciple of Petipa, who viewed the male dancer only as a support for the ballerina's artistry. As a result of this rupture she was no longer welcome at the Opéra. In March 1932 she bade the Opéra farewell as Giselle.

Now her years of wandering truly began; paradoxically, it was now that she attained the peak of her artistry. Two years earlier she had appeared at the London Coliseum in Nijinska's *Paysage Enfantin*, a trifle in which she was in Nijinska's words, "so light with those lovely, elegant pointes, perfect pirouettes, and long sustained arabesques." In 1931 she danced at the Teatro Colón in Buenos Aires. Fokine himself rehearsed her in *Les Sylphides*, *The Firebird*, *Carnaval*, and *Schéhérazade*. The last, one of Tamara Karsavina's finest roles, was a vehicle for the display of pictorial qualities—never Spessivtseva's forte.

Spessivtseva's gleaming talent was muted and tarnished in these roles. In 1932 she appeared in London with the newly formed Camargo Society, established to fill the void left by Diaghilev's death. She performed *Swan Lake* Act II and *Giselle* with the first English Albrecht, Anton Dolin, and attained the summit of her glory, artistry—and despair.

She was thirty-seven, totally alone, without artistic guidance or protection; her innermost feelings of unfulfillment shattered her self-confidence. The next five years unfolded as a dismal coda to her career. By an irony of fate, she associated herself with the Ballet Russe Classique, a small company organized by Victor Dandré as a replica of Pavlova's troupe. Now Spessivtseva was obliged to follow in the footsteps of Anna Pavlova and compete with her legend, while in her private life her own Dandré appeared in the guise of Leonard Braun, an American businessman. He became her father figure, manager, and common-law husband. This relationship, which lasted until Braun's death in 1942, provided financial security and friendship, but it did not alleviate Spessivtseva's emotional torment.

In October 1934 she made her debut with Dandré's troupe at the Theatre Royal in Sydney in a program that included *Les Sylphides*, *Carnaval*, the Grand Pas Classique from *Raymonda*, and the Dance of the Hours from *La Gioconda*. But Spessivtseva's struggle to be equal to her talent could never be won in the face of such unequal odds, both artistic and psychological. These performances must have taken a tremendous toll. In November, during the Dance of the Hours, Spessivtseva—frustrated, depressed, and paranoid—broke down on stage.

She struggled on for several years, attempting to form her own company, giving her last performance in July 1937, at the Teatro Politeama Buenos Aires. And then the denouement of her tragedy: the Hudson River State Hospital for the Insane at Poughkeepsie.

The "weeping spirit" that she had created on stage finally merged with the mysterious sources from which it so enigmatically arose.

Giselle, mid-1970s

NATALIA BESSMERTNOVA

BESSMERTNOVA'S STAGE IMAGE, especially in Romantic arabesques or jetés, strikingly recalls Olga Spessivtseva's: the same "Persian" face and suffering dark eyes, smiling, if at all, with a hint of tears. Her ideally long-lined body seems frail; her strong yet slender and unmuscular legs, well-developed ankles, and marvelously shaped feet with moderately etched insteps afford her both soaring jumps and sharp, dynamic turns. But Bessmertnova's most amazing characteristic is her thin arms, long out of all proportion. They soar upward and bend at the wrists like long stems that have broken at the place where they bear the flower, imparting a nuance of vulnerability and femi-

nine submissiveness to her dancing. Together with her charged, floating jump, these qualities define Bessmertnova as the ideal incarnation of the true Romantic ballerina. In one sense, however, this ease of categorization and her lyrical gift were something of a handicap to her; at the outset of her career Bessmertnova was limited to the old Romantic repertory—*Giselle*, *Les Sylphides*—and to neo-Romantic miniatures.

Two qualities rarely found together are combined in her dancing: lightness and a legato flow of movements. During the 1960s her technique surpassed that of Natalia Makarova, her Leningrad rival, although like Spessivtseva's her style was remarkably aloof and dreamily detached, as if she were engaged in an invisible interior struggle. Her appeal stemmed precisely from her seemingly "doomed" frailty, yet her plasticity differed from Spessivtseva's in its erotically tinged Orientalism, its sensual languor, subdued and enticing. This quality somehow softened her aloofness and singled her out as a most seductive and appealing ballerina among her tempestuous Russian colleagues.

N ATALIA IGOREVNA BESSMERTNOVA was born in Moscow on July 19, 1941, into a family that was not part of the ballet world. Her infatuation with dancing began in childhood, grew through amateur performances at school and at a Young Pioneers club, and finally bloomed at the Moscow Choreographic School, in which she enrolled in 1952.

Bessmertnova was a product of Moscow training, but, strangely enough, the coarse Bolshoi style never rubbed off on her. She seemed to be the offspring of St. Petersburg's classicism rather than of Moscow's spectacular gaudiness. At the Moscow Choreographic School she studied under Kozhukhova and Sofia Golovkina. Only Bessmertnova's exceptional physique and her innate aristocratic finesse enabled her to resist the show-stopping vulgarity that was Golovkina's hallmark.

In June 1961 the young Bessmertnova gave her graduation performance in *Etude*, a choreographic miniature set to Liszt, and in a variation from *Don Quixote*. Just two weeks later she performed the Mazurka and the C-sharp-minor Waltz from *Chopiniana* at the Bolshoi. What eventually was to be appreciated as Bessmertnova's personal allure puzzled her first audience: her gangly, adolescent thinness, her angular awkwardness, and her air of reverie somehow sounded an echo of the distant past. After her performances her admirers would pore over old dance books and antique Romantic etchings, hoping to establish the legitimacy of her style. Her impact was potent, especially in the Waltz, where her mysterious delicacy and lingering flights and landings, scarcely touching the boards, evoked for the audience the legendary Romantic shades. At times her image even looked stilted, as if overburdened by historical associations.

At one of her early performances I remember someone saying: "She resembles a primrose desperately striving to blossom out. Will she?" Watching the young Bessmertnova invariably proved to be a moving and poignant experience,

and each such experience foreshadowed her greatness as Giselle.

The still-budding ballerina took part in the 1961 Bolshoi tour of the United States, Canada, and England. She danced Autumn in *Cinderella*, one of the potential brides in *Swan Lake*, and one of Juliet's friends in *Romeo and Juliet*. Clement Crisp in London noted her as strikingly unusual in the trio of swans from *Swan Lake* Act II. Words like "magic, dreamy grace, the beauty of aloofness," began to appear in Bessmertnova's notices.

By about 1963 she was bringing a more significant profile to her exaggeratedly expressed Romantic qualities. She seemed so charmingly old-fashioned, so unlike the flamboyant Bolshoi style, that she was the talk of balletic Moscow: "Bessmertnova is like a Chopin melody bursting by mistake into a broadcast of a soccer game. This is a ballerina who has emerged from the visions of Heinrich Heine or Degas, or even as the blue Picasso dancer magically brought to life," Vadim Gayevsky observed.

In 1963 she made her long-awaited debut in *Giselle*, coached by Leonid Lavrovsky. One must be aware of the atmosphere at the Bolshoi in the 1960s and the cult of Ulanova's naturalistic Giselle in order to do full justice to Bessmertnova's innovative portrayal. Compared with Ulanova's interpretation, it seemed iconoclastic throughout. Bessmertnova's image was a far cry from Ulanova's simple, light-hearted peasant girl; rather, she evoked a shy, frightened bird. Her Giselle was a quaint creature from the start—odd, utterly detached from the world, she seemed to contain within herself the seeds of inevitable tragedy and doom. She was the most tragic, anguished, elusive Giselle on the Soviet stage.

Her characterization seemed to be motivated less by Albrecht's betrayal than by the perpetual anxiety and pain of a predestined Wili pining for her natural state. In Act I she diligently followed the order of the mime scene, but her downcast eyes, her reluctant manner of dancing, and her brittle arms breaking at the wrists all implied her fate. Bessmertnova accentuated not so much Giselle's timidity as her morbid strangeness; her attraction to Albrecht was rooted in her anticipation of spiritual union with a kindred soul. Her mind seemed to vacillate between the reality she was compelled to face and her inner twilight world. Her unpredictability created a special aura of suspense in the mad scene, which Bessmertnova danced with abandon and delirium.

In Act II Bessmertnova seemed to accept death as her

Right: Odette, 1970
Below: Giselle, with Mikhail Lavrovsky as Albrecht, 1976

OPPOSITE
Top: Shirin in *The Legend of Love*, with Maris Liepa as Ferhad, 1965
Bottom: (left) Anastasia in *Ivan the Terrible*, with Vladimir Vasiliev as
Ivan, mid-1970s; (right) Anastasia, with Yuri Vladimirov as Ivan,
1975

natural though transcendent condition. Opaque and elusive, she created an image of mystic intensity. This Giselle rescued her Albrecht from the vengeance of the Wilis not for love but in memory of their former spiritual kinship and the hopes that had died with her earthly aspect. She seemed to enjoy her spectral state, flitting amid the throng of her ghostly companions, beyond love or hatred, forgiveness or revenge.

Bessmertnova's mystical interpretation deepened from one performance to the next, while her Albrechts (Mikhail Lavrovsky or Maris Liepa) carried on the traditional drama of repentance that she seemed to transcend. Possibly only Baryshnikov, her partner at the Kirov during the early 1970s, matched her Giselle perfectly. Such an unworldly, Romantic figure might well have ignited Baryshnikov's poetic imagination and haunted his Albrecht. In fact, in their performances Giselle seemed to be the figment of Albrecht's turbulent emotions; only the white sepulchral flowers hinted at the physical reality of their relationship.

Like Spessivtseva, Bessmertnova reached an artistic summit as Giselle that she was never able to attain in other roles, although she was remarkable in many. One such role was Leili in Goleizovsky's *Leili and Mejnun* (1964). In this ballet Bessmertnova portrayed an Oriental princess who loves the poet Kais, called Mejnun ("the possessed"), although she is betrothed to a wealthy man. As if testing the twenty-three-year-old ballerina's ability to alter her established Romantic image, Goleizovsky's choreography deliberately deprived Bessmertnova of her soaring jump. Her plasticity was placed in the context of stylized but erotic movements recalling ancient Persian miniatures. Unlike Vladimir Vasiliev's psychologically profound Kais, Bessmertnova's characterization was elusive, more the incarnation of diffident unrequited passion than anything else. In her first duet with Vasiliev, a stream of flowing neoclassical steps, Bessmertnova's appealing bashful femininity could be sensed in the way she timidly yet passionately clung to her beloved. Her Leili was a visual metaphor of Oriental sensuality; her success in this role stemmed from the perfect balance of her subtlety and the implicit qualities of Goleizovsky's choreography.

Unlike many other Soviet ballerinas, Bessmertnova's personality was revealed in the element of pure dance rather than burdensome drama-ballet. Choreography that served simply to advance the plot rather than to illuminate emotional states tarnished the luster of her talent: in Leonid Lavrovsky's full-length *Romeo and Juliet* she looked awkward and restrained, but her personality radiated in his condensed television version, which paraphrased the theme without spelling out the whole story. Portraying characters was always less congenial to her than evoking the metaphysical essences of the legendary heroines. At times she herself seemed to be the reincarnated shade of Taglioni or Pavlova.

The Oriental princess Shirin in Grigorovich's *Legend of Love* (1965) was a one-dimensional copy of Leili. The choreography called for a frolicsome Oriental character with a soubrettelike, coquettish air, which was unfortunately beyond Bessmertnova's range. She is not, in fact, a dancing actress. Her characterizations become larger-than-life projections only when the choreography eschews a definitive dramatic message; only then can her stage image intimate facets of girlish diffidence and subdued eroticism.

In Grigorovich's schematic creations for the Bolshoi, Bessmertnova has often seemed at a loss and miscast. This is all the sadder because in Petipa's academic repertory (as revised by Grigorovich) her projection seems to lose its power. Her Florine in Grigorovich's first *Sleeping Beauty* (1963) and her Aurora in his second version (1973) were simply unconvincing. Her self-absorbed, rather dolorous Florine was out of place in the festive atmosphere of the Act III divertissement, and her Aurora was a startlingly gloomy and arrogant princess. The favorite of the fairies and recipient of their gifts, she seemed to have been told only of the curse of Carabosse. The elegiac flavor of her image was poignant but inappropriate in the Rose Adagio, and in the final pas de deux her Aurora seemed unable to forget a past that marred the happiness of the present.

In Petipa's ballets Bessmertnova has overemphasized her Romantic projection, at times allowing the audience to forget that, rare among genuine Romantic ballerinas, she commands a first-rate academic technique. (At her graduation exams her impeccably executed forty-eight fouettés had astounded the Bolshoi old-timers.) This emphasis on the Romantic element was actually damaging to the balance Petipa struck between the dramatic plot and the choreography it was meant to serve. In this respect her characterization of Odette-Odile was especially inadequate. In both Gorsky's and Grigorovich's productions of *Swan Lake* Bessmertnova neglected the stylistic requirements. She lent a morbid grace to her Odette by accentuating her "weeping wrists," evoking "the image of a crane's wings rather than a swan's," as one critic observed. She brought a nervous, staccato rhythm to the sequence of slow ronds de jambe and sissonnes in the Act II adagio, as if their legato design positively annoyed her. Moreover, in this act she underscored Odette's doom so potently as to obliterate the ensuing development of the drama, which ought to be full of subtle transitions from despair to hope, or from resignation to the triumph of love in death. Her Odile looked like Odette in different clothes; she even managed to add a touch of rue to her temptation of Siegfried. A mournful stranger, she gazed at the Prince, her dark eyes expressing hidden pain and anxiety.

Bessmertnova's inadequacies were even more poignant in *Don Quixote*. She attempted to portray Kitri abstractly, unfortunately rendering the Spanish scamp anonymous and bland. Her Romantic style gave the entire ballet a misleadingly ethereal aspect. Gayevsky incisively observed that "through her characterization, Bessmertnova singlehandedly returned Gorsky's Spanish theatricality to Petipa's Romantic original. Bessmertnova's Kitri is essentially the Dryad, if it is possible to imagine a dryad hopping around with castanets or performing thirty-two fouettés." It was, in fact, hardly possible at all; Bessmertnova's remote Kitri did not fit the mischievous atmosphere of Gorsky's *españolada*.

Her appearance in *Don Quixote* proved that her theatrical impulse was limited, a fact that Grigorovich (perhaps because he is her husband) always seemed to disregard. He cast his wife in all his productions, to her obvious detriment: *The Nutcracker* (1966), *Spartacus* (1968), *Ivan the Terrible* (1975), and *Angara* (1976). Repeating what he had done with Vasiliev, Grigorovich exploited Bessmertnova's unique qualities to cover his own choreographic deficiencies. But unlike Vasiliev, whose multifaceted theatricality enabled him to sparkle in the midst of Grigorovich's inflations, Bessmertnova was bound to be defeated by these roles.

In *Spartacus* her Phrygia, the cardboard lover of the Roman slaves' cardboard leader, was given the most hackneyed choreography to convey dramatic truisms. In *Ivan the Terrible* she desperately strove to imbue with her charming vulnerability the Tsarina's trite circuits of glissades and arabesques. I have been told that in Grigorovich's most recent ballet, *Angara*, with its melodramatic plot unfolding against the background of a hydroelectric plant under construction, she portrayed "a rather conventional Soviet girl through the concoction of balletic trivialities." Grigorovich's new version of *Romeo and Juliet* was a work of sense-less and banal choreography in which Bessmertnova, outlandishly costumed in a Romantic tutu, performed neo-classical steps laced with vulgar realistic movements. Shown in New York in September 1979, her Juliet, in my view, proved to be Bessmertnova's most deplorable defeat, almost enough to annihilate her balletic image for all time.

Her Masha in *Nutcracker* was the most compelling role Grigorovich gave her. To this portrayal Bessmertnova brought facets of her Giselle—her introverted character, her intense inner life full of hopes and poetic insights incompatible with reality. Bessmertnova's frail, dark-eyed Masha recalled Natasha Rostova in *War and Peace* with all her whimsical individuality. She conveyed the vulnerable sensitivity of a childish soul on the threshold of illusionless maturity, responding perfectly to Tchaikovsky's music.

The distinctiveness of Bessmertnova's rare talent turned out, in a way, to be an artistic disadvantage. Throughout her career she remained ill at ease in the Bolshoi's large-scale full-length productions. She was unable to diversify her projection, to prevent a certain monotony from creeping into the evening-long works. Her subtle talent resonated with poetic force in shorter pieces such as *Le Spectre de la Rose* or *Ondine*. In *Spectre* even her poses were fascinating, and not only because of their evocative resemblance to those of the glorious Romantic ballerinas of the past. Her nervous intensity and air of charmingly frail femininity, as she stood at the window pensively gazing at the moonlit garden, made the Spectre seem to be a visible extension of her subtle erotic reverie.

Among her contemporaries in Russia, Bessmertnova seems to be the only ballerina who might be able to evoke Anna Pavlova's image on the screen. She was a candidate for the role in an Anglo-Soviet film biography, but, regrettably, she was not chosen. Undoubtedly, she would have been in her element, giving us fresh insights into Pavlova's *Dying Swan* and *La Nuit*, for one aspect of Pavlova's art, intensely tragic and poetically evocative, was fully refracted through Bessmertnova's image.

Strangely enough, these qualities of Bessmertnova's dancing were not made use of at the Bolshoi in the seventies, the years that should have been her artistic peak. In later years she has not created anything to match her great achievements of the early sixties—Giselle and Leili, with which she will always be identified.

THE IDEAL SOUBRETTES AND INGENUES

Vera Trefilova · Irina Kolpakova
Ekaterina Maximova

ТРЕФИЛОВА.

8776

VERA TREFILOVA

PORCELAIN COMPLEXION, black hair, beautiful pale gypsy face and black velvety eyes—she looks at you from the glossy postcards that St. Petersburgers used as Easter greetings or party invitations. She might be mistaken for a dramatic actress or an operatic diva, but in fact Vera Trefilova was the ballerina of whom Cyril Beaumont said: "She danced with such self-command, confidence, and ease, with such ravishing precision, subjugating her body to her will so perfectly, that she made the audience appreciate as never before the beauty of geometry in dance, performed by a true classical ballerina."

VERA ALEXANDROVNA TREFILOVA was born in 1875 in Vladikavkaz, a provincial Russian town, into a family with an established theatrical pedigree. Her mother was an actress, and her godmother was one of Russia's greatest actresses, Maria Savina. In 1887 Trefilova rehearsed the role of Aniutka in a St. Petersburg production of Tolstoy's drama *Power of the Dark*. Had the Tsar's censors not banned the play, perhaps the youngster would have followed in the footsteps of her mother and godmother. But Cecchetti's powerful jumps and whirlwind pirouettes, seen by Vera when she was eight, had already made such an impression on her that she decided to commit herself to ballet. In 1884 she was accepted into the Imperial Theatre School by her future teacher Ekaterina Vazem, who saw the promise in the girl's slightly flabby legs, her strong back, natural turnout, and remarkably harmonious lines. Obviously Trefilova's encounter with Vazem had a great effect on her development as a dancer. A mediocre actress but an impeccable technician, Vazem subjected her pupil to the rigor of her own method, shaping the young Vera in her own image. Trefilova progressed slowly and never really developed any sense of dramatic projection.

When she joined the Maryinsky corps in 1894, Trefilova was given small demi-caractère parts: a confidante of Swanilda in *Coppélia*, a gypsy girl in *Paquita*, one of the twenty-six butterflies in *Les Caprices du Papillon*, and ensemble roles in operas such as *Carmen* and *Faust*. The atmosphere at the Maryinsky was intensely competitive. The lean, sportive virtuoso Legnani reigned supreme, although she was challenged by the sparkling young Kschessinskaya and by Olga Preobrajenskaya with her strong pointe work and fabulous legato. All the coveted places were more or less divided among these ballerinas, and it was only in 1898 that Trefilova appeared in her first role as a soloist, Hymen in Ivanov's *Acis and Galatea*. (She had previously performed the Silver Fairy in *Sleeping Beauty*, one of the cygnets in *Swan Lake*, and the Peasant pas de deux in *Giselle*.) Nikolai Bezobrazov wrote at the time: "Trefilova has a certain appeal on the stage, her dancing is correct; but she is somewhat poor in terms of dance sweep, and her port de bras is rather deplorable."

Trefilova herself was aware of her limited technique. As she recalled in 1926, "Although my toes were strong, and I was able to execute many intricate steps, the pirouettes in attitude in *Giselle* and the piqués en tournant eluded me. In 1897 I decided to take classes from Maestro Cecchetti." She continued to polish her technique, enhanced by Cecchetti, in the classrooms of La Scala with Caterina Beretta and then with Rosita Mauri in Paris. Just before she was promoted to ballerina in 1906, she began to work with Nicolas Legat, who pronounced her "an ideal soubrette." Under his guidance she danced the Canary Fairy and the White Cat in *Sleeping Beauty*, the Flower Seller in *Marco Bomba*, the river Congo in *Pharaoh's Daughter*, Hail in *The Seasons*, and Columbine in *The Nutcracker*. By all reports she danced these roles properly but without inspiration, concentrating more on technical survival than on artistic projection.

In the early 1900s Trefilova's position at the Maryinsky was jeopardized by an influx of talented young dancers. She was now being pushed to the periphery not only by Preobrajenskaya and Kschessinskaya but by Pavlova, Egorova, Vaganova, and Sedova (whose ballon rivaled Nijinsky's, but whose total lack of individuality prevented her from becoming a great ballerina). Like Egorova, Trefilova was saddled with small parts for years; but even in the roles suitable to her (Swanilda in *Coppélia* or Teresa in *The Cavalry Halt*), her effect was muted, as if she were afraid to put her individual stamp on them. The critics usually complained about her insufficient dramatic projection but were enthusiastic about her impeccable tours and swift jumps.

Clockwise from top right: The Street Dancer in *Don Quixote*; Graziella; unidentified role; The Danse Manu in *La Bayadère*, all 1890s

When compared with her young colleagues, such as Lidia Kyasht or Tamara Karsavina, Trefilova's technical superiority was obvious. In his review of *La Source* in December 1902, Alexander Pleschayev remarked: "Misses Trefilova, Kyasht, and Karsavina had a great success. It goes without saying that in terms of technique and care for details, Miss Trefilova surpassed both still-budding ballerinas."

As artistry became Trefilova's major concern, the critics noted her "awakening personality" more frequently. About *Le Roi Candaule* in 1903 Valerian Svetlov said that Trefilova, depicting "*la naissance du papillon* as a charming little choreographic picture, was a ravishing, beautiful, and modest butterfly, infusing the role with a chaste feeling of the joyful awakening of life."

From 1902 to 1905 Trefilova continued to establish herself as a soubrette, adding to her repertory Pierrette in *Les Millions d'Arlequin*, the pert Giannina in the Perrot-Petipa *Naiad and the Fisherman*, and Emma in *The Harlem Tulip*, revived especially for her in 1903 by Alexander Shiriayev. Again she enthralled Svetlov, her severest judge:

> She danced as a genuine, accomplished ballerina; moreover, as a quite exceptional one, with her own approach and grace, endowed with highly developed technique bordering on sheer virtuosity. What is most precious about her is the flawless reciprocity of her expressive arms, legs, and torso; everything creates harmony, nothing insults the eye, each movement is correct, each pose is perfect. Her attitudes and arabesques seem to be carved images; her rhythms and tempos are never in conflict with the orchestra. She is the embodiment of classicism and musicality.

In 1903 and 1904 Trefilova rehearsed with Petipa himself; he, too, found her "utterly musical . . . a ravishing talent." Petipa coached her in the Tyrolean pas de trois from *The Magic Mirror* (his last ballet), in which she replaced Pavlova, and then in *Naiad and the Fisherman*, *Coppélia*, and *Graziella*, where her soubrette quality shone. The pupil never failed to express her unfeigned gratitude for the old maestro's care. Her devotion was all the more commendable in light of the official anti-Petipa attitude of the Maryinsky administration. During a benefit performance for the corps de ballet on the occasion of Petipa's jubilee in December 1903, although the directorate had ordered that the curtain not be raised and that no wreath be presented to Petipa in sight of the audience, Trefilova challenged the administration. Petipa recalled in his memoirs: "[Trefilova] and the other dancers revolted against such harsh orders, pushed aside the obedient functionary of the director [Teliakovsky], and literally dragged me by the arms out onto the stage, where the wreath was presented to the accompaniment of loud and prolonged applause and shouts of 'Bravo, Petipa! Bravo!'" Her loyalty was limitless: when the general infatuation with Duncan and Fokine was at its height, Trefilova remained true to Petipa's academic standards. In her interviews she did not spare critical barbs for her artistic adversaries: "I do not see any art in running barefoot" and "I have only seen Fokine's *Une Nuit d'Egypte*. Well, everyone has his own way of having a good time."

She rehearsed *The Sleeping Beauty* with Petipa in 1904. Aurora became her best role; no one since Carlotta Brianza had revealed the purity of academic dance so perfectly as Trefilova. *Sleeping Beauty* was followed by Nicolas Legat's *The Fairy Doll* and the role of the Tsar Maiden in *The Little Humpbacked Horse*. In his unpublished memoirs Nikolai Soliannikov recalled 1905 as the year when Trefilova "shone in the irresistibility of her flawless technique and noble charm."

Nevertheless, having attained the summit of academic virtuosity, Trefilova underwent a unique metamorphosis. Before 1905 she had constantly attempted to extend her range by perfecting her technique, knowing that technical weakness hampered her ability to discover a personal touch for each role. After 1905, at the peak of her artistry as an instrumentalist, Trefilova seemed not only to outgrow her soubrette status but to lose interest in it. Certainly she often danced Aurora, but now Giselle and Odette-Odile stirred her artistic ambition. In 1906 she finally made her debut in *Swan Lake*.

It is interesting to note that in his original 1895 production Petipa cast Trefilova as a peasant girl (Act I) and a black swan; her ability, appearance, and potential had earned her no more. Ten years later her Odette was praised for its excellent legato, purity of line, and perfection of movement. She was criticized for her extreme detachment, which verged on impassivity, but despite all the rebukes Trefilova did not alter her interpretation. She was adamant about her reserved approach—not because she could not act, but because she simply considered histrionics irrelevant to the role. Vera Krasovskaya incisively noted: "Trefilova's mellifluous, singing legato took on unexpectedly poignant shadings in the lyrical, sorrowful adagio of Odette and Siegfried, while her face remained inscrutable, like that of a musician absorbed in the sound of his own violin. Thus she viewed the performing act of a ballerina, and the cognoscenti of instrumental dance esteemed her point of view."

Trefilova performed *Swan Lake* for the last time in January 1910; shortly before this performance, the *St. Petersburg Gazette* reported: "[She] is in the heyday of her glory. Now she displays all the polished facets of her dance gift, revealing not only dazzling virtuosity but also a definite personal stamp and integrity of choreographic image." But her last *Swan Lake* turned out to be her final appearance on the Maryinsky stage. At the age of thirty-five, Trefilova suddenly retired from the stage at the peak of her career. Krasovskaya offers this explanation: "An adversary to the innovations of Fokine, she simply favored eternal balletic values over newfangled ones. She preferred to worship one god, and at the time of Fokine's triumph her departure from the Maryinsky was both a challenge to the new trend and a kind of capitulation to it."

During the 1910s her only link with the ballet world was her marriage—her third—to Svetlov, formerly her merciless adversary. She began to give lessons; during the war she would put on all her woolen clothing and exercise in her room at night, using the rails of her bed as a barre. In 1921 Diaghilev coaxed her out of retirement to dance in London as an alternate to Spessivtseva in *The Sleeping Princess*. Before going abroad, she took private classes with her old teacher Nicolas Legat. In the West no one remembered her, although she had undertaken many tours at the beginning of the century.

Destitute and nervous, she arrived in London a few days before the first performance. Her inner turmoil increased when she faced Pierre Vladimiroff's innovation for Aurora: the famous two pirouettes en dedans, ending in the "fish dive" into Desiré's arms, repeated three times in the grand adagio of the last act. This "stunt" infuriated her, Petipa's fervent champion; she refused point-blank to depart from the original choreography, pronouncing it unclassical, an acrobatic feat.

Forty-six years old, Trefilova was terrified of appearing in public after a ten-year hiatus. Sergei Grigoriev recalled:

On the eve of her performance, Diaghilev was awakened in the middle of the night by a violent pounding on his door. There stood a Savoy Hotel porter, as pale and stammering as if he had just seen a ghost. The man handed Diaghilev a letter from Trefilova. It said: "If you do not release me from my contract, which I signed all unaware and which requires me to appear in *Sleeping*

Beauty at my age, at a time when I have lost all technical skill, this very night I will kill myself, and you shall be responsible for my death." Diaghilev answered neither Trefilova's letter nor her incessant telephone calls; and the next evening, looking as if she were sixteen, she triumphed in the role of Aurora.

Trefilova and Spessivtseva were both partnered by Vladimiroff, and a certain rivalry sprang up between them. Knowing that sustained balance was not Spessivtseva's forte at that time, Trefilova one night held a balance in the adagio of the Act III pas de deux for what seemed like minutes. Spessivtseva told friends it was merely a trick: Trefilova had simply balanced herself against Vladimiroff's thigh. Word of this accusation quickly reached Trefilova; as Anton Dolin recalled:

Naturally, she was furious. "I will show you how true this is!" When the moment in the ballet came for the celebrated arabesque, Vladimiroff, who had been warned beforehand, moved away to the other side of the stage, leaving Trefilova standing perfectly and most wonderfully poised on one pointe in a supreme arabesque position for as long as she wanted and for that one occasion with a complete disregard for the music. The audience went wild with amazement and an audible gasp went through the theatre, ending in a frenzy of applause. I was there, on stage, and saw it myself.

Her Aurora in 1921 became Trefilova's undisputed artistic victory—some cognoscenti even preferred her to Spessivtseva. Arnold Haskell wrote that "it was Trefilova who moved me, and whom I shall always identify with the role." Moreover, Haskell saw logic in her performance. Lydia Lopokhova recalled her Aurora as "the daintiest little creature, though with very strong legs and feet, and she had a noble turn of the head such as I have never seen in any other dancer. . . . Trefilova, with her classical style and with the Olympian sureness of her stagecraft, was utterly suited to Petipa's choreography, and I think she was my choice of the two Auroras."

She repeated her London success as Aurora in Paris in May 1922. André Levinson wrote in *Commedia*:

Mme Vera Trefilova, whom Paris applauded yesterday for the first time, is a perfect dancer. . . . She had been one of the purest glories of the Imperial ballet. Her technique is absolute . . . it is the complete expression of a harmonious being. In the adage the interplay of curves and vertical lines is of incomparable purity: she unfolds her dance like an opening blossom. Giddy jumps and outbursts of passion are not for her. If Pavlova is a bird, she is a flower. She is at once the instrument and the musician: a dancing Stradivarius. In the coda of the pas de deux she introduced a series of thirty-two fouettés (the hardest and prettiest of pirouettes) taken from *Swan Lake*. Well, she did only twenty-eight and allowed herself to glide downstage instead of "biting" the floor, for she was too emotionally involved.

In November 1924, at the age of forty-nine, Trefilova danced with Diaghilev's troupe in Monte Carlo, astounding the audience with her "unheard-of pirouettes." In the late 1920s, when her technique began to fade, she frequently performed choreographic miniatures, like her famous "Japanese number," *Madame Butterfly*, charming the audience with her brittle, chiseled lines and her "chastity of dancing," as Levinson once remarked. But in the thirties her health was suddenly shaken: the years of perpetual work took their toll. She suffered constant misery from many illnesses but continued to give ballet classes. Among her pupils were Anton Dolin, Mia Slavenska, and Margot Fonteyn. She died in Paris on July 11, 1943, and under the German occupation her death went unnoticed. But in Russia her name has always been synonymous with the "artistic integrity, dance brilliance, and stylistic mastery" that Levinson described, and which Vera Trefilova represented throughout her life.

Aurora in *The Sleeping Beauty*, late 1950s

IRINA KOLPAKOVA

VERA TREFILOVA'S "instrumental" spirit seems to have been reborn in Irina Kolpakova, the latest outstanding technician in the long lineage of the Imperial ballet of St. Petersburg. Like Olga Preobrajenskaya's, Kolpakova's artistry derived more from perspiration than from inspiration. The critic Valeria Tchistiakova aptly noted: "Kolpakova took the entire one hundred percent of her potential and made of it three hundred percent." An ideal soubrette-ingenue, with a marvelously proportioned doll-like body and chiseled arms and legs (although lacking extraordinary extension or beautiful feet), she became a great ballerina thanks to a combination of willpower and fervor. One of

the last pupils of Agrippina Vaganova, Kolpakova shines equally in Romantic and classical styles, with special elegance and precision. Among the ballerinas of her generation Kolpakova is the most polished and flawless classicist.

IRINA ALEXANDROVNA KOLPAKOVA was born in Leningrad on May 22, 1933, into a family affiliated with the ballet world. Kolpakova's mother had studied ballet, though she never performed professionally. Her friendship with Vladimir Ponomarev, one of the greatest teachers of the Leningrad Choreographic School, enabled her to place her daughter there in 1942. Irina participated in several amateur performances during the war years and began her studies on a steady basis when Leningrad was liberated in 1945. At various times her teachers were Lidia Tiuntina, Elena Shiripina (one of Makarova's teachers), and finally Vaganova. At her graduation performances Kolpakova danced the leading role in Vaganova's *The Dove of Peace* and alternated Florine and Aurora in *The Sleeping Beauty* Act III.

In 1951 she joined the Kirov company as a soloist and was soon given several small roles: the Breadcrumb Fairy in *The Sleeping Beauty*, one of the two cygnets in *Swan Lake* Act II, and a solo in the Grand Pas of *La Bayadère* (1951); Fairy Candide in *The Sleeping Beauty* and the Mistress of the Dryads in *Don Quixote* (1952); the Prelude in *Chopiniana* (1953); Florine, Maria in *The Fountain of Bakhchisarai*, Masha in *The Nutcracker*, and *Cinderella* (1954). In each role she was correct but uninspired, showing no gleam of individuality and little promise of future greatness. She was promoted because of her link with Vaganova, who was deified in the Russian balletic pantheon after her death in 1951; but Kolpakova was unable to compete with either the refined elegance of the young Alla Osipenko or the potent impetuosity of Alla Shelest.

Kolpakova's breakthrough occurred at the beginning of 1956, when the Leningrad critics and balletomanes began to single her out as a budding instrumentalist endowed with considerable projection. In the same year, her fifth season at the Kirov, she made her debut as Aurora, an event that might rightly be viewed as the birth of a great ballerina.

Kolpakova did not attempt to mimic Shelest or Dudinskaya; she remained true to her profound faith in the validity of Petipa's choreography, whose range of meanings would grow organically out of absolutely polished and properly rendered dancing. As Aurora she never sought to limn a psychological state, nor did she capitalize on her youth. She did not distinguish herself with the finesse of Fonteyn, the most poetic Aurora I ever saw—Kolpakova's charm was more subdued than compelling. Nevertheless, so impeccable a balance of instrumental dance qualities, responding to the music as the equivalent of the choreography, was unique at the Kirov at that time. Act I was particularly praiseworthy: Kolpakova executed every enchaînement so flawlessly that the underlying structure of Petipa's choreography was elucidated. Moreover, she orchestrated the steps with such vividness that her Aurora seemed to express all the qualities the fairies had bestowed upon her in in-

fancy: the sharpness of her pas de chat and pirouettes, frisky and alert as a bird, recalled the variation of the Breadcrumb Fairy; her soft développés echoed those of the Lilac Fairy; the brio of the coda maintained the spirit of the Fairy Violente's dynamic tours chaînés and sissonnes. Kolpakova's dancing was, in fact, a visual demonstration of *The Sleeping Beauty*'s symphonically arranged choreography, reaffirming it as an encyclopedia of classical ballet and the most perfect possible expression in dance of Tchaikovsky's music. Curiously enough, Kolpakova's impersonal approach worked to her great advantage; her lack of projection seemed quite appropriate in the context of her performance.

Had Kolpakova created nothing but her Aurora, she would still be considered a great ballerina. However, her early instrumental maturity was awesome but somehow disquieting: a gift of such caliber could blossom only in the environment of plotless neoclassical or classical dance. One can only imagine Kolpakova sparkling in Balanchine's *Symphony in C*, *Concerto Barocco*, and *Donizetti Variations*, the ballets she was truly born to dance; instead, she was limited to the Kirov's repertory of drama-ballets, in which she often looked one-dimensional and superficial. Her Pannochka in Lopukhov's *Taras Bulba*, Tao-Hoa in *The Red Poppy*, and the Beloved One in Igor Belsky's *Shore of Hope* were cardboard figures, which could have been brought to life only by a large dose of inspired histrionics, such as Kolpakova has never had at her command. The single exception to this uninspired sequence was Katerina, the sweet heroine of Grigorovich's *The Stone Flower*, a role that brought out Kolpakova's own personality. Her good-natured Katerina was mild, frail, unobtrusively feminine, softly shaded with the stylized elements of Russian folk dance. Unfortunately, in the 1957 production Kolpakova's portrayal paled in comparison with Osipenko's graphic sharpness and sensual power as the Mistress of the Copper Mountain. Kolpakova obviously needed a much more inventive choreographer than Grigorovich, one who could interpret the music rather than merely illustrate it.

Kolpakova danced her first Giselle in 1959. She varied the dramatic accents in Giselle's character, looking now dovelike and innocent, now flirtatious and even mischievous, especially in later years when her Albrecht was Mikhail Baryshnikov, whose youthful ardor seemed to ignite her theatrical instincts. But in comparison with the modern dramatic approach of Makarova or Bessmertnova, Kolpakova's peasant girl seemed utterly old-fashioned and unimaginative. The cognoscenti might enjoy Kolpakova's purity, her academic port de bras and lightning entrechats, but the champions of balletic expressiveness found her Giselle inane and flat. In *A Dance Autobiography* Makarova observed that in *Giselle* Kolpakova's "dry, academic approach always seemed offensive in relation to the ballet itself, to the unpretentious story of first love, first deception, death, and farewell beyond the grave."

In 1961 Kolpakova gave the Leningrad audience a pleasant surprise: her Shirin in Grigorovich's *Legend of Love*. Among the many mediocre roles Kolpakova danced during the 1950s and early 1960s (Desdemona in Chabukiani's *Othello*, the Confidante in *Raymonda*, Nina in Fenster's *Masquerade*) her Shirin was exceptional for its radiant and potent projection enhanced by extraordinary neoclassical artistry. She excelled in the stilted attitudes, doelike jumps, and aerial splits; her ever-changing port de bras, tinged with languid Oriental playfulness, was quite astounding. Moreover, she brought to her half-child, half-adolescent heroine her own soubrette quality of enticing femininity. For the first time all these aspects of her personality emerged from the facade of her frigid beauty.

After her portrayal of Shirin, Kolpakova's admirers expected her to have another success in Lavrovsky's *Romeo and Juliet*, but her Juliet was utterly conventional and anemic. Unlike the daring Makarova, whose portrayal only underscored the discrepancy between her modern projection and the antediluvian choreography, Kolpakova proved totally unable to bring the decrepit design to life.

Unsuited as she was to the scheme of Soviet dramaballet, Kolpakova came into her own in the crystal purity of Russian academicism. In the 1960s *Raymonda* became one of her major achievements. She approached the role as a purely stylistic challenge, conveying wonderfully the coquettish verve of the pizzicato and the languid reverie of the waltz variations as well as the demi-caractère nuances of the adagio and the Grand Pas.

Unlike her glorious predecessor Natalia Dudinskaya, Kolpakova was never tempted to instill a special bravura into *Raymonda*'s brilliance. Rather, she seasoned the crystalline precision of Petipa's design with rare ethereal qualities, making her Raymonda the most romantic and dreamy on the Kirov stage. Clad in a pink tutu, sparkling and fresh, she seemed to toss off the pas de bourrée of her entrance, alternating the flowing runs on pointe with airy attitudes, pirouettes, and jumped emboîtés. With rare sensitivity to the stylistical differences of each variation, Kolpakova pre-sented them as the fluctuating moods of a maiden who anticipates her every meeting with her betrothed. She was especially effective in the dreamy second variation with a scarf and in the pure Romantic dance of the dream-adagio.

In the pas d'action and the ensuing adagio with Abdul-Rakhman she maintained her elusive detachment; her self-absorption seemed to shield her from the advances of her ardent admirer. Unlike Semyonova, Dudinskaya, or Plisetskaya, Kolpakova never highlighted the traditional arrogance of her heroine; rather, she seemed self-sufficient, alone in the middle of a magic circle with no admittance for others.

After her success as Raymonda—in fact, throughout the 1960s—Kolpakova seemed frozen in the frame of her sparkling, icy beauty. To the gallery of her Kirov portrayals she added Kitri (1965), Nikiya in the Kingdom of the Shades scene (1965), and the Fair Maiden in Jakobson's *The Country of Wonders* (1968). All were failures, or at best repetitions of earlier characterizations.

During this period Kolpakova was perceived as the incarnation of Kirov academicism, but her single performance in December 1969 of Igor Tchernichov's neoclassical one-act *Romeo and Juliet* revealed a completely new aspect of her art. Tchernichov's ballet was a romantic drama of soaring, blind passion, abounding with eroticism in both the terre-à-terre combinations and the lifts. Its choreographic innovations, too daring for the prim Kirov stage, paralleled those of choreographers like John Neumeier and Glen Tetley. To the Soviet eye, this choreography blatantly overstepped the bounds of decorum, but Kolpakova courageously took her chance, stepping into the role originally designed for Natalia Makarova. As Juliet she unveiled for the first time her passionate nature and ardent femininity. The critics were forced to acknowledge her dramatic talent, but unfortunately the ballet was banned after the first performance.

Continuing to explore this side of her talent, in 1971 Kolpakova undertook the role of Eve in Natalia Kasatkina and Vladimir Vasilyov's *The Creation of the World*. The ballet was based on the French caricaturist Jean Effel's unremarkable series of biblical satires and was choreographed to Andrei Petrov's equally unremarkable music, but out of these elements came an unusually sophisticated, lively work. Kolpakova was partnered by Mikhail Baryshnikov as Adam—perfectly matched children of Paradise, passing together through the ordeal of knowledge and maturity. Once again, as she had in *Romeo and Juliet*, Kolpakova went beyond

Clockwise from top: Maria in *The Fountain of Bakhchisarai*, early 1960s; Aurora, early 1960s; *Les Sylphides*, early 1960s; Katerina in *The Stone Flower*, late 1950s; Giselle, mid-1960s

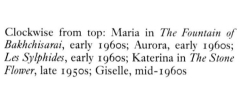

THIS PAGE & OPPOSITE
Raymonda, early 1960s

Aurora, mid-1950s

flawless pointe work and exemplary port de bras. Baryshnikov's partnership obviously inspired her to the point of total transformation, her customary coldness disappearing in an outpouring of genuine lyricism. Like a leafless branch on a limb, she clutched God's hand, then slowly opened her arms like the petals of a flower. Awakening, she proved as curious as Adam. Awed contemplation of the unknown creature was not enough to satisfy her, and she darted impatiently toward him. They approached each other like two awkward puppies, then froze in bewilderment until Eve, taking courage, put her finger into Adam's astonished mouth, and the duo launched a playful dance competition.

Until his defection in 1974, Baryshnikov danced frequently with Kolpakova. Each performance amazed the audience as he brought out the unexpected colors of her new lyrical palette. In this partnership one always sensed an attitude of fraternal confidence and mutual care. During the three years of their fruitful partnership Kolpakova's dancing became ever more personal and expressive. Baryshnikov's defection was a hard blow to her, both professionally and personally. Her work at the Kirov was affected; for three years she seemed too depressed to undertake anything new, except for the Dream Bird in Igor Belsky's *Icarus* (1974) and Boris Eifman's *Divertimento Brillant* (1975), in which her partner was Yuri Soloviev.

It was Soloviev who replaced Baryshnikov as Kolpakova's regular partner. With Soloviev as Romeo, she revamped her portrayal of Juliet in Lavrovsky's *Romeo and Juliet*. Her biographer Marina Ilyicheva has noted: "Her dreamy Juliet still retained something of the passionate Juliet of Tchernichov's ballet. Now her pale, frail Juliet displayed a character of unparalleled persistence and vehemence, vibrant with tragic pathos in Act III."

Kolpakova's most recent dramatic role was the Spanish Infanta in Leonid Lebediev's one-act *Infanta* (1976), set to Kosholkine's music. In neoclassical choreography Lebediev recounted the poetic legend of the unrequited love of a page (Soloviev) for his mistress. Ilyicheva reports: "[Lebediev] boldly disregarded Kolpakova's subtle lyricism, compelling her to reveal temperament and passion hampered by severe ethical inhibitions."

Soloviev's suicide in 1977 was another hard blow for Kolpakova. According to unofficial sources from Russia, the emotional shock of Soloviev's death overwhelmed her far more than had Baryshnikov's flight. She seemed withdrawn and even began to speak of curtailing her career, though despite her age her technique had not deteriorated. In 1977 she portrayed Nele in Glebov's *Tyl Eulenspiegel*; in 1978 she appeared as Maria Taglioni in the old *Pas de Quatre*.

As late as 1981 she still made occasional appearances in her old roles. In 1982 she had a tremendous success in Paris during the Kirov engagement there. Arlene Croce reported:

> We are given the pleasure of seeing Irina Kolpakova perform with Sergei Berezhnoi a little pas de deux from Offenbach's *Le Papillon* arranged by Pierre Lacotte. Kolpakova's only appearances this season have been in the Romantic revivals and pastiches of the repertory. In her late age—she is now fifty—she has become the queen of sylphs; her grand impalpable style has never seemed more secure. Kolpakova does not offer us illusion in place of a technique that she no longer possesses; she offers us the mysterious extension of that illusion which her technique has always sought to fulfill, even at its height. When Kolpakova lands from a grand jeté and throws up her back leg to make us think she has jumped higher we are instantly pleased by the illusion, and we don't think of the jumping she used to do twenty years ago. Now, as then, the separate facets of her technique are precisely in scale one to another. Like Ulanova at the same age, Kolpakova makes you concentrate on what she does, not on what she doesn't do. She judges every effect, and yet she doesn't shrink or fake in the interests of "style"—she appears to dance with the freedom of the day she was born. Kolpakova refreshes my faith in Kirov ballerina style and its possibilities of expression.

Rumor has it that Kolpakova is preparing to become the Kirov's chief choreographer. Although she has no experience as a composer of dances, her political profile and Party membership make her a reliable figure in the eyes of the Kirov's Party supervisors. If this should come to pass, the reins of management and artistic policy will be in female hands for the first time in the two-hundred-year history of the Maryinsky-Kirov.

Icarus, 1979

EKATERINA MAXIMOVA

H AD SHE BEEN BORN more than a half-century earlier, Ekaterina Maximova undoubtedly would have
been the ideal interpreter of Petipa's butterflies and Nicolas
Legat's dolls. She is, in fact, the most cheerful and impish
of Soviet ballerinas, the most perfect soubrette or *ingénue
comique* the Bolshoi has ever had. Her physique combines
mischievous feminine charm with the exceptional endowments of a terre-à-terre virtuoso. Her doll-like Mediterranean face signals wit and mischief; with her chiseled,
extremely beautiful legs, well-shaped feet, arched insteps,
and extraordinary extension she performs effortlessly any
terre-à-terre combination; her moderately high but light
leaps reveal the carefree spirit of a frisky baby ballerina.

At the drama-oriented Bolshoi the soubrette is simply
not taken seriously; mere entertainment cannot express the
moral or ideological message that is the raison d'être of
most Bolshoi productions. In cumbersome, grand-scale
spectacles Maximova's merry persona seems out of place;
her struggle to adapt her gift to the Bolshoi's needs and
repertory reflects the vicissitudes of her long career.

E KATERINA SERGEYEVNA MAXIMOVA was born in
Moscow on February 1, 1939, entered the Moscow
Choreographic School in 1949, and graduated in 1958.
Her teacher was Elizaveta Gerdt, who had also trained

Plisetskaya and Shelest. Gerdt apparently imparted her special Petersburg finish and grace to her talented pupil, whose charming verve attracted attention in the small parts she danced at the Bolshoi while still a student: Amour in *Don Quixote* and supporting roles in the *Nutcracker* divertissement.

On joining the company in 1958, Maximova danced the solo with bells in *The Fountain of Bakhchisarai*, the *Swan Lake* pas de trois, Columbine in *The Bronze Horseman*, the Mazurka and Prelude in *Chopiniana*, the Water Fairy in *The Little Humpbacked Horse*, and Jeanne in *The Flames of Paris*. Except for *Chopiniana*, these were secondary assignments, although the critics praised her excellent timing and precise beats and turns. From the start the young Maximova danced with gusto and abandon, unconcerned with stylistic strictures or dramatic requirements. The radiance of her youth and her technical flamboyance brought her immediate and uproarious success. Gamboling through the Bolshoi's awkward *Chopiniana*, she looked like sunshine on drab, faded wallpaper.

In 1959 Maximova danced Katerina in Grigorovich's *The Stone Flower*, making quite a stir in the Moscow ballet world. Unlike Kolpakova's downtrodden yet courageous serf, Maximova's Katerina was a touching adolescent on the brink of maturity; she imbued the part with an innocence and fey grace that the Bolshoi perceived as a manifestation of budding lyricism. (Only Marina Semyonova abstained from this judgment, warning that "Maximova is a wonderful ingenue forced into the wrong *emploi*.") She began to be coached by Galina Ulanova, and it was Ulanova who encouraged her to undertake *Giselle* under her supervision.

Although in her interviews Maximova invariably thanked her coach for "priceless advice and inspired lessons of artistry," their collaboration seemed to be fruitful only in terms of Maximova's promotion, for she began to be regarded as Ulanova's successor. Ulanova trained Maximova in the Stanislavsky method, even compelling her to read the novels of Turgenev in order to understand the conventions of Romantic art. Maximova diligently followed these instructions; as a result, her performances of *Giselle* were marred by slavish mimicry and were unconvincing and disturbing. Although technically she mastered the choreography with ease, the critic Alexander Demidov maintained that "Giselle's world was simply alien to Maximova."

Nevertheless, her early Giselle in the sixties was marked by a touching frailty and genuine French grace. But despite Ulanova's instructions to dramatize the action, Maximova's portrayal showed anything but tragic intensity. At times the Mad Scene seemed even incongruous, greatly at odds with so frolicsome and lively a character. In Act II she remained the vivid spirit, regardless of the purity of her Romantic technique and stylistic sensitivity. Maximova's joyful nature and zest broke through; nothing could eradicate that.

During her twenty-year career Maximova continued to work on her Giselle, gradually shedding what she had borrowed from Ulanova. Although it never became her most representative role, she did bring to it a suggestion of the soubrette that made it a Russian parallel to the Giselle of the French ballerina Liane Daydé, who caused a sensation in the Russian ballet world of the 1950s.

The official acclaim for Maximova's Giselle may have misled the young ballerina about the magnitude of her lyrical gift. Following in Ulanova's footsteps, she undertook Maria in *Fountain of Bakhchisarai* and Odette-Odile. But as Maria she overacted, unduly emphasizing the childishness of the princess; and as Odette, her movements lacked fluidity. Her Odette brought to mind an image of a timid, adorable child, a baby-swan. Throughout the White Adagio she arduously sought to convey the grievances of her enchanted princess, but her plaints were belied by her energetic ronds de jambe, willful sissonnes, and soaring jumps. The swan image was not truly realized. Even Odile eluded her, despite the precision of her thirty-two fouettés, which looked like a bravura classroom exercise.

In 1963 Maximova began to prepare Cinderella with Ulanova, who had excelled in the role in the 1940s. Her debut in January 1964 was a milestone in her artistic growth. She followed Ulanova's instructions respectfully, but Maximova's lively dancing was not compatible with the realistic style of the mime episodes that depicted Cinderella's wretched plight. Her exuberance gave the naive fairy tale an air of spontaneity in the spirit of vaudeville. The famous partnership of Vladimir Vasiliev and Maximova was forged in this ballet, in which they complemented each other in their sensitivity to balletic comedy. It was in *Cinderella* that Maximova's true artistic personality was first unveiled. She revealed her forte: a combination of virtuosity and innocence, a prima ballerina's attack and a childlike vulnerability, bravura and the slightly awkward playfulness with which she swept through the most intricate terre-à-terre sequences.

Maximova's baby ballerina character could take on various shadings: the childish selfishness or narcissistic self-infatuation of her cruel and capricious Ballerina in *Petrushka*; the carefree glee and inoffensive shrewdness that brought her innocently wicked and conniving Swanilda and

Kitri in *Don Quixote*

OPPOSITE
Top: *Walpurgis Night*, with Vladimir Vasiliev, 1960s
Bottom: (left) Cinderella, mid-1960s; (right) Aurora in *The Sleeping Beauty*, 1981

Top: (left) Phrygia in *Spartacus*, with Vasiliev, 1960s; (right) Kitri
Above: Giselle, with Vasiliev as Albrecht, early 1970s

Lise to life; or the innocent flirtatiousness she displayed in Goleizovsky's *Mazurka* to Scriabin, as she radiantly and deftly lifted her skirt or playfully bent forward.

In 1965 Maximova appeared as Kitri in Gorsky's *Don Quixote*, a tremendous challenge and calculated risk while Maya Plisetskaya still reigned as the Bolshoi's supreme Kitri, setting an unattainable standard of style and bravura. To Maximova's credit, she never ventured to mimic her glorious predecessor's irresistible femininity or unparalleled technical feats. Nevertheless, Maximova's approach was not unlike Plisetskaya's: disregarding the old-fashioned naiveté of the plot, she attacked Gorsky's choreography with sheer abandon and untrammeled confidence. Each movement and step looked appropriate and spontaneous, free of contrived histrionics. She was merely a "cheerful daredevil" who reveled in guileless pranks and unaffected eccentricity. So convincing was she that some critics thought Kitri was the dancer's self-portrait; in fact, Kitri was the product of her theatrical and balletic maturity. Offstage, Maximova is introverted and serious.

Maximova adapted her gift for comedy, her soubrette persona, and prima ballerina bravura to the stylistic needs of each act. In Act I she was a mischievous scamp, sparkling in her cocky mime and dance dialogues with Basil. In the Dream Scene of Act II she tinged the Romantic sequences with a subtle touch of irony; and in Act III she paraded her triumphant aplomb, effortlessly executing the cascades of whirlwind pirouettes.

Alexander Demidov has pointed out one of the most salient characteristics of Maximova's style: "In her interpretation, the jetés and the leaps do not impress us with their airiness or their speed; the moment we wait for is when she lands, and the pose with which she ends the whole movement. It is as though through her jeté we come to appreciate the beauty of her movement at stage level. And it is here that she creates the fantasy and illusion."

Her terre-à-terre brilliance and charismatic radiance contributed to the French flavor of Maximova's Aurora in Grigorovich's second version of *The Sleeping Beauty* (1973). Wearing a blonde wig and a whimsical rococo costume, in Act I she appeared to be a refined counterpart of her Cinderella, innocent and impish, an Aurora who "suddenly learned the old minuet style with its slightly mincing grace," as Vadim Gayevsky put it. This touch of French style tinged her Rose Adagio and her Act III variation; she swept through Petipa's patterns with consummate elegance and finesse.

From 1965 on, with her husband Vasiliev as her partner, Maximova danced in many of Grigorovich's productions designed along the lines of the Bolshoi's grand style. Maximova's soubrette quality and the verve of her dancing seemed to be stifled, especially in *Spartacus* (1968). The role of Phrygia contained none of the choreographic complexities of Giselle or even Cinderella, nor was she so fully drawn a character. Instead of portraying Phrygia as the strong-willed companion of the Roman hero, as Grigorovich's scheme demanded, Maximova highlighted the childish aspects of the heroine.

But in the fairy-tale element of Grigorovich's *Nutcracker* Maximova obviously felt much more at ease. Her Masha was an introverted, intelligent girl, touching in her shy infatuation with the ugly Nutcracker and in her position on the threshold of adolescence. It was obvious that the evolution of this highly sensitive girl, passing from "children's games to the dawn of love," as one critic noted, had a powerful effect on Maximova's theatrical instincts.

The 1970s proved to be the artistic acme of Maximova's career. She was highly acclaimed during her engagements in France, Italy, and South America, although it would seem that such universal recognition did not appease her artistic curiosity.

The Vasiliev-Grigorovich feud and Vasiliev's ensuing estrangement from the Bolshoi made Maximova also feel something of an outcast. Seeking to chart her own course, she began with great determination to capitalize on her soubrette or comic potential. In 1978 Dmitry Briantsev mounted for her a one-act ballet after Shaw's *Pygmalion*, with Professor Higgins transformed into a ballet teacher. Although the choreography was no better than mediocre, "Maximova shone with the skill of a comedienne born on pointe, swimming in the comic element with charming abandon, as if it had been her legitimate genre for years," as a reviewer in *Soviet Culture* maintained.

In 1979 Briantsev staged another one-act ballet for Maximova, *The Old Tango*. In this, one critic reported, "[she] demonstrated her keen sensitivity to the genre of balletic parody and rich theatricality. Her personality radiates in the adagio with the Diva."

Apparently it is balletic comedy that attracts Maximova now. In 1980 she had a new success in Briantsev's *The Hussars' Ballad*, as Shura Azarova, the famous nineteenth-century woman who acquired a scandalous reputation by joining the Russian army en travesti. Her most recent role, Natalie in *The Swiss Milkmaid*, a Romantic comedy created in the 1830s and now restored by Pierre Lacotte, was "a minor theatrical gem," "the triumph of wit and exuberance," the Moscow reviews reported.

THE
DECORATIVE
BALLERINAS

Tamara Karsavina
Alla Osipenko

Studio portrait, 1920s

TAMARA KARSAVINA

STARDOM CAME TO TAMARA KARSAVINA as the leading ballerina of the Diaghilev troupe, whose emblem she became along with Vaslav Nijinsky. It is doubtful that her talent would have flourished with such splendor in Russia had she not found herself, by a twist of fate, at the center of those innovations and experiments that so decisively altered the course of Russian and Western ballet.

Karsavina, only five years younger than Pavlova, made her debut at the Maryinsky in 1902, three years after Pavlova's; but in the 1910s, when both had achieved international acclaim, Karsavina was frequently listed as one of the "gifted youngsters" of the new generation. This definition did contain a grain of truth: the images of the two ballerinas and their approaches to dance differed as strikingly as if there were a gulf of decades between them. This was the result not so much of any inequality of their technical qualifications or artistic projection as of the fact that Pavlova incarnated the essence of St. Petersburg classicism while Karsavina was a product of the Western trends invading Russian art at the beginning of the twentieth century.

As a ballerina, Karsavina is hard to label: she was not an instrumentalist, a lyrical ballerina, or a soubrette. The great Romantic roles of Giselle and Odette never added to her glory; moreover, at a time when her name and Pavlova's enjoyed equal recognition in Western Europe, she was still regarded by the Russians as a promising debutante. Vera Krasovskaya has written:

> Pavlova's fame had a democratic appeal, whereas Karsavina's was elevated in ballet gourmet circles. The most refined poets eulogized her, while the public at large preferred Pavlova, who was capable not only of captivating the audience but of penetrating the depth of human emotions. Karsavina's aesthetic range was far narrower, and her qualifications as a classical ballerina were rightly contested by many partisans of Russian academic training. While the Paris audience treasured Karsavina as a major adornment of the Saisons Russes, where she created the image of the fatal enchantress of irresistible beauty, the St. Petersburg public and critics quite often belittled her as an inadequate dancer. For the Parisians she immediately became the Muse of

contemporary ballet, while the Russians continued to regard her as poorly trained. Some of her contemporaries still believe that Karsavina's reputation outdistanced her technique.

But one of Karsavina's qualities was praised by all the critics: her beauty, which was more Mediterranean than Russian; with her graceful, indolent movements and her dark, velvety eyes that suggested both a fascinating directness and a touching modesty, she was to be compared to the women of Greuze, Murillo, and Caravaggio. She had well-shaped feet and a considerable extension, although her physique was quite ordinary. Akim Volynsky characterized her jumps: "Despite her diligent, seemingly rather high leaps, her elevation was heavy. The legs would get off the ground with ease, but the torso remained rigid and somehow immobile, without thrusting upward or vibrating. Her arms never modified the dances; she displayed a poor port de bras." In Russia, despite her relatively high jump, Karsavina was considered a terre-à-terre ballerina, but her plasticity made every pose strikingly picturesque. Krasovskaya described her as "a mistress of pictorial stylization."

In *Theatre Street*, her intelligent and generally reliable autobiography, Karsavina recalled her thorny career at the Maryinsky with enviable objectivity and charming modesty. Her critical attitude toward her own weaknesses, and the sober light of common sense she shone on events in St. Petersburg and in the Western ballet world, reveal her sharp mind and immense cultural sophistication, rare among Russian dancers. Her perceptive essays testify that in her artistic practice, control prevailed over inspiration. She was able to make much use of her innate advantages and conceal her shortcomings, which seem to have been numerous at the outset of her career.

THE DAUGHTER of the renowned Maryinsky character dancer Platon Karsavin, Tamara Platonovna Karsavina was born in St. Petersburg on February 25, 1882. She grew up in a family that respected both classical ballet and the spiritual values of the Russian intelligentsia. Her brother,

Lev Karsavin, became a religious philosopher of note: his debates with his colleagues, at which the young Karsavina assisted, shaped her analytical mind and broadened the range of her interests. The family tradition led her to the Choreographic School in Theatre Street, where she first studied under the supervision of Gerdt and Johannsen and then perfected her technique with Nicolas Legat.

Her first steps on the Maryinsky stage were rather shy and awkward. A string of minor debuts as a member of the corps, which she joined in 1902, were not especially promising. From 1902 to 1904 she diligently performed a number of insignificant roles: the Emerald in *Bluebeard*, a Flower Vendor in *Don Quixote*, one of Swanilda's confidantes in *Coppélia*, one of the Fresques Reanimées in *The Little Humpbacked Horse*, and the pas de deux from *Les Millions d'Arlequin* with Mikhail Fokine. Eventually she was given the pas de trois in *The Harlem Tulip*, the Peasant pas de deux in *Giselle*, and the pas de trois in *Swan Lake*. In 1904 she was promoted to the rank of coryphée.

Her dancing was uneven, arousing the critics sometimes to praise but sometimes to bitter rebuke. Reproaches for sloppy pointe work, imprecise positions, and inadequate arms were invariably juxtaposed with appreciation for Karsavina's grace and picturesque plasticity. She had many fans in the balcony, but the severe balletomanes in the stalls continued to castigate her for her poor turnout and slipshod pirouettes. After her appearance as a Spanish girl in Legat's *The Fairy Doll*, Svetlov called her "pigeon-toed" and said that she was unable "to sustain the correct attitude."

By 1905 Karsavina found herself in the middle of the artistic combat being waged in Russian ballet. Petipa's champions attacked her technique and her "slack temperament and mannerism," but it was precisely her decorative qualities and reserve that aroused the admiration of Diaghilev and Teliakovsky, who detested "Petipa's tedious routine," as he put it in his diaries. Karsavina's mannerism was, in fact, ill suited to roles that demanded austere, precise, and brilliant classicism. "Karsavina's ability to create on her own was put on trial in Petipa's *The Trials of Damis*," Svetlov remarked ironically in 1905. "Her dances and acting were cute. But since the pieces in this bagatelle are mostly 'pedestrian'—passe-pied, courantes, musettes, sarabandes, gavottes—it is rather difficult to evaluate Miss Karsavina's aptitude for dancing even minor classical ballets."

In December 1906 Karsavina made her debut in *The Little Humpbacked Horse*. Unfortunately, the intricate role of the Tsar Maiden proved to be beyond her ability, although an anonymous critic noted that "she did the best she could." The large-scale Russian manner of presentation and the taxing academic combinations, requiring pointes of steel, were obviously too much for her. But her refinement, the Oriental serenity of each pose, and the intriguing aloofness of her beautiful face imparted a brand-new flavor to the role. Benois and Diaghilev were thrilled; they pronounced her the bearer of a new kind of sex appeal, both impassive and potent. Yet even they hardly saw in her the future queen of the Paris Saisons Russes; nor did Fokine, immersed at the time in his experiments with Pavlova. Nevertheless, on March 8, 1907, Karsavina performed the C-sharp-minor Waltz in Fokine's new version of *Chopiniana*, then appeared in *Une Nuit d'Egypte* and *Eunice*. After 1907 she often danced in the Fokine ballets in which Pavlova had the leading roles. She was appreciated as a spectacular and useful prop; the critics regarded her with a slightly insulting indifference. Juxtaposed with Pavlova's magnetic projection in *Chopiniana* or *Eunice*, even Karsavina's charm lost its power.

When Diaghilev organized his first Paris season in 1909, he intended to employ Karsavina as a garnish for Pavlova's stellar role. But Pavlova arrived late, after her own tour of Berlin, Vienna, and elsewhere, allowing Karsavina to score the first triumph. Today it seems that Karsavina's instantaneous success in Paris was predestined, regardless of Pavlova. Long before opening night at the Théâtre du Châtelet, one member of the press described Karsavina as "the elusive, thoughtful beauty who seems wafted by infinite grace." In the context of the Diaghilev repertory, which emphasized a pictorial effect that rivaled painting itself, Karsavina's decorative qualities had more appeal for the audience than Pavlova's subtle lyricism and ethereal magic. Pairing Karsavina with Nijinsky in "L'Oiseau de feu" (the Blue Bird pas de deux from *The Sleeping Beauty*), Diaghilev did not err. Karsavina's magical bird was the perfect match for Nijinsky's impetuous prince; together they took Paris by storm. She was equally successful in her other roles that season: as a Confidante in *Le Pavillon d'Armide*, as a Slave in *Cléopâtre* (the revised *Une Nuit d'Egypte*), and as one of the three ballerinas in *Les Sylphides* (Diaghilev's new name for *Chopiniana*).

During the second Paris season (1910) Karsavina consolidated her reputation in three new roles—Columbine in *Carnaval*, the Firebird, and Giselle. As Krasovskaya wrote:

Columbine seemed to combine all the facets of the female characters flashing through Fokine's choreography for *Carnaval*. She recalled the careless Estrella, the languid Chiarina, and the elusive, mysterious Butterfly. Her fluctuating moods came and went in the course of her innocent romping. Curls flirtatiously spilling over drooping shoulders, her bosom peeping out of a low-necked bodice, the tip of her foot appearing from under the large flounces of her skirt, arms whose frailty seemed to be emphasized by the puffed sleeves of her blouse—every detail connoted refined femininity.

The decorative appeal of Karsavina's Columbine was enhanced by the featherly lightness of her dancing; even her terre-à-terre technique took on a special lacy quality thanks to the spirit of fun and elegant play that informed her portrayal. In a sense, Columbine conveyed the essence of Karsavina's art, an art of impish theatricality and refined entertainment. Pavlova's intense portrayals elicited an emotional response from the audience, but Karsavina's stylizations were never intended "to penetrate beneath the skin of the public," as Volynsky once noted. And this perfectly suited Diaghilev, whose aesthetic creed considered art an activity of *homo ludens*. Many of the St. Petersburg poets and painters also preferred Karsavina to Pavlova, whom they regarded as a perpetrator of old-fashioned histrionics. Diaghilev in particular appreciated Karsavina's ability to create a stylized mask that provided pure visual delight, titillating the eye with its subtle eroticism.

Nevertheless, when choreography and music blended appropriately, Karsavina's roles became more than decorative. Her Firebird was a great artistic achievement, the first of her Oriental heroines (Zobeïde in *Schéhérazade*, the Sultan's favorite wife in *Islamey*, the title role in *Thamar*, the Queen of Shemakhan in *Le Coq d'or*). Decorative qualities certainly prevailed when as the Firebird—clad in transparent harem pants and wearing a crown adorned with feathers and pearls from beneath which her golden plaits emerged—she crossed the stage like a flash of lightning, looking like "a fiery phoenix," as Alexandre Benois said. Her Firebird, in fact, was described by Krasovskaya as "a modification of the Odette-Odile image from *Swan Lake*. . . . Its genuine lyricism was replaced with abstract female qualities, arranged in the key of symbolist poetry. The bird-maiden from a Russian fairy tale manifested herself as a symbol of femininity, devoid of human traits." But there was an additional dimension that lent a unique grandeur to

Karsavina's portrayal: the power of formidable Oriental sensuality that foreshadowed the femmes fatales of Theda Bara's silent films. Like Nijinsky's androgynous creations, Karsavina's Firebird resonated in the erotic twilight that enveloped Paris during the 1910s.

The 1910 Paris season also saw Karsavina's first Giselle, with Nijinsky as Albrecht. She had learned the famous role from her St. Petersburg teacher Yevgenia Sokolova and had hoped to have Pavlova's help in rehearsal. But Pavlova, annoyed by Karsavina's assignment, refused to coach her. Nijinsky also demonstrated an insulting indifference. Lacking artistic guidance, Karsavina "took the part in another key," Svetlov observed. "In her interpretation there enters no deep tragedy. On the contrary, it is the lyrical song of a woman's grief, sad and poetic. The pathos is tender, restrained. The mad scene is an almost timid complaint. In the second act, in all of her dances there is something soothing, almost a quiet satisfaction, a submission to fate and a hope for a happier future."

Physically, Karsavina fit very well into Benois's nostalgic decor, with its autumn landscape, castle on a distant crag, and deep-blue moonlit forest. According to her contemporaries, Karsavina created a Giselle more refined and decorative than Pavlova's passionate, heartbroken peasant girl. And in Benois's view she "almost outshone Pavlova," an opinion that was shared even by Pavlova's partisans. The critics reporting back to St. Petersburg wrote that "each of her movements, each attitude, seemed to rival the etchings of the old masters."

Karsavina's impish Columbine and her stylized, reserved Giselle were reflected in two new roles that she undertook in 1911—the Young Girl in *Le Spectre de la rose* and the Ballerina in *Petrushka*. She danced both roles with Nijinsky; both became legendary. Her dreamy Young Girl was an asexual, decorative embodiment of the Freudian wish-dream. Paired with Nijinsky's sexual ambivalence as the image of sublimated desire, Karsavina's Young Girl teased the imagination of the sophisticated audience.

The effect of her Ballerina was different. A silly, cute doll with oversized eyelashes and carmine spots on her cheeks, she evoked an image of female temptation in the guise of an impassive mechanical toy. In the fatal puppet drama, unfolding at the behest of the Magician as the replica of a human tragedy, the Ballerina's tempting charm was only a catalyst. But Karsavina implied something more profound—a concept of the same latent erotic power that was to inform the characters created by Dietrich and Garbo in

Left: Odette, 1915
Bottom: (left) *La Sylphide*, 1910s;
(right) Medora in *Le Corsaire*, 1910s

OPPOSITE
Top: The Page in *Fiammetta*, early
1910s
Bottom: (left) Pas de trois in *Le
Pavillon d'Armide*, 1907; (right)
Armida in *Le Pavillon d'Armide*, 1908

Т. П. КАРСАВИНА

Above: Armida, 1907
Right: The Ballerina in *Petrushka*, 1913

Above: The Sugar Plum Fairy in *The Nutcracker*, 1920s
Left: *Le astuzie femminili*, 1910s

Clockwise from top: Columbine in *Carnaval*, 1910; Lise in *La Fille mal gardée*, 1910s; *Le Spectre de la rose*, mid-1910s; Zobeïde in *Schéhérazade*, 1912

OPPOSITE
The Firebird, 1910s

THE DECORATIVE BALLERINAS

the movies of the 1920s and 1930s. This image was enthusiastically saluted in Europe; but Karsavina's visual metaphors were either misunderstood or simply rejected in St. Petersburg—the Russian mentality does not tolerate sexual ambiguity.

In St. Petersburg, Karsavina's refined Armide was perceived as a weak copy of Pavlova's passionate enchantress. Even after the triumphs of her third season with Diaghilev, Karsavina had to make tremendous efforts in Russia to achieve comparable recognition among her compatriots. Her situation was made more difficult by the fact that after 1910 she inherited Pavlova's repertory. When she made her Petersburg debut in *Giselle* in 1910, her decorative qualities, appealing picturesque poses, and stylized finesse were disparaged for "debilitated dramatism" and "pinched lyricism." After her *Swan Lake* Volynsky accused her of poor turnout, lack of sustained balance, sloppy pointe work, sugary sentimental posing, and, strangely enough, inadequate musicality.

The fact was that Petipa's academic roles were too much for her technique, which was already weakened by her work in Fokine's impressionistic style. Dancing with an emphasis on decorative posing and with neglect of the academic rules certainly had a bad effect on her Odette-Odile (1908), Raymonda (1909), and Aurora (1911). Although the unexacting public in the top balcony saluted Karsavina as the most attractive flower in the Maryinsky hothouse, she was intelligent enough to realize that simultaneous success in the works of Fokine and Petipa was beyond her training and technique. Pavlova did not succeed in this either, although alongside her Nikiya and Giselle she created Fokine's Dying Swan, and captivated the entire world. Karsavina's masterpieces were lesser roles—the Young Girl in *Spectre*, Columbine, the Firebird, the Ballerina in *Petrushka*—and her triumph extended only to Paris and London. Had Karsavina remained at the Maryinsky, her career might have deserved no more than a footnote in the history of Russian ballet.

In Pavlova's repertory, Karsavina's most successful role was her Nikiya in 1910. The critics noted the plasticity of her Oriental arms, the expressiveness of her shimmering dark eyes, her reserve in the mime scenes—and the weakness of her pointe work in the Kingdom of the Shades.

She brought more theatricality to such soubrette roles as the Sugar Plum Fairy in the *Nutcracker* and Isabelle in *The Trials of Damis*; these were characters similar to Columbine. But their choreographic value was insignificant,

although in this familiar element Karsavina demonstrated far more elaborate technique. Even Volynsky approved of the precision of her pas de bourrée and the elegance of her glissades as Isabelle.

Karsavina's collaboration with Fokine, in whose ballets she continued to shine, gradually lost its vitality. Fokine became ever more self-indulgent, while over the years, as Karsavina confessed, his style became detrimental to her classical technique. Years earlier she had rejected Fokine's proposal of marriage; after *The Dream* in 1915, she broke her artistic ties with the choreographer in whose creations she had attained the summit of her artistic maturity.

In 1915, when Karsavina was only thirty and at the peak of her career, she began to polish her artistry in a purely classical repertory—*Paquita, Don Quixote, La Fille mal gardée, Sylvia*, Petipa's *Nénuphar*—seeking to husband and enrich her classical technique and to reaffirm her status as a genuine exponent of the Maryinsky tradition. The Revolution and ensuing social cataclysm shattered Russia; otherwise she might indeed have succeeded in mastering the Petipa style at its best. By all reports, from 1915 to 1918 she grew as an instrumentalist despite the drastic artistic decay of the Maryinsky during the regime of Nicolas Legat. In May 1918 she closed the Maryinsky season in *La Bayadère*; in July, with her second husband, the British diplomat Henry Bruce, and their infant child, she left Russia at the risk of her life.

The last decade of her career was a premature artistic sunset. She rejoined Diaghilev's company to dance in Leonide Massine's ballets—she was the Miller's Wife in *The Three-Cornered Hat*, the Nightingale in *The Song of the Nightingale*, and Pimpinella in *Pulcinella*. She also danced the pas de deux in Massine's *Le astuzie femminili* to the music of Cimarosa.

Apparently, the repertory of the Ballets Russes left her thirsting for "the spring water of Petipa's choreography," as she confessed in 1925. The previous year she had admitted with bitterness that "our ballet is slightly exhausted. Its seeking and striving for new paths was too impetuous. Having indulged in the extremes of modernistic trends, the development of our ballet frequently took on new forms, defying the essence of ballet as art."

In 1924 she appeared in New York with Pierre Vladimiroff, but the tour was a failure. According to Felia Doubrovska, Karsavina "did the choreography herself, and they danced in Carnegie Hall, but without scenery, without corps de ballet. At the same time Pavlova was dancing at the

Metropolitan Opera House with her own company, performing a repertoire of works which audiences used to like. . . . In Europe Karsavina had success everywhere, but in America, with a bare stage at Carnegie Hall, it was a mistake. She and Vladimiroff left New York after one week." To make things worse, she was advertised not as a ballerina but as "a bird," and, as Doubrovska recalled, "people came expecting to see her fly instead of dance."

Her American failure hurt Karsavina deeply. She returned to Europe to dance with various companies (including Diaghilev's in 1928) but never regained her former brilliance.

In 1931 Karsavina retired from the stage. She wrote her illuminating memoirs *Theatre Street* as well as many theoretical essays and recollections that reflect her profound intelligence. She died in London in 1978, one of the last venerable relics in the glorious pantheon of Russian ballet, where she had her own special niche. Vera Krasovskaya wrote: "More than anyone else she embodied the idea of Fokine's heroine as a tempting fraud and a dangerous enchantress. She was an ideal dancing actress, reveling in balletic tradition, a refined stylist, keenly sensitive to the achievements of Diaghilev's followers and similar artistic trends."

Odette, mid-1950s

ALLA OSIPENKO

I N THE 1950s and 1960s Alla Osipenko was the most decorative ornament of the Kirov stage, with a more Western artistic profile than her illustrious colleagues displayed. She was endowed with the most refined physique, an ideally molded body whose elongated lines started from beautifully shaped legs and chiseled feet, to continue through a well-proportioned torso and swanlike neck crowned with a head regally placed on equally regal shoulders. Clad in a tutu, standing motionless on pointe, Osipenko called to mind an extraordinary tropical flower on a long stem. Distinguished by a precious musicality, Osipenko was a mistress of adagio, the contours of her long-limbed body seeming to flow and stretch upward with an authentic Russian legato.

By physique and technical qualifications—high jump, enormous extension, and sculptural completeness of arabesques and attitudes—she perfectly defined the term "Romantic ballerina." Unfortunately, she was unable to make much use of her natural elevation: soon after her debut on the Kirov stage she suffered a serious injury that never healed, the pain of which caused her to fear jumping.

Nevertheless, Osipenko's beauty seemed to presage a great success in Petipa's realm of sprites and enchanted princesses. But she possessed a unique trait: despite her flawless legato in movement, the lines of her body constantly strove to take on a graphic or etched character uncovering the special tension and dynamic play of the muscles. This made her better suited to the neoclassical style than to St. Petersburg academicism, a disposition that was reinforced by Osipenko's unusual artistic projection: her stage image was reserved and queenly, aloof to the point of indifference. The inner tension of her projection won out over the traditional tempestuous Russian outpouring of emotions. She was indeed a distinctive ballerina, resisting any label; but within the confines of the meager Kirov repertory her career developed with difficulty.

ALLA YEVGENIEVNA OSIPENKO was born in Leningrad on June 16, 1932. With Irina Kolpakova she became one of Vaganova's last pupils at the Leningrad Choreographic School. She was immediately accepted into the Kirov corps de ballet upon her graduation in 1950, the year in which she won a gold medal at a competition of young dancers in Prague.

Osipenko's early roles (the traditional confidantes of ballet heroines and the like) called attention only to her unique body. She seemed to dance with a kind of sluggish remoteness that Russians thought of as a lack of individuality. At a time when the Kirov audience was shifting its favor from Dudinskaya's bravura to Shelest's expressivity, Osipenko was regarded as a majestic yet anemic ballerina. The exacting Leningrad public, while enthralled by her decorative glamour, was unable to predict the roles in which she would excel. Neither Odette-Odile nor Nikiya, Aurora nor Giselle, seemed to suit her rather somnambulistic gift. Her pleasure in dancing seemed almost selfish, without any concern for dramatic impact or the response of the viewer.

But in 1952 Osipenko danced the Lilac Fairy in Konstantin Sergeyev's revised *The Sleeping Beauty* and instantly became the talk of the Leningrad ballet world. Her performance, in fact, was truly a revelation, all the more miraculous in that this secondary role was suddenly made so vivid that it overshadowed Dudinskaya's Aurora. The effect derived not so much from the tempting charm or puzzling regal remoteness of her Lilac Fairy (Shelest's was of the same mold) as from the special significance of the image. Osipenko's lines seemed to "sing" in the slow développés à la seconde of Lopukhov's variation. Her épaulement was impeccable, her arms eloquent and commanding as she abrogated the Fairy Carabosse's spell and imperiously directed the Prince toward his encounter with Aurora. Every ingredient of Osipenko's characterization conveyed the powerful energy of refined eroticism: this Lilac Fairy was a metaphor of irresistible female power, inaccessible and challenging. Her potent confidence and the authority with which she guided the action made her the mistress of the fairy tale. Her portrayal, in fact, expanded Petipa's design by transforming it into something more meaningful that teased the imagination by its mystery. It added a piquant note to the question of what role would perfectly fit her puzzling dance gift and unorthodox personality.

During the 1950s she performed Odette-Odile, Nikiya, and Raymonda. The critics called her "a virtuoso musician who could master the score yet remain unmoved by its emotional depth." This observation was, in my view, beside the point. Unlike Dudinskaya or Kolpakova, Osipenko was not a pure instrumentalist, excelling only in technique seasoned with a soubrette spice. Her decorative appearance and reserved manners gave an added dimension to her visual image, appealing more to intellectual than to sensual perception. This dimension imperiously demanded deciphering, regardless of any ballet's plot. Her dancing did not clarify a plot or her character's state of mind but rose into the sphere of pure abstraction.

From the outset more often disparaged than praised, Osipenko sought to overcome her natural manner by making it more "Russian," more emotional. The problem was that she was unable to add an intellectual dimension to the classical roles, although her technique was superb. Even her Odette, immersed in grief and dreamy detachment, somehow appeared wingless, despite her flexible swanlike arms. Moreover, she was of such spectacular noble beauty and dignity that she seemed miscast in the drab Kirov production. Her Nikiya also looked alien to the Oriental element of *La Bayadère*, but in the Kingdom of the Shades her lingering tours en attitudes and arabesques conveyed such peace and austerity that the grim conventional rocks in the background seemed superfluous.

Osipenko's strength lay precisely in her ability to illuminate the abstract nature of classical dance. Leonid Jakobson was the first choreographer to use her unusual projection by capitalizing on her sculptural appeal and subtly erotic energy. In his cameo ballets *The Kiss* and *The Eternal Idol*, Osipenko was indeed a sculpture in motion, enigmatic and challenging; but the effect of her roles was deadened by the ostentatiously spectacular yet shallow choreography. She obviously needed roles with dramatic content that could be elevated into an intellectual dimension.

In 1957 she danced the Mistress of the Copper Mountain at the premiere of Grigorovich's *The Stone Flower*. Five years later came her Queen Mekhmene-Banu in his *The Legend of Love*. However unimportant and imitative these ballets may seem today, in each role Osipenko was stunningly beautiful and mysterious. As the Mistress, clad in black tights with malachite stripes and dark green spots, she skillfully alternated the vibration of her flowing, stretching lines with the intensity of their graphic sharpness. She reveled in the acrobatic, mercurial movements, looking like a nimble lizard, while retaining her impassivity, as if her feminine psyche were at war with her animal substance. The ease with which she orchestrated these conflicting elements in her nature deepened the perspective of the part, rendering it elusive and enigmatic. The choreography was meant to illustrate a didactic principle of the Russian fairy tale, the superiority of the artist to sexual temptation; but Osipenko's image was the opposite: the power of woman to stimulate man's creativity and imagination.

In *Legend of Love* her characterization was even more profound. She seemed unconcerned with the plot, in which Mekhmene-Banu sacrificed her beauty to save her sister Shirin from a fatal disease, only to fall in love with Shirin's lover, Ferhad. The sharp dynamism of Osipenko's impeccable legs rending the air with a scissorlike movement, the utter tension of every inch of her flexible muscular body, had the impact of a balletic Phaedra. Confronted by Ferhad (portrayed by Nikita Dolgushin as a sensitive, intellectual artist), Osipenko's tragic heroine represented the fatal force of destructive sensuality. The critics praised her performance, recognizing her rare ability to transform the concrete into the abstract and imbue her characterizations with the blood of Greek tragedy.

In the 1960s Osipenko's talent was not so much nurtured or encouraged as exploited by the Kirov. In the pedestrian, one-dimensional choreography of *The Pearl*, Konstantin Sergeyev's *The Man*, or Igor Belsky's *The Shore of Hope*, Soviet choreographers employed her merely as a decorative prop, ignoring the metaphorical potential of her stage image. During the twenty years of her career at the Kirov, not a single ballet was mounted specifically for her. The fact that many great Soviet dancers shared her lot did not soothe the bitterness of her artistic life. She had to vegetate for a decade before she got the chance to demon-

strate the true dimensions of her gift, and when this happened at last, it was not at the Kirov but at the Maly Theatre.

The breakthrough occurred in 1971, in Igor Tchernichov's imaginative ballet *Cleopatra*. Contrary to Soviet drama-ballet tradition, the choreography did not narrate the story but rather unfolded as a series of evocative scenes that only implicitly referred to the legendary love of Marc Antony and Cleopatra. The neoclassical solos and duets of the principals expressed not so much the power of their passion as their thwarted attempt to maintain the delicate balance between two hostile civilizations: the Roman—cold, pompous, prematurely decadent—and the Egyptian—full of Oriental suavity, calm, and wisdom.

Keenly sensitive to this conflict, Osipenko brought to her Egyptian queen an aura of Oriental sagacity and quietude. Like Alla Shelest's Cleopatra in Fokine's *Une Nuit d'Egypte*, Osipenko's heroine was a mythical figure, vaguely glimpsed through the haze of past centuries. Tchernichov's choreography, with its remarkable balance of classical and neoclassical patterns, suited her perfectly, because it related the story only remotely or implicitly. Osipenko was released from the disconcerting necessity of clarifying the kind of plot that had compelled many a ballerina to indulge in traditional histrionics.

Bursting into swift développés à la seconde alternating with swirling promenades on pointe and torso contractions, rising and subsiding like an ocean wave, Osipenko poured forth her muscular energy while her face maintained an expression of enigmatic reserve. At times she looked like a mask from an Egyptian sarcophagus, serene and passionless. This Cleopatra was two-sided: one aspect was sensual and tempestuous; the other, sage and imperturbable. The strength of her portrayal stemmed from these conflicting elements. Cleopatra's impetuous sensuality threw her into Antony's arms, but she seemed to foresee the death of passion, its vanity in the face of eternity. Her fluctuations of mood, shifting from fury and passion to total indifference, puzzled and inflamed her Antony (John Markovsky); in the most erotic passages of their duets Cleopatra still maintained the distance of detachment. Osipenko thus put an ancient legend into the perspective of a modern drama of existential alienation.

Osipenko was especially great in Cleopatra's solos, unfolding the intricate combinations as a kind of interior monologue, pinpointing the discord between the power of her passion and her keen sense of doom. Her Cleopatra seemed to find respite only in the return to a state of

Taglioni's Flight, with John Markovsky, early 1970s

OPPOSITE
Top: The Lilac Fairy in *The Sleeping Beauty*, 1950s
Bottom: Cleopatra (Tchernichov), early 1970s

Left: Queen Mekhmene-Banu in *The Legend of Love*, 1960s
Below: Concert number to music of Pink Floyd, with John Markovsky, late 1970s

Rehearsal with John Markovsky, 1970s

nonbeing: at the end of the ballet she froze in the attitude of the Sphinx over Antony's dead body, a symbol of Oriental wisdom impassive in its petrified form.

Cleopatra had a great effect on Osipenko's creativity, which found its outlet in neoclassical dance. It suddenly illuminated her Kirov period with the merciless light of wasted time and encouraged her to leave the company, although the actual break was due to her unhappiness over restrictions placed upon her partnership with her husband, Markovsky.

She took her chance, realizing that available choreographers beyond the Kirov orbit were few. The third decade of Osipenko's career saw her affiliated with the Company of Choreographic Miniatures under the artistic direction of Leonid Jakobson, another nonconformist exile from the Kirov. Unfortunately, the enfant terrible of Soviet ballet was simply interested in adapting Osipenko to his often absurd and naive concepts, while her iconoclastic personality and special projection demanded more attention from her choreographer, or at least a less selfish approach. The collaboration was uneven, as Osipenko continued to rebel against the confines of explicative choreography. She looked pinched and subdued in *Prometheus* (set to a Bach toccata); clad in black tights, she obediently portrayed an eagle tearing the Greek giant's liver to pieces. As the Firebird she was asked to demonstrate her decorative femininity and bizarre aloofness through a series of whimsical lifts in the duet with the Tsarevich, and that was all. As if to mock her flowing, singing line, Jakobson deprived Osipenko of any movement whatsoever in *Taglioni's Flight*, where, attired in a Romantic tutu, she smoothly alternated the positions of the grand jeté, supported by black-clad porteurs who were invisible against the black backdrop. Thus the immortal symbol of Romantic flight was reduced to the image of Osipenko being carried around the stage like a spectacular prop.

Apparently the most imaginative of Jakobson's short ballets was *The Minotaur and the Nymph*, an erotic combat between the gorillalike, low-browed Minotaur in black and the Nymph in white. With her loose-flowing hair and languid plasticity, the Nymph was a metaphor for frail femininity confronted by the crushing force of male aggressiveness. As if sensing that the concept was a truism, Osipenko deliberately enriched her image with a stylization borrowed from the nymphs depicted on black-figured Greek vases.

Osipenko obviously relished the freedom she felt in small-scale ballets. The more abstract the choreography, the more the various facets of her personality broke through it. She was magnificent in Georgy Alexize's *Syrinx*, an abstract choreographic parallel to the inflections of Debussy's music for the flute. Even if the audience was unfamiliar with Ovid's tale of Syrinx (the nymph whom the gods rescued from Pan by turning her into a reed), Osipenko's dancing suggested the peacefulness of plants and their unity with nature. The flowing lines of her body lengthened, stretched upward, or curved from the imaginary freshness of the brook. But at the same time her movements connoted something grander than the image of a growing reed, something that resists any precise definition and is possible to create only in music and ballet.

In recent years Osipenko has continued to strive for a new dimension in ballet, working with such experimental Soviet choreographers as Boris Eifman and Leonid Lebediev. She gave a series of imaginative portrayals, such as Nastasia Filippovna in Eifman's *The Idiot* and the Siren in Mai Murdmaa's *Prodigal Son*, with Baryshnikov as her partner during some of his gala performances at the Kirov in the spring of 1974. Osipenko and Baryshnikov were a perfect match in terms of their musical sensitivity and striking ability to imbue their choreographic poems with layers of meaning. Baryshnikov called her "the most modernistic, most neoclassical classical ballerina." But in the Soviet environment her fresh and dazzling dance gift was her personal undoing. A determined and unmalleable personality, she was doomed to suffer in the iron grip of socialist realism.

DANCERS WITHOUT CATEGORY

Vaslav Nijinsky · Rudolf Nureyev

Mikhail Baryshnikov

Albrecht, 1910

VASLAV NIJINSKY

LIKE ANNA PAVLOVA, Nijinsky is a legendary figure of Russian ballet, thoroughly publicized and scrutinized. A survey of critical Nijinskiana would constitute a bulky volume in itself. His life and achievements have been recorded in profuse detail, as has his complex relationship with Serge Diaghilev, whose intuition and flair guided Nijinsky's genius. The pens of hundreds of ballet critics and historians have described his now legendary performances. There are continuing attempts to reconstruct his choreography, on the assumption that it was a comparable manifestation of his genius, though arguments to the contrary have been strongly advanced by those who played leading roles in the artistic life of the Ballets Russes. But, ironically, this avalanche of accounts has only made Nijinsky's personality, both as a man and as a dancer, more elusive. Even the date of his birth remains questionable: according to Nijinsky's birth certificate he was born in Kiev on December 17, 1889; but his sister, Bronislava, maintained that Vaslav was born on February 28, 1889.

The landmarks of his life—his resounding glory, his too-brief career, his madness—could have served as subject matter for one of Alexandre Dumas's Romantic melodramas. In fact, this is the tone that predominates in the most popular biography of Nijinsky, written by his wife, Romola. This book, first published in 1933 and recently reissued in one volume with her later biography, *The Last Days of Nijinsky*, is mostly a skillful fictionalization. It abounds in intentional distortions and misinterpretations, especially in the years leading up to 1913, a period of which Romola simply had no firsthand knowledge. Furthermore, she presented Nijinsky's premature artistic decline and ensuing insanity as a cruel consequence of the revenge of Diaghilev and worldwide homosexual circles, the devastating power of which she publicly equated with that of the Vatican. The book was invariably perceived as fiction by Nijinsky's colleagues and collaborators in both Russia and the West. Unfortunately, this biased picture of Nijinsky has prevailed and was strongly reinforced by Richard Buckle's critical biography (1971), in which the copious facts were interpreted in the same melodramatic fashion.

The intimations of miracle and scandal that pervaded Nijinsky's artistic and personal lives were too tempting for many of his biographers. The impression of him as a mass of contradictory extremes stemmed partly from the striking discrepancies between the private Nijinsky and his devastating stage persona. Fyodor Lopukhov's account of his classmate as a mentally and emotionally retarded dunce unable to cope with the multiplication tables is not apocryphal; it has been confirmed by firsthand witnesses. When this awkward, shy, inarticulate youth was introduced into the glittering high society of Paris by Diaghilev, Misia Sert labeled him "an idiot of genius." This image did not tally with that of a "volcano of sensuality" with an "irresistible body," as he was often described by the critics. Through his electrifying plastique Nijinsky evoked visions of untrammeled passion, languorous longing, and sexual ambivalence on stage. The powerful impact of his danced poems created an atmosphere of awe and disbelief that made his fervent champions view his every role as a further manifestation of genius.

One of Nijinsky's most authoritative biographers, Vera Krasovskaya, interpreted his Albrecht as "the embodiment of a doomed hero. His encounter with Giselle mystically anticipated his confrontation with the Wilis. He centered his projection around the drama of personal solitude and fate." On the other hand, Fyodor Lopukhov, a witness to Nijinsky's triumphs, seriously disputed his Romantic genius in *Giselle*. In Lopukhov's view, the nature of Nijinsky's expressiveness lay rather in a grotesque, eccentric manner of presentation. For Lopukhov (as well as for Stravinsky and Benois) Nijinsky remained unsurpassed as Petrushka, Tyl Eulenspiegel, and the Golden Slave in *Schéhérazade*. For all her hostility toward "Diaghilev's pet," Anna Pavlova expressed a similar opinion.

Nijinsky was an unclassifiable dancer indeed. For a Romantic hero (and the repertory at the beginning of the century was exclusively Romantic) he was "somewhat stocky," as Lopukhov recalled, "his legs too short and muscular, his calves and thighs rather bulging and athletic"—as can be seen in any of his photographs. This kind of physique was the direct opposite of the standard danseur noble as exemplified by Pavel Gerdt. Also, Nijinsky's pale face with its prominent cheekbones, Oriental eyes, and feminine mouth, did not suggest anything regal or noble.

A son of the Polish dancer-comedians Thomas Nijinsky and Eleonora Bereda, Vaslav was raised only by his mother, who enrolled him in the Imperial Theatre School in 1898. He studied in the classes of the Legat brothers and was honored with the Didelot stipend, bestowed upon the most talented pupils. As a senior, he studied with Mikhail Obukhov. Nijinsky became the talk of St. Petersburg very early on, the critics predicting a glorious future for this precocious virtuoso, whom they pronounced a miracle. In 1906, while still a student, he excelled in a ballet interlude in Mozart's *Don Giovanni*, partnering Trefilova or Pavlova; and at his graduation performance in 1907 he shone in Fokine's one-act *Flight of the Butterflies*.

For Nijinsky, Fokine devised a new type of changement de pieds. Bronislava Nijinska recalled: "Nijinsky surprised everyone when, after jumping straight up in the air from fifth position, he did not return to the same spot but instead leaped sideways across the stage. Immediately he repeated this amazing sideways changement de pieds that had never been executed in this manner before, jumping from side to side several times. With each pas he covered a wider span of the stage until with his fourth and last jump he flew more than fifteen feet."

Even before Nijinsky officially joined the Maryinsky company, Obukhov showed off his prize pupil in various pas de deux and pas de quatre, leading one critic to note: "His jump is enormous; his ballon is so extraordinary that it makes him seem to fly in the air like a bird. His entrechats and pirouettes are daring and precise—he executes them effortlessly." Another singled him out as "a classical dancer of pure style, endowed with rare natural abilities."

In May 1907 Nijinsky joined the Maryinsky as a soloist. His strong and exuberant partnering won him the favor of the most prominent ballerinas: during his first season he danced with Julie Sedova and Lidia Kyasht (pas de deux from *Paquita*) and with Tamara Karsavina (the Peasant pas de deux from *Giselle*). At the end of the year he appeared as Colin in *La Fille mal gardée* and as the Prince in *The Prince Gardener*, partnered by Matilda Kschessinskaya. Svetlov's acclamation of his entrechats huit and his fabulous ballon added to his fame and tempted Kschessinskaya to take him with her to Paris in 1908, the trip which never took place.

According to the reviews covering the beginning of his career, Nijinsky impressed the critics mainly with his technical brilliance; his theatrical projection seemed to be muted or totally lacking. In November 1907 he captivated the St.

Petersburg balletomanes with his "incomparable" brisés volés as the Blue Bird (with Lidia Kyasht as Florine). Apparently this was the first role in which the innovative, even revolutionary approach of the eighteen-year-old Nijinsky was plainly evident. Bronislava Nijinska underscored this in her vivid description of one of the most spectacular moments in ballet history:

> The birdlike wings were part of his dancing body; his arms did not bend at the elbow, but the movement as in the wing of a bird was generated in the shoulder; the movements of the dancing body were the movements of a bird in flight. . . . He was creating his dance-image of a Blue Bird, an image that had become a living entity, part of himself. . . .
>
> Nijinsky flies on in an enormous leap, a prolongated grand assemblé. The arm-wings are open wide, extended. The Blue Bird soars—two light motions of the shoulders, a flutter of the wings, and the Blue Bird seems to linger in its flight. A slow sweeping movement of the arm-wings, as if gathering new strength, and then a strong upsweeping movement of the wings create the impression that the Blue Bird is rising still higher in its flight. Then smoothly, imperceptibly, Nijinsky comes down on half-toe only to fly upwards again.

Nijinska was the only one among her brother's contemporaries to have given us a penetrating analysis of his brand-new style of concentrated dancing, which was to become a trait of classical ballet in the twentieth century:

> One of the amazing features of Nijinsky's dance was that it was impossible to perceive when he was finishing one pas and when he was starting the next. All the preparations were concealed in the shortest possible time, the very instant of the foot touching the floor of the stage. On a background of persistently repeated entrechat six, entrechat huit, entrechat dix, a whole range of movements played in the body of Nijinsky—vibrating, trembling, fluttering, flying. It seemed that after each entrechat Nijinsky did not come down to touch the floor. . . . It was one continuous glissando in which all the entrechats flowed together in an upward flight.

From November 1907 to March 1908 Mikhail Fokine managed to get Nijinsky to work on two new roles: the White Slave in *Le Pavillon d'Armide* and the Dark Slave in

Une Nuit d'Egypte (later to become *Cléopâtre*). Curiously enough, these roles, in which Nijinsky was to take Paris by storm in 1909, went almost unnoticed in Russia. Nijinsky's ability to invest his portrayals with his sensual fantasies must have been still dormant, or else the Imperial ballet, with its ideal of asexuality, might already have rejected him. At the Maryinsky he was perceived only as an impeccable virtuoso. The administration's belligerent conservatism never aroused the subconscious resources that fueled his magical transformations on stage; the old Maryinsky style failed to provide the picturesque and imaginative theatricality to which he responded: only in the charged, stimulating atmosphere of Diaghilev's seasons could Nijinsky's talent blaze with so blinding a light that its glow illuminated the entire world of Western art.

The subconscious sources that fed Nijinsky's creativity were as unique as they were morbid. Twenty years after his last performance, in a revealing preface to Nijinsky's *Diary*, the prominent psychoanalyst Alfred Adler convincingly traced the dancer's schizophrenia to the dominant escapist tendency of his personality as well as to his indulgence in frustrated vanity and the feelings of inferiority that make a person retreat from social life. As the antidote to disappointing reality, Nijinsky sought the imaginary world of the stage—a soothing alternative, an escape and an outlet for the pent-up energy of the androgynous essence that he repressed in everyday life. Alexandre Benois pointed out Nijinsky's keen attention to his stage garb, when "having put on the costume he gradually began to change into another being, the one he saw in the mirror. He became reincarnated and actually entered into his new existence as an exceptionally attractive and poetic personality." As Edwin Denby explained, writing about photographs of Nijinsky: "Looking at him, one is in an imaginary world, entire and very clear, and one's emotions are not directed at their material objects but at their imaginary satisfactions."

The collaboration with Fokine in 1907–08 was a catalyst in Nijinsky's artistic development. Two aspects of Fokine's choreography seemed to have aroused Nijinsky's imagination: the freedom from rigid classical patterns, and the visual richness, which made Nijinsky feel part of an elaborate imaginary world. The unorthodox choreography, which encouraged the free movement of an unfettered body, released Nijinsky's subconscious resources, enabling him to saturate the steps and combinations with hidden energy. As the slaves in *Pavillon d'Armide* and *Une Nuit d'Egypte* Nijinsky overwhelmed Diaghilev, who understood imme-

diately the nature of the dancer's gift, his ability to charge his technical perfection with sensuality and the energy of subconscious drama. The two slaves were the first of a series of Nijinsky characters, submissive yet tempestuous creatures dependent on the whim of another being, of which Petrushka was the most tragic. Fokine's Romantic reverie *Chopiniana* (*Les Sylphides*), which had its official premiere in March 1908, stirred another pole of Nijinsky's imagination—his subconscious craving for ideal love, pure and asexual, which would subsequently lead to his infatuation with Tolstoy's Franciscan philosophy, his hatred for Diaghilev's "demons of sensuality," and his religious bigotry.

In May 1909 Nijinsky dumbfounded the Parisians at the Théâtre du Châtelet with his unprecedented virtuosity in *Le Pavillon d'Armide*, calling to mind the legendary technical feats of Auguste Vestris. Bronislava Nijinska observed:

> . . . his whole body is alive with an inner movement, his whole being radiant with inner joy—a slight smile on his lips . . . his long neck bound by a pearl necklace . . . a light quivering of his small expressive hands among the lace cuffs. This inspired figure of Nijinsky captivates the spectators, who watch him spellbound, as if he were a work of art. . . .
>
> Suddenly, from demi-pointe preparation, Nijinsky springs upwards and with an imperceptible movement sends his body sideways. Four times he flies above the stage—weightless, airborne, gliding in the air without effort, like a bird in flight. . . . He soars upwards, grand échappé, and then he soars still higher, in a grand jeté en attitude. Suspended in the air, he zigzags on the diagonal (three grands jetés en attitude) to land on the ramp by the first wing. . . . With each *ralentissement* in the air the audience holds its breath. . . .
>
> Throwing his body up to a great height for a moment, he leans back, his legs extended, beats an entrechat sept, and, slowly turning over onto his chest, arches his back and, lowering one leg, holds an arabesque in the air. Smoothly in this pure arabesque, he descends to the ground. Nijinsky repeats this pas once more, like a bird directing in the air the course of its flight. From the depths of the stage with a single leap, assemblé entrechat dix, he flies towards the first wing. . . .
>
> [He] ends the variation in the middle of the stage, close to the footlights, with ten to twelve pirouettes and

a triple tour en l'air, finishing with the right arm extended forward in a révérence.

In the Blue Bird pas de deux from *The Sleeping Beauty* (dubbed "L'Oiseau de Feu") Nijinsky repeated the wonders of his elevation, enhancing his ever-growing reputation as a "soaring angel." The snobbish, refined Parisian audience responded keenly to Nijinsky's ambiguous sexuality. What was most appealing was that, as Elizaveta Timeh (a celebrated actress and Fokine's original Cleopatra) told me, "He by no means looked effeminate. On the contrary, his robust body with its strong neck and muscular, overdeveloped legs indicated a sexual power that in everyday life he was rumored not to possess. His superpotent projection stirred the audience of both sexes equally. His strong body seemed, through dancing, to be transformed into something larger than life."

During this first season the Paris reviews were full of curious animal imagery: Nijinsky was compared to a panther, a lynx, a tiger; to a "head-wagging simian creature"; to a fish thumping at the bottom of a boat; to a rabbit caught by the bullet of a hunter. His dances and portrayals were larger-than-life projections and larger than dance per se. He affected his audiences viscerally, imaginatively, and subconsciously—a unique power, though perhaps Nijinsky himself was not aware of it. It made him the first ballet superstar, the first dancer to display to the Western audience two of ballet's most potent qualities: its kinetic thrill and beauty and its nonrepresentational symbolic means.

Oddly enough, after his return to St. Petersburg, Nijinsky seemed to lose all the glamour of the "reincarnated Vestris," as he was frequently called in Paris. He was depressed and confused, deeply hurt by the attitude of the Maryinsky directorate, which frowned upon his affair with Diaghilev and sought to punish the impresario's favorite. The wonder boy of Paris enjoyed no more advantages in St. Petersburg than a regular member of the corps de ballet; he was fined for coming late to rehearsal and was cast mostly in such ossified pieces as *La Fille mal gardée* and *Le Roi Candaule*. Instead of sparkling in Fokine's innovative works, he appeared as Vayou, God of the Wind, in Petipa's *Talisman*, as revived and condensed by Nicolas Legat in 1909. Nijinsky once again demonstrated his fabulous ballon, but critics noted that he looked "extinguished and drab." Svetlov, who had seen him in Paris, speculated that after Diaghilev's experiment "Nijinsky felt pinched in our old-fashioned routine." No wonder that at the beginning of 1910 he frequently shirked his work, saying he was unwell.

He seems to have reawakened in the spring of 1910, when Diaghilev got him to rehearse the new roles specially designed by Fokine for the second Paris season—Harlequin in *Carnaval* and the Golden Slave in *Schéhérazade*. He was also scheduled to dance Albrecht in *Giselle*, which was being staged for Pavlova, and two cameo roles in the divertissement called *Les Orientales* ("Kobold" to Grieg and "Danse Siamoise" to Sinding). According to Sergei Grigoriev, Nijinsky choreographed the "Kobold" himself, the beginning of his self-assertion as a choreographer. It was first performed in St. Petersburg in February 1910.

The second Paris season focused on Nijinsky's unique ability to project not so much an individual character as "the states of being in which character is inherent but not precisely determined: the somnambulistic but rapturous longing of *Les Sylphides*; the animalistic force of nature in *Schéhérazade*. . . . In Nijinsky's hands each . . . became a gloriously physical consummation of fundamentally metaphysical conceptions," as Dale Harris has aptly written. His mercurial, teasing Harlequin was the quintessential masked rogue, the very spirit of Romantic irony brought to life by his scintillating technique. "A beautiful feline beast, strong and ingratiating," said André Levinson in his review of Nijinsky's Golden Slave, which was an embodiment of sheer physical desire even more powerful than his Dark Slave in *Cléopâtre*. Only his Albrecht (with Karsavina, as it happened) failed to earn much acclaim; this brooding character seemed pallid in comparison with the feral power of his portraits of sheer sexuality.

Back in Russia Svetlov complained that "Nijinsky, who has given rise to a whole critical library about himself in the West, does not perform here. To tell the truth, what is he supposed to do in our petrified repertory, with its meaningless cavaliers serving only as props for the ballerinas in pas de deux and pas d'action?" And indeed, the louder the fanfare of Nijinsky's Parisian triumphs sounded, the more strained and melodramatic his relationship with the Maryinsky became. There may be some truth to the gossip that Diaghilev tried his best to jeopardize Nijinsky's position at the theatre and even to instigate his dismissal. At any rate, Nijinsky was so late for the opening of the fall season of 1910 that his salary was suspended. His first appearance, in *Giselle*, did not occur until January 1911, and that turned out to be his last performance in Russia.

His Albrecht provoked a scandal: the severe Dowager Tsarina Maria Fyodorovna, whose Victorian prudery was rivaled only by her ignorance, waxed indignant over Nijinsky's yellow tights, which he wore without covering trunks.

Top: Ballet interlude in *Don Giovanni*, 1906
Above: (left) The White Slave in *Le Pavillon d'Armide*, 1909; (right) Vayou in *Le Talisman*, 1909

Above: The Danse caucasienne in *Le Festin*, 1909
Right: The Mulatto Slave in *Le Roi Candaule*, 1906
Below: The Danse siamoise in *Les Orientales* (Fokine), 1909

The Golden Slave in *Schéhérazade*

OPPOSITE
Clockwise from top: Portrait, 1910s; The Golden Slave in *Schéhérazade*, 1910;
Petrushka, 1912; The Danse siamoise, 1909

Above: *Le Spectre de la rose*, with Tamara Karsavina, 1911
Right: *Chopiniana*, 1908

Above: *L'Après-midi d'un faune*, 1912
Right: Tyl Eulenspiegel, 1916

His vehement insistence on retaining the costume led to his dismissal from the Maryinsky. He pronounced a bitter opinion of the Russian public, which "views the ballet theatre as a drinking house without any care for its real artistic attributes," and accused the Maryinsky directorate of neglecting him.

Nijinsky's St. Petersburg career lasted only three years. His rupture with the Maryinsky strengthened his tie to Diaghilev's enterprise and his total personal dependence on the great impresario. As an artist Nijinsky benefited from this union, but he suffered as a man. His separation from his mother, his life in an alien milieu under Diaghilev's vigilant control, and the burden of ever-increasing celebrity crushed his utterly introverted nature. But the more he shrank into himself and the more unsociably he looked at the world around him, the more devastatingly the energy of his suffering poured forth on the stage.

During the third Ballets Russes season (1911) Fokine designed three great roles for Nijinsky: in *Narcissus*, *Le Spectre de la rose*, and *Petrushka*. The technical tricks in which these roles abound capitalized on Nijinsky's unique qualifications. For example, *Spectre* displayed his rare ankle-muscle stamina as well as his ability to take off effortlessly after being strained by an unabated stream of sissonnes, alternating with entrechats six, coming from and to a closed fifth position.

In creating *Petrushka* for Nijinsky, Fokine achieved a kind of malicious psychoanalysis. Unquestionably, the role was designed with an eye to Nijinsky's bizarre offstage behavior—his mechanical gestures, wooden manner, impassive face (as deadpan as Buster Keaton's). What is more, the similarity between Petrushka's relationship with the Old Magician and that of Nijinsky and Diaghilev was surely meant to arouse the dancer's complex inner mechanism. His suppressed resentment, his self-pity—all the facets of a "trapped soul"—were to surface and stun the audience with the force of his pain.

Fokine's experiment was more than successful. As Petrushka, Nijinsky displayed the tragic facet of his genius. According to Alexandre Benois, he miraculously managed to express Petrushka's "pitiful oppression and his hopeless efforts to achieve personal dignity without ceasing to be a puppet." Nijinska described her brother's performance:

When Petrushka dances, his body remains the body of a doll; only the tragic eyes reflect his emotions, burning with passion or dimming with pain. The heavy head,

carved out of a wooden block, hangs forward, rolling from side to side, propped on the shoulder. The hands and feet are also made of wood, and Vaslav holds his fingers stiffly together inside black mittens like wooden paddles. His feet are wooden feet in black boots, dangling loosely at the end of sawdust legs. The soft knees bend suddenly under the weight of the body, the knock-kneed legs sway from side to side, and the wooden dangling feet dance freely. Petrushka dances as if he is using only the heavy wooden parts of his body. Only the swinging, mechanical, soulless motions jerk the sawdust-filled arms or legs upwards in extravagant movements to indicate transports of joy or despair.

We can only wonder at the impact of Nijinsky's Petrushka. The rare balance between his stunning virtuosity and his impassive appearance had an almost surreal effect. His total identification with Petrushka, which stemmed (as Fokine had intended) from his sense of his relationship with Diaghilev and from his deep-seated inferiority complex, added an element of poignancy to the characterization which was further enriched by the resonance of Russian culture, with its time-honored theme of the spiritual superiority of the oppressed.

Quite a different aspect of Nijinsky's personality was displayed in *Le Spectre de la rose*. *Spectre* was a powerful metaphor for sexual ambivalence: a flower represented by an athletically built youth. Nijinsky's muscular but androgynous body soared in the air, embodying the inebriating power of perfume or, in a broader sense, a young girl's vague longing for sexual fulfillment. But, besides this disturbing, teasing sexual element, "he seemed to the audience to float slowly down like a happy spirit," as Edwin Denby has noted in his illuminating essay "Meaning in Ballet." "He seemed to radiate a power of mysterious assurance as calmly as the bloom of a summer rose does. . . . For Nijinsky in this ballet the leaps and the dance were all one single flowing line of movement, faster or slower, heavier or lighter, a way of moving that could rise up off the ground as easily as not, with no break and no effort. It isn't a question of how high he jumped one jump, but how smoothly he danced the whole ballet."

SINCE NOVEMBER 1910 Nijinsky had been working on his own ballet, *L'Après-midi d'un faune*, which launched his brief and controversial career as a choreographer, part of his effort to assert his independence from Diaghilev. It is impossible for us to judge Nijinsky's talent as a choreographer, because of his four ballets—*Faune* (1912), *Jeux* (1913), *Le Sacre du printemps* (1913), and *Tyl Eulenspiegel* (1916)—only *Faune* has come down to us in anything like its original form. The others may have been lost because Nijinsky's audacious innovations defied too drastically the aesthetic standards of the time or because, as intensely personal manifestations of his art, they could be sustained only with the immediate participation of their creator. In any case, after Nijinsky's rupture with Diaghilev, the impresario made no effort to preserve these difficult and unpopular ballets in the repertory.

In her deeply revealing *Early Memoirs*, Bronislava Nijinska has dispelled the legend that Diaghilev was the initiating spirit behind Nijinsky's daring productions. According to his sister, Nijinsky began to compose his *Faune* in November 1910 and, after ninety rehearsals, completed the ten-minute piece in April 1912. The ballet was a personal and utterly iconoclastic experiment, challenging even Diaghilev's aesthetic creed. The sensual longings of a creature half-beast, half-human, extended the leitmotif of primitive instinct and feral passion that so lavishly colored Nijinsky's portrayals of the Golden Slave and Narcissus. What distinguished Nijinsky's design from Fokine's picturesque endeavors was its innovative static expressiveness.

According to his sister's memoirs, Nijinsky himself described *L'Après-midi d'un faune* as his attempt to "move away from the classical Greece that Fokine likes to use . . . [his] sweetly sentimental line in the form or in the movement." Nijinsky's choreographic patterns mimicked or suggested the bas-relief forms of an archaic Greek frieze, a sequence of static, stylized configurations. It is curious that, unlike many dancer-choreographers, Nijinsky did not capitalize on his own virtuosity; in fact, he absolutely negated it. His choreography was intentionally devoid of any dance steps; nor was it a descriptive parallel or visual supplement to the music.

On the contrary, the discrepancy between the vague fluidity of musical sequences and the emphasis on half-conscious animal gestures, in the Egyptian confrontation of a frontal torso with head, hands, and legs in profile, was immensely daring. The disturbing incompatibility of the music and the choreography caused an uproar at the premiere. Only a few people in that audience—Auguste Rodin among them—were conscious of the revolutionary approach to ballet that Nijinsky represented. Rodin pointed out that in Nijinsky's ballet "form and meaning are indissolubly wedded in his body, which is totally expressive of the mind within."

Ironically, Diaghilev disapproved of *Faune*, although a decade later he would lead his company in the direction that Nijinsky's choreographic intuition had foreshadowed. The artistic independence and challenge that Nijinsky asserted in *Faune* "marked the beginning of the break with Diaghilev," as Nijinska has noted.

In 1913 Nijinsky supplied Diaghilev with two new works, *Jeux* and *Le Sacre du printemps*, whose audacity gave rise to the most conflicting critical verdicts in the history of ballet. In each of them Nijinsky sought to realize a ballet in which the plot would be, in his words, "universal or nonexistent."

In *Jeux* the plot was truly minimal, more implicitly conveyed than fully drawn. The meeting of two girls and a young man, all in quest of a lost tennis ball, and their ensuing flirtatious games, served Nijinsky as a pretext to saturate his composition with the stylized movements of tennis players.

Nijinsky called *Jeux* "an apologia in plastic forms for a man of 1913"; as such, it justified his goal. But the setting of angular, sportive, staccato movements (such as the sideways and upward swing of both arms across the body) to Debussy's impressionistic, melodious score, in a romantic, twilight stage atmosphere, created many discrepancies. The ballet did not emerge as a unity, because Nijinsky's choreography emphasized the kinetic appeal of movements as their ultimate value, and their individual impact not only extended beyond the plot but in fact seemed to annihilate it. Nijinsky's design foreshadowed the shift in modern ballet from expressive content to independence of choreographic forms. Vera Krasovskaya has noted a certain similarity between Nijinsky's structure and that of Balanchine's *Episodes*: "The frontal exposure of dancers, based on the exclusive use of the second position, is identical in both ballets, as well as the plasticity of angular lines and intentionally charged poses. The faces of the performers are equally immobile, as if investing the body with the exclusive right to expression."

In *Le Sacre du printemps* Nijinsky went even further. The libretto referred to the primitive pagan rites of pre-Christian Russia and, to an extent, activated Nijinsky's constant interest in the uncontrollable sensual elements in human nature. On the other hand, Stravinsky's avant-garde music compelled him as a choreographer to provide an equally iconoclastic design that would diverge drastically from established dance forms. By resorting to the elements of Russian ritual dance, Nijinsky in fact created a new dance vocabulary. His artistic task was all the more difficult because in *Sacre* he sought the balance between music and choreography that had eluded him in *Faune* and *Jeux*. *Sacre* was a pure experiment in the dance laboratory of Nijinsky's body and imagination. Its daring, disturbing character confounded even the composer; it was only half a century after the riotous premiere that he acknowledged Nijinsky's endeavor as "the most talented choreographic parallel" to his music.

Nijinsky's choreography was based on turned-in feet and clumsy, uncouth movements, including clenched fists, torso contractions, hunched shoulders, and a heavy walk on slightly bent knees. It was full of wild, uncoordinated jumps and sporadic hopping and pounding. Unlike the design of *Faune* or of *Jeux*, it was not an arrangement of stylized movements but an elemental dance of explosive primitive energy.

In *Sacre* Nijinsky rejected the principles of classical symmetry that were the basis of Petipa's and Fokine's choreography. He filled the stage space with groups of dancers performing different patterns "hatched in isolation from the other groups, like those spontaneous fires that break out in haystacks," as one Parisian critic noted. A kaleidoscopic ensemble, the groups were meant to convey the spirit of pagan madness and the fermentation of uncontrollable instincts.

Jacques Rivière in his famous article on Nijinsky's *Sacre* wrote: "By breaking up movement, by returning to the simplicity of gesture, Nijinsky has restored expressiveness to dancing. All the angularities and awkwardness of this choreography keep the feeling in. . . . Nijinsky makes the body itself speak. It only moves as a whole, as one block, and its speech is expressed in sudden bounds with open arms and legs, or in sideways runs with bent knees and with the head lying on the shoulder. . . . This is a biological ballet. It is not only the dance of the most primitive men, it is the dance before man. . . ."

Nijinsky's choreography was an energetic rejection of Fokine's picturesque aesthetic, which had nourished Diaghilev's artistic policy during the first decade of the Ballets Russes. A pioneer, Nijinsky drastically turned dance in the direction of nonpictorial expressiveness. In 1931 Fokine, in his article "The Sad Art," attacked Martha Graham's deviation from neoclassical forms in ballet, but his accusations of mannerism were in fact indirectly aimed at Nijinsky's

innovations in *Sacre*, to which Graham's expressionism traced its artistic lineage.

NIJINSKY'S sudden decision to marry the dancer Romola de Pulszky in Buenos Aires in 1913 resulted in his painful break with Diaghilev. The twenty-four-year-old husband paid a high price for his independence, finding himself weighed down by his many responsibilities: his career, his pregnant wife, his mother and mentally ill brother to support in St. Petersburg. Nijinsky's total inability to make choices and decisions, his childish impatience, and the unremitting pressures of everyday life all took their toll of his delicate inner resources. His paralyzing fears and deep-rooted inferiority complex came ever closer to the surface, as life tested his endurance by pouring upon him an avalanche of failure.

With Bronislava Nijinska he organized a company of seventeen dancers. Their first independent tour in London (March 1914) was a fiasco that devoured Nijinsky's scanty savings. In 1914, with Romola and their infant daughter, Kyra, he was trapped by the outbreak of the war in Budapest, where the little family was forced to remain until 1916. Nijinsky's total isolation in an alien environment where he neither spoke the language nor had a stage to provide an outlet for his emotional life must have accelerated the process of inner disintegration. The escapist tendencies of his subconscious, bereft of creative sublimation, caused him to withdraw ever deeper into insanity.

A temporary truce with Diaghilev provided a soothing respite before Nijinsky's total collapse. In April 1916 he made his New York debut at the Metropolitan Opera House in *Petrushka* and *Le Spectre de la rose*. His success was enhanced by the premiere in October of his last ballet, *Tyl Eulenspiegel*. Nijinsky designed this eighteen-minute ballet as a Rabelaisian comedy of masks in which the episodes were connected by the pranks of the daredevil Tyl. In many ways the structure, mime devices, and ideological message recalled *Petrushka*: Tyl, like Fokine's puppet, cheated death, parading his lively, indestructible spirit in the finale. "The keynote of Nijinsky's interpretation was gaiety," Carl Van Vechten wrote. "He was as utterly picaresque as the work itself; he reincarnated the spirit of Gil Blas."

Nijinsky, still resisting his approaching collapse, attempted without success to choreograph his first long-cherished abstract ballet, to the music of Bach. On September 26, 1917, he performed *Petrushka* and *Spectre* for the last time. In 1919, before a small audience in a Swiss hotel, he suddenly improvised an awesome antiwar dance—his last public appearance as a dancer. The rest of his story, until his death on April 11, 1950, is to be found in the pages of psychiatric reports, not those of ballet history.

Psychologically, his Tolstoyan obsession with Russian Orthodox piety and God, which left so heartfelt an imprint on his *Diary*, can be seen as a desperate search for a father figure to replace Diaghilev. His cubist drawings with their perpetual nightmare of concentric circles seem to reflect his pathetic meandering through the maze of his own soul. Physically, he long outlived his own epoch. In postwar Vienna he watched Galina Ulanova perform with a small group of Soviet dancers, to whose technical flamboyance he had contributed enormously, though he was unaware of this.

RUDOLF NUREYEV

Arlene Croce once said of Nureyev, "[He] is the kind of dancer who causes categories to have a nervous breakdown." He truly resists the customary classifications or comparison even to the most brilliant of his fellow dancers, standing apart from and above them by virtue of his awesome persona. He is an enigma, a bundle of contradictions, the most Russian among his Russian colleagues and at the same time the most Western, the most controversial and magnetic. Like Nijinsky and Pavlova, he belongs entirely to dance. In his younger days he was the very personification of ballet in both Russia and the West. Robert Helpmann once remarked that in his time there have been three artists whom audiences wanted to perform forever, never to leave the stage: Pavlova, Callas, and Nureyev.

At the dawn of his flamboyant career Nureyev was more a danseur noble than anything else: his physique was almost ideal, except that his legs were a bit short in proportion to his elongated torso set on narrow, boyish hips. He was endowed with rare muscular elasticity, a soft plié that imparted an ingratiating feline quality to each of his movements, and a regal carriage which seemed to envelop the stage at the moment of his entrance. The features of his highly expressive face, more than merely handsome, are mobile, able to convey rapid transitions from sorrow to anger, from amorous languor to passion or fury. Nureyev's face and body are wondrously capable of expressing the essence of human feelings, a quality invaluable in dance, an art meant to evoke rather than depict, to suggest more than to explain.

On the other hand, from the very beginning Nureyev's "oversized" dance manner—too exuberant, tempestuous, and sensual even for the Russian taste for uninhibited expression—did not complement his noble physique but inexplicably almost obliterated its effect, adding a demi-caractère flavor to his dancing. The paradoxical combination of his princely looks and his explosive, edgy style toppled all the classical criteria established by Russian academic training.

Nureyev's uniqueness has often been attributed to the fact that he is the only Tartar among the great Russian dancers. As he wrote in his autobiography: "Our Tartar blood runs faster somehow, it is always ready to boil. And yet it seems to me that we are more languid than the Russians, more sensuous. . . . We are a curious mixture of tenderness and brutality—a blend which rarely exists in the Russian (perhaps that is why I discover such a strong affinity with many of Dostoevsky's characters). Tartars are quick to catch fire, quick to get into a fight; unassuming, yet at the same time passionate and sometimes cunning as a fox. The Tartar is in fact a pretty complex animal."

Be that as it may, his Oriental explosiveness and the unpredictable energy of his abrupt shifts from legato to staccato, from voluptuous languor to emotional outburst, made him extraordinary even in comparison with the legendary "scorching sensuality" of Vakhtang Chabukiani. That the young Nureyev was compared so frequently to Chabukiani is both valid and revealing.

Another quality that distinguishes Nureyev's art is his unquenchable thirst for performing, which seems never to be fully assuaged. As it did for Pavlova and Nijinsky, the stage provides Nureyev with his very identity and the framework of his "real" life. But his ardent devotion to dance, it seems, does not give the final clue to the riddle of his puzzling, electrifying personality; one must also consider his overpowering theatricality, his unique sense of stage space, his self-discipline and rare willpower. It is amazing that a young dancer—endowed with flexible, well-stretched muscles and rare extension but lacking a natural jump or coordination—could shatter the academic mold of the Kirov after only three years of classical training. If the

idea of a ballet superstar connotes a personality able to add a touch of pagan frenzy and visceral excitement to classical choreography and create madness in the air, a powerful ability to stir up the subconscious of the audience and feed its hidden hungers, then Nureyev is the only true heir to this title, first held by Nijinsky. Neither Vasiliev nor Baryshnikov, in many respects Nureyev's peers, can equal him in this.

His early performances still haunt the imagination of those Russians who succumbed as I did to his animal magnetism. In my view, this quality should not be equated with his potent sex appeal. The latter is a rather dubious concept anyway in terms of classical ballet, which is concerned with harmony and platonic beauty, responding to our profound yearning for purity and stability in an impure, ever-changing world. Since his first public appearances, Nureyev has demonstrated not so much the possible extension of classical male dancing within the limits of perfect form as the potential range of kinetic expressiveness in general, the scale of sensual impact, emanating from the plastic metaphors that his body has created on stage. He was the only Russian male dancer—as Plisetskaya was the only ballerina—who knew how to thrill and perplex, to captivate and infuriate, to present the most unbelievable or bizarre in ballet with inimitable authority. His devastating impact was the product of his personality, which made his questionable technique a secondary issue, and of the social and psychological climate of the 1960s, in which his image reverberated with special vitality.

N UREYEV WAS BORN on the eve of World War II, on March 17, 1938, into the family of an itinerant political instructor in the Soviet army. He grew up in Ufa, the capital of the Bashkir Soviet Republic. It is truly hard to imagine a city and circumstances more distant from the world of dance than those surrounding the young Nureyev. His ever-increasing passion for ballet developed despite hardship and the cultural stagnation that marked every provincial town in postwar Russia. Before Nureyev, not a single great Russian dancer had come from such a "godforsaken" place.

His childhood impressions of a ballet performance at the Ufa Opera House overwhelmed him. At the age of eleven, in spite of his father's prohibition, he took his first ballet lessons at the Ufa Scientists Club from a former member of Diaghilev's company, Udaltsova. Within four years he was participating in performances at the Ufa Opera House as a mime, super, or character dancer. In May 1955 he came to Moscow to perform in a special festival called "A Decade of Bashkir Art." He took Asaf Messerer's classes at the Bolshoi and, encouraged by this illustrious teacher, soon proceeded to Leningrad to enroll in the Vaganova School.

In August 1955, at the age of seventeen, Nureyev passed the entrance exams to become a student of the sixth grade. Like Baryshnikov a decade later, Nureyev was fortunate enough to enter the class of Alexander Pushkin, who fostered the extremely talented but raw student and indeed became a second father to him. Pushkin helped him develop his jump and reinforced his coordination. What Nureyev achieved during his three years at the Vaganova School was miraculous—a miracle born of his unremitting effort and extraordinary willpower. The story of his zest, devotion, and singleminded persistence—he was known to spend sixteen hours a day in the classroom—is still told and told again at the Vaganova School.

His reputation as a rebel preceded his fame as a dancer. His classmate Elena Tchernichova told me about the young Nureyev:

"Rudi is a high-strung person, with keen feelings for justice and common sense. His early reputation as a temperamental, intractable young man derived mostly from his tempestuous persistence and independent enterprise, which he utilized to make reality conform to his own criteria. He was possessed by dancing and, aware of his technical inadequacy, tried his best to catch up to the classical standard. He was anxious to learn from the famous masters of the Kirov and sneaked into the theatre to see the night performances, although it was forbidden by school regulations. He frequently skipped lessons unrelated to his profession, using the time to work on his own, in the classroom, on his slowly increasing technique. That was really the only way he could condition his body and arm it with all the tricks that students usually had nine years to acquire. He had only three years and naturally didn't want to waste a minute. Instead of winning approval, his devotion and independence infuriated the bureaucratic management. But Pushkin was aware of Rudi's real motivations and defended him in every way possible."

His first student performances (as Acteon in the "Diana and Acteon" pas de deux from *Esmeralda*, Albrecht in the Act II pas de deux of *Giselle*, Siegfried in the Act II adagio of *Swan Lake*, and the Slave in the *Le Corsaire* pas de deux)

immediately drew from him the special quality that was to become his hallmark: he lent to each of his performances a hint of an imminent explosion. His dancing seemed to arise from nowhere and to end as spontaneously as it had emerged. More often than not he would burst onto the stage like a wild animal released from a cage, at a peak of bubbling exultation, outpouring energy, or agonizing tension. And this physical state Nureyev conveyed to the audience with a miraculous thrust. The similes of "leopardlike grace" or "lynxlike attack" which were routinely used to describe him were indeed legitimate, but they only partially suggest his impact. At times the overwhelming thrill the audience got from his attack and execution of the steps was mixed up with a sense of puzzlement; for instance, he performed saut de basque vertically, toward the floor, so that one invariably wondered how he would manage to land. His positions after tours were always blurred. One never knew whether he would end a sequence with his back to the audience or at some incredibly bizarre angle. His beats were seldom precise and his cabrioles could hardly be called exemplary; he never achieved the perfect terre-à-terre technique necessary to excel in Bournonville's choreography.

His graduation performance in May 1958, at which he danced the "Diana and Acteon" and *Le Corsaire* pas de deux and a solo from Nina Anisimova's *Gayane*, aroused a storm of raving enthusiasm in the audience. It was not only Nureyev's animal magnetism that distinguished him from the rest of the dancers but the fact that he looked nothing like a graduating student. The public was confronted with a mature artist with his own style, approach, and even individual technique, strikingly singular against the severe background of the Kirov. It would be fair to say that if there ever was a danseur noble totally alien to the entire Kirov generation of "academicians" from Konstantin Sergeyev to Boris Bregvadze and Vladilen Semyonov, it was the young Nureyev. He was an odd bird in the flock indeed, not only because he was not a "neat" dancer (which he was never to become) but also because the viewer was so transfixed by the sweeping scope of his movements, his confidence and feline grace, that even the most vigilant eyes failed to catch his technical imperfections. They were in fact of no importance, given the thrill of his presence.

Photographs of Nureyev give only a hint of his kinetic scale. The magnetic impression stemmed not from his spectacular posing or the execution of this or that step but from the inimitable way he swept through the choreography as a whole, reveling, pulsating, transfiguring himself as if in a state of trance. The camera always fails to catch the moments of ecstasy so central to his art; this is why picture albums of Nureyev are disappointing to anyone who has felt powerfully drawn into the electrifying hurricane of his dancing.

During his first season at the Kirov (1958–59) Nureyev danced various classical or demi-classical roles: Frondoso in *Laurencia* (his company debut), Basil, Albrecht, Solor, the Blue Bird, and Armen in *Gayane*. Each was transformed by his flamboyance; each bore the mark of his frenetic energy and "irresistible peculiarities," as his technical flaws were called by his fans. As the Blue Bird, however, he seemed earthbound; the exhausting sprint of brisés volés taxed him to such a degree that one cannot understand how he managed to captivate the Parisian audience when he danced this role with the de Cuevas company after his leap to freedom.

Nureyev has often described himself as a genuine product of the Russian school in terms of his concept of ballet as dance-drama. This approach implies the total identification of the dancer with the role, in which he seeks to discover and explore his true self. In this respect Nureyev's involvement in his roles is satisfying and absolute. Like Makarova, he always seeks emotional truth in a performance, no matter how elusive that truth may be. But at the beginning of his career the passion for movement and even for life with which he invested ballet's formal language seemed insufficient to him. That he was so far from being a "correct" dancer constituted an additional challenge, spurring him on to eliminate his imperfections. That is why his primary concern at the Kirov was *how* to dance, not *what* to dance.

Nothing seemed further from the customary Russian theatricality than Nureyev's projection in his early portrayals. It was even hard to relate to them as characterizations in the traditional sense, since in each role he simply poured forth his intoxicating joy of dancing, his cocky bravado, and his teasing sexual ambivalence. But in dramatic terms his Albrecht differed little from his Siegfried, and his Solor resembled his Armen. To a certain degree his characterizations were utterly monotonous, although one was always impressed by his unbridled outbursts of energy—his dashing manèges, when he lingered on high demi-pointe, palpitating with the impatience and delight of a young thoroughbred before the race, and then burst into a string of sauts de basque. One also recalls the unique sense of

freedom he magically brought to the stage, the energy with which he bit into a choreographic phrase, and his seemingly invincible bravura.

Nureyev's drastic modification of the classical roles was both rebellious and awesome; it implied a hint of risk and danger that immediately ignited the audience. He did not just parade his dislike for the conventional mime devices, a time-honored ingredient of Russian classical ballet. He eliminated them. Sometimes he would challenge the audience (and the Kirov management!) by leaving the stage in the middle of an ensemble scene because there was nothing for him to dance at that point. He was truly a "rebel without a cause," arousing great indignation from part of the audience; but his reaction to rebukes was simply "I am a dancer, not a mime." In *La Bayadère* he never bothered to portray the warrior designed by Chabukiani; rather, an unfocused violence and passion, laced with a touch of effeminate Oriental mannerism, marked his pantherlike, space-cleaving jumps. Solor's Act II variation had been choreographed by Chabukiani for himself, in total accordance with his strong, logical design. When Nureyev danced it, his kinetic impact was felt but served no dramatic purpose. The emotional frenzy he introduced into the Kingdom of the Shades somehow did not ring true in the abstract tonality of a spectral no-man's-land. Moreover, Nureyev's detractors could fairly claim that he was not much of a stylist. Indeed, stylistic sensitivity has never been his forte.

In *Swan Lake* Nureyev seemed rather one-dimensional and slack in his partnering. The outpouring of unmotivated sensuality that suddenly pervaded his Act III variation was as perplexing as its brio was captivating. As Frondoso, he seemed to "wake up" only in the bravura Act II variation, which he imbued with absolutely authentic Spanish cockiness. In *Don Quixote* he simply marked time through Acts I and II, waiting for the pyrotechnics of the final pas de deux.

During his brief but dazzling career at the Kirov, Nureyev partnered all its leading ballerinas. Shelest and Kolpakova were his Giselles; Dudinskaya was his Laurencia and Nikiya. His performances with Shelest, whose control and tragic intensity so marvelously contrasted with Nureyev's ardor and *sauvagerie*, were unforgettable. What they evoked was always more than an illumination of the plot; the effect was somewhere beyond it, magically transposed and elevated to abstract, poetic visions. The impact was different with Dudinskaya, whose support contributed greatly to Nureyev's swift promotion. Their special chemistry on stage was fed by mutual competition and the inspiration he brought to her. His enthusiasm and overflowing energy ignited the middle-aged yet still strong ballerina, who seemed to experience an artistic rejuvenation. Second to none at the Kirov, Nureyev had the magical power to cast an invigorating spell on his ballerinas and make them realize their hidden potential. In the *Le Corsaire* pas de deux Alla Sizova revealed her stunning, flamboyant vitality and femininity, but only when Nureyev was her Slave.

Needless to say, his iconoclastic approach to classical tradition, combined with his obvious technical flaws, made his status at the Kirov somewhat precarious. Paradoxically, though, it gave him a special advantage. His performances were like bullfights, with Nureyev and the audience as bull and toreador. The issue of this combat was unpredictable. His very appearance on the stage seemed to stir up an atmosphere of violence and danger; the cruel tension in the anticipating audience boosted Nureyev's self-confidence and electrifying magnetism. This sense of a perpetual duel with the audience intensified Nureyev's impact and eventually brought his harshest detractors under his spell. As one of them, Elizaveta Timeh, once said to me in those early days: "His dancing is not perfection, but what he achieves on stage is more than ballet."

Despite the inadequacy of his classical technique, Nureyev had a considerable effect on the profile of male dancing at the Kirov. He was the first to spin out the grande pirouette on high demi-pointe, to make his legs look longer. Like Plisetskaya's snaking arms in *Swan Lake*, Nureyev's daring trick aroused much indignation from the purists; but fifteen years later, when Baryshnikov executed his ideally balanced grande pirouette on very high demi-pointe, it was accepted as routine.

Occasionally his attempts to break with tradition held a hint of scandal. In *Don Quixote* he was the first to shed Basil's ugly puffed breeches, which disfigured the lines of his legs, and to change them for white tights. Elena Tchernichova told me:

"The intermission lasted forty minutes, while the management pleaded with Rudi to stick with the old costume. It seemed as though Nijinsky's 'cause célèbre' was being revived, with hilariously funny overtones. But Rudi won this preposterous battle. The leading dancers of the old generation—Askold Makarov in particular—urged Boris Fenster, the chief choreographer at the Kirov in those days, to tame the 'effete and vulgar rebel.' To Fenster's credit he uttered this verdict: 'Nureyev marks the beginning of a new era in male dancing. *Your* days are numbered.'"

Nureyev's defection during the Kirov's 1961 engagement in Paris was, of course, the ultimate act of rebellion. When Konstantin Sergeyev and the KGB supervisors attempted to lure him back to Moscow for a fictitious concert performance, all the hidden themes of his life seemed to come into dramatic focus: Sergeyev's jealousy and vindictiveness, Nureyev's own pent-up resentment, his instinctive desire to grow as a dancer and an artist, and his avid interest in everything new, which the West represented for him.

It was Nureyev who launched the series of Russian defections that has so considerably altered the landscape of Western ballet over the last two decades. Invisible threads of fate seem to link him with the two other great fugitives from the Kirov. In 1961 Makarova was allowed to dance her first Giselle in London specifically in order to provide a new sensation to cover for Nureyev's absence. This performance, which otherwise would not have taken place, brought her Western recognition and her subsequent ties with London and the Royal Ballet. When she herself defected in 1970, she made her debut on British television with Nureyev, dancing the *Swan Lake* Act III pas de deux; and Makarova in her turn helped to arrange Baryshnikov's debut in New York four years later.

Nureyev's instant popularity in Europe was largely due to the tremendous publicity that surrounded him, the Russian who preferred the challenges of artistic freedom in the West to the comfortable stability of Soviet servitude. But the impact of publicity should not be overrated—an overnight sensation is the least enduring thing in the Western world if it is not based on real artistic achievement. Nureyev's development as a dancer and his ever-increasing appeal were stimulated, too, by the psychological climate of the sixties. His appearance in the West could not have been better timed: his compelling, iconoclastic personality and his flamboyant, challenging style responded perfectly to the rebellious spirit of the day.

Arlene Croce has remarked:

When he arrived in the West, it was at a moment of upheaval in public morals and popular culture. Nureyev's behavior on- and offstage appeared related to a new trend, and he may even have instigated it, in part. It was amazing how many British rock stars suddenly turned up looking like him. He has never really belonged to the Royal Ballet; he has said that he is an interloper wherever he goes and that he will go anywhere if he is asked. I'm not even sure that he belongs to the dance

Top: (left) Frondoso in *Laurencia*, with Natalia Dudinskaya as Laurencia, late 1950s; (middle & right) Albrecht, with Irina Kolpakova as Giselle, 1960　Bottom: (left) rehearsal, 1950s; (right) The Blue Bird in *The Sleeping Beauty*, 1961

Top: (left) Romeo, with Margot Fonteyn as Juliet (MacMillan), 1960s; (right) Siegfried, with Fonteyn as Odette, 1960s
Bottom: Armand, with Fonteyn as Marguerite, 1975

Right: *Diana and Acteon* pas de deux, 1963
Below: *Les Rendezvous* (Ashton), 1970

OPPOSITE
Top: Basilio in *Don Quixote*, with Lucette Aldous as Kitri, early 1970s
Bottom: The Slave in *Le Corsaire*, 1969

El Penitente (Graham), 1970s

profession, and it's always a bit of a surprise to see him turn up for his entrances on cue.

He was an interloper indeed. In his twenty years in the West he has experimented and collaborated with choreographers both major—Balanchine, Robbins, Ashton, Taylor, Graham, Béjart—and minor—Rudi van Dantzig and John Neumeier. At times his choices seemed arbitrary, but the unevenness of his artistic achievement was balanced by his extraordinary wild-animal quality, by the larger-than-life stage images that hit the audience in the viscera and teased its subconscious. The ever-growing Nureyev craze of the 1960s widened the limited circle of ballet-goers; he did for ballet (once assumed to be an elitist art) just what Maria Callas had done for opera—he made it a popular entertainment. His extravagant, at times idiosyncratic behavior offstage only helped to reinforce his superstar image. And although it seems almost impossible to separate Nureyev's personality from his technical qualities as a dancer, one nevertheless can say that his nomadic life has served him as a school of professionalism. To those who missed his salad days in the 1960s, his increasing perfection in the filmed ballets—*Romeo and Juliet*, *Don Quixote*, and the autobiographical *I Am a Dancer*—testifies to his artistic progress with authority and pride.

In the West Nureyev's technique developed rapidly, thanks to his characteristic talent for absorbing the best of each school and style, be it Danish (especially at the beginning of his career under the influence of Erik Bruhn) or British. The result was a fascinating though odd conglomeration of different choreographic devices variously incompatible with his Russian training. Moreover, the velocity of his progress—a product of his tremendous willpower rather than of gradually conditioned muscles—and the staggering number of performances he gave each year (from two hundred to three hundred) inevitably resulted in notorious technical flaws, even at his artistic peak. His biographer John Percival noted: "There were plenty of people to point out that if Nureyev jumped high, he sometimes landed heavily, and that his tours en l'air were not always strictly vertical." Certainly, the precision and purity of Russian style never did run in his blood; classicism, in a broader sense, was always alien to his unconfined personality. Nor did he ever reveal any strong affinity for Balanchine's neoclassical revamping of Petipa's technique; his performances in *Theme and Variations* (1962) and *Apollo* (1967) aroused much controversy. In my opinion, Nureyev is the latest incarnation of passionate romanticism in ballet, the purveyor of the "sensual exaltation" that Akim Volynsky once thought to be the main appeal of the art. Facets of such irresistible personalities as Chabukiani, Mordkin, and Vladimiroff have been refracted through Nureyev's stage images.

Characteristically, the most profound and compelling of Nureyev's projections came from the pantheon of romantic heroes: Siegfried and Albrecht, Armand in Ashton's *Marguerite and Armand*, Romeo in MacMillan's *Romeo and Juliet*, Des Grieux in MacMillan's *Manon*, the Slave in *Le Corsaire*. In whatever style, be it Ashton's, Petipa's, or MacMillan's, Nureyev tested his potential; he tried to surpass himself as a charismatic personality. To a certain extent he subjugated each style to his forte and to his essentially Russian theatricality, at times outré and overblown—his "oversized grimaces," exaggerated expressions of grief or sorrow, evoked memories of the close-ups in silent movies. An undefinable hint of camp creeps into some of his balletic images and is especially obvious in his intriguing screen portrayal of the legendary Rudolph Valentino.

Nureyev's persona is indeed rather excessive, motivated more frequently than not by his own narcissistic needs and self-involvement. He is truly unmatched in his ability to fill the stage space with the vibrations coming from his electrifying presence, pushing his colleagues to the periphery. When he organized "Nureyev and Friends," his mini dance festivals in Paris and New York, his attitude toward himself as the focus of each performance remained valid regardless of the brightness of the stars who surrounded him. They served as a glamorous frame, of minor interest when measured against his artistry.

Nureyev's tendency to consider his performance a one-man show strikingly recalls Auguste Vestris's pre-Romantic creed "*ballet, c'est moi*" and the legendary prerogatives of Romantic prima ballerinas like Taglioni or Grisi. His cantankerous behavior and tiffs with his partners come from the same source. Even some devices of his style—the exaggeration of his poses or his runs across or around the stage, dazzling in their winged swiftness and lightness—hark back to the mannerisms of those illustrious ancestors.

The romantic thrust and ebullient confidence of Nureyev's image, reinforced by his inquiring artistic nature and ever-increasing professionalism, endowed him with a revolutionary aura in the ballet world of the last two decades. In the sixties his salutary influence and vitality were powerfully felt, especially in British ballet. His achievements included the mounting of Petipa masterpieces such as the Kingdom of the Shades scene from *La Bayadère* (1963) and the Grand Pas from *Paquita* (1964); his success in bringing the British corps de ballet within the reach of Russian academic standards; and his own interpolations (more arbitrary than imaginative) into the canonized Royal Ballet versions of *Swan Lake*, *Sleeping Beauty*, and *Giselle* (Siegfried's Act I solo, Prince Florimund's Act III solo, the baroque vignettes with which he adorned Albrecht's Act II variations).

But Nureyev's most conspicuous contribution to Western ballet came from his unique partnership with Dame Margot Fonteyn, the kind of artistic marriage indeed made in heaven. Their collaboration of many years was a rare phenomenon of mutual inspiration and creative interaction. Fonteyn ennobled and to some extent tamed Nureyev's unrestrained vigor, while his frenzy stirred the ballerina, already in her forties, to imbue her Giselle and Odette with hitherto unseen vitality and poignant lyricism. Their contrasting yet compatible individualities were complementary; or, rather, they blended in an unprecedented artistic osmosis. Thanks to their irresistible chemistry, the eternal values of the Romantic ballets once again cast their enduring magic spell.

Fonteyn's noble reticence, the subdued sacrificial tonality of her lyricism (like Ulanova's but more subtle and multifaceted), her fascinating control and precision—all these qualities were subtly intensified through Nureyev's outbursts of sensual emotion: passion, anger, despair, pain. When juxtaposed, Nureyev's physical exuberance and Fonteyn's spiritual predominance made visible the fundamental poetry of Romantic ballet. The antagonism of sensual and spiritual antinomies, *le diabolique* and *l'angelique*, temptation and sacrifice, love in death—all the metaphysical aspects of Romantic conflict underlying the dramas of Odette and Siegfried, Giselle and Albrecht—were powerfully illuminated by the poetic radiance and full-blooded vitality of the Fonteyn-Nureyev partnership. The chiaroscuro of their portrayals in *Giselle* or *Swan Lake* took on the most refined and contemporary finish.

The finale of Sir Frederick Ashton's *Marguerite and Armand*, designed as a modern incarnation of old Romantic theatre, epitomized the characteristic art of this duo: the sublime simplicity of Fonteyn in the death scene was juxtaposed with the passion of Nureyev "running in a great arc across the back of the stage, his cloak flowing behind him, only to disappear into the wings and then at the last moment to arrive again at the front of the stage, hurling the cloak from him and rushing to take the dying Marguerite in his arms. Nothing but running across the stage, but what he makes of it!" (John Percival). It is hardly an exaggeration to say that in the 1960s and the early 1970s Fonteyn and Nureyev together created the most engaging Romantic theater in all of twentieth-century ballet.

The intensity and power that distinguished Nureyev's own performances and his partnership with Fonteyn frequently proved to be a destructive element in the transcriptions of the Russian classics (*The Nutcracker*, *Raymonda*, *The Sleeping Beauty*, *Swan Lake*, and *Don Quixote*) that he mounted for various Western companies. To a certain extent his choreographic schemes were the reverse of his Romantic image. Like most of the great Russian dancers, he is not a genuine inventor but a capable stage director and restorer. But unlike Chabukiani, Vasiliev, or Baryshnikov, Nureyev has often sacrificed his choreographic skill and stylistic sensitivity to his inflated self-interest as a dancer. By focusing the action on the male principals in *Raymonda* (American Ballet Theatre, 1975) and *Sleeping Beauty* (National Ballet of Canada, 1972) he inevitably disrupted the firmly maintained balance between choreography and music so characteristic of Petipa's compositions. Ideal vehicles for the ballerina, these works resisted his "male chauvinist" encroachment, particularly when, defying Tchaikovsky's or Glazunov's intentions, Nureyev appropriated for his own purposes the music they had written for female variations. *The Sleeping Beauty* somehow managed to withstand his revisions, but his *Raymonda* at ABT degenerated into an extended divertissement loosely attached to a farfetched plot.

No matter how many imperfections, great or small, may mar Nureyev's productions or performances, they can never seriously detract from his glory as a pathfinder, which he deserves as no one else in Russian ballet since the era of Nijinsky and Pavlova. Nor can they tarnish the miraculous phenomenon of his unparalleled creativity, represented by more than seventy roles and many productions, on almost every major Western ballet stage.

The scope of such activities over a twenty-five-year career has inevitably included an omnivorous assimilation of all choreographic styles as well as some dubious choices and lapses of taste. He was miscast in Martha Graham's expressionist *Lucifer* (1975) and almost grotesque as Prince Myshkin in Valery Panov's nonsensical transcription of Dostoyevsky's *The Idiot* (Berlin, 1979). Nureyev's miscalculation was painfully obvious when he tackled Nijinsky's three most famous roles with the Joffrey Ballet in a program of Diaghilev revivals (1979). The Spectre of the Rose, the Faun, and Petrushka all came to him too late, at a time when he was unable to demonstrate the unlimited virtuosity and powerful histrionic abilities the roles demand. Even in the heyday of his career Nureyev could hardly have been labeled a "dancing actor," the sine qua non for Petrushka. Arlene Croce was harsh but accurate in describing his underdog puppet as "waggling, flapping, hunching like a small boy in need of a bathroom, and turning up a piteous little face." His heavily fluttering Spectre, ostentatiously ignoring the Girl and displaying slipshod port de bras, only distantly suggested the androgynous appeal and Freudian overtones that are vital to the role. He was indeed a spectre of the Spectre. And while his broad-shouldered, lithe, sensuous Faun did exhibit the necessary feral quality and adolescent sexuality, he arbitrarily split the stream of Nijinsky's flowing design into segments, not always coherent or meaningful.

By the mid-1970s, Nureyev's worn-out muscles had considerably affected his technique. He has paid a high price for his lifelong, burning obsession with dance, for his never-ending balletic marathon, and for his dazzling fame. With customary vehemence he still claims that his dancing is unimpaired and that he plans to continue performing until he reaches the age of fifty, but his most recent appearances testify that he has sadly depleted his technical resources. What lies ahead only Nureyev knows. He is reluctant to leave the stage, but his appointment as artistic director of the Paris Opéra Ballet, and the success of his new version of Petipa's *Raymonda* there, seem to suggest that he will curtail his dance career. His nondancing film role in *Exposed* suggests possible new directions, although in interviews he insists that his film activities serve only as "a break between performances." Should we ever again see such an avalanche of dazzling creativity, however, we will unavoidably be seeing another artist, not the man whose once-in-a-century gifts shattered the old choreographic and aesthetic standards of Western ballet. That Rudolf Nureyev no longer exists.

Apollo, 1978

MIKHAIL BARYSHNIKOV

The legendary Nijinsky was on everyone's mind at Mikhail Baryshnikov's graduation performance in the spring of 1966. Although rumors about Alexander Pushkin's new prodigy had already ignited the audience's expectations, Baryshnikov's variation from the *Corsaire* pas de deux greatly exceeded them—no one was prepared for the absolute classical perfection of his grande pirouette, flawlessly balanced with the leg raised to ninety degrees, or his double tours en l'air, which he executed with such effortless brio.

The pandemonium in the audience, which was mesmerized by the kinetic power, elegance, and classical pre-cision of the young graduate, matched the frantic enthusiasm that had attended Rudolf Nureyev's early appearances. But Baryshnikov was of an entirely different nature. His personality did not project sexual energy, nor did it hit the viewer in the solar plexus. Rather, his appeal came from an incredibly pure classical technique, enhanced by an impish charm. His lightness in the most intricate sequences, his coordination, balance, precision, and musicality—all were second nature to him, and all contributed to creating the image of a poet of the classical dance, who seemed to be testing its limits and possibilities. The rare freedom with which he passed from one movement to another gave the impression of a body dancing reflexively, without control or mental effort. The effortlessness of his jumps and turns recalled Yuri Soloviev's, but in artistry and charm he far surpassed the latter. Like Nijinsky, Baryshnikov knew how to blend movements, linking steps and preparations into one long sequence of dance that overwhelmed with its kinetic charm and power.

After his debut Baryshnikov was immediately pronounced a wonder, and the aura of legend hovered over each turn of his career in Russia and in the West.

MIKHAIL NIKOLAYEVICH BARYSHNIKOV was born on January 27, 1948, in Riga, the capital of Latvia, into the family of a Soviet army officer, Nikolai Baryshnikov. In 1960 his mother, Alexandra Kiseleva, brought the twelve-year-old Misha to the Riga State Choreographic School, where he progressed so quickly that after only two years he was promoted to the advanced class. In 1964 one of his senior colleagues took Baryshnikov to the Vaganova School in Leningrad, where he was immediately accepted and placed in Alexander Pushkin's class, as if to fill the void left by Pushkin's most illustrious pupil, Rudolf Nureyev, who had defected to the West in 1961.

Pushkin's influence on Baryshnikov's artistic growth would be difficult to overestimate. With his exceptional pedagogic gift Pushkin stimulated Baryshnikov's natural coordination and increased the amplitude and elevation of his strong yet only moderately high jump. Pushkin proved to be Baryshnikov's spiritual mentor as well. Pushkin's background stemmed from the legacy of the nearly extinct prerevolutionary intelligentsia, whose cultural standards became the measure of his pupil's attitude toward life, the ballet, and art in general. He inculcated in Baryshnikov a tremendous respect for, and an eagerness to absorb, Russian culture. Moreover, Pushkin developed in Baryshnikov the intellectual and artistic curiosity that made him determined to explore the aspects of Western culture from which Soviet artistic life had for many years been isolated.

In 1967 he was taken into the Kirov company as a soloist, bypassing the corps de ballet. But Baryshnikov presented something of a problem to the administration, because he could not easily be cast in any of the traditional balletic categories, and the Kirov regulations were as strict about this as they had been under Petipa in the last century. His limitless technique was not a factor in deciding the roles Baryshnikov might perform, but his physical qualities

were: his supple, elongated muscles and soft plié seemed to orient him toward lyrical-Romantic roles. On the other hand, his short stature, his boyish face with its wide expressive range, and his generally playful disposition seemed to indicate demi-caractère possibilities. But his body was too perfect a classically polished instrument to be limited to the demi-caractère repertoire (of which the buffoon in Konstantin Sergeyev's version of *Swan Lake* is an example). Pushkin, apprehensive about how the Kirov might employ Baryshnikov, warned him: "They can make you squander your technique on assorted pas de deux for years."

Baryshnikov was difficult to cast for another reason: the way in which he infused ordinary enchaînements with flamboyant vitality by integrating the main movements and the linking steps. This unusual manner of execution, his speed, and his brio confused or even annoyed his Kirov colleagues. Some of the established soloists complained that they could hardly see his "darting tricks," although others asserted that Baryshnikov had nothing less than a perfect technique. Moreover, the drama-ballet-oriented Kirov policy seemed to preclude Baryshnikov's being correctly employed in the future.

His first season at the Kirov (1967–68) illustrated these problems. For his debut he danced the Peasant pas de deux from the first act of *Giselle*, in Petipa's original choreography, executing the stream of beats and cabrioles as if they were child's play. He stole the show. I remember hearing someone in the audience say: "He is like Ariel, the spirit of youth that makes one feel younger." Soon afterward, he appeared as the Blue Bird in *The Sleeping Beauty* and as the Romantic Poet in *Chopiniana*. In both roles Baryshnikov was miscast. Compared with Yuri Soloviev, Baryshnikov lacked natural ballon—the capacity to appear to hang in the air—so that his flitting bird looked heavy and contrived, while in *Chopiniana* the necessary mixture of meditative reticence and mannered solicitude eluded him completely. He successfully executed the choreography that Fokine had created for Nijinsky, but he never went beyond a merely correct performance. The Poet was one of the very few roles that he was never to master, even in later years in the West.

During this first season he usually performed in mixed bills dancing pas de deux (*Le Corsaire* or *Don Quixote*, for instance) that had been threadbare even in Petipa's time.

Baryshnikov's physical appearance, his irresistible youthful charm, his confidence and buoyancy all proved to be something of a trap. He could too easily be used to represent the official image of Soviet youth, who appeared in ballet after ballet. In 1968 Oleg Vinogradov offered Baryshnikov a role of this type: the rather abstract yet zany Soviet student in *The Mountain Girl*, based on a prose epic by the prolific Caucasian writer Rasul Gamzatov. In the primitive, acrobatic choreography of the early Vinogradov, Baryshnikov was radiant, bursting into the dizzying rivoltades, beats, double tours en l'air, and other breathtaking feats that brought him his early glory. In *The Mountain Girl* he danced opposite Natalia Makarova, a first harbinger of their fruitful collaboration in the West.

The lighthearted barber Basil in Petipa's *Don Quixote*, which he danced during his second season (1968–69), was the only part in the Kirov's classical repertory that suited Baryshnikov's talent. It was the first role in which he made the Leningrad audience fully aware of his impish charm and extraordinary sense of humor. He took the silly old plot as a pretext for a stream of bravura dancing, performed with a mocking, mischievous air, and he deliberately departed from the traditional approach, which prescribed a realistic portrayal of Basil as a cunning rogue. Instead, he performed Basil's pranks as if purely for the sake of making playful mischief. This carefree, ebullient Basil seemed uninvolved in the absurdities of the plot, and the most virtuoso passages were performed with insouciance.

This unusual approach was disparaged by Baryshnikov's most fervent champions, who regarded his iconoclasm as a sign of his artistic immaturity. His keen sense of irony also seemed too daring and even eccentric. Very few in the audience felt that Baryshnikov's intellectual approach to the artificiality of *Don Quixote* shed witty modern light on a well-worn classic.

The shortage of roles available to Baryshnikov at the Kirov caused him to seek other opportunities in collaboration with nonconformist choreographers. One of these was Igor Tchernichov, whose one-act *Romeo and Juliet* (Berlioz) had its premiere in December 1969. Baryshnikov's portrayal was a cascade of showstopping pyrotechnics, but it also brought about the essence of Shakespeare's headstrong youth—his challenging, romantic bravado and his sardonic wit. Especially memorable and evocative was his rendition of the "Queen Mab" sequence: with his back to the audience, he suddenly burst into a double-and-a-half tour en l'air without preparation, landing in arabesque facing the audience, and, a split second later, throwing himself into an enchaînement of lightning pirouettes and beats performed at top speed.

The year 1969 brought Baryshnikov a surprise: Leonid

Jakobson choreographed *Vestris* for him, for that year's international competition in Moscow. This cameo ballet evoked the legendary image of Auguste Vestris, the virtuoso and a powerful dramatic dancer of the eighteenth century. Both aspects of Vestris were imaginatively pinpointed by Baryshnikov in his portrayal: dressed in waistcoat and gold-colored tights, he paraded an unparalleled technique and potent theatricality that dumbfounded the Moscow jury. The panel included Galina Ulanova, Alicia Alonso, and Maya Plisetskaya, who was especially amazed by the spectacular lightness with which Baryshnikov shifted from the most complex classical sequences to compelling, grotesque pantomime. The extraordinary sequence of momentary masks—the broken-down courtier, the brazen upstart, the arrogant nobleman—revealed the unique talent of the young dancer.

Baryshnikov won a gold medal for his performance. The dramatic potential he displayed in *Vestris* seemed to open new perspectives for his career. When the Kirov appeared in London in August 1970, the British critics pronounced him a genius, but the administration seemed uninterested in his future. The next year, neither Konstantin Sergeyev's *Hamlet* nor Oleg Vinogradov's *The Prince of the Pagodas* presented any real challenge. *Hamlet* was genuine Soviet kitsch, a farrago of pointless clichés. To his credit, he refused to dance the ballet after two performances, citing the production's utter inconsistency. More frustration followed with *The Prince of the Pagodas*. Although set to music by Benjamin Britten, the choreography proved to be merely a tour de force of circus tricks and showstopping acrobatics. Baryshnikov was despondent over the result, at a time when no meatier roles seemed likely to appear.

But one soon came from an unusual quarter: in 1971 Baryshnikov startled the Leningrad television audience with his potent portrayal of the toreador in Sergei Yursky's dramatization of Hemingway's *The Sun Also Rises*. His stage presence, his glances, and his movements combined with his vitality and special energy to bring his torero to vivid life.

Also in 1971, Moscow's Natalia Kasatkina and Vladimir Vasilyov mounted their *Creation of the World* for Baryshnikov. He was a charming and amusing Adam—it seemed that comedy was perhaps his true forte. As a baby he was hilarious, paying childish attention to his own feet, taking his first shaky steps, frolicking excitedly with the little angels—every action was both touching and comical. Then, as the "child" grew up, he gradually became independent of his progenitor and guardian angels. Fully coordinated at last, he began to dance, launching into the most startling sequences, in which his virtuosity seemed to recognize no limits. When, in a fit of passion, he threw himself into a string of rivoltades, instead of landing in the ordinary fashion he shifted in the air before landing, thus beginning another set.

In the course of the ballet Baryshnikov depicted Adam's maturation from child to adult: the progress of his relationship with Eve gave the whole a poignant, lyrical tonality. Gradually his appealing insouciance gave way to vulnerability and real tenderness. Dramatic genius, even more than virtuosity, marked this portrayal.

In *The Creation of the World* Baryshnikov convinced the audience that he possessed the artistic maturity to master Albrecht and Siegfried, roles previously considered beyond his range. To this day he has never danced Siegfried, but 1972 saw his Albrecht. He was coached by the Kirov traditionalist Vladilen Semyonov, but Baryshnikov's interpretation was wholly modern. For him, Giselle was an object of romance, a first love whom he never intended to deceive. An irresponsible, flirtatious youth, he gave no thought to the problems of class.

The first act gave him very little to dance but allowed him to display his histrionic instincts. One was amazed by the clarity of the motivation of his behavior. His chaste love left him entirely unprepared to meet its consequences. Giselle's death was an emotional shock—grief-stricken, almost numbed by this unexpected blow, he bent over his dead love as if facing the mystery of death for the first time.

The second act also proved anything but traditional. The ardent youth came to the moonlit forest in search not of forgiveness but of a solitude in which he might evoke the image of his remembered love and indulge in a poetic vision of the Wilis' grove, a realm beyond life and death. Baryshnikov displayed a stunning sensitivity to the second act's symbolic richness. He interpreted the dance "marathon" not as the Wilis' curse but as their challenge, a competition of two equal adversaries. He was determined to do more than just survive the ordeal: he saturated diagonals—glissade, cabriole, coupé, assemblé, entrechat six repeated three times—with a tremendous thrust, even violence, exploding into vehement jumps and imbuing the beats with a strong energetic impulse. In executing cabrioles he threw his torso back to 60 degrees (instead of an academically approved 45-degree angle), giving the familiar enchaînement a new dimension.

The tours en l'air, pirouettes, and chassés of the second part of the variation, meant to indicate Albrecht's exhaus-tion, breathed his vigor and indomitability; his tours en l'air leading directly into dazzling renversés were equally powerful. The two diagonal series of swift brisés, usually seen as a plea for Myrtha's mercy, were danced with a bent torso, at enormous speed. They flashed like lightning, and their kinetic power suggested this Albrecht's courage and unwillingness to surrender. The last touch Baryshnikov added to the farewell scene was also unusual: moving away from Giselle's grave, he strewed the white flowers on the ground in a line that seemed to mark the last, indissoluble link between them, a symbol of their indestructible love.

The title of Honored Artist of the Republic was bestowed on Baryshnikov at the end of 1973, when he was engaged in a rather taxing enterprise—a special gala performance at the Kirov focused on him. Allowed his choice of music and program, he chose choreographers who opposed the artistic policy of the Kirov or simply were not in official favor. He spent the entire winter of 1973–74 working with two of the most daring young Soviet choreographers, Georgy Alexidze and Mai Murdmaa. The program consisted of three one-act ballets: *Daphnis and Chloe* and *The Prodigal Son*, both newly remounted by Murdmaa, and Alexidze's *Mozartiana*, set to Mozart's *Les Petits Riens*. But despite all his efforts, Baryshnikov's gala enjoyed a *succès d'estime* at best.

The terre-à-terre choreography of *Daphnis and Chloe* precluded the kind of pyrotechnic display the public was eager to see. Moreover, Daphnis was a vapid role, neither dramatic nor comic, and even Baryshnikov's charm and youthful ardor could barely compensate for its emptiness.

Had Murdmaa's *Prodigal Son* not been measured against Balanchine's masterpiece (which had produced quite a stir during the New York City Ballet's Russian tour in 1962), the ballet's inconsistency might not have been revealed so dramatically. The choreography was designed as a pure-dance parallel to Prokofiev's score, which lost sight of the dramatic essence of the music. Shunning stylized pantomime and a logical unfolding of the plot, Murdmaa was left with a trite story about a disagreeable youth who returns to his loving father after a string of crazy escapades. Baryshnikov danced flawlessly, but nothing could bring the ballet to life.

Baryshnikov's radiant talent, his lightness and zest added a jubilant luster to Alexidze's *Mozartiana*, a lively ballet with Balanchinian overtones that was the most successful piece on the program.

Baryshnikov perceived this gala as a failure, and his sparkling personality seemed to be quenched at most of his performances during the spring of 1974. Restless, and understandably so, at twenty-six, he began to consider the alternatives. The Kirov routine was stifling. He dreamed of collaborating with Western choreographers as Plisetskaya and Vasiliev had done, but what was obtainable to them at the Bolshoi seemed impossible under the repressive Kirov management and Leningrad's severe KGB. In June 1974 he embarked on a Canadian tour with a group of Bolshoi "Stars" supervised by Raissa Struchkova and Alexander Lapauri. Baryshnikov and Irina Kolpakova were the only true stars; the programs were a shabby potpourri of excerpts and threadbare divertissements.

On June 29, 1974, Baryshnikov performed a true act of improvisation by defecting in Toronto. His first two years in the West were full of anguish, anxiety, and remorse for deserting the Kirov and his friends: "The phantom of Russia pursued and haunted me like a hangman, always invisibly watching my steps and making my new life almost unbearable," he once told me.

After his initial appearances with American Ballet Theatre he was instantly granted superstar status. He danced the *Don Quixote* pas de deux, the Kingdom of the Shades scene from *La Bayadère*, and *Giselle*—all with Makarova. For the first time in his career he was subjected to thorough critical scrutiny, as in an article on "The Ballet Superstars" by Tobi Tobias:

> One of the unspoken premises of classical dancing . . . is that each gesture or pose has a Platonic (or perfect) model that the ordinary dancer is striving to imitate; more often than not, Baryshnikov manages to look like the model come to life. At any given moment of dancing, each part of his body seems to be moving in complement to the rest; this grace is never studied, but so absolute it seems natural. The images he creates in space—even at top speed—are clear, and however extravagant his expenditure of energy, he appears to hold some still in reserve. Baryshnikov is a master of rapid, spirited turns and can vary the action of the working leg against the supporting leg—a feat that looks like circus trickery when tried by all his lesser imitators. His elevation—the ability to achieve height and breadth in space—is remarkable not just for the surprises he creates by changing the shape of a leap in mid-air, but for its look of effortlessness.

Or as Arlene Croce wrote in her *New Yorker* piece "Glimpses of Genius":

Baryshnikov is able to perform unparalleled spectacular feats as an extension of classical rather than character or acrobatic dancing. . . . He gets into a step sequence more quickly, complicates it more variously, and prolongs it more extravagantly than any dancer I've ever seen. . . . Perhaps his greatest gift is his sense of fantasy in classical gesture. He pursues the extremes of its logic so that every step takes on an unforeseen dimension. His grande pirouette is a rhapsody of swelling volume and displaced weight. He does not turn; he is turned—spun around and around by the tip of his toe.

Baryshnikov's Western career to date can be divided into three periods: the experimental years (1974–77), the Balanchine seasons (1977–79), and the ABT era, in the capacity of artistic director, a post he assumed in 1979.

During his first three years in the West Baryshnikov pounced omnivorously on an enormous repertoire, taking on twenty-two new roles; his book *Baryshnikov at Work* handsomely records these accomplishments. Their variety was staggering, ranging from Western stagings of the classics to Tudor, Balanchine, and Robbins, from Roland Petit and John Butler to Twyla Tharp and John Neumeier. But the more he danced James in *La Sylphide*, Solor in the Kingdom of the Shades, Albrecht in *Giselle*, and Siegfried in *Swan Lake* (in both Erik Bruhn's modernized version with the National Ballet of Canada and the traditional version with the Royal Ballet in London), the more he felt that these roles, no matter how brilliantly performed, were merely sounding a coda to his Kirov period.

During his early years in the West, few members of the audience, breathlessly following his rapid, spirited turns on stage or the wonders of his elevation, understood that what they were seeing was, in a way, merely the glittering façade of a superb artist. Arlene Croce, who regarded him as a "one-man revolution," once remarked that "Baryshnikov's dancing is in his showmanship. His acting tends to be a cover for his personality, not a revelation of it." In comparison with Nureyev's sensuality and tempestuousness, Baryshnikov seemed to hold back. He was quite conscious of the uniqueness of his unparalleled classical technique and potent theatrical instincts. He could have capitalized on them for years; but the intensity with which he absorbed the cultural life of the West was accompanied by a drastic re-evaluation of the Russian approach to ballet as dance-drama. The realistic mode, though dramatically effective, now ceased to compel him intellectually. The evolution of Baryshnikov's career in the West reflected his inner need

Clockwise from top: *Flames of Paris* pas de deux, with Olga Vtorushina, mid-1960s; Adam in *The Creation of the World*, early 1970s; *Don Quixote* pas de deux, with Nelli Kurgapkina, late 1960s; *Don Quixote* pas de deux, 1969 (First International Ballet Competition, Moscow)

Above: Albrecht, with Gelsey Kirkland as Giselle, 1975
Left: Colin in *La Fille mal gardée*, with Kirkland as Lise, 1974

OPPOSITE
Clockwise from top right: *Le Spectre de la rose*, 1976; *Push Comes to Shove*, 1976; *Vestris*, 1976; Petrushka, 1976

Left: Rubies in *Jewels*, with Patricia McBride, 1979
Below: Melancholic in *The Four Temperaments*, 1979

OPPOSITE
Clockwise from top right: *Tarantella* (Balanchine), 1979; Romeo (MacMillan), 1975; Franz in *Coppélia*, 1975

Top: *Other Dances*, with Natalia Makarova, late 1970s
Above: (left) *Follow the Feet*, 1983; (right) *Nine Sinatra Songs* (Tharp), with Elaine Kudo, 1984

to go beyond what was for him a stale aesthetic. He was not afraid to jeopardize his prestige as a superstar by tackling sometimes rather controversial choreographic styles; he cared more about artistic fulfillment than about success. To some extent he began to struggle against his image as an impeccable virtuoso in order to reveal the human subject, the personality concealed behind his show-stopping tricks. This struggle led him to explore two seemingly contradictory directions: an "instrumental" style, in which the dancer's body creates the choreographic images without direct reference to a plot, and a style of more emphatic personal projection.

His first forays into these "new" areas were at ABT. In Balanchine's *Theme and Variations* in October 1974 he realized, as he later wrote, that "the characterization is . . . in the steps, which have to be performed without any 'interpretation.'" This new attitude, so alien to the Russians, predominated throughout his "pre-Balanchine period," and each of his various roles stimulated it differently. In Roland Petit's *Le Jeune Homme et la mort* in January 1975, Baryshnikov's perception of the metaphysical drama triggered his own pent-up dissatisfaction or anger, which colored his portrayal with a very disquieting tone. In John Neumeier's *Hamlet Connotations* and John Butler's *Medea*, both premiered at ABT in January 1976, Baryshnikov seemed to have reached a crossroads. Plot took second place to choreography in these works, but neither attained the level of inventiveness or poetry worthy of Baryshnikov.

He continued to dream of a ballet that would make no reference to his Russian background and found it at last in Twyla Tharp's *Push Comes to Shove* (January 1976). In choreography that bordered on parody of the classical lexicon, Baryshnikov found his freedom, displaying unprecedented virtuosity and spontaneity, and a talent for improvisational comedy that he had never before revealed to the American audience. His mastery of Tharp's choreographic shenanigans was unexpected and breathtaking, an exploration of the seemingly limitless possibilities of Baryshnikov's art. His charming sense of humor shone through every sequence. The audience relished his exuberance and insouciance; as Arlene Croce noted in *The New Yorker*, "the dancing gives us more of Baryshnikov, the twentieth-century 'American' Baryshnikov, than anything else he has done so far. . . . His personality does not go behind a cloud, as it often does when he isn't dancing; it continues to radiate."

Baryshnikov's fascination with Nijinsky led to his essaying *Le Spectre de la rose* (December 1975) and *Petrushka*

(June 1976) at ABT. These ballets each presented serious technical problems to Baryshnikov; *Spectre* was especially challenging because of his lack of natural ballon. Rather than attempting to imitate Yuri Soloviev's effortless flight—flittering, flickering, and vanishing like a subtle perfume in the air—Baryshnikov invested the elaborate sequences of beats and sissonnes with his natural fluidity, to create an image of refined sexual ambivalence. Where Soloviev teased and dumbfounded, Baryshnikov conjured up a vision of youthful grace that was poetic and serene.

Petrushka was a different story. Baryshnikov's physical qualities—his sharp features, distant eyes, his flexible body—were right for the role, but he was conscious of the danger this advantage might entail. He could easily capitalize on his physicality and give the traditional dancer-playing-a-doll-performance, but he sought the poignant emotional coloring that would transform a cartoon figure into a suffering human soul. This vivid characterization eluded him at first, but eventually he achieved a miracle of theatricality, the underdog of Russian folklore giving way to the tormented child, longing for affection and sympathy. His angularity and touching awkwardness evoked a score of emotional shadings, from jubilation to grief, humiliation to triumph, in a manner reminiscent of Chaplin.

Baryshnikov's strong affinity for tragedy, which in my view constitutes the major facet of his personality, was confirmed in 1979 when he danced the Pushkinesque visionary Hermann in Roland Petit's one-act ballet *The Queen of Spades*. Hermann is a soul-torn daydreamer, lost between fantasy and reality, an ambitious neurotic caught up in the drama of fallacious dreams. Baryshnikov reveled in Petit's compelling choreography, which conjoined expressionistic, bravura show-stoppers that conveyed Hermann's maniacal passion for gambling with charged mime that suggested the character's sporadic moments of self-evaluation and scrutiny. His intensely dramatic transitions from insanity to normalcy showed that Baryshnikov had not entirely abandoned the dramatic storytelling ballets of his Russian past.

His sensitivity to drama revealed itself anew in his own productions of *The Nutcracker* and *Don Quixote*, which he mounted for American Ballet Theatre in December 1977 and March 1978, respectively. His approach to *The Nutcracker* obviously grew out of the traditional Soviet view of the ballet as a fairy tale for adults, which was not that of the original Maryinsky production conceived by Petipa and choreographed by Lev Ivanov. Baryshnikov tried to resolve some of the discrepancies between music and subject, drawing on the experience of his Soviet predecessors—Lopukhov and Vainonen in the 1920s and 1930s, Grigorovich and Tchernichov in the 1960s. In an interview broadcast to Russia by the Voice of America, he said: "*The Nutcracker* was more of an experiment as a director to me. I paid tribute in it to all the previous experiments in Russia. The interpretation was mine."

Baryshnikov's design had a strong dramatic message, investing Clara's godfather Drosselmeyer with the traits of a Hoffmannesque conjuror who initiated Clara into the miracles of Christmas night, a crucial event in the development of a childish soul that bids farewell to illusions. The theme of disenchantment is quite meaningful to Baryshnikov himself, who struck a very personal note in his *Nutcracker*.

His revival of *Don Quixote*, choreographically more consistent than *The Nutcracker*, was also an experiment in stage direction. Baryshnikov revised the Petipa-Gorsky legacy, picked the best from each, and seasoned his composition with a dash of the irony that had marked his earlier interpretation of Basil. By restoring the original title, *Don Quixote or The Wedding of Basil and Kitri*, Baryshnikov paid tribute to Petipa and Gorsky, who conceived the ballet as dance comedy with vaudeville gags. *Don Quixote* was a sparkling entertainment, more consistent and spectacular than Baryshnikov's *Nutcracker*, reflecting his own affinity for comical scenes and merrily orchestrated dancing.

In the summer of 1978 Baryshnikov startled the ballet world by joining George Balanchine's New York City Ballet. Ever since the company's second Russian tour in 1972, Balanchine's choreography had been a source of inspiration for Baryshnikov. Like many of his Russian colleagues, he considered Balanchine's work to be the legitimate descendant of St. Petersburg classicism, refined and elevated to the aesthetic standards of the twentieth century. In joining Balanchine's unique ensemble, he seemed to be returning to the Maryinsky in its new incarnation, which, in its turn, gave a special meaning to his defection from Russia.

NYCB's enormous repertory offered Baryshnikov a challenge that was no longer posed for him by the thoroughly explored classics—in Balanchine's neoclassical works Baryshnikov could test himself in a new style and technique. Encouraged by his successful experiences with *Apollo* and *Prodigal Son* in Chicago and with *Theme and Variations* at ABT, he thought that the transition from Petipa's idiom to Balanchine's would be smooth, and counted on his own highly concentrated dancing and innate coordination to

cope with Balanchine's densely packed choreography and syncopated rhythms. But probably the most tempting challenge was that of mastering NYCB's cool style, so different from that of his Russian background. It almost seemed that Baryshnikov had joined the company in order to erase his virtuoso image.

His fifteen months with Balanchine proved both fruitful and taxing. The ballets deriving from Balanchine's Russian heritage, such as *Prodigal Son, Coppélia, Harlequinade, The Nutcracker*, and *The Steadfast Tin Soldier*, provided an easier transition for Baryshnikov than the choreographer's more daring works.

The fury and vulnerability of the *Prodigal Son* were immediately apparent in Baryshnikov's first solo, with its impetuous leaps and lightning turns. His portrayal, less stylized and more spontaneous than Edward Villella's, was seasoned with a strong dash of humor when he was obliged to contend with the advances of the towering Siren.

Baryshnikov's interpretation of Balanchine's *Apollo*, in the slightly truncated version that he danced in Paris and Chicago in 1978 and in the more drastically abbreviated one introduced at the New York City Ballet in May 1979, was on a par with the brilliance of his *Prodigal Son*. In the Chicago Ballet Festival production, Baryshnikov gave a passionate portrayal of the temperamental god of libretto and myth. Although some critics expressed dissatisfaction with his "angry-young-man style," to others his effort to humanize the majesty of Apollo with Russian impetuosity seemed a legitimate and compelling way to convey the transformation from frenzied youth to magisterial god. In *Apollo* Baryshnikov embodied the work's major idea—self-discovery through dancing.

The Nutcracker, Harlequinade, The Steadfast Tin Soldier, and *La Sonnambula* were all related to Baryshnikov's Russian past. Using him in these works was perhaps Balanchine's tribute to the Maryinsky, their common alma mater. To each Baryshnikov brought his personal magic, that piercing lyrical touch that so animated his Harlequin *mal aimé* and warmed the angular mechanical movements of his Tin Soldier. In *La Sonnambula* he created one of his most poignant and moving characterizations. The Poet is virtually a mime role, but it brought out Baryshnikov's sense of drama and style, offering him the opportunity to create a character like Goethe's Werther, a love-smitten Romantic soul longing for his feminine ideal. His portrayal was measured, in total harmony with the stylized nature of the ballet.

Despite his seemingly boundless technique, Baryshnikov's performances in other Balanchine ballets—*Rubies, Symphony in C, Donizetti Variations, The Four Temperaments*—were flawed. In the magnificently structured ensemble ballets, his usually dazzling stage presence was muffled; technical survival took precedence over projection. In *Symphony in C* even his priceless coordination failed him; in *Donizetti Variations* he was liable to lose his timing. The breakneck speed at which the complex choreography of these works had to be performed required special training that Baryshnikov was unable to absorb within such a short period of time. In order to execute Balanchine's inventions with his customary technical brilliance, he should have had many long and drudging hours of rehearsal, but he was committed to learning a dozen ballets at a time. The strain on his muscles was so severe that in order to keep up, he could only dance perfunctorily.

There were times when his projection was sufficiently potent to compensate for his technical inadequacy, as in *A Midsummer Night's Dream*. Baryshnikov's Oberon was mischievous and slightly arrogant, coldly calculating each step in his amorous combat with Titania. In the variation, however, one of the most taxing of all Balanchine's male roles, he was slipshod and strained, unable to master the exceedingly intricate combinations of turns and jetés à la seconde. He could unleash his virtuosity only in a work like *Tchaikovsky Pas de Deux*, choreographically similar to Petipa's academic style and therefore more comfortable for him. He also excelled as the Costermonger in *Union Jack* and in *Stars and Stripes*, although he did not feel much affinity for either ballet.

In 1976 at ABT, Jerome Robbins had created *Other Dances*, an elegant and lyrical plotless pas de deux, for Baryshnikov and Makarova. When he joined the New York City Ballet, Baryshnikov added to his Robbins repertory *Dances at a Gathering, Fancy Free, The Four Seasons*, and *Opus 19 / The Dreamer*. Perhaps his most successful portrayal in these works was his spry and sprightly "second sailor" in *Fancy Free*, which he performed only once, at a benefit for the School of American Ballet in May 1979. The role was a gem, a showcase for his verve, hilarious tricks, and virtuoso brilliance.

Robbins designed two ballets for Baryshnikov at NYCB: *The Four Seasons*, set to Verdi's ballet music for *I Vespri Siciliani* and *I Lombardi*, and *Opus 19 / The Dreamer*, to Prokofiev's First Violin Concerto. In *The Four Seasons* Baryshnikov was the focus of the autumnal bacchanale, a vaudeville stunt man showing off his technique with sparkle

and élan. He reeled off his unique grand pirouette with the free leg bent in every attitude, and with sautés on his working leg. At times he would freeze in mid-pirouette à la seconde and then continue spinning, the epitome of concentrated speed and impeccable balance.

The anguished protagonist of *Opus 19 / The Dreamer* seemed to be adrift in the dim realm of the subconscious, a world inhabited by faceless creatures and a menacing woman. His muscular arms and quivering torso, his powerful leaps and turns, added up to a vision of tormented masculinity. His pas de deux with Patricia McBride, the emotional climax of the ballet, was performed without emotional coloration; Baryshnikov achieved his effects not through technical skill or theatricality, but by means of the purely intellectual control that he had achieved while he was assimilating Balanchine's style.

Baryshnikov's withdrawal from the New York City Ballet in the fall of 1979 launched a new period in his career, one that is hard to analyze not only because it is still in progress, but also because the circumstances of his present life make it difficult to predict the direction in which he will travel as an artist.

In September 1979 he was appointed artistic director of American Ballet Theatre, where he has continued the policy of his predecessors, Mikhail Mordkin, Lucia Chase, and Oliver Smith, blending the traditions of Russian and American ballet into a new artistic unity. His interest in dancing the classics has subsided, at least for the present. His performances away from ABT have been kept to a minimum, only partly because of the injuries that have befallen him. (The most serious, a knee injury in 1982, condemned him to inactivity for the major part of that year, except for a brief appearance at Spoleto.)

The year 1979 was crucial for Baryshnikov. Arlene Croce noted that he had met "every feasible challenge that the Western ballet repertory holds and has been far afield in search of new stimuli." Unexpectedly, he sought those stimuli in the domain of mass media, participating in two television shows—*Baryshnikov on Broadway* in 1980 and *Baryshnikov in Hollywood* in 1982. The fervent enthusiasm with which he has discussed these programs with me seems to relate more to his psychological needs of the moment than to the dubious artistic results. To a certain degree, these programs were an extension of his film debut in *The Turning Point* in 1977, which had disappointed him and made him seek out employment in television, which offered, it seemed, more exciting possibilities. His desire to experiment beyond purely classical forms was powerful enough to make him disregard the indisputable flaws of both shows, especially those of *Baryshnikov in Hollywood*, the vapidity of which could challenge the silliness of the most nonsensical soap opera. *Baryshnikov on Broadway*, in spite of its triviality, provided an unprecedented glimpse of a classical virtuoso in Fred Astaire's tap shoes, but its sequel gave us the shadow of a great dancer writhing in the void. For Baryshnikov the venture was not a failure, because he enjoyed the creative process per se, and indulging his artistic curiosity meant much more to him than the fact that the product was deplorable. His virtuosity and his clean-cut, ingratiating appeal may have accelerated the expansion of the ballet audience. Still, these shows got Baryshnikov nowhere as an artist.

The new stage roles Baryshnikov created from 1980 to 1984 seemed only to confirm the correctness of his choice of television as a laboratory. He appeared with Britain's Royal Ballet in Frederick Ashton's *Rhapsody*; he portrayed Don José in a French television version of Petit's *Carmen* with Zizi Jeanmaire and later at ABT with Makarova. He indulged himself in the frenzied sensuality of *The Wild Boy* in MacMillan's inept and vulgar choreography, and he tried to be amusing in an insipid pas de deux for two male dancers called *Follow the Feet*, by John Meehan. These roles were not all total failures, although they could hardly be said to have added new luster to Baryshnikov's image; nor did the alterations and modifications he brought to ABT's versions of *Giselle* and *Swan Lake*. Eliminating the peasant pas de deux, an integral part of the first act of *Giselle*, proved detrimental to the Perrot-Petipa Romantic structure. Baryshnikov's experimental crossing of ABT's Maryinsky-oriented *Swan Lake* with the Kirov recension only made clear the shortcomings of both. His latest choreographic version of *Cinderella*, mounted to Prokofiev's music in collaboration with Peter Anastos, did not greatly enhance Baryshnikov's prestige as an imaginative choreographer. Only when displayed in the playful, lyrical atmosphere of Twyla Tharp's new ballets *Once Upon a Time* (later called *The Little Ballet*), set to Glazunov's music, and a composition set to Frank Sinatra songs, did Baryshnikov's dance genius express itself with its customary power.

It is impossible to predict what lies ahead for Baryshnikov and where his artistic curiosity will lead him. This unfinished period of probing and experimenting will perhaps mark another turning point in his own career, and he will enrich us yet again with the thrill of his unique artistry. He recently said to me: "No matter what I try to do or explore, my Kirov training, my expertise, and my background call me to return to dancing after all, because that's my real vocation, and I have to serve it."

DANSEURS NOBLES

Pavel Gerdt · Vasily Tikhomirov
Konstantin Sergeyev
Nikita Dolgushin · Yuri Soloviev

Prince Désiré in the original production of *The Sleeping Beauty*, 1890, with Carlotta Brianza as Aurora

PAVEL GERDT

PAVEL GERDT WAS not only the prototype of the danseur noble, the "blue cavalier" of Russian ballet; he was unique among his generation. He made his debut at the St. Petersburg Bolshoi Theatre in 1860, at a time when Petipa's choreographic career was getting under way. He ended his activity under the direction of Nicolas Legat in 1916, during the period of Diaghilev's glorious Saisons Russes, the triumph of Anna Pavlova on two continents, and the swelling exodus of the Maryinsky's stars to the West. In the course of half a century, Gerdt was the partner of all the famous Russian ballerinas, from Maria Surovshchikova-Petipa to Anna Pavlova, to whom he taught the soaring leap of Taglioni and Grisi.

The son of a Russified German, Johann Heinrich Gerdt, Pavel was born on November 22, 1844. He entered the Petersburg Theatrical Institute on a government scholarship and graduated in the spring of 1864. He had the good looks of a danseur noble, a natural balletic prince: he was tall, well-built, blond, blue-eyed, possessing noble features and astonishingly beautiful legs. He had a marvelous turnout, natural coordination, and—amazingly for his incredibly sculptural but not very muscular legs—a huge jump.

Ekaterina Vazem, who first had the honor of dancing with Gerdt at the age of sixteen, recalls in her memoirs that in 1868, at a rehearsal of Mazilier's ballet *Jovita, or the Buccaneers*: "The conductor Bogdanov asked Gerdt, who was executing a variation with huge jumps, whether he couldn't wait just 'a bit in the air, please, I have a little pause here.'" Nonetheless, Gerdt's manner was reserved and gracious; he avoided showy tours de force and was a matchless partner.

Gerdt studied with Alexander Pimenov, a pupil of the great Didelot, and with Jean Petipa, Marius Petipa's father, a master of the old pantomime and a student of Vestris. In the senior classes, Gerdt was drilled by Marius Petipa himself and by Christian Johannsen, a pupil of Bournonville who had been appearing in St. Petersburg in danseur noble roles since 1841. Gerdt's teachers combined in themselves the best traditions of European ballet, which the young dancer greedily imbibed. As early as 1857 Petipa took notice of Gerdt, then thirteen years old, in a student performance, in a classical pas de trois with the "Russian beauty"

from Paris, Ekaterina Friedberg (for whom Jules Perrot had staged *Le Corsaire* in 1856).

At the St. Petersburg Bolshoi, Gerdt was used at first more in a classical capacity than in pantomime. In the 1860s he danced in many of Perrot's Romantic choreodramas, which had a unique balance of dancing and pantomime well suited to the major facets of Gerdt's talent. Endowed with superb technique, a skillful partner with an extraordinary mimetic gift, Gerdt felt confident with the elements of the old Romantic ballet. Unfortunately, the great days of this style were past.

In the spring of 1866 Gerdt danced the cunning Colin with the "ideal soubrette" Klavdia Kanzireva as Lise in Dauberval's *La Fille mal gardée*. In September 1867 he made a spectacular debut as the fisherman Matteo in Perrot's masterpiece *The Naiad and the Fisherman*, partnering the blond, steel-pointed virtuoso Ekaterina Vazem, also a debutante. The role of Matteo remained Gerdt's for twenty-five years, as did another great Romantic part—Albrecht, which he first danced in 1870. With an eye to Gerdt's exceptional jump, Petipa enlarged his variation in Act II of *Giselle* to include cabrioles and assemblés. Thirty years later, at the beginning of the twentieth century, Gerdt performed *Giselle* with Anna Pavlova.

After Saint-Léon's departure in 1869, Marius Petipa became the chief choreographer of the Imperial Ballet. He wanted to create ballets that would combine Perrot's dramatic impact with Saint-Léon's choreographic inventiveness. For this he needed a male dancer who possessed both ballet and mime technique. But the male dancers of the 1870s resembled those of the 1840s, when the Romantic ballet was in flower and the ballerina ruled the stage. The male dancer was relegated to the role of porteur, and male dancing was generally treated with disdain. Petipa himself shared Théophile Gautier's opinion: "What could be more repulsive than the spectacle of a man showing off like a doorman, his red neck, his muscular arms, his calves and his whole heavy frame shaken by jumps and pirouettes."

In the 1850s and 1860s Petipa himself had performed mime roles; Lev Ivanov did them in the 1870s. In the pas de deux or the full-scale pas d'action, the miming hero would be replaced by a danseur noble, of whom flawless mastery of partnering technique and classical training was demanded. Gerdt possessed a happy combination of both. He often stepped in for Ivanov when the ballerina needed a nimble partner, for although Ivanov was extremely musical, a true professional, he was so nearsighted that he often dropped his ballerina. In the first St. Petersburg staging of *Don Quixote* in 1871, Gerdt replaced Ivanov as Basil in the pas de deux (with Alexandra Vergina as Kitri)—a piece that subsequently became one of his specialties. In Petipa's *Camargo* (1872) Gerdt portrayed Auguste Vestris, dancing the classical waltz with Adele Grantzow as Camargo, while Ivanov performed the Count de Melin. In this small role, said Vazem, Gerdt "seemed to bring to life the image of the illustrious virtuoso of the eighteenth century, a graceful, flippant gentleman, a china bibelot that suddenly became animated." He stepped in for Ivanov as Solor in the Act II pas de deux of *La Bayadère*, with Maria Gorshenkova as Gamzatti.

Ekaterina Vazem recalled one of Gerdt's partnering feats in Petipa's *Trilby*:

> In the adagio I had a spot where, having done two tours on pointe, I used to stop for a moment as if planted there, balanced on Gerdt's hands. As always, I lingered on after the tours, when I heard an incredible burst of applause that quite surprised me since there had never been an ovation at this point before. In fact, the pas itself was rather ordinary. After I finished the adagio and raced into the wings, I expressed my amazement to the people there. And what did I learn? It turns out that at the "critical moment" in the dance when I was stopped, my cavalier, relying entirely on my mastery, had stepped back three paces with no warning whatsoever, folded his arms, and invited the audience to express its appreciation for a ballerina sustaining her balance with no support. Balletmaster Petipa was ecstatic at this deception.

It is no wonder that in the 1870s, at the time of Petipa's early masterpieces, Gerdt was the only male dancer to be singled out by the press. From 1864 to 1916 he almost singlehandedly ruled over the entire repertoire, which was truly enormous. In 1871 Petipa choreographed the one-act ballet *The Stars*, in which Gerdt portrayed Apollo, for Gerdt's benefit performance—an honor bestowed on no other male dancer. During this era he shone as Albrecht, Valentin in the Perrot-Petipa *Faust*, Oberon in Petipa's *A Midsummer Night's Dream*, Gringoire in *Esmeralda*. In these Romantic roles Gerdt was inimitable as both a mime and a dancer. His Gringoire "displayed the whole gamut of feelings, from naïve simplicity at the beginning to heartfelt grief as he wept for Esmeralda at the end," an anonymous critic noted. Describing his mime, the ballet historian Mikhail Borisoglebsky wrote: "He used the conventional lexicon of gestures to perfection. No one could rival the way he bore himself on stage; no one could equal his carriage. Always spectacular, with extraordinary makeup, he appeared on the stage as its cheerful master. His rare skill as a makeup artist stemmed from the fact that he drew marvelously and devoted his leisure hours to painting."

Gerdt's career developed quite smoothly and without disruption. Showered with favors by higher-ups, he took Russian citizenship in 1868, which further reinforced his status at the Bolshoi Theatre. In 1871 he married the talented soloist Alexandra Shaposhnikova, with whom he had three daughters (among them Elizaveta Gerdt, the future teacher of Shelest, Plisetskaya, and Maximova) and a son. Unlike many of his colleagues, Gerdt was never in need: his salary was the highest in the company. He was given honorary hereditary citizenship in 1890 and, in 1901, the title of Premier Danseur to His Majesty. As Vazem wrote in her memoirs: "He was by nature an extremely good, responsive man, always sympathetic to 'the less fortunate' and ready to help whenever he could, despite his ingrained German prudence and punctiliousness. . . . In Gerdt's home there was always a feeling of family warmth; he was hospitable and loved to play cards. At parties in his house, one would see Lev Ivanov, various balletomanes and others who were connected with the ballet in one way or another."

But in the 1880s, despite his obvious prosperity, Gerdt became somewhat displeased with his situation, because Petipa made much use of his mimetic gift but disregarded his dance abilities. Gerdt, at the peak of his artistic maturity, dreamed of portraying the full-blooded Romantic characters. In 1880, when at the behest of Tsar Alexander II Petipa revived Filippo Taglioni's *La Fille du Danube*, Gerdt as Count Rudolph "moved the audience to tears by the dramatic force with which he sought his beloved [Vazem], drowned in the Danube." One critic noted that "Gerdt had the rare privilege of being applauded merely for his mime abilities, through which he depicted the despair of the loving heart." Another, writing in the *St. Petersburg Gazette*, said: "As a dancer, Gerdt has been long appreciated; but in *La Fille du Danube* he brilliantly showed what an incompa-

Clockwise from top right: *The Goldfish*, late 1860s; *The King's Command* (Petipa), 1880s; Solor in *La Bayadère*, mid-1880s; *The Trials of Damis*, late 1890s

257

rable actor he is. The mad scene was acted with genuine theatricality, realistically, with a good sense of measure. The dancer is a real artist." Twenty years later, in an interview given on the eve of his festive thirty-fifth anniversary gala in 1900, Gerdt recalled Rudolph as his most beautiful part.

In the 1880s, though, such roles were very scarce. Gerdt was frequently miscast: for instance, as Conrad in *Le Corsaire*, whose imperious, tempestuous character eluded him; as the immobile, faceless Norwegian captain in Petipa's *The Daughter of the Snows*; or as the Roman centurion Lucius in his *La Vestale*. He scored his greatest success in the Romantic ballets, to the style of which he was especially sensitive: in *Giselle*, *A Midsummer Night's Dream*, and *La Fille mal gardée*. In 1888 a reviewer of *Giselle* remarked: "In the wonderful pas de deux, our premier danseur Gerdt, who dances rather infrequently, was able to demonstrate all his elegance, refinement, and ease in performing every step, the pirouettes renversés in particular." In 1885 Petipa revived *Fille* for Gerdt's benefit performance, with Virginia Zucchi as Lise. In his review Bezobrazov wrote: "When Gerdt appeared in Act I, many in the audience could not believe they were seeing a dancer who was celebrating a twenty-five-year career. They thought he himself was twenty-five, so young and fresh he looks! As for his dancing, he was remarkable in his variation in the pas de deux, borrowed from *Esmeralda*. The variation does not abound in tricks, but every step he performed was marked by the elegance and finish of an elaborate classical style. His mime was also impressive, and in this he was the equal of the prima ballerina."

Twenty-five years after his debut Gerdt appeared as the first Prince Desiré in *The Sleeping Beauty* (1890), and later as Prince Coqueluche in *The Nutcracker* (1892), and Siegfried in *Swan Lake* (1894). Both Desiré and Siegfried were developed by Petipa with an eye to Gerdt's diminished technique. Desiré was almost a mime role, limited to one variation in the third act, "a song" consisting of short jumps that Petipa felt would give the impression of the Prince's boyish exultation. Contemporary accounts indicate that the forty-six-year-old Gerdt conveyed this amazingly well: "Gerdt dances only a few bars in *Sleeping Beauty*, but how beautifully he does them." He was less successful as Prince Coqueluche, the cavalier of the Sugar Plum Fairy in the *Nutcracker* pas de deux. Perhaps he was hampered by his terrible costume: a high helmet-cap exaggerated the size of his head, while his legs looked truncated because his tunic hung down to his knees.

Desiré and Coqueluche did not transcend the status of the *chevalier servant*, but in *Swan Lake* Tchaikovsky, at least, aimed at something more. The score makes Siegfried a participant in the drama on the same level as Odette; he divests himself of illusions and perishes together with her. Nevertheless, Ivanov and Petipa did not grant Gerdt a single independent passage. There was no variation in the Act III pas de quatre (later restaged as the "Black Swan" pas de deux), and even in the Act II adagio Ivanov gave Siegfried's friend Benno some of the partnering, probably to alleviate the strain on the debilitated Gerdt. And his physical appearance hardly tallied with the concept of Siegfried as a romantic youth: Gerdt presented him as a middle-aged German, complete with beard and mustache. This Siegfried was basically a partner, executing several elegant pas in the waltz with the brides, striking the pose of passive admirer in the pas de quatre for Odile, Rothbart, Benno, and himself. But the mime did not suffice to convey Siegfried's drama, and it is not surprising that at the premiere Gerdt was overshadowed by his ballerina, Pierina Legnani.

In 1900 Petipa cast Gerdt as the Marquis Damis and as Bacchus in two Glazunov ballets, *The Trials of Damis* and *The Seasons*. As Damis, Gerdt repeated all the mannerisms of his Vestris in *Camargo*. As Bacchus, dressed in a Greek tunic with a wreath of grape leaves on his head, the now heavy, almost sixty-year-old dancer looked like a caricature, unable to cope with the dash of Glazunov's bacchanale. At this time, he tried to capitalize on his extraordinary dramatic abilities, which were as strong as ever. He had been quite impressive as the Saracen Abdul-Rakhman in Petipa's *Raymonda* (1898), so picturesque and temperamental that ten years later Diaghilev wanted to open his Paris season with Gerdt in this role—"one of your most brilliant," as he wrote to the elderly dancer.

Gerdt was not destined to share Diaghilev's glory, but at the beginning of the century his name was firmly linked to that of Pavlova, who was his pupil and partner. A contemporary account indicated: "Everything that Pavlova had—lightness, grace, elegance, the ability to control her hands, to give meaning to movement—all came from Gerdt's schooling." At a time of public enthusiasm for Italian technical tricks, Gerdt drew Pavlova's special attention to the positioning of the hands, the body, the turning of the head, and épaulement. This gave to her chiefly Romantic characteristics the academic finish necessary for work in Petipa's style.

Gerdt frequently partnered Pavlova in character dances like the Ural dance in Saint-Léon's *The Little Humpbacked*

Horse. In this piece, based on high sauts de basque, teacher and pupil seemed to compete in the springiness and force of their jumps. "He is a phenomenon as an artist," the *St. Petersburg Gazette* said of the fifty-eight-year-old Gerdt. "Yesterday he was filled with youth and . . . showed such boldness and such great expansiveness that the applause was stormy. Executing the Cossack cabrioles with the sylphide Pavlova, Gerdt simply flew through the air." Actually, character dance had long been his forte. He had danced the Cracovienne and the mazurka from Glinka's *A Life for the Tsar* for decades. "Who could have said that this gracious, nimble, handsome Polish Pan," said the *St. Petersburg Gazette* in August 1902, "was an artist who has been performing on stage for forty-three years?"

But the character dance, too, began to fade gradually, although Gerdt remained a mime and actor to the end of his life. In his last performance, as Gamache in *Don Quixote* on November 27, 1916, Kitri was performed by his pupil Tamara Karsavina. She left an objective and enchanting portrait of her teacher in her memoirs:

The most interesting part of his lesson began when the necessary routine of exercises had been got through. He then worked the steps into short consecutive dances. Often he reconstructed parts of old ballets, long gone from the stage. Great dancers of the past lived again, evoked by him. There was some kind of magic for me in coming into the succession of the great art revealed through my Master. When, the lesson finished, a maid would come in with a large handbell, we trooped out unwillingly, all steaming hot, looking forward to tomorrow, when perhaps the dance with a shadow [from Perrot's *Ondine*], the masterpiece of Cerrito, would be gone through again.

His skill in transmitting the special qualities of any balletic style was Gerdt's undisputed forte as a teacher. Nevertheless, according to Alexander Shiriayev, Gerdt never developed the strictly defined professional method that so happily marked the pedagogy of his own instructors, Johannsen and Petipa. As Shiriayev confessed: "Gerdt was never able to explain exactly what a student should do to execute the movement in obedience with the academic canon. He used to say: 'Repeat my movements, spin out the pirouette the way I do. I can by no means put my talent into your body.'"

Gerdt died on July 30, 1917, a veteran of the Imperial Ballet and a most remarkable participant in its glorious accomplishments.

Lucien in *Paquita*, with Maria Gorshenkova and Felix Kschessinsky, 1881

Conrad in *Le Corsaire*, 1912

VASILY TIKHOMIROV

V ASILY TIKHOMIROV was the patriarch of the danseurs nobles of Moscow as Pavel Gerdt was of St. Petersburg. Gerdt himself fostered Tikhomirov; from his outstanding teacher the pupil adopted a slightly dated manner of performing, harking back to the traditions of French training epitomized by the legendary Auguste Vestris. At the beginning of the twentieth century, when Gerdt's career declined and Tikhomirov's took wing, they were perceived in Moscow and St. Petersburg as "inspired anachronisms." In his memoirs Fyodor Lopukhov recalled: "Even in everyday life Tikhomirov's gait and carriage savored of the third position canonized by the old French school. From Cecchetti and the Italian training, he bor-rowed only the technique of the grande pirouette, though he modified it slightly: he executed it not 'at random,' as Cecchetti taught, but from the same third position, with the arms reminding one of the knobs of copper samovars dating back to the epoch of Alexander I." His technique was extraordinary: he could do twelve or fifteen pirouettes on the spot, combining high demi-pointe with high cou-de-pied. He was endowed with a springy, soaring jump that Akim Volynsky likened to a "lion's thrust." Volynsky frequently took Tikhomirov's jump as an example of the difference between the dancers of Moscow and St. Petersburg: "The Moscow dancers used to jump for the sake of jump-ing. . . . A dancer rocketed upward with a big thrust, as though anticipating the following trajectory of flight that must lead him back to earth. . . . In St. Petersburg, on the other hand, Nijinsky flew away rather than soared up, seeming to extend himself in the air."

Tikhomirov displayed a spectacular virility, but his sculpturesque poses looked stilted and even mannered. His pupils (among them Pavlova's partners Alexander Volinine, Laurent Novikov, and Mikhail Mordkin) adopted his powerful movement style, though they rejected the mannerism of "the old marquis," as they called him. As Conrad in *Le Corsaire* or Solor in *La Bayadère*, with his long curls, black mustache, Herculean torso, regal carriage, and large gestures, he exemplified the nineteenth century's ideal of male beauty. In Petipa's ballets, crowded with gallant cavaliers and princes, incarnations of the ladies' dreams, Tikhomirov created stage characters with an impressive vitality.

VASILY DMITRIEVICH TIKHOMIROV was born on March 17, 1876, in Moscow, into a poor family, and entered the Moscow Theatre School on August 25, 1886. His mother's friend, the Bolshoi ballerina Maria Svetinskaya, impressed by the boy's musicality and interested in his future, arranged his acceptance to the school as a scholarship student.

At this time the Moscow School was a citadel of balletic routine and boredom. Nevertheless, Tikhomirov's fervor and technical abilities were highly appreciated and rewarded: in 1891, at the request of his teacher Mikhail Cheremukhin, the fifteen-year-old student was sent on scholarship to the Imperial Theatre School in St. Petersburg. From 1891 to 1893 Tikhomirov took Pavel Gerdt's classes and observed those of Johannsen, Petipa, and Cecchetti. In May 1893, at the age of seventeen, he made his debut in the classical pas de deux from Petipa's *Paquita*. The famous critic Pleschayev noted: "He is quite an alert, elegant, and exquisite partner." Tikhomirov's early success was enhanced by his appearance in the classical pas de deux from Perrot's *Gazelda*. The tall, handsome, well-trained dancer was offered the position of soloist at the Maryinsky, but he resisted the temptation, not wanting to jeopardize the supremacy of his teacher Gerdt. He preferred to return to Moscow, where he would have no rivals at the Bolshoi, thanks to the advantages of his St. Petersburg training.

Unfortunately, in the last decade of the nineteenth century the Bolshoi repertory did not abound in classical ballets, and those that were performed had deteriorated under the awkward guidance of the chief choreographer, Jose Mendez. Nevertheless, Tikhomirov's debut in the pas de deux in Mendez's revival of Francois-Michel Hoguet's *Robert and Bertram*, with one of the most talented Moscow ballerinas, Lubov Roslavleva, made "the audience literally moan in rapture," according to his wife, Ekaterina Geltzer. Tikhomirov's exceptional physical attractiveness, his noble manners, technique, and musicality, distinguished him from the general run of Moscow male soloists. Until the appearance of Gorsky and Mordkin, Tikhomirov enjoyed continuous success, though he did not get to dance much besides the *Coppélia* pas de deux and the *Esmeralda* pas de six.

When he appeared in Mendez's utterly dilapidated *Esmeralda*, the critic in the magazine *Artist* rebuked the production but praised Tikhomirov: "In the pas de six the young dancer Tikhomirov stands out strikingly. He is a genuine classical dancer, a rare phenomenon in the ballet of our time." Mendez's revivals of *The Magic Slipper* (*Cinderella*, 1894) and his *India* (1900) seemed disappointingly trivial to Tikhomirov, but his effect in these hapless roles was so tremendous that he managed to defy the Moscow tradition of having ballerinas en travesti perform such male roles as Franz in *Coppélia* and Colin in *La Fille mal gardée*. In 1895 he danced Lucien in *Paquita*; in 1896, Frantz and Colin; in 1897, Lord Wilson and Ta-Hor in *Pharaoh's Daughter*, Mars in Clustine's *The Stars*, and Akhmed the Pasha in Perrot's *La Péri*; in 1898, Prince Charming in a new version of *Cinderella* and Matteo in *The Naiad and the Fisherman*.

Tikhomirov's roles, in fact, included the best of the contemporary male Bolshoi repertory, and in them he singlehandedly produced a revolution in Moscow male dancing. Before him, no one had ever done ten pirouettes or sixteen entrechats six, which he executed with utter ease, as if for fun. He was the first dancer in Moscow to perform thirty-two grandes pirouettes in the second position, in the crisp, academic manner. The precision of his beats and the swirl of his turns were also unprecedented. But if his accuracy, noble attack, and charming care for his ballerina were signs of his St. Petersburg training, the sweeping gestures and exaggerated dynamism he imparted to each role were true to the Moscow grand manner. Tikhomirov was indeed the father of the virile and dynamic male dancing emblematic of the Bolshoi.

In 1898 Clustine reshaped the pas de deux from *Le Corsaire* with an eye to Tikhomirov's technique, which the critics found "amazingly acrobatic." The reviewer in the *Moscow Leaf* was quite indignant that "Mr. Tikhomirov, holding the knee of Miss Djuri with one hand and her

Top: Petronius in *Eunice and Petronius*,
1916
Bottom: (left) Mars in *The Stars*, 1897;
(right) the Grand Pas from *Catarina*,
1895

OPPOSITE
Top: (left) *The Naiad and the Fisherman*,
with Ekaterina Geltzer, 1900s; (right)
Ta-Hor in *Pharaoh's Daughter*, 1910s
Bottom: Concert numbers, with Geltzer,
1911

waist with the other, walks quietly between the corps rows and carries the ballerina around."

One cannot say how Tikhomirov's style would have evolved in later years had he not found himself whirled into the vortex of those administrative and artistic reforms that drastically altered the whole landscape of Russian ballet at the beginning of the twentieth century. In January 1899 the Moscow premiere of Petipa's *The Sleeping Beauty*, staged by the old maestro's talented but impetuous disciple Alexander Gorsky, scored an enormous success. Tikhomirov was the Bolshoi's first Blue Bird, unveiling at last the precision of his brisés volés and entrechats, taking the Moscow audience by storm. His Blue Bird, followed by his Prince Desiré, was the epitome of Petipa's academicism, establishing a standard against which a whole generation of Moscow danseurs was to be measured. "No one among Moscow dancers," writes Tikhomirov's biographer, Natalia Roslavleva, "could convey the elegance, nobility, and academic finesse of the part [of Desiré] the way Tikhomirov did. In a tribute to Tikhomirov celebrating his thirty-year career, Ekaterina Geltzer included Prince Desiré among his four greatest roles."

Upon his arrival in Moscow, Gorsky was at first quite tolerant of classical dance and gladly cast Tikhomirov in his revivals. In December 1900 Tikhomirov performed Basil in Gorsky's version of Petipa's *Don Quixote*. As the bawdy barber, he thrilled the audience with his triple ronds de jambe en l'air and even more with his thirty-two grandes pirouettes in the final pas de deux, his working leg impeccably maintained parallel to the floor. But next to the seductive theatricality of Mordkin's Espada, he seemed only to be a master of stylized acting with its clichés of mime and static gallantry. The character of the shrewd *pícaro*, demanding vivid realistic strokes to bring him to life, definitely eluded Tikhomirov. After the premiere of *Don Quixote*, the collaboration between Gorsky and Tikhomirov was doomed. The more the restless innovator became immersed in his experiments with "realistic ballet-drama," the more Tikhomirov was relegated to the periphery, and the more difficult it was for him to assert himself as an artist and as a master of classical movements. During the first decade of the twentieth century Gorsky used Tikhomirov in his own ballets mostly as a decorative prop rather than as a classical dancer of the highest caliber. From performance to performance Gorsky reduced more and more the male dance passages in his versions of the classical ballets. Thus in *Giselle* he abolished Albrecht's Act II variation, where once Tikhomirov had excelled in a flurry of cabrioles and beats. In Gorsky's 1911 production dancing with Vera Karalli or subsequently with Sofia Fedorova, Tikhomirov cut a reserved, noble, and spectacular figure. The reviewer in the magazine *Theatre* wrote: "Mr. Tikhomirov portrays Albrecht in a simple manner, without excessive emphasis in the scenes demanding an outburst of dramatic temperament. The slightly cold tonality given to Gautier's wretched protagonist is compensated by the inner strength and vitality of his characterization." In 1916 Pleschayev compared the figures of Karalli and Tikhomirov, who froze over her in his special mournful pose, with "the marble monuments in the cemetery of Père Lachaise in Paris or in Campo Santo in Genoa."

In Gorsky's ballets Tikhomirov was treated as a spectacular living monument, with insulting and persistent indifference to his unique dance qualities. In *Salammbô* he portrayed the arrogant Numidic general Narr-Avas, a role that was mostly mime. Only in the last act did he have a small classical solo, in which "his dignified grace shone," as an anonymous critic wrote. "Mr. Tikhomirov is a dancer of the old training, endowed with a special beauty of movement. He is a genuine rival of Gerdt, the most accomplished classicist in St. Petersburg." But in Moscow Gerdt's rival had to make do with Gorsky's *Eunice and Petronius* (1914), in which the noble Roman Petronius did little more than walk around the stage, miming or striking stylized antique poses. To make matters worse, he was in the second cast, as a substitute for Mordkin. In *Raymonda* (1909) and *Le Corsaire* (1912) Gorsky was less harsh to him. As Jean de Brienne, Tikhomirov recalled "a medieval statue of a knight, brought to life" (Roslavleva), but in spite of his monumental stature he impressed the audience with his leonine leaps and "diamondlike" beats, which he demonstrated in his one variation as a cavalier in the Dance of the Hours. His jump was distinguished by a unique takeoff and landing, almost miraculous considering his Herculean body. His entrechats were dazzling, proverbial at the Bolshoi since his appearance as the Beam of Sunshine in Gorsky's *The Little Humpbacked Horse*: "Clad in a golden costume," wrote Roslavleva, "Tikhomirov literally sparkled in the variation. According to his contemporaries, he performed the beats at such speed that they were invisible, fusing into a glittering line of gold." His majestic appearance and technique made his Jean de Brienne the most impressive adornment of the picturesque medieval tapestry Gorsky attempted to reproduce in *Raymonda*.

His portrayal of Conrad in Gorsky's revival of *Le Corsaire* (January 1912) harked back to the characterization shaped by Petipa himself in St. Petersburg in the 1860s. Tikhomirov created a picturesquely impressive noble pirate, "a lithograph perfectly illustrating Byron's hero, magically brought to life" (Victor Iving). Tikhomirov's Conrad was a multifaceted character: courageous and monumental among his fellow-pirates, but timid and vulnerable in the scenes with Medora (Geltzer), especially in the adagio, choreographed anew by Gorsky to a nocturne of Chopin. He "thrilled the audience with his eloquent poses and powerful partnering, abounding in high lifts, and moved with the freshness of his passion for Medora" (Victorina Kriger).

But if in Moscow he was somewhat lost in the gigantic shadow of the young Mordkin, in St. Petersburg his exemplary classical style was highly appreciated, when he danced at the Maryinsky with Geltzer. "Tikhomirov is an amazing cavalier and partner. He is strong, nimble, graceful, and precise; he is sensitive to the intentions of the ballerina and very cooperative in the partnership. . . . A better cavalier is hard to imagine. As for his grande pirouette in the variation of the last act of *Don Quixote*, this is a masterpiece of male dancing," Svetlov wrote in 1910. Tikhomirov's style now began to influence the manners of male dancers in St. Petersburg, where he himself had been fostered. His grande pirouette, regarded as a great feat and seldom performed at the Maryinsky in those days, overwhelmed the young Pierre Vladimiroff, who confessed that he "attempted to mimic Tikhomirov's potent virility and dashing virtuosity even in small details."

Perhaps only his partnership with Geltzer, mutually stimulating and fruitful, mitigated the hardship of Tikhomirov's service under Gorsky, no matter how he admired Gorsky's artistic flair and audacity. If the measured academicism that he advocated in coaching his frantic partner mellowed her extremely eccentric dancing, Geltzer's flamboyance, on the other hand, ignited Tikhomirov's reticence. From this striking confrontation stemmed the effect of "ice and flame" that so lavishly colored the classical duets that they frequently performed at concerts in Moscow and St. Petersburg.

In 1911 Tikhomirov and Geltzer captivated the audience at London's Alhambra Theatre. His dominant stage presence and impressive jumps greatly contributed to the interest in Russian ballet and classical dance aroused in England by Pavlova's and Diaghilev's seasons. The Alhambra management offered Tikhomirov the chance to stay in London and open his own ballet school, but he preferred to return to the Bolshoi. In 1914 Anna Pavlova invited him

to be her partner in an abbreviated *Giselle*, *Les Sylphides*, the Glazunov *Bacchanale*, and the pas de deux from *Don Quixote*, for her tour of Germany. Victor Dandré recalled: "In spite of his great height and corpulence, Tikhomirov's dancing revealed an extraordinary lightness." This report is all the more amazing because his years of minimal dance activity had taken their toll on Tikhomirov's technique and appearance. He had grown heavy; his legs lost their slenderness. In 1911, during a guest appearance in *La Bayadère* at the Maryinsky, the prop elephant on which he sat fell to pieces under his weight. The critics complained after his participation in Geltzer's St. Petersburg gala in April 1913: "Tikhomirov demonstrated again his unparalleled stamina by carrying Geltzer, far from ethereal, on his outstretched arms, as if she were a feather. As a dancer he looks a bit flabby; therefore, despite his excellent classical stature his variation looked grotesque."

At the centenary celebration of the Bolshoi Theatre in 1925, Tikhomirov performed James in *La Sylphide*. The following year he danced Phoebus in the "back-to-Petipa" version of *Esmeralda* that he mounted for Geltzer. In his portrayal of Phoebus he mingled the Romantic traits of Petipa's noble hero with the merciless, shallow seducer Mordkin had created in Gorsky's version. He seemed to anticipate the peculiar blend of harrowing melodrama and inane cardboard Romanticism that would become typical of the Soviet drama-ballet.

Tikhomirov's performing career lasted until 1927, when he created the Soviet captain in the first Soviet dramaballet, his own *The Red Poppy*. In the 1920s he spent most of his time teaching and coaching at the Moscow Ballet School, where he had given his first class in 1894. He never stopped defending and reinforcing the principles of Petipa's academicism in the struggle against the proletarian critics who demanded the eradication of the Imperial flower. However unimaginative or priggish his classical revivals were (*La Bayadère* with Gorsky in 1923, for which he restored the original Kingdom of the Shades scene; *The Sleeping Beauty*, a production that lasted at the Bolshoi from 1924 to 1934; Act II of *La Sylphide* in the Taglioni-Petipa version; *Esmeralda*), no matter how awkwardly he modified or even damaged Gorsky's productions in the twenties, Tikhomirov paved the way for the restoration of Petipa's legacy in Moscow and inspired the younger generation to transcend and rework it. He died in Moscow on June 20, 1956. His *Red Poppy* may have been the herald of the entire thrust of Soviet ballet, but Vasily Tikhomirov as a great Russian danseur noble had nothing in common with it.

Frondoso in *Laurencia*, 1939

KONSTANTIN SERGEYEV

AMONG THE danseurs nobles of the Soviet era, Sergeyev stands out as the *beau ideal*. He was of medium stature, well shaped and virile, with beautiful and expressive features, suave manners, and a regal carriage. His contemporaries regarded him as the perfect ballet prince, and his innovative style blazed the trail for a number of highly gifted successors.

His technique was outstanding: he had great ballon and landed without a sound; his double cabrioles and double tours were combined with spectacular poses. Especially amazing were his jumps, marked not so much by the impetus or elevation Yermolayev attained as by lightness and effortlessness. Sergeyev got off the ground without any visible muscular strain and froze like a sculpture in the air. His rare command of the grammar of classical dance was enhanced by his marvelous musicality and unusual sensitivity to his partners. Asaf Messerer recalled: "Without any excessive bustle Sergeyev seemed in constant motion: his support of the ballerina never revealed any tension, and in his partnership he seemed to be dancing as well. With his neck, arms, and head, he followed and complemented the dancing of his partner and her mood. As for the solo pieces in a variation or a coda, he threw himself into dancing with abandon and passion. His every movement was so impeccably delivered that even a short piece, meant to last for a couple of minutes, acquired dramatic dimension, which is a very rare case among male dancers."

Natalia Makarova, who danced with Sergeyev in his last *Giselle* in 1962, incisively characterized his style: "He was able to partner a ballerina without giving the impression of supporting her. He could sense the point of her balance and still maintain his distance. And he never exerted unnecessary strength when directing me, literally with one hand, so that I never felt myself bound to my partner—I felt simultaneously free and yet in his control."

Konstantin Mikhailovich Sergeyev's career developed in a most unusual way. He was born in St. Petersburg in 1910, the son of a worker in a light bulb plant. His infatuation with ballet began relatively late, when he was fourteen. In 1924 he began to take the evening course at the Leningrad Choreographic School, studying with Spessivtseva's partner Victor Semyonov, whose favorite pupil he soon became.

During his four years at the school he made such progress that in 1928 he was invited to join the small company that Joseph Kschessinsky was touring all over Russia. Over the next year and a half the young Sergeyev got to perform Siegfried, Albrecht, the Slave in *Le Corsaire*, Gringoire in *Esmeralda*, and other roles. In September 1929 he returned to the school a mature artist and passed the exams. On June 5, 1930, he danced the young Chinese coolie in Zakharov's *The Red Poppy* on the erstwhile Maryinsky stage.

For Sergeyev, the decade of the 1930s was an uninterrupted trajectory of success. His new artistic approach to Petipa's legacy, his extraordinary technique and powerful projection, made him a pioneer who singlehandedly changed the performing style of the Russian danseurs nobles of his own and later generations. After warming up in a number of smaller roles (the Spirit of Ocean in *The Little Humpbacked Horse*, the Blue Bird in *The Sleeping Beauty*) he tackled the whole Romantic repertory of the Kirov. Such roles as the Youth in Lavrovsky's *Etudes symphoniques* (1929–30) and the Poet in *Les Sylphides* brought out an unusual lyricism and Romantic impetuosity. Unwilling to be only the ballerina's passive escort, he shifted the focus to the challenging rivalry of partners. In fact, Sergeyev followed the trail blazed by the generation of danseurs nobles that had emerged after Pavel Gerdt (Andrianov, Vladimiroff, Obukhov, Semyonov), but he surpassed them by the flawless balance of his exemplary physique and classical technique.

Sergeyev was the first Russian danseur noble who employed this balance to do full justice to the dramatic consistency of the old ballets. A perfect product of Russian schooling, he shared the native belief that art is morally purifying and cathartic and the inclination to view ballet as dance-drama. He had been educated in the traditions of pantomime and so-called "balletic realism" and was concerned above all with the psychological approach to character—its realistic justification.

Sergeyev's critics and biographers unanimously agree that his brilliance as a dancer was inseparable from his dramatic ability. In the 1930s he became a vociferous champion of the Stanislavsky method, vigorously transplanting dramatic realism to the ballet stage. During his great days in the 1930s and 1940s he portrayed the entire gallery of drama-ballet principals, so comfortable did he feel in this milieu: the actor Mistral in Vainonen's *The Flames of Paris* (1932), Prince Vaslav in *The Fountain of Bakhchisarai* (1934), the composer Lucien Rubempré in Zakharov's *Lost Illusions* after Balzac (1936), and Ostap in his *Taras Bulba* (1941). Most of these roles have sunk into oblivion with the productions that contained them; the entire approach became outdated with the end of the epoch that had fostered Sergeyev's aesthetic creed. In the 1950s and 1960s my generation perceived him as an overacting anachronism. Many dancers at the Kirov, such as Dolgushin, Baryshnikov, and Makarova, could not help treating him with irony. Makarova still remembers her embarrassment at the sight of Sergeyev, her Albrecht, shedding real tears on stage when they danced *Giselle* together.

However old-fashioned or even preposterous his theatrical means might seem today, Sergeyev's grandeur lay precisely in the way he reshaped, expanded, and dramatically justified the roles of Siegfried, Albrecht, Jean de Brienne, and Desiré. To a certain extent his portrayals served as a springboard for the imagination of many extraordinary dancers at the Kirov in the 1960s and 1970s (Nureyev, Dolgushin, Baryshnikov) who transcended Sergeyev's achievement as one might a parental legacy.

Sergeyev's new versions of Petipa's famous roles cost him tremendous effort. His Siegfried, for instance, took several decades before it acquired a form close to the contemporary one. He worked on this role throughout all the readaptations of *Swan Lake* at the Kirov: first the Petipa-Ivanov canonical version of 1895 (1932); then Vaganova's production (1933); Lavrovsky's uncompleted prewar transcription; Lopukhov's (1945); and finally Sergeyev's own recension (1950). He was determined to transform the originally rather inane suitor of Odette and Odile into a dynamic Romantic hero, supplied with a dramatic profile and meaningful—not just show-stopping—choreography.

Although Vaganova's *Swan Lake* was a collection of extremes, it somehow proved a considerable breakthrough as a revision of the Petipa-Ivanov production. Sergeyev gave Siegfried the daydreaming spirit of Hamlet in the clothing of a nineteenth-century German count. His sensitivity matched his neurotic complexes and vulnerability. The lake of swans appeared to be *le paysage de son âme*, a dreamland for which he yearned. Odette was not real, either, but part of the ideal world that crumbled in the finale. Appearing first in carpet slippers with an old volume of poetry in his hands, this Siegfried resembled Goethe's Werther, limning the drama of incompatibility between dream and reality with inimitable sincerity and bitterness.

Sergeyev diversified the choreography by adding to the Black Swan pas de deux variation a string of double assemblés and grands jetés; but mostly, as in Petipa's time, he had to make do with "the language of the deaf-mutes" (as dancers sometimes call pantomime). Vaganova's staging, attuned to the official Soviet ideology, was meant to unmask the futile lives of the idle aristocracy of the nineteenth century. Sergeyev's portrayal, however, as many critics pointed out, failed to complete this ideological mission. The romantic appeal of his hapless daydreamer was so potently convincing that he seemed to advocate the "obsolete" spiritual values rather than to undermine them. A yearning for the sublime and a kind of spiritual languor pervaded Sergeyev's partnership with Ulanova.

But the role was still in the process of becoming. It took shape in Lopukhov's 1945 production, which laid the groundwork for Sergeyev's own rendition. Apparently he was also influenced by Gorsky's version, which he had frequently performed in Moscow in the 1930s. Now his characterization took on more convincing consistency, and, more important, a dramatic evolution occurred: the carefree rake of Act I, smitten and transfigured by his sudden passion for Odette in Act II, was seduced by Odile in Act III and finally expiated his betrayal by his death in Act IV. Choreographically, the role was now considerably enlarged: Siegfried participated in the Act I waltz and pas de trois and also danced a new variation to music Petipa had deleted from the original score.

All these components were put together in Sergeyev's own production of 1950, in which the action centered on the tribulations of Siegfried. To intensify the dramatic evolution, Sergeyev drastically reshaped Act I. To entertain their Prince, Siegfried's friends and courtiers danced the waltz, the newly choreographed Danse des Coupes, and the polonaise; he was amused by a zany Shakespearean jester and presented with an arbalest. From the original Sergeyev preserved only Petipa's pas de trois, as somewhat altered by Nicolas Legat in 1904. Sergeyev gave Siegfried a new bravura variation to depict his cheerful disposition and a newly designed contemplative solo to suggest his Romantic ennui and his ripeness for his encounter with Odette. Thus, Act I set the stage for all that followed.

Ivanov's Act II was left intact, except for the deletion of an explicative pantomime describing Odette's plight. Siegfried's reactions to Odette and the dramatic accents conveyed in the adagio served as a commentary on the action.

In Act III Sergeyev emphasized Siegfried's detachment from the phalanx of potential brides and his immersion in his dreams of the Swan Queen. As if to reinforce this state of inner isolation, only the pas de deux was illuminated; the festive crowd faded into the dark background, symbolizing the disarray of Siegfried's mind. The variation that Sergeyev choreographed for himself seemed to grow out of the Prince's exultation. His biographer Prokhorova writes:

> Sergeyev soared in big jetés with enviable ease. At times he seemed to hang in the air as if enjoying a kind of airy pause. His large, encompassing jumps were alternated with a whirl of turns. Standing erect on one leg, he pulled the other one high, bent at the knee, to embark on his turns, at first flowing slowly and then accelerating more and more. No sooner did they reach a climax than he suddenly interrupted them by freezing into a sculpturesque pose, which immediately was followed by spectacular, weightless double tours en l'air, executed at breakneck speed—three or four within the time usually necessary for one.

In the coda he covered the stage with a series of grands jetés. Prokhorova wrote: "They did not gravitate to the ground but rather seemed to dissolve in the air. By slackening the tempo he imparted a delayed character to his airy circles. In the finale, arms outstretched upward, he complemented his jetés with double tours and froze in arabesque."

The most dramatic detail that Sergeyev introduced in Act III was a bouquet of white flowers, an emblem of Odette's and his own purity. Odile threw the flowers in Siegfried's face, expressing her contempt for their symbolic meaning. (Baryshnikov reproduced this detail in his piecemeal revision of *Swan Lake* for ABT in 1980.)

Sergeyev was the first Soviet choreographer to impose consistent reforms on the last act. He increased the intensity of the drama and enhanced its cathartic possibilities by reinterpreting the thunderstorm sequence, deleted by Petipa but reintroduced by Vaganova in 1932. Siegfried was now involved in the combat with Rothbart, and his adagio with Odette emphasized his repentance and yearning for redemption.

Quite daring for the puritanical Soviet stage was Sergeyev's attempt to give a visual interpretation to the *Liebestod* motif in Tchaikovsky's music. The libretto called for Odette to throw herself into the lake and Siegfried to follow her, while the thunderclap and lightning turned Rothbart to stone. From the depths of the lake a cliff would rise to reveal the dead Siegfried, over whom Odette would be seen grieving in a mournful arabesque penchée. Unfortunately, the censor prescribed an optimistic finale which prevented Sergeyev from realizing his unorthodox design: Siegfried killed Rothbart, nullified his evil spell, and was happily united with the liberated Odette.

The gallery of characters Sergeyev created in the 1930s was outstanding artistically and technically, but most of them no longer seem vital when viewed from a contemporary perspective. Only one competes with his Siegfried in artistry. Still radiant through the haze of years is his Albrecht, a role on which he worked for thirty years. To a certain degree, this portrayal was an artistic paradigm for the young dancers of the 1940s and 1950s, against which they measured their own endeavors. He performed it first in March 1928 and for the last time in July 1962. With such Giselles as Ulanova, Dudinskaya, Chauviré, Nadia Nerina, and Makarova, he varied the details and shadings of his interpretation; but his approach to the ballet as a psychological or even sociological drama always predominated.

Physically and technically, Sergeyev's Albrecht represented a powerful reference to the Romantic tradition, tracing its lineage to Lucien Petipa. He was, above all, an exemplary danseur noble. His aristocratic mien shone through his disguise in his manner of wearing his cloak; in his elegant, slightly arrogant carriage; and, most important, in the distance he maintained in his dealings with the peasants in Act I, including Giselle herself. He retained his noble bearing even after his beyond-the-grave experience. Released from the pangs of remorse, his purified Albrecht could have happily wed Bathilde had she appeared in the cemetery, as Gautier's original libretto had her do.

His "social" approach notwithstanding, Sergeyev lavished on this role a profusion of meaningful details, all in the service of potent dramatic consistency. Many of them are still seen in contemporary productions: for instance, the white flowers strewn on the ground. Unlike the role of Siegfried, Albrecht never required elaborate choreographic revision by Sergeyev; it has been expanded considerably since the 1880s. Sergeyev's direct predecessors and his teachers Boris Shavrov and Semyonov as well as his colleagues Chabukiani and (especially) Yermolayev had already developed certain passages to the point of choreographic tours de force. Nevertheless, Sergeyev choreographed the Act I variation (hitherto mostly a mime passage) as a "dance response to Giselle's solo." He also gave Albrecht much more to dance in Act II.

Sergeyev's grandeur as Albrecht stemmed from the

Right: Romeo, with Galina Ulanova as Juliet, 1940
Below: Prince Désiré in *The Sleeping Beauty*, with Natalia Dudinskaya as Aurora, early 1950s

OPPOSITE
Clockwise from top right: Siegfried, mid-1950s; Albrecht, early 1950s; Frondoso, mid-1950s; The Prince in *Cinderella*, mid-1950s

Top: (left) The Prince in *Cinderella*, with Dudinskaya, late 1940s; (right) Lenny in *The Path of Thunder*, with
Dudinskaya as Sari, 1957
Above: Siegfried, with Dudinskaya as Odile, 1951

perfect balance between the logic of his dramatic portrayal and his romantically stylized dancing. However one-dimensional or naive his psychological insights might seem today, the core of his characterization is still valid. This Albrecht loved Giselle sincerely, but social prejudices overwhelmed them and led to her death. His ensuing remorse was mitigated only by his pardon by the shade of Giselle. Sergeyev transfigured this design through the subtle Romantic stylization of Act II. In the adagio he never indulged in powerful high lifts, because they had been unknown in the Romantic era. Instead, he sustained his ballerina almost invisibly, so that she seemed to float in the air.

The dynamic, rebellious drive that Chabukiani had instilled into the duet and variation was subdued. Sergeyev's effortless jumps, the pianissimo of his cabrioles and uniquely silent landings, were in keeping with the atmosphere of the production. His soaring leaps alternated with flowing, swift tours chaînés that devoured the stage. Mikhail Mikhailov recalled in his memoirs: "His arms drooping, the dancer seemed to move slowly in a foggy haze. As if to evoke the Albrecht-Giselle duet from Act I, he executed a big, passionate soubresaut, his arms reaching out for Giselle. A mysterious force seemed to drive him and lift him into the air. He hovered in the bleak moonlight and landed, exhausted, only to leap again and complete the whole sequence with several decelerating pirouettes en attitude. The movement gradually died away through the final pose on high demi-pointe."

During his encounter with the Wilis Sergeyev emphasized his sorrow and his belated pledge of fidelity to Giselle, rather than the challenge of combat. He performed the traditional double cabrioles with a suave legato, alternating them with coupé-assemblé as a soft preparation for an explosion of entrechats six. He burst into beats, his arms stretched upward in despair. The second part of the variation was given an elegiac tone. Sergeyev extended his arms to Giselle as if he were dancing only for her. "He would bring the most subtle pianissimo to an intricate combination of assemblés and entrechats, as if he were wandering soundlessly in the predawn mist," Mikhailov recalled. The soft assemblé was followed by grandes pirouettes, performed with increasing speed and climaxing at the musical fortissimo. The reluctance with which Sergeyev executed the high, lingering jeté entrelacé and the big diagonal, echoing the first part of his variation, suggested Albrecht's inner disarray and pain. As if overcoming it, he darted toward Giselle, his arms open, bursting into effortless double

pirouettes. He ended the variation with a final pirouette, corresponding to the music's fortissimo, and fell exhausted by Giselle's grave. Over the years, he altered this finale: he would interrupt the swinging pirouette and freeze, his arms pressed against his chest, recalling Giselle's gesture in the Mad Scene.

His farewell to Giselle was replete with compelling dramatic detail: as she vanished into the grave, he caressed her hands, pressed them to his cheek, warmed them with his breath; even after she had disappeared he continued to caress the air. The finale varied from one performance to the next: sometimes Albrecht tossed himself about the stage in a state of ecstatic torment, as if still pursuing Giselle's shade; at other times he moved away in reverie, strewing the white flowers, or fell dead by Giselle's grave.

Sergeyev's third great classical role, less dramatic yet equally significant, was Prince Desiré in *The Sleeping Beauty*. He first performed Desiré in October 1932, in a slightly modified version of Petipa, but the role took final shape in Sergeyev's own production, which had its premiere at the Kirov in March 1952. This version is still considered classical, despite its considerable departures from the Petipa original. To the largely mime role of Desiré, originally designed for the fifty-year-old Pavel Gerdt, Sergeyev added a new Romantic dimension, supplying it with an imaginative dance characterization.

Sergeyev had begun revising the ballet in 1942, in Perm, with a new Act III variation for Desiré which was approved by Fyodor Lopukhov, the first choreographer to modify Petipa's masterpiece. This ebullient solo was incorporated into the 1952 version, as was an Act II variation that displayed Desiré's willful, dynamic nature. The latter began with various jumps and continued with small glissades and cabrioles from traveling upstage and twice-repeated jetés en tournant, ending in attitude croisé. They were complemented by pirouettes into fourth position, preceded by linking steps such as sissonne en tournant, performed with uplifted arm and the torso slightly bent forward, as the step had been executed in the days of Louis XIV.

Desiré's impressionable nature, moved by the Lilac Fairy's tale and his vision of Aurora, was expressed in a new adagio for the Prince and his dream princess in which the traditional promenades alternated with a series of high lifts (nonexistent in Petipa's original staging) meant to suggest Desiré's growing infatuation with the vision. The energetic element of his character was demonstrated in a newly choreographed episode called "The Combat with Carabosse."

The action of this passage was set on different stage levels, a transparent curtain dividing the conflicting worlds of the belligerent Carabosse, standing guard with her throng of mice and dwarfs, and Aurora's spellbound realm of immobile courtiers. The duel between the Prince and the evil fairy took place on an illuminated spiral staircase.

Sergeyev also introduced a new bravura variation into the wedding pas de deux in Act III. It began triumphantly with big cabrioles en avant alternating with the fireworks of double pirouettes, soutenu en tournant along the front of the stage, and double pirouettes ending in fifth position. In the coda the sissonnes en tournant and jetés entrelacés encircling the stage were combined with low jetés en tournant and a whirl of tours chaînés, complemented by a big jeté en tournant.

On January 11, 1940, Sergeyev danced his first Romeo in Leonid Lavrovsky's *Romeo and Juliet*, with Galina Ulanova as Juliet. Into the choreography of a typical dramaballet, which consisted mostly of recurrent pantomime and poorly developed dance sequences, Sergeyev instilled the energy and lyricism of his earlier Romantic roles. He insisted that Prokofiev expand the music devoted to Romeo, who was originally conceived as a supporting role. He still had only one variation, but Sergeyev made the role a convincing stylization of an ardent, love-smitten Renaissance youth. The portrayal grew out of a hundred dramatic details, meticulously developed and acted with inspiration, a potent visual manifestation of vulnerable romantic love doomed by social prejudice and senseless hostility. The impact of his tempestuous Romeo matched that of Ulanova's most lyrical Juliet. None of their followers or imitators could pour forth such a richness of shadings, such a combination of genuine lyricism and tragic pathos, as did Ulanova and Sergeyev in the 1940s and 1950s.

The dramatic emphasis he gave Romeo was a function of Sergeyev's strong faith in ballet as choreodrama. Over

the years this attitude evolved into an aesthetic creed, carefully nurtured and thoroughly realized in the ballets he choreographed at the Kirov: *Cinderella* (1946), *The Path of Thunder* (1957), *The Distant Planet* (1963), and *Hamlet* (1970). He was quite proud to call himself a disciple of Petipa, a lineage he proved in his restorations of *Raymonda*, *Swan Lake*, and *The Sleeping Beauty*. But unlike Petipa, the master of the entire academic vocabulary, Sergeyev's choreography never went beyond conscientious arrangements of classical clichés or dry specimens of socialist realism. All of his ballets are now forgotten.

As artistic director of the Kirov, Sergeyev reduced the repertoire to revisions of Petipa's works and pedestrian drama-ballets, banning any experiments in neoclassics or modern dance. But thanks mainly to his effort and fervor, the Kirov in the 1960s was the best classical company in the world, with the most sensitive and polished corps de ballet and impeccable academic style. It still maintains a lofty standard of pure classicism in the Petipa style, as the 1982 Paris engagement so happily demonstrated. On the other hand, this vociferous traditionalism gradually became a vise that cramped the artistic development of many gifted dancers. Some, like Alla Osipenko, Yuri Soloviev, and Nikita Dolgushin, realized their potential only in part—they were stifled in the prim, hothouse atmosphere of the Kirov. A few survived artistically by going West. Paradoxically, Sergeyev's policy should be credited in part for the defections of Nureyev, Makarova, and Baryshnikov, who gave Western ballet a new vitality. How ironic that Sergeyev made this indirect contribution to Western culture, which he has never been able to fully appreciate!

To punish Sergeyev for Makarova's leap to freedom in 1970, the Party supervisors dismissed him from the Kirov. Now in his early seventies, he is artistic director of the Vaganova School, running it with his customary fervor and iron hand.

Hamlet in *Reflections* (Dolgushin), 1973

NIKITA DOLGUSHIN

O F THE CONSTELLATION of gifted dancers that illuminated the austere Kirov with dazzling light in the
1950s and 1960s, Nikita Dolgushin was the most refined,
intellectual, and iconoclastic star.

Dolgushin's physique was truly impressive: long-legged,
long-necked, with extremely expressive and beautiful arms
and a small head, a slightly elongated Mediterranean face,
and blazing black eyes. Dolgushin at times seemed like a
living statue. His elegantly reserved manners, regal carriage, and imperious though suave gestures gave him the
air of an accomplished Romantic dancer, the flawless Prince
of Petipa's ballets. Moreover, he was endowed with such

powerful dramatic projection that he was regarded as "the
most spectacular and gifted actor among dancers." His artistic evolution and career kept pace with the development
of Soviet ballet in his time.

N IKITA ALEXANDROVICH DOLGUSHIN was born in
Leningrad on November 8, 1938, into a family of
Russian intelligentsia. He entered the Leningrad Choreographic School in 1950 and graduated in 1959, having
been a student of Mikhail Mikhailov and Alexander Pushkin. His schoolmate Elena Tchernichova told me: "Nikita's

extraordinary personality revealed itself very early at the school through his extremely controlled, or, rather, intellectual, attitude to each choreographic task, however insignificant it was. He had to do so, because he was a sickly adolescent, struggling with some emotional problems and constantly suffering from migraine headaches. Because any physical overstrain was detrimental to his health, he never managed to develop his technical potential to the perfection of a real virtuoso. His terre-à-terre technique, though precise and elegant, lacked the swiftness favored at the Kirov; his ballon was not remarkable. He compensated for these flaws by developing an extreme control over each movement, which precluded any spontaneity. Every step was calculated, measured, elegantly shaped. But Dolgushin's real strengths lay in his precious individual projection, in the consistency of his dramatic designs and that 'intellectual reticence' that constituted, in my view, his major charm."

These qualities manifested themselves at Dolgushin's pregraduate performance in 1958 at the Kirov, at which he danced Kasyan Goleizovsky's miniature *The Poet and his Muse*. Dolgushin's dramatic response to Goleizovsky's choreography, with its Romantic emphasis and sharp, angular elements of neoclassicism, was spellbinding. With his head covered by a blond "Liszt" wig, he looked like the popular image of a tempestuous composer in a state of inspiration, groping the air with his long fingers as if seeking the first chord of the famous "Liebestraum." His Muse, Natalia Makarova, clad in a Romantic white tunic, loomed behind him in arabesque, as if directing and igniting his imagination.

The Leningrad audience was immediately struck by the artistic compatibility of Dolgushin and Makarova, and even more so when they danced a concert version of Act II of *Giselle* as their graduation performance in 1959. Dolgushin's Albrecht was refined and rather cool, thanks to his unusual reticence and concentration. He seemed to test his ability to feel, which had been crushed by the weight of reason. His perfunctory support of Giselle and brooding detachment strongly conveyed the impossibility of their union even beyond the grave. "Notes of nervous expressionistic alarm rang through the elegiac lament of the pas de deux. The languid lyricism of a century-old masterpiece was treated to a slightly daring contemporary interpretation," noted Vera Krasovskaya, saluting the appearance of the talented young couple.

Dolgushin's portrayal of Albrecht in the full-length *Giselle* in 1960 brought a brand-new intellectual and dramatic dimension to a role that had been considered Sergeyev's exclusive property. Dolgushin was the first Kirov dancer to challenge the standard Sergeyev had set. He had everything necessary: his attractive, aristocratic physique implied nobility and finesse; his impressive technique served the choreography of Perrot and Petipa perfectly. He never indulged in show-stopping tricks; every step and movement revealed precision and an appealing sensitivity to the Romantic style.

But the truly innovative aspect of Dolgushin's characterization stemmed from his projection and approach, which defied the Kirov tradition. In many ways Dolgushin's portrayal was strongly encouraged by the warmth of Khrushchev's liberal thaw, which led the dancer to seek new moral values in the old Romantic masterpieces. He interpreted *Giselle* as an existential drama; like Vladimir Vasiliev at the Bolshoi, Dolgushin rejected the threadbare idea of Albrecht as a merciless aristocrat whose character derived from his social position. His attitude was to some extent a rebellion against the Marxist determinism that had held the Soviet arts in an iron grip.

Dolgushin portrayed Albrecht as a Hamlet figure, a tormented intellectual for whom the simplehearted peasant girl embodied Rousseau's natural, uncorrupted, guileless ideal. In Act I he was an ardent observer, not a rake; his love for Giselle seemed to be based more on intellectual curiosity than on passion. He enjoyed Giselle's timid, slightly awkward reactions to his wooing, as a refined intellectual might be "turned on" by the spontaneity and straightforward behavior of a country girl. His winning of her gave him proof of his magnetic, if devious, intellectual power. With amazement blended with a touch of disdain, he watched the cheerful abandon of Giselle and her country companions, innocently enjoying their simple life. His mimed comments on his bucolic fling, addressed to Bathilde and the courtiers, were as carelessly cruel as his sorrow over the dead Giselle was thoughtful and compelling.

In Act II he was not so much concerned with escaping the vindictive Wilis as he was enchanted by the mysterious reappearance of his dead love and blissful at the possibility of their reunion. In his confrontation with Myrtha he remained the slightly scornful aristocrat, defying death and savoring challenge. Dolgushin left the audience with the feeling that Albrecht's midnight experience had not touched his heart but would merely feed his future fantasies.

Dolgushin's interpretation differed drastically not only from the Kirov's established standard but even from that of Nureyev, with whom he frequently alternated. Nureyev's

Tartar ebullience and passion were more familiar to the Kirov, an echo of Chabukiani's fervor; but Dolgushin's approach represented a rebellion against the institution's aesthetic creed. Such audacity was punished in a rather cruel way.

Only a few critics welcomed Dolgushin's radical portrayal, but at the Kirov his romantic looks and technique convinced his colleagues that a new Sergeyev had appeared. Feya Balabina, Sergeyev's ex-wife, expressed her rapture too openly; she suddenly re-experienced her youthful vision of the ideal danseur noble and went up to Dolgushin's dressing room, weeping and kissing his hands, convinced that he was the very reincarnation of Sergeyev. These cries of ecstasy over Dolgushin may have been displeasing to the "original," who had to come to terms not only with his own advancing age but also with the thought that his replacement had already appeared. In Sergeyev's relations with Dolgushin there was an element of irrepressible and ill-concealed envy.

Dolgushin's debut as Siegfried only compounded Sergeyev's anger. Dolgushin's Prince was a melancholy, neurotic character whose inability to love brought about his defeat by Rothbart. In Act IV this hapless Siegfried, lost between reality and dreams, experienced so devastating a despair that his story took on a truly tragic dimension. This pessimistic approach, so alien to the official Soviet optimism, was unacceptable to Sergeyev as artistic director. Baryshnikov has described a rehearsal in the late 1960s at which Sergeyev even opposed Dolgushin's manner of holding his bow and arrow, "as if gravitating toward the grave." "Cheer up," Sergeyev would say, "head for the sun, for the sunshine illuminating your life."

But it was sunshine that was definitely lacking, both in Dolgushin's approach to the classics and in his career at the Kirov. Maliciously referring to his "not-so-convincing classical training," Sergeyev managed to saddle the younger dancer with the *Swan Lake* pas de trois and various demi-caractère roles. Dolgushin rebelled, giving portrayals that were slightly vulgar or grotesque. He even went so far as to make his mime role in Sergeyev's *The Path of Thunder* a blatant parody of the choreographer's own ingratiating style. Elena Tchernichova recalled: "Sergeyev accused Nikita of sheer hooliganism and threatened to dismiss him."

In 1961 Dolgushin left the Kirov and moved to Novosibirsk, where his career continued until 1966. Fortunately the condition of cultural vacuum so endemic to Soviet provincial life did not exist in Novosibirsk, where he found a group of talented young dancers and choreographers who were experimenting beyond the official boundaries of Soviet arts. It was here that Oleg Vinogradov, now the director of the Kirov, began his career. Stimulated by his collaboration with Dolgushin, Vinogradov choreographed the first Soviet neoclassical transcription of Prokofiev's *Romeo and Juliet*, introducing to the provincial stage combinations not unlike the vocabulary of Jerome Robbins or even Glen Tetley. "Dolgushin's Romeo," his colleague Evgeny Poliakov, now Nureyev's assistant and coach at the Paris Opéra, recalled in an interview with me, "was truly iconoclastic, a composite of seemingly incompatible qualities, fiery passion and intellectual control. He was both poet and philosopher, a multifaceted personality through whom the richness of the Renaissance was refracted." Dolgushin's daring interpretations were accepted quite enthusiastically by the local critics. Especially interesting, by all accounts, was his Poet in Fokine's *Chopiniana*, whom he portrayed as a Romantic demiurge of the evanescent spirit world.

Dolgushin began to choreograph in Novosibirsk, excelling in particular in his version of some fragments from Lopukhov's *Ice Maiden* (1964). The Novosibirsk theatre, artistically less restrictive than the Kirov, became Dolgushin's choreographic laboratory, which subsequently helped him to mount a few highly imaginative one-act ballets at the Maly Theatre in Leningrad.

By 1966 Dolgushin felt he had outgrown Novosibirsk, which he left to join a small experimental company in Moscow, the Young Ballet, affiliated with Igor Moiseyev's Folk Dance Institution. From there, he thought, it would be easier to renew his ties with the Kirov. With the Young Ballet he continued to expand the field of experimentation and the daring assertion of his individual style. Igor Tchernichov, still at the dawn of his choreographic career, mounted for him a plotless one-act ballet that had been banned at the Kirov. Dolgushin's tragic intensity and severity transformed this cameo set to Albinoni into a poem about the discord between sensual longing and religious ecstasy.

In Moscow Dolgushin's intellectual attitude imparted a slight touch of irony to his performances of the old Petipa warhorses, especially the final pas de deux of *Don Quixote*, in which he alternated utterly spectacular movements and exaggerated theatrical poses, underscoring their "campy" character. As he himself confessed, in that pas de deux he intended to evoke the image of a gilded, glittering girandole.

In 1968 the prodigal son attempted to return to the Kirov. Sergeyev permitted him to appear in *Legend of Love* with Alla Osipenko and in *Giselle* with Makarova. His per-

Left: Franz in *Coppélia*, with Tatiana Fesenko as Swanilda, early 1970s
Below: The Grand Pas from *Paquita*, with Fesenko, 1975

OPPOSITE
Top: (left) rehearsing a concert number by Mai Murdmaa to music of Villa-Lobos, late 1960s; (right) Albrecht, with Natalia Makarova as Giselle, 1960s
Bottom: The Torero in *Carmen Suite*, with Valentina Mukhanova as Carmen, 1972

formances were among the most dazzling I had ever seen in Russia. Not only did Dolgushin seem to be at the peak of his technical and artistic maturity, but his presentation was very Westernized, drastically differing from his Kirov colleagues. To the precision and suavity of movement that had formerly constituted the core of his style, he now added a new finesse, a stunning ability to be meaningful and powerful at any moment of action. The intensity of his pauses, charged looks and poses, economical yet significant gestures, and appealing emotional reserve at times suggested more than his most bravura sequences. His ability to draw one into the electrifying field of his intellectual energy could be compared to that of the young Paul Scofield.

In *Legend of Love* his frail, flexible, tempestuous Ferhad recalled a prince from the Arabian Nights. He skillfully suggested the heat of Oriental passion cooled by the control of a sober mind. He held back in the duets with Shirin, as if still re-examining his feelings, and then burst into leaps of untrammeled sensuality in his variation. In the dream scene with Mekhmene-Banu (Alla Osipenko) he was both inscrutable and tantalizing, the eternally unattainable goal of her feverish imagination. His partnership with Osipenko was unique; they brought such intensity and tragic pathos to their duet that *Legend of Love* unexpectedly took on a new and poignant dimension. It is truly disheartening to think that this partnership was never allowed to develop further.

As for *Giselle*, Dolgushin's emphasis on the psychological incompatibility of Albrecht and his beloved came into more salient relief than it had in 1962. In *A Dance Autobiography* Makarova mildly criticized Dolgushin for his over-intellectual characterization. She recalled him in Act II as "the image of some mad Greek hero driven by the furies" but also noted that "the contours of the naïve, romantic drama about love and repentance became blurred and distorted." Nevertheless, it is my own opinion that Dolgushin's approach actually deepened the contemporary perspectives of the part. With cold curiosity his Albrecht watched Giselle's mad scene as if envying the emotional climax he himself could not achieve. In his encounter with Giselle's spirit, he seemed to be trying to recapture the freshness of his feelings for her. His intellect seemed to be ignited only during his confrontation with the hostile Wilis; and as the night waned, he seemed to droop, as if withdrawing again into the fortress of his mind.

Of course Dolgushin's daring interpretation aroused the indignation of the Kirov Art Committee and of Sergeyev himself. The latter accused Dolgushin of an exces-

sively neoclassical, Westernized, and even effeminate manner, and slammed the Kirov doors on him. Several years later, driven by a desire to portray Hamlet that was apparently more powerful than his resentment, Dolgushin appeared in Sergeyev's full-length ballet, but even the impact of his stage presence seemed weakened, and no amount of expressive miming could bring the cardboard design to life.

Many of Dolgushin's colleagues viewed his career at the Maly Theatre as a gradual artistic decline. Makarova maintained that at the Maly he "did not achieve anything of significance because no one created for him roles worthy of his talent, and the great promise that he had shown at the beginning of his career remained unfulfilled." But Makarova left Russia in 1970 and was simply unaware of the variety of Dolgushin's work at the Maly and the special qualities he revealed as a choreographer.

From 1968 to 1981 Dolgushin danced many classical and neoclassical roles at the Maly. The company run by the young Oleg Vinogradov distinguished itself in the 1970s with far more experimental verve than the Kirov, in such fresh and spectacular productions as *The Yaroslavna*, set to Boris Tishchenko's highly imaginative score, choreographed by Vinogradov, and directed by Yuri Lubimov (1974); Nikolai Boiarchikov's *Three Cards* after Pushkin's *The Queen of Spades*, set to Prokofiev (1973); Boiarchikov's *Tsar Boris* after Pushkin's *Boris Godunov*, again set to Prokofiev (1978), and Vinogradov's revision of *Romeo and Juliet*. Dolgushin played Prince Igor and Tsar Boris in a lofty, tragic key. The intensity of these portrayals was enhanced by his unique ability to imbue each movement and pose with his intellectual energy. The line of his elongated, muscular body, brittle and energetic, his expressive face and his power in repose—all evoked the image of a soul in torment. His Tsar Boris was an especially powerful characterization. The fully drawn transition from power-mad maniac to repentant murderer gave Dolgushin's protagonist the grandeur of Macbeth.

Other classical roles that Dolgushin danced at the Maly included the Prince in Igor Belsky's *The Nutcracker* (1971); Colin in Vinogradov's *La Fille mal gardée* (1971); Frantz in Vinogradov's *Coppélia* (1973), and James in Bournonville's *La Sylphide* (1975), revived by the Danish choreographer Elsa von Rosen. Colin and Frantz were unexpected triumphs, revealing Dolgushin's flair for comedy. As Colin, he was especially successful, matching his clownish escapades with impeccably performed virtuoso show stoppers, permeated with a sense of light romantic comedy.

Dolgushin's James came from the same mold as his

Albrecht. His characterization rivaled Erik Bruhn's for poignance and refinement. Dolgushin presented the naive conflict of dream and reality as a consequence of his hero's introverted, slightly neurotic nature. In Act I he portrayed James as a contemplative, phlegmatic lad immersed in reverie; in Act II, the confrontation with the sylphides aroused his tempestuous Romantic temperament, muted in everyday life. As James, Dolgushin proved to be an impeccable stylist, never overacting or indulging in spectacular technical tricks. He executed his high jumps without soaring and without preparation, in obedience to Bournonville's principles, and emphasized small-scale technique, imparting a special polish and precision to circuits of beats and tours.

A keen sensitivity to the genuine Romantic style marked Dolgushin's revival of the original *Giselle* (1973). He maintained a delicate balance between the archaic mimodrama of Act I and its Romantic antithesis, the spectral, airy style of Act II, creating a refined stylization of the old ballet without giving it the air of a museum piece. The same stylistic finesse distinguished his reconstruction of Petipa's famous Grand Pas from *Paquita*, whose frontal compositions breathed the Cartesian *lucidité* and elegant crispness of classicism. As the cavalier, Dolgushin intentionally eschewed any of the technical tours de force that others had interpolated in the 1920s. His noble dancing harked back to the affected artistry of Petipa's cavaliers—Pavel Gerdt, Nicolas Legat, Samuil Andrianov. Dolgushin's stylized manner was an elegiac sigh for their outmoded art.

At the Maly Dolgushin successfully continued his choreographic career, mounting several ballets to music of Tchaikovsky—*Concerto in White* (1969), *Contemplations* (1970), *Mozartiana* (1970), *Romeo and Juliet* (1971). He also choreographed Rodion Tshchedrin's *Chamber Suite* (1971) and the divertissement from Gluck's *Clytemnestra* (1972). Rare for Russian ballet, Dolgushin's compositions are virtually or entirely plotless and, even more amazing, totally free of Soviet provincialism. His style is hard to define. When it resembles that of John Cranko or of Jerome Robbins, it happily combines graphic sharpness with Russian fluidity of movement, and more frequently than not the dramatic intensity grows out of the contrast of these elements. Although a serious knee injury in 1980 has curtailed Dolgushin's dancing, his promising choreographic efforts suggest that his artistic potential is by no means exhausted.

The Blue Bird in *The Sleeping Beauty*

YURI SOLOVIEV

I RECALL VIVIDLY the last time I saw Yuri Soloviev dance at the Kirov, in Igor Belsky's ballet *Icarus* in the spring of 1974. Heavy, with athletically developed legs and thighs that gave his stocky body a squarish look, he seemed weary and fatigued, as if he were performing against his will. In the perspective of his luckless career at the Kirov, the role of Icarus took on special symbolic meaning; the youth's fatal attempt to achieve his freedom seemed to anticipate the dénouement of Soloviev's own life.

Shortly before my departure for the United States, I met Soloviev on the Nevsky Prospect after a rehearsal at the Vaganova School. He had a slight limp and a stern, impenetrable expression on his face. We exchanged several short phrases—"The knee started bothering me again . . . I hope it will be all right. . . . Are you leaving us for good? Well, give my regards to the kids, let them enjoy their lives; as for us, we'll remain here to rot and slave for *them*. . . ."

On January 15, 1977, Yuri Soloviev died from a self-inflicted shotgun wound at his country place in Sosnovo, a three-hour drive from Leningrad. In the same month I received a letter from Russia reporting the tragedy:

Another misfortune befell the accursed theatre whence dancers flee either beyond the Iron Curtain or into nonexistence. Some of them slowly go berserk from a harassing mixture of self-contempt and self-pity. Yuri's death is utterly mysterious: he went to the country and got lost for three days—there was no phone, of course, in his wooden cottage. Tatiana [Legat—Soloviev's wife] raised an alarm when Yuri missed a rehearsal. Someone went to Sosnovo immediately. The hut stood buried under the snowdrifts like an icy tomb.

He began to knock at the door and bang his fists on the windows—only the echo reverberated. As he broke open the door, a strong smell of onions came to his nose. In the kitchen there were several plates lavishly filled with chopped onion. Beside them stood empty vodka bottles. Why did he slice onion? To kill the stench when he was discovered? Very strange, because the ferocious cold at the house had prevented his decomposition. Yuri was found under a blanket, heaped up with some cloths and rags—he lay stiff, covered with his frozen blood, a bullet hole in his temple. In his hands he clasped his old hunting rifle.

It is not hard to guess why he committed suicide. At the age of thirty-seven he had nothing worth justifying his efforts, his pain and drudgery. His career was ruined; he had no courage to defect, although it was said that during his last tour in Italy he was planning to take a leap to freedom. He was not happy with his family, suffered from solitude and sexual frustration. As a result the Kirov is bereft of its last Prince, and Yuri's death seems to be the most sinister stroke on the canvas of its dismal decay.

SOLOVIEV'S PHYSICAL QUALITIES—his short stature and cherubic face, his thick, strong thighs and far-from-beautiful swollen muscles—did not invest him with the legitimate authority of a danseur noble. Nevertheless, thanks to his exceptional classical technique, the Kirov allowed him to undertake such roles as Siegfried, Solor, Albrecht, and Desiré. He possessed the natural soaring ballon of Nijinsky; moreover, he was able to maintain a legato quality rare among male dancers, never being caught in abrupt transition from one step to another. It was said that Soloviev danced musical sequences, lending a special fluidity to each of his roles. He used to mark the choreographic units softly so as to blend them into a flowing entity. This special legato gave a unique look to his chaînés, which were like curling clouds, and to his precise but supple pirouettes. His beats were high and strikingly large and were frequently compared to coloratura trills or *gruppetti*.

His tireless ballon erased the distinction between take-off and landing. His flight seemed effortless; he soared upward with his particular force and lingered in the air, as if the air itself could support him. In his leaps and turns his impeccable feet, with high-arched insteps and well-pointed toes, helped to elongate his rather short legs.

YURI VLADIMIROVICH SOLOVIEV was born in Leningrad on August 10, 1940, into a working-class family. Before her marriage his mother had attended the

Vaganova Choreographic School, which Yuri entered in 1949. Unlike Nijinsky, he was not considered especially gifted until he reached the advanced classes of Boris Shavrov (a former partner of Spessivtseva) and Alexander Pushkin. Because he was so short, the administration was determined to expel him, but Shavrov arranged for him to be given a trial term.

In 1957 he danced the *Swan Lake* pas de trois with Natalia Makarova and Alla Sizova at a pregraduate performance at the Kirov. In this virtuoso piece Soloviev displayed his polished technique, noble carriage, and innate sense of ensemble. His miraculous ability to flutter above the stage was especially striking. He danced the same role in September 1961 at his New York debut in the old Metropolitan Opera House. John Martin of the *New York Times* singled out the pas de trois as "magnificently danced."

For his graduation performance in 1958 Soloviev prepared the Blue Bird from *The Sleeping Beauty*, Acteon in *Diana and Acteon*, and the pas de deux from the Petipa-Vaganova *Esmeralda*. His flowing high jumps and lightning turns as Acteon could not compensate for his inconsistent portrayal of the mythological hunter, but his Blue Bird was a revelation. It remained Soloviev's masterpiece in the 1950s and 1960s, on a level with Bessmertnova's Giselle, Plisetskaya's Odette and Kitri, and Vasiliev's Mejnun.

The uniqueness of Soloviev's Blue Bird lay in the fact that it not only demonstrated his sheer virtuosity but also displayed such artistry that it clarified the hidden meaning of Petipa's choreography. In 1890 Petipa himself had defined this piece as "the ecstasy of a bird in flight, swimming in the untrammeled freedom of the air." In a broader sense it might be interpreted as a song of love in the language of beats and brisés dessus-dessous. Sweeping through the choreography with an unparalleled fusion of ballon and legato, Soloviev made both symbolic meanings visible. This Blue Bird did not just fly: he soared, with soft, hardly discernible landings that did not disrupt the high trajectory of his flight. The powerful strokes of his winglike arms seemed to propel him into the air. Beginning a jeté entrelacé, he slowly spread his body in arabesque, landing gradually in a final sequence of beats; he would gain height with each thrust, potently lingering in the air, and his brisés dessus-dessous, performed with a slightly curved torso, seemed to cap this flight of exultation.

Thanks to his tremendous success as the Blue Bird at his graduation performance, Soloviev was immediately accepted at the Kirov as a leading soloist, but his unorthodox physique created many complications in casting. During his first seasons he was assigned insignificant pas de trois and pas de deux in *Laurencia* and *Raymonda*. The Kirov seemed to be limiting its use of him to his purely instrumental gift, but this made him an invaluable part of the now legendary ensembles of the late 1950s and early 1960s: e.g., *The Sleeping Beauty* with its incomparable cast of Kolpakova as Aurora, Vladilen Semyonov as Desiré, Osipenko as the Lilac Fairy, Soloviev as the Blue Bird, and Makarova as Florine, with the best soloists as fairies and Igor Tchernichov as one of the four cavaliers.

His third season (1960–1961) was crucial for Soloviev. His repertory increased considerably, including not only small roles—a troubadour in *Raymonda*, the Spirit of the Ocean in *The Little Humpbacked Horse*, the Peasant pas de deux in *Giselle*—but also the Soviet Youth in Belsky's *Leningrad Symphony*, Desiré in *Sleeping Beauty*, and the Poet in *Chopiniana*. In 1962 and 1963 he danced Siegfried, Albrecht, Harlequin in Fokine's *Carnaval*, Ferhad in Grigorovich's *Legend of Love*, and Man in Sergeyev's *The Distant Planet*.

Even at the outset of his career Soloviev's dance profile and the problems of his artistic growth at the Kirov were quite apparent. His technique took on more classical finish, but it was seen mostly in small show-stopping virtuoso pieces like the Peasant pas de deux from *Giselle*, when this little early gem of Petipa's was restored in 1960. It was sad to witness the discrepancy between his unprecedented technique and his muted personality—a gap that was all the more noticeable when he was miscast, as he was in *Chopiniana*. The poetry of reticence and Romantic detachment that Makarova and Dolgushin conjured up was alien to Soloviev. His Poet looked earthbound.

In a sense Soloviev was trapped by his physique—his pleasant, open, "country boy" face, his solid body and powerful, muscular legs. He could easily be cast as a sterling Soviet youth, one of the stereotypes that embodied the official image in so many ballets—the conqueror of the cosmos or of the virgin lands of Siberia. Ironically, these cardboard roles were anticipated somewhat in Soloviev's portrayal of the stone-cutter Danila in Grigorovich's *The Stone Flower* (1957). Although the role provided a certain amount of choreographic meat, Soloviev's lack of the potent projection that had distinguished Igor Tchernichov and Vladimir Vasiliev in the role left his Danilo anemic and two-dimensional. When this kind of social mask functioned in the choreographic vacuum of *Distant Planet* or Belsky's *Shore of Hope*, Soloviev's efforts to bring abstractions to life were doomed. Only in Belsky's *Leningrad Sym-*

Above: Albrecht, early 1960s
Right: Prince Désiré in *The Sleeping Beauty*, 1964

Top: The Youth in *Leningrad Symphony*, late 1960s
Above: The Cosmonaut in *The Distant Planet*, with Natalia Makarova as The Planet, mid-1960s
Right: The Slave in the *Corsaire* pas de deux, with Kaleria Fedicheva, late 1960s

Above: The Slave in the *Corsaire* pas de deux, early 1970s
Left: Kino in *The Pearl*, with Alla Osipenko as The Pearl, 1965

phony did Soloviev overcome the choreographic clichés and put an individual stamp on his portrayal of the protagonist. The appealing vulnerability that shaded his sustained jumps softened the ostentatious virility of the character; his image expanded the role, transforming it into a more complex metaphor. Praising his portrayal of a "positive hero," the critics somehow overlooked Soloviev's rare ability to write choreographic poems with his body, both masculine and vulnerable. He would have been very successful in plotless dance; but, unfortunately, that genre was unpopular at the Kirov at the beginning of the sixties.

As for the classical roles, he generally seemed to be at a loss with them, especially with Albrecht. It seemed that he was not sensitive to the new psychological approach that marked Dolgushin's and Vasiliev's interpretations; rather, he perceived the role impersonally. His flawless dancing, particularly in Act II, was at odds with his diligent yet amateurish pantomime. He simply illustrated the plot when his partner was Kolpakova or Sizova; when paired with Makarova, he was unable to take fire from the spark of her inspiration and feverish lyricism.

As Desiré in *Sleeping Beauty* he was more convincing: the lack of dramatic conflict and the minimum of mime in the role suited his introspective, phlegmatic nature. Surrounded by the Romantic entourage of the Nereids in Act II, his visionary Prince pensively followed the Lilac Fairy toward the encounter with his dream lady yet was attractive and moving. The role of Desiré, dramatically inexpressive, limited to partnering until the pyrotechnics of the final variation, was here saturated with contemplative peace, lyrical detachment, and unobtrusive fragility.

One might have expected that these qualities would make him a perfect Siegfried, but this was not the case, because in *Swan Lake* Soloviev found himself in a field of balletic drama alien to his temperament. He was at his best in Act II, where he overacted less and seemed to respond to the subtle lyricism of the adagio. But as a whole his portrayal revealed a puzzling inconsistency, in the quaint transitions from Siegfried's youthful mischief at the beginning of Act I to his brooding melancholy, and in the Act III pas de deux, in which he played Siegfried as a foppish rake, almost intoxicated with Odile's amorous wiles. What is more, the explosion of despair at his farewell to Odette in Act IV seemed somehow unmotivated, since the amazing virtuosity of his Act III variation, with its rare combination of double tours en l'air with double assemblés en tournant, a symbol of Siegfried's exultation over his infatuation with Odile, indicated the Prince's fickle nature.

Soloviev's failing seemed to be not only an inability to respond to the dramatic conflict but also an inaptness in shaping and developing the role. In a broader sense this perplexing awkwardness may have reflected his confusion about his own identity, which he was apprehensive about revealing. This kind of personal disarray marked many of his roles during the 1960s, despite his perfect technique and the body that he molded into elaborate, exemplary forms (photographs of Soloviev already graced many Soviet manuals of classical dance). Soloviev's personality did at times manifest itself in his portrayals in the most puzzling way. It seemed that one was observing the inner controversies of a complex human being, refracted through the characters of Solor, Ferhad, and Cinderella's Prince.

The stalwart warrior of *La Bayadère*, so eloquently impersonated by Vakhtang Chabukiani and Boris Bregvadze, one of the most talented Kirov dancers in the fifties, in an ostentatiously virile manner, seemed like an unsuitable role for Soloviev. Nevertheless, his Solor was a significant addition to his gallery of classical protagonists, a composite of the vulnerable but virile Youth of *Leningrad Symphony* and the dreamy Desiré of *Sleeping Beauty*. Remarkably convincing in the dynamic variation with a bow, he was moving as Nikiya's timorous lover and touching as a youth mesmerized by Gamzatti and unable to withstand her erotic attraction. But in the Kingdom of the Shades he was a shining knight of love, united with his dear one beyond the grave. As Solor, Soloviev did not repent ostentatiously or wring his hands as he did in *Giselle*. Plunged into an opium-induced reverie, he seemed to be cutting his ties not only with reality but with his own life. This gave a special tragic meaning to the Kirov production, which has long ended with the Kingdom of the Shades scene, the last act having been truncated in 1919.

Equally significant was his Ferhad in *Legend of Love*, possibly the most complex role Soloviev ever danced. The choreography, including two variations, three duets, and three *terzetti*, realized Soloviev's potential, and the paucity of mime enabled him to avoid overacting. His appeal stemmed from the fusion of his skilled dancing and his effeminately stylized Oriental plasticity. In many ways his Ferhad, chastely adoring the Princess Shirin and victimized by the passion of her sister, Mekhmene-Banu, might have been Solor's twin.

Another aspect of Soloviev's puzzling individuality was manifested in his Prince Charming in Sergeyev's *Cinderella*. In the 1960s Vladilen Semyonov had imparted to the Prince the impersonal luster of an abstract danseur noble; Soloviev's interpretation restored the vivid, mischievous spirit of the original design. His Prince exploded the decorum of the court ball with swift beats that were more dramatically apt than any of his vague histrionics. The encounter with Cinderella seemed to stir his dormant emotional resources and initiate him into early maturity. His impassive features took on a melancholy cast, as if he were dismayed by the surge of his first amorous feelings. What had struck one as incongruous and farfetched in *Swan Lake* here looked absolutely legitimate and natural: in particular, the assertiveness that animated the Prince's dizzying galop with its large split jetés that encompassed the stage and suggested a fairytale chase in magical boots. But his final adagio with Cinderella was suffused with a feeling of peace, conveying the Prince's recaptured inner balance with reality.

These three roles seemed to refract facets of Soloviev's personality that many choreographers simply disregarded. The iconoclastic Leonid Jakobson merely made use of Soloviev's virtuosity in his Land of Wonders (1968); he preferred to experiment with Baryshnikov's theatricality, so much more striking and compelling than Soloviev's. Georgy Alexidze miscast him as the villain Aegisthus in *Oresteia*, ignoring his natural endowments. Igor Tchernichov's attempts to employ Soloviev in his daring neoclassical ballets *Bolero* and *Romeo and Juliet* never came to pass, at least partly because Soloviev's own phlegmatic nature paralyzed his initiative. But even in rehearsals one could see the extent to which Soloviev reveled in the neoclassical element. Tchernichov's choreography, based on a fusion of classical steps, acrobatics, and expressionistic poses, demanded a powerful release of emotional energy that apparently stirred the dancer's hidden psychological springs.

Unfortunately, at the peak of his artistry Soloviev was doomed to self-repetition. Unlike the energetic, effervescent Baryshnikov, Soloviev was not a fighter, and the debilitating atmosphere of corrosive passivity at the Kirov took its toll on his dancing and his mind. In *A Dance Autobiography* Makarova said correctly: "No one nurtured Soloviev's soul or fostered his mind; no one ever produced a ballet to tap his inner world. This was a Stradivarius which played beautifully but never sang. Rudi and Misha had Pushkin; Vasiliev had Yermolayev to pull the individuality out of him. Yuri had no one. And he was too weak to break through to self-realization in isolation." Moreover, his indolent and in many ways frustrated nature only aggravated the problems he faced.

In the 1970s Soloviev had two roles that were like gusts of fresh air in the stifling hothouse atmosphere of the Kirov: *Le Spectre de la rose* and God in Kasatkina and Vasilyov's inventive, farcical *Creation of the World*. His interpretation of *Spectre* again warranted the proclamations of a "new Nijinsky" that had been made after his now legendary Blue Bird. Fokine's technical tour de force came so easily to Soloviev that even Baryshnikov's Spectre, seen years later at American Ballet Theatre, paled in comparison. His natural short "takeoff" and unequaled ballon, as well as a certain affinity with the androgynous nature of Fokine's choreographic image, enabled Soloviev to provide a striking visual reincarnation of the "victorious attack of rose perfume" that, in Jean Cocteau's words, Nijinsky's image allegorized. Through Soloviev's dancing the substitute of a rose for a man in Fokine's choreography vibrated with poignant sexual ambivalence.

In 1972 his appearance as God in *Creation of the World* overwhelmed the Leningrad audience. In this role he gave the first indication of his extraordinary comic gifts: dressed in a long white shirt, with a beard, light brown hair, and a round, trusting face, Soloviev's God resembled a hapless Russian peasant. He simpleheartedly pined away amid his submissive subjects in his neat paradise filled with ox-eyed daisies. He created the world virtually out of boredom, and the way he inspected his thoroughly mundane household or flew up into the clouds over the heads of his host of angels was hilariously comical. He instilled the same funny verve into his breathtaking cascades of dizzying leaps and split jetés, which he seemed to perform as a joke, a way to kill the oppressive ennui of heaven. It is regrettable that Soloviev was never to mine this comic vein by dancing Tyl Eulenspiegel or Mercutio.

After *Creation of the World* Soloviev did not dance any significant role except for the tormented Page in Leonid Lebediev's one-act ballet *The Infanta* (1977), based on Cervantes's tale of a servant's thwarted love for his royal mistress (Irina Kolpakova). I have been told that in this cameo Soloviev astounded the audience with sudden outbursts of tragic temperament and passionate despair, totally unlike his customary good-humored or impersonal stage image. It would seem that his last role only proved that he was at the height of his artistic powers when he died. His death interrupted the tradition of danseur noble at the Kirov.

THE DANCER AS "SUPERMAN"

Mikhail Mordkin · Pierre Vladimiroff

Alexei Yermolayev

Vakhtang Chabukiani · Vladimir Vasiliev

Bacchanale, 1910

MIKHAIL MORDKIN

MIKHAIL MORDKIN, notorious for the onstage slap with which Anna Pavlova once rewarded his capricious partnering, was undoubtedly one of the most colorful figures in Russian ballet and indeed a great master of male dancing. He was a typical product of theatrical Moscow, alien to the classicism of St. Petersburg, an outstanding dancer and an equally remarkable dramatic actor. Fyodor Lopukhov devoted to him the most enthusiastic pages in his memoirs:

For me, Mikhail Mordkin is the pre-eminent Russian dancer; no one could compete with him in the rarest and most spectacular balletic category—the heroic. Athletically built, with an impeccable body, inspired face, and big, fascinating eyes, Mordkin was an ideal of male beauty on the stage. He possessed a striking dramatic gift, knew how to wear the most exotic attire, and captivated the audience with his picturesque poses and grand-scale gestures. Like no one else, he was able to fill the huge Bolshoi stage with movements as powerful as a Greek god's, arousing a storm of applause. I cannot help but resent Diaghilev's "promotion" of Nijinsky, which made him a god of dance and stole this legitimate title from Mordkin. In my view, by the aggregate of all his qualifications, Mordkin definitely surpassed Nijinsky. As an actor, Mordkin was rivaled only by Chaliapin, whose stage presence and potent projection resembled his. Little wonder that Stanislavsky valued Mordkin's theatrical instinct highly and frequently invited him to teach the technique of stage movement at the Moscow Art Theatre. In their turn, Mordkin's dramatic devices were shaped under the influence of Stanislavsky's theory.

This panegyric, rather biased in terms of the Nijinsky-Mordkin comparison, echoes that of Akim Volynsky, who proclaimed indifference to male dancing in general but wrote enthusiastically about Mordkin: "His stage projection, with its power, abundant means, and straightforward emotionality, stands unparalleled in Russian ballet. It would be legitimate to claim that Mordkin proved himself a first-rate tragedian, substituting for antediluvian, ridiculous pantomime the emotional depth of genuine acting. What striking plasticity, what freedom of movement, what lingering poses that convey sculpturesque monumental power! Mounet-Sully, Coquelin, Salvini, and Rossi might vie with his plastic art."

Nevertheless, it was not only Mordkin's plasticity and rare virile beauty that constituted his main artistic resource. The range of his dancing was also magnificent: he possessed a huge jump, spectacular turns, and the regal carriage of a danseur noble. The way he exploited his physical qualities and training truly distinguished him as a performer.

MIKHAIL MIKHAILOVICH MORDKIN was born in Moscow on December 9, 1880. He entered Vasily Tikhomirov's class at the Moscow Theatre School in 1890. At his pregraduate debut in Clustine's version of *La Fille mal gardée* in September 1899, he took the Moscow audience by storm. The reviewer for the *Moscow Observer* wrote that Mordkin was "the best Colin on the Moscow stage—he was so alert, handsome, graceful in dances and expressive in pantomime."

Thanks to his extraordinary achievements, Mordkin became a soloist at the Bolshoi upon his graduation in 1900 and was quickly promoted to the rank of principal dancer. Perhaps no other Russian male dancer except Nureyev and Baryshnikov achieved such a high and steady trajectory of permanent success, and no one realized his potential with more intensity and fullness than Mordkin.

His youth, technical exuberance, and dramatic ability immediately made him a strong rival of Tikhomirov, who at that time dominated the Bolshoi's male contingent. But this rivalry was of no importance, since from the outset, Mordkin showed himself to be a controversial dancer. Tikhomirov epitomized an old-fashioned noble style similar to Gerdt's, but Mordkin's approach was influenced by the theatrical innovations of his native city—in particular, those of Stanislavsky. Unlike Tikhomirov, Mordkin viewed classical dance only as a vehicle for dramatic expression, to the point, at times, of neglecting the value of the steps themselves. It is not surprising that in spite of his unique qualifications as a danseur noble, Mordkin seemed to eschew the classics. At the dawn of his Bolshoi career he frequently performed *Swan Lake* and *Giselle*, but in mastering the old repertory he was concerned less with technique than with dramatic projection. He was intent upon establishing the psychological credibility of the characters, although in Petipa's day they had never been regarded as serious dramatic parts. Nor were the ballets themselves perceived as realistic dramas; they were performed more in the stylized mode of opera than as realistic drama-theatre. Both approaches were given equal rights during the Soviet era; as a dancing actor, Mordkin may be considered the predecessor of this artistic trend.

But it is noteworthy that unlike such Soviet dancers as Yermolayev and Chabukiani, who followed in Mordkin's footsteps without having seen him on the stage, he never attempted to enrich the vocabulary of his classical roles with bravura tricks; mainly he sought to fill the stage space not with the conventional mime devices of Petipa's time but with a plasticity saturated with straightforward emotional projection. Moreover, in his early years Mordkin's rebellious spirit spurred him to a parody of Tikhomirov's academic style—the aesthetic of nineteenth-century male dancing with its pompous posing, regal but wooden gait, and sweeping gesticulation. The spirit of defiance urged him to extremes: in *Le Corsaire*, his stalwart Conrad suddenly let out a scream; in *Don Quixote* (in which he danced both Espada and Basil) "his wild jumps and frantic stamping were at odds with the artistic purpose of the ballet, bordering on caricature," as the critic Nikolai Vashkevich observed. By emphasizing the elements of Spanish folk dance that Gorsky had introduced into Petipa's choreographic vocabulary, Mordkin vulgarized Petipa's style and distorted his creation, an *españolada* that was never intended to be a realistic Spanish comedy.

In terms of rhythm and tempestuous presentation, Mordkin and Geltzer were kindred spirits. But unlike the ballerina, a genuine instrumentalist who sought the balance of pure dance and dramatic expression in classical roles, Mordkin imbued his roles with an exaggerated emotionalism that time and again treated the dumbfounded St. Petersburg audience to "outbursts of temperament and frenzied enthusiasm hardly appropriate in the frame of traditional presentation" (Volynsky). However, what in St. Petersburg was perceived as an infringement upon academic norms was seen in Moscow as highly relevant and legitimate. In the early thirties, when Alexei Yermolayev

succeeded in fusing Mordkin's flamboyant expressionism with his own sheer virtuosity, he created the "big sloppy style" that was the hallmark of later generations of Bolshoi dancers.

Mordkin achieved a balance between dramatic consistency and balletic conventions only in the productions of Alexander Gorsky. Like Geltzer, Mordkin resented Gorsky's campaign against the academic style, especially after Gorsky turned him into a handsome prop in *Gudule's Daughter*. In contrast to Petipa's Romantic concept of Phoebus as a noble cavalier, Esmeralda's savior, Gorsky presented him as a primitive ruffian, a formidable product of medieval Paris. The minimal dancing that Mordkin was given reduced his virile figure to a colorful member of a motley crowd, which certainly hurt the dancer's ego.

Despite his furious resistance, Gorsky never ceased to regard Mordkin as a spectacular, decorative ornament. He was colorful and picturesque as Espada in *Don Quixote* (1900), King Hitaris in *Pharaoh's Daughter* (1905), an Indian warrior in *Nur and Anitra* (1907), and Mato, leader of the mercenaries, in *Salammbô* (1910). (As Nur he wore light chain armor over a silk tunic; golden bracelets adorned his ankles and naked arms; a mane of hair flowed from under a turban and spread freely over his shoulders.) In all these ballets pictorial expressiveness, temperamental movement, and pantomime reinforced one another, illustrating the plot and its main emotional leitmotifs—hatred, passion, wickedness. Several of Mordkin's concert numbers as preserved on film recall the technique of the early silent movies. Dance, if included at all, served the same illustrative purposes. Mordkin's unique gift was a fascinating ability to fuse the three components: pantomime, decoration, and dance.

But one of Mordkin's portrayals stood apart: Mato in *Salammbô*, the role that observers called his masterpiece. The character of the muscular warrior, impetuous in love and hatred, marvelously matched Mordkin's personal qualities: his indefatigable hot temper, arrogant virility, and indomitable pride. Mato's passion for Salammbô (Geltzer), the chaste priestess of the goddess Tanit, was as unbridled as his ambitious desire to conquer Carthage, which he expressed in his powerful sword dance. But in the heat of the night, when Salammbô appeared in Mato's tent to trade her virginity for the goddess's sacred veil, the tamed savage fell asleep on her breast. Lopukhov claimed that Mordkin's inspired interpretation elevated this transcription of the Samson-Delilah legend to the level of tragedy. He imbued

Clockwise from top right: The Fisherman in *Love Is Nimble*, mid-1910s; *The Gypsy*, mid-1910s; King Hitaris in *Pharaoh's Daughter*, with Vera Karalli, 1905; *The Legend of Azyiade*, mid-1910s

Дорогая Женя!
Поздравляю
тебя со днемъ
рожденія, и желаю
всего лучшаго.
Всегда тебя
Изд. Фот. К. Фишеръ.
Москва

Мордкинъ.

46

М. Мордкинъ

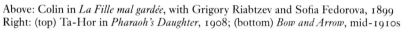

Above: Colin in *La Fille mal gardée*, with Grigory Riabtzev and Sofia Fedorova, 1899
Right: (top) Ta-Hor in *Pharaoh's Daughter*, 1908; (bottom) *Bow and Arrow*, mid-1910s

OPPOSITE
Top: (left) Siegfried, c.1900; (right) Hermes in *The Stars*, c.1900
Bottom: (left) Espada in *Don Quixote*, 1900; (middle) *The Legend of Azyiade*, mid-1910s;
(right) unidentified role

the extremes of Mato's behavior—from rebellion to submission—with rare emotional verve. Volynsky wrote in his review of *Salammbô*: "One could forgive his excesses, because his daring and colorful portrayal brought Mato to life through the glare of his fiery temperament." Nicolai Vashkevich wrote that Mordkin "seemed to scatter sparks when his infuriated, powerful savage attacked the throng of bestial people, and to generate a quiet light when he sought Salammbô's love." The audience was overwhelmed by the death of Mato on the steps of the terrace where Salammbô celebrated her betrothal to the general Narr-Avas. According to Volynsky, Mordkin demonstrated "the purely physical tragedy of a beautiful body, suffering and torn to pieces, with awesome power." Lopukhov recalled in his memoirs how "terrifying and moving Mordkin was when, blinded, with his heart cut out, he kept staggering to his feet until he suddenly fell dead." Fyodor Chaliapin and many dramatic actors came to watch the way Mordkin acted this famous scene.

Nevertheless, by 1909 Gorsky's downgrading of classical dance had apparently exhausted Mordkin's patience. Despite his tremendous success as Mato, Mordkin left the Bolshoi and exchanged his star status for three wandering years in Europe and America, first in Paris with Diaghilev in the spring of 1909 and then with Anna Pavlova during the following summer in London, in February and March 1910 in America, and in April 1910 back in London. During the first Diaghilev season Mordkin danced a czardas with Sofia Fedorova in *Le Festin* and René de Beaugency in Fokine's *Le Pavillon d'Armide*. In Pavlova's enterprise he served as a substitute for Nijinsky, whom Diaghilev had forbidden to travel with the refractory ballerina. During the summer of 1909 they astounded London. In his memoirs Sergei Khudekov recollected: "Mordkin and Pavlova were born to dance together. He was as great a master of spectacular movement as she. They sparkled in small-scale ballets, compact and efficient in their nomadic life; both were endowed with extraordinary temperament, all the more enchanting when Pavlova's frail grace was displayed against the background of Mordkin's virile beauty. And so Pavlova's strong statement that as a dancer Mordkin is not inferior to Nijinsky cannot be accounted for only by her infatuation with her partner."

At the Metropolitan Opera House in New York the duo danced *Coppélia*, an abridged *Giselle*, the *Bacchanale*, and *The Legend of Azyiade*, the last two mounted by Mordkin. Their success in the *Bacchanale* was so enormous that "they swept the audience almost literally out of their chairs," wrote Carl Van Vechten. The finale, in which Pavlova seemed to hover in the air, circling round and round Mordkin, was also irresistible. His success was not overshadowed by hers. A particular triumph of his was the so-called bow and arrow dance, in which "he shot arrows from a huge bow behind his shoulder. The celerity, the grace, the rhythm of terpsichorean feats were indescribable in their effect" (van Vechten).

After the American tour Mordkin's reputation, reinforced by the triumph of his *Bacchanale* in London, began to grow. As a bacchant he was sensational indeed. According to Pavlova's conductor Walford Hyden, "It was the first time the London audience had ever seen anything of the kind, an authentic Bacchanale danced in a frenzy of abandon to the spirit of revelry and drunkenness." But apart from the *Bacchanale*, where Mordkin displayed the beauty of a Greek god, his own fiery temperament, and untrammeled freedom in movement, he created no significant choreography, although he composed several ballets during the next two decades.

After his rupture with Pavlova in 1911, he continued touring in America and London, but his solo performances were a pale shadow of their triumphant and tempestuous partnership. Mordkin's widow, Bronislava Pojizka, recalled in a 1976 interview with me: "They were incomparable in their artistic union, and they were aware of it, though they tried to convince themselves and others that it was not so. Their reasons were different: Pavlova was motivated by the vindictive feelings of a loving yet rejected woman. Mordkin was driven by his ambitious desire of not sharing his success with her." According to Kathleen Crofton, whom I interviewed in the spring of 1977, Pavlova often regretted her break with Mordkin. She frequently mentioned him to the men of her company as an example of real artistry.

After three years of wearisome touring, Mordkin returned to Moscow. At the urgent request of the director of the Imperial Theatres, Teliakovsky, he rejoined the Bolshoi company, where he really belonged. In October 1912 he once again performed Mato in *Salammbô* and then various roles in Gorsky's new ballets: the static part of the knight Sonnewald in *Schubertiana*, the Norwegian Fisherman in *Love Is Nimble*, the mime part of Petronius in *Eunice and Petronius*. Gorsky persisted in employing Mordkin as a dancing actor, and only "his enormous success made him put up with his lot," wrote Geltzer in her memoirs. He was most effective as the Fisherman, whose slightly uncouth and awkward dances contributed to the creation of a stern Northern character.

Apparently these roles encouraged Mordkin to seek new perspectives, while the appreciation of the public ignited his truly unlimited ambition. His collaboration with the Moscow Art Theatre in 1913 was not an aberration. After he mounted an interlude in Molière's *Le Malade imaginaire* for the theatre, he began to perceive the ballet stage as secondary in his artistic life. He became more involved in teaching Duncanesque free plasticity and rhythmic calisthenics and experimenting with the "different ways of plastic presentation of the body on stage." Had he happened upon Ted Shawn in those years, they would have understood each other perfectly.

His unlimited confidence and ambition helped him to uphold his aesthetic principles with admirable consistency. The success of his *Bow and Arrow* dance in America encouraged him to choreograph a few short pieces for himself, such as his famous solo *The Italian Beggar*, to Saint-Saëns. The beggar walked onto the stage in rags and tatters, giddy with hunger and desperate for alms. Rejected, he began a frantic dance of despair (including tours chaînés and even pirouettes) which ended with his death. Despite its obvious choreographic eclecticism and melodramatic flavor, the piece scored an enormous success, even in St. Petersburg, when Mordkin danced it at Sedova's farewell benefit performance in October 1916. His unprecedented expressiveness and colorful acting overwhelmed the St. Petersburg audience.

When Mordkin danced standard pas de deux in these years, the critics were amazed at the meaningful emphasis he put on each step, although they disparaged him for his lack of ease. But by 1916 Mordkin was no longer in his first youth and apparently had lost his interest in classical parts. His ties with the Bolshoi weakened. In 1918 he broke with the company, but four years later he returned to present several mixed-bill programs and his own versions of *Coppélia*, *La Fille mal gardée*, *Carnaval*, and *Les Sylphides*, which he had revised and shown in his own school in Georgia (1920–21) and then in Moscow (1923). Unfortunately, these productions were a potpourri of sloppily patched-up odds and ends from different versions; inevitably, they were unsuccessful.

Discouraged by his failure, Mordkin decided to capitalize on his American reputation. At the end of 1923 he moved to New York, to begin a new twenty-year period in his artistic career. He organized the Mikhail Mordkin Studio of Dance Arts and a small company, to implant the traditions of Russian ballet in a different soil. During the 1926–27 season, the Mordkin Ballet toured the States with Vera Nemtchinova and Pierre Vladimiroff; and out of this company, with the assistance of Mordkin's most devoted pupil, Lucia Chase, gradually emerged American Ballet Theatre. In the last twenty years of his life Mordkin achieved more as a choreographer and champion of classical dance in America than as a great dancer, although at the age of sixty he portrayed an old fisherman in his *The Goldfish*, Marcellina in *La Fille mal gardée*, and other roles—the dignified and brilliant sunset of an outstanding dancer and artist, who died in New York on July 15, 1944.

Paquita pas de trois, 1909

PIERRE VLADIMIROFF

PIERRE VLADIMIROFF made his debut at the Maryinsky in September 1911 in the *Swan Lake* pas de trois, as a replacement for the dismissed Vaslav Nijinsky. He immediately aroused a flurry of conflicting opinions in the Russian press; some critics regarded him as Nijinsky's legitimate successor, while others thought him only a weak copy. In 1912 he spent three months with the Diaghilev company and reaffirmed his identification with Nijinsky by replacing him in *Cléopâtre* during the troupe's London season. His amazingly sensual Slave made a stir; to Vladimiroff's credit, his portrayal was not just an imitation of his illustrious predecessor's. But in the perspective of the de-

velopment of Russian male dance the juxtaposition of their names seems farfetched and inaccurate. Representatives of entirely different generations, they were strikingly dissimilar in their approaches to classical dance, artistic projection, and style. Like Mikhail Mordkin, Vladimiroff was a prototype of a brand-new, ostentatiously virile and heroic trend.

Although the comparison of Vladimiroff to Nijinsky may seem dubious, the fact that Vladimiroff was amazingly gifted, a perfect example of the danseur noble, is indisputable. "Pierre Vladimiroff is distinguished by the manly beauty of a strong youth, endowed with sculpturesquely shaped muscles; his high jump is spectacular and powerful," noted the exacting André Levinson. Vladimiroff possessed an explosive temperament; his turns were swift and precise (his grande pirouette was proverbial among St. Petersburg balletomanes); his beats were likened to lightning and fireworks. As the Slave in *Le Corsaire*, he would cover the enormous Maryinsky stage with three powerful leaps.

Levinson wrote that the young Vladimiroff was "obsessed by the idea of a competition with Nijinsky, whose performances he never failed to watch." Vladimiroff indeed sought to rival Nijinsky, whose legend was enhanced by the news of his Parisian triumphs. Nijinsky's ghost, lurking behind Vladimiroff's back, was vindictive: the latter's characterizations were frequently criticized as grotesque distortions of Nijinsky's highly individual portrayals. In fact, Vladimiroff's effeminate, mincing Albrecht or his clownish Harlequin (in Fokine's *Carnaval*) had nothing in common with Nijinsky's work. This slightly comical combat with the absent Nijinsky was the only distressing blemish on Vladimiroff's splendid career, which progressed so swiftly that in 1914, only three years after his debut, Levinson pronounced him "the finest classical dancer in the world."

THE DANCER who won fame in the West as Pierre Vladimiroff was born Pyotr Nikolaevich Vladimirov on February 1, 1893, in St. Petersburg. He was enrolled in the Imperial Theatre School in 1902 and quickly acquired a reputation as a "rebel," an impudent, brawling hooligan. In 1906, during a student performance at the Maryinsky, Vladimiroff stuck his tongue out at the audience, infuriating Teliakovsky, the director of the Imperial Theatres. This waywardness and sedition marked his whole career at the Maryinsky. Boris Shavrov, a pupil of Vladimiroff who became a leading dancer in the 1920s, recalled in an interview with Vera Krasovskaya: "His temper was violent, a genuine Cossack from the river Kuban. At the school he once broke a glass door with his fist because he did not want to take a piano lesson. At the Maryinsky he threw a silver cigarette case into the face of the administrator Alexander Krupensky, saying: 'There are plenty of such bureaucrats as you; but such a dancer as I am may be unique.' Vladimiroff loathed Andrianov, considering his style obsolete, despite the fact that he was Gerdt's son-in-law and had noble manners. On the other hand, he worshiped Fokine."

Vladimiroff was instantly acknowledged by the critics:

in 1909, after his student appearance in the pas de trois from *Paquita*, he was praised by an anonymous critic as "a future classical artist of the noblest mold. No exaggeration; his lightness and elegance are beyond belief; his stride is large; his face is expressive." Matilda Kschessinskaya chose the promising pupil of Fokine and Obukhov as a partner (as she had previously selected Nijinsky), unaware of how difficult he would be to control.

Like Mordkin, from the outset Vladimiroff renounced the canonized mannerisms of the Russian danseurs nobles from Pavel Gerdt to Andrianov. His Prince Siegfried in *Swan Lake* (1913) captivated viewers with flights that the critics praised as "powerful and high," but annoyed them by an outrageously iconoclastic portrayal. He seemed to gibe openly at the old conventional pantomime, breaking its patterns with the gestures of a cocky urchin, ridiculing Siegfried's noble manners. In her essay on Vladimiroff, Krasovskaya quotes Boris Shavrov's account of three St. Petersburg Siegfrieds: "In the Act II coda Nicolas Legat executed an assemblé when accentuating the posé en croisé following each of his jumps. Adrianov performed a series of sissonnes fondues. Vladimiroff introduced several grands jetés in a row, causing a great scandal: 'How could the Prince bounce around as if he were a peasant?' Such was the reaction to Vladimiroff's innovation."

The point was that Vladimiroff was not concerned with the character of a traditional Romantic prince. On the contrary, he was attempting to convey a sense of Siegfried's heroic, willful nature through a series of dynamic movements and steps. When a classical role resisted his recarving, he simply ignored it. According to Shavrov, "Vladimiroff introduced a few innovations into strictly academic parts, some of which extended beyond the art of dance to the realm of sheer circus. For instance, he invented a new support for the Slave in *Le Corsaire*: lifting Medora (Smirnova) up to his chest, he took her bodice in his teeth and spread his arms. Some of his new lifts increased the impact of a portrayal and became an essential ingredient. For instance, he introduced the ballerina's jeté entrelacé at the beginning of *Giselle* Act II as a substitute for her being carried from one place to another by her partner: lifted upward by Vladimiroff, she seemed to be poised in the air."

Vladimiroff's development, in fact, suffered from the choreographic paucity of the Petipa-Fokine repertory, in which the ballerina reigned supreme and his potential could be only partially realized. During his early years at the Maryinsky Vladimiroff danced one of the four cavaliers in

Above: *Les Sylphides*, with Anna Pavlova, 1926
Right: *Paquita* pas de trois, with Elizaveta Gerdt and Elsa Vil, 1909

Left: (top) unidentified role; (bottom) Siegfried, with Tamara
Karsavina as Odile, 1913
Above: Harlequin in *Carnaval*, early 1910s

Raymonda (1911); the pas de trois from *Paquita* (1912), in which, said Volynsky, he demonstrated "fiery beats" and light jumps all over the stage; both the Merchant and the Slave in *Le Corsaire* (1914); and Albrecht to Tamara Karsavina's Giselle (1914). In this partnership, observed Levinson in his review, "with his eaglet flights Vladimiroff entirely overshadowed the ballerina, who lacked any natural elevation."

From the reviews of the 1910s it is hard to say how original Vladimiroff's portrayals were or to what extent they reflected his artistic approach. Most likely, he concentrated more in these years on dance per se, striving to shine as brightly as his ballerinas or even to eclipse them. At times his characterizations attempted to combine incompatible traits: his Albrecht, for example, whose effeminate manner seemed to preclude the heroic stance that he took in the Act II variation. But he was absolutely unique as the Merchant and the Slave in *Le Corsaire*: according to Levinson, "Vladimiroff and Egorova overwhelmed the audience with the bravura of their Pas d'Esclave. . . . With his swift jumps Vladimiroff skimmed over the stage on the diagonal and, while running, lifted his partner high over his head. . . . The impetus attained its climax when, repeating the same diagonal, the dancer landed with all his might with his legs bent and crossed, the torso upright, instead of a traditional landing on one leg. Vladimiroff was also an unusual partner in the adagio from the Act II pas de six, in which his flowing, feminine arabesques paralleled Preobrajenskaya's."

Vladimiroff was well aware of his unique talent and daring, and the directorate of the Maryinsky was afraid he might defect to Diaghilev. Vladimiroff took advantage of the situation: he started in 1911, as a member of the corps, with a salary of 600 rubles a month; by 1913 he commanded 3000 rubles a month; in 1917 he received 500 rubles for each performance. Spoiled by the directorate, he behaved boldly and insisted on arranging his own schedule. In 1914, after dancing the *Paquita* pas de trois with Agrippina Vaganova and Elsa Vil, he refused to give an encore, despite the persistent demands of the audience. His partners repeated the piece without their cavalier, who stood in the wings and laughed!

Vladimiroff's flamboyant stunts were both physically daring and defiant of tradition, and they aroused conflicting opinions. For instance, Volynsky complained about Vladimiroff's reluctance to portray the ideal cavalier Petipa had intended, virile yet conventional. But it was the very con-

ventionality of the characters that annoyed Vladimiroff. His tempestuous, restless nature compelled him to revamp the elements of male dance as formed by Petipa as an appendage of the ballerina's art. Krasovskaya analyzed Vladimiroff's changes as "the encroachment of Fokine's style on academic patterns. Stylized details began to sneak into the canonized movements: the Oriental cross-legged posture, the free plastique of the arms, folded on the chest or pressed against the shoulders in the Oriental way. At the same time, the heroic emphasis was manifested in the way the tempos speeded up, the leaps became swifter, and the turns more dynamic."

However irrelevant or iconoclastic Vladimiroff's efforts might have seemed in the 1910s, in many roles his new energy and verve were overwhelming and convincing. Thus, one of his undisputed masterpieces was the god Vayou in Petipa's *Talisman*, a role he inherited from Nijinsky as revised by Nicolas Legat in 1909. As Vayou he exploded Petipa's petrified academic patterns with movements borrowed from acrobatics and calisthenics. And Solor, hitherto no more than a supporting cavalier, was transformed by Vladimiroff into an exotic Indian hunter afflicted by passion and remorse, and prone to emotional outbursts. In his memoirs Nikolai Soliannikov, recalling Karsavina and Vladimiroff in the Kingdom of the Shades scene, described the special electrifying dynamism that lent tragic grandeur to their duet.

But when Vladimiroff imposed his style on Fokine's creations, the effect was often sheer nonsense. In *Carnaval*, instead of depicting the stylized Harlequin of Fokine's intention, Vladimiroff presented a mask of the Italian commedia dell' arte. Levinson observed that "his exaggerated briskness and inappropriate high jumps were at odds with Fokine's picturesque vignette." Nevertheless, the cascade of intricate jumps in the episode called "The Lark Catching," and the swirl of his pirouettes, thrilled the audience with their sheer kinetic power. Performing the Nijinsky roles in other Fokine ballets (*Les Sylphides*, *Cléopâtre*, *Le Pavillon d'Armide*), Vladimiroff only exacerbated the incongruities, arousing mixed feelings in the audience. On the one hand his swift, spectacular tours en l'air, the perfection of his pirouettes and cabrioles, and the way "his subtle body," in Volynsky's words, "shifted from the pas fouetté to the sculpturesque sustained arabesque" were irresistible in their athletic force. On the other, the same sportive approach, the cold glitter of his gymnastic skill, the exhibition of technique for its own sake, were regarded as disruptive of

Fokine's style and detrimental to its impact. Vladimiroff was frequently criticized for his inability to uncover poetic values in Fokine's refined vignettes, transforming them instead into inexpressive tours de force. Nijinsky's sensuality had vibrated through Fokine's creations, extending their significance; but Vladimiroff, heroic and impetuous, flattened them and made them one-dimensional.

Volynsky excoriated Vladimiroff's performance in *Le Spectre de la rose* as "uninspired athletic exhibitionism"; but other critics and choreographers (Levinson, Lopukhov) did not agree that his athletic style should be equated with a lack of inspiration. They enthusiastically described the momentum of Vladimiroff's "inspired flights" in Fokine's *Eros*, where with one huge jump he crossed the stage to land on his knee near the girl asleep on a sofa. "The seething whirl of derisive pirouettes accompanied by the finger-snapping," as Levinson wrote, of his Harlequin were indeed prompted by his inspiration and emotional involvement in the performance. Contrary to Volynsky, Vladimiroff did not so much distort the meanings of Fokine's stylized characters as shift them into a different sphere. For example, the choreographer's image of Eros as a slightly effeminate, Praxitelean ephebus, with half-bent knees and hands rounded over the head, did not correspond to Vladimiroff's tempestuous personality.

By nature straightforward and strong, Vladimiroff was never really at home in Fokine's whimsical garden, but he did pave the way for the experiments of Yermolayev and Chabukiani in the 1920s and 1930s. Had he not left Russia when he did, he certainly would have spread his wings in the choreography of Goleizovsky and the young Balanchine or perhaps have been the first among the pioneers of the new style of male dancing. But the timing was not favorable. In the autumn of 1919 Vladimiroff left Russia with Felia Doubrovska, whom he married in 1920. His temporary union with Diaghilev's company did not enhance his career. In November 1921, in London, he danced a role he had rejected at the Maryinsky, Prince Florimund in *The Sleeping Beauty*, and introduced the famous fish dive that so infuriated his Aurora, Olga Spessivtseva. In 1922 he left Diaghilev and toured extensively in Europe with Doubrovska. He appeared with Karsavina in New York's Carnegie Hall in 1924 and was described by one critic as "a flamboyant and confident partner." He returned to Diaghilev in 1925 as a replacement for Anton Dolin and then performed with Adolph Bolm's company. In 1927 he became Pavlova's partner and danced with her for four years, until her death in 1931. The repertory was a mixed bag—Clustine's *Dionysus*, Sergei and Nicolas Legat's *The Fairy Doll*, Fokine's *Les Sylphides*. But one of his greatest roles with Pavlova was Albrecht. Pavlova favored him and, as Doubrovska remembered, often compared his appealing virility and partnering skill with Mikhail Mordkin's.

In January 1934 Vladimiroff joined the faculty of Balanchine's new School of American Ballet. "It was just by chance that this distinguished dancer became available to the school," writes Balanchine's biographer Bernard Taper. "At the time the school was being formed, he happened to be in New York, as a member of a small troupe which Lifar had brought to America, and became dissatisfied with it. Balanchine had always admired Vladimiroff greatly and thought it very lucky that the school had been able to obtain his services. . . . For the inexperienced American students who would be joining the school henceforth, merely to see the way Vladimiroff comported himself was an essential lesson in the fundamental tradition of classical dance." In October 1967 Vladimiroff retired after thirty-three years of teaching, having produced a number of talented dancers, including Edward Villella. It was Vladimiroff who inculcated in the young Villella the ostentatiously virile manner of presentation that became a hallmark of his energetic and inspired style.

Three years after his retirement, Pierre Vladimiroff died in New York on November 26, 1970.

Solor in *La Bayadère* (Gorsky), mid-1930s

ALEXEI YERMOLAYEV

IN RUSSIA the name of Alexei Yermolayev is synonymous with male virtuosity in ballet, thanks to the accounts of contemporaries who saw him execute unprecedented technical feats. He was indeed a new Cecchetti of the 1920s and 1930s, a Soviet Vestris, who had a considerable influence on the flamboyant style of such dancers as Vladimir Vasiliev and Alexander Godunov.

According to Soviet ballet historians, Yermolayev's theatrical instincts happily matched his great virtuosity; but his performances preserved on film (for instance, his Tybalt in *Romeo and Juliet*) somehow contradict this statement. Unlike Chabukiani, Ulanova, and Semyonova, Yermolayev was a proponent of histrionic exaggeration. Nevertheless,

his virtuosity is undeniable; the artistry of all male dancers from the 1940s to the 1960s was measured against it.

ALEXEI NIKOLAEVICH YERMOLAYEV was born in St. Petersburg on February 23, 1910. From his early childhood he evinced a rare musical talent and dreamed of a professional career as a pianist. In 1926 Alexander Glazunov accepted him as a pupil in the Leningrad Conservatory; but Yermolayev's penchant for ballet, which he had also been studying for several years, prevailed over his predilection for the piano.

In the early 1920s Yermolayev had studied for six months

at Akim Volynsky's private ballet school. Disappointed by the female supremacy there, he auditioned for the Leningrad Choreographic School. Fyodor Lopukhov, who presided over the entrance committee, enrolled him immediately in the second class, although Yermolayev's physical qualifications did not meet the standard of the erstwhile Imperial stage. He resembled Pierre Vladimiroff: an athlete of medium stature, with overdeveloped torso and arms and strong legs, endowed with rare ballon, swift turns, and natural coordination. During his school years he succeeded in increasing his potential as no one else among his colleagues.

As a student, Yermolayev was a pure product of the modernistic trend of Soviet ballet in the twenties, with its infusion of acrobatics and athleticism into academic dance. To a certain degree he viewed classical ballet as a kind of sport; his motto was "Jump and turn as high and as fast as possible." From his teachers he took the best: Christianson conditioned his back to execute twenty consecutive pirouettes on the spot; Victor Semyonov taught him to soar up softly and land soundlessly; Vladimir Ponomarev reinforced the coordination of his torso, legs, and arms. In his last year at the school Yermolayev attended Lopukhov's class of acrobatics and artistic calisthenics. His ardent champion Yuri Slonimsky wrote that "Yermolayev, photographed in flight, could easily be taken not for a dancer but for a record holder in the high jump."

For five years he labored at the school as no student ever had before. His later career was distinguished by many virtuoso feats amazing even by the standards of our own day—triple sauts de basque, triple pirouettes, jetés en tournant at breakneck speed, triple cabrioles, fourteen consecutive traveling soubresauts.

Yermolayev was not secretive about the sources of his stunning technique. He considered regular exercises at the barre the most efficient way to achieve virtuosity. "At the barre," he said in interviews, "one can condition the whole body by developing the muscles, their elasticity, the flexibility of the torso, turnout and extension." To increase the muscular strength of his legs and develop a powerful, swift leap combining high flight and a silent landing, he took class wearing cloth belts filled with small shot tied around his waist and ankles. He would increase the weights as he tried to produce higher jumps—and of course during performance the leaps were easier for him.

At his graduation performance Ponomarev had the sixteen-year-old Yermolayev dance Vayou, god of the winds, in Petipa's *The Talisman*, which previously had been resurrected for Nijinsky and for Vladimiroff. "The prologue took place in heaven," Slonimsky wrote. "Spirits of heaven wove the traditional lace of the classical waltz, then froze in attitudes of respect and submission as sonorous drums and trumpets announced the appearance of a hurricane—the god Vayou. Clad in whimsical Oriental attire, Yermolayev swept through the air over the bent heads of the corps, leaping into the wings and reappearing a split second later with another high leap. His jumps and turns, reverberating in the musical leitmotifs of the orchestra, enveloped the stage with the sultry breath of a tornado."

To achieve this spectacular effect Yermolayev, guided by Ponomarev, devised a new way of executing the grand jeté on which Petipa's choreography was based. In order to imbue the step with the utmost expressive value, he would thrust his working leg not forward but upward, pulling his entire body up to it. Once aloft, he seemed to push off again, using the air itself as a springboard. This produced an inimitable illusion of uninterrupted flight over the stage, as Yermolayev soared upward, rending the air with his chest, with both legs fully stretched, his right arm uplifted, and his back arched. The circuit of grands jetés was immediately followed by a cascade of pirouettes, complemented by a special movement he invented himself. It derived from the traditional pas de ciseaux—the leap in which a dancer opens and closes his legs, imitating scissors. Into this intricate step Yermolayev introduced a beat.

Yuri Slonimsky wrote that "the young dancer, like a hurricane, swept aside the old canons and stereotypes." The opinion of the audience was split: Yermolayev's champions saluted the wonder of his highly concentrated energy; but his adversaries thought his dancing "a barbarian vehicle" that turned the noble art of classical ballet into a set of circus tricks. Both sides were right. Like any pioneer, Yermolayev was somewhat obsessed; he desired to revamp the fundamentals of male dancing, but he never knew where to stop. (Maya Plisetskaya called this quality "a little folly.") Revising old roles, he often overembroidered the choreography, to the detriment of music and style. But when music, style, and Yermolayev's own virtuosity were in balance, real wonders occurred, as in his Blue Bird. Lopukhov charged the seventeen-year-old prodigy with this complex role, a gamble that paid off. In the first part of the variation— sissonne, failli, and assemblé repeated six times up and down on the diagonal—Yermolayev startled even Maryinsky veterans Nikolai Soliannikov, Joseph Kschessinsky, and Ekaterina Vazem as he transformed sissonne alternating with assemblé into a brand-new step, sissonne soubresaut,

Above: Li Shan-fu in *The Red Poppy*, 1949
Left: (top) Vayou in *Le Talisman*, 1926; (bottom) the Cavaliere
Ripafrata in *Mirandolina*, 1949

Left: (top) Tybalt in *Romeo and Juliet*, early 1950s;
(bottom) Basil in *Don Quixote*, mid-1930s
Below: Abdul-Rakhman in *Raymonda*, 1945

Above: Yevgeny in *The Bronze Horseman*, late 1940s
Right: Philippe in *The Flames of Paris*, 1933

soaring above the stage with his legs pressed together so long that it seemed inevitable that he would fall. According to them, even Nijinsky had never produced such a virtuoso stunt.

In the third part of the variation Yermolayev performed seven high entrechats six with widely open beats, then a double tour en l'air, landing in arabesque allongée. The soaring entrechats and the open beats produced an impression of sustained ballon in the air. In the coda he executed the twenty-four brisés front and back, alternating with pirouettes, at such breakneck speed that they poured forth in an incredible sparkling torrent of movement.

As Vayou and the Blue Bird, Yermolayev outstripped Nijinsky's legendary ballon technique, and all the roles of the classical repertory seemed to be within his range. However, when in 1927 he undertook Siegfried in *Swan Lake*, his revolutionary approach resulted in a fiasco. By nature Yermolayev, with his athletic legs and torso and his coarsely virile warrior's features, was a far cry from a danseur noble. Nevertheless, he attempted to depict Siegfried as a Romantic poet, appearing in felt slippers, with a book in his hands, on his face the brooding yet mischievous look of a hybrid of Mercutio and Hamlet. He adorned Siegfried's one variation with triple tours en l'air that were at odds with Tchaikovsky's music. As a technical feat his triple tours were unparalleled in the history of ballet. (To achieve them, Yermolayev miraculously managed to push off not only through his arms and legs but through his torso, shoulders, and neck.) But artistically it was to no avail. Yermolayev himself recalled in an interview: "I was spinning out these powerful, physically exhausting tours to the accompaniment of the most lyrical and languid violin solo." Into the jubilant coda of Act III he introduced big cabrioles en avant and en arrière. His ballet shoes, rubbed with chalk and powder, raised clouds around the stage, as if Prince Siegfried were beating the dust out of his slippers.

Yermolayev freely admitted that Siegfried was "beyond" him. But what roles were his own domain? He sorely needed a choreographer to create for him the heroic or demi-caractère roles of which he dreamed—Spartacus, Icarus, Robin Hood, Tÿl Eulenspiegel—but these were unacceptable to the socialist realism of the 1930s. Yermolayev was fated to do no more than repeat his astounding tricks or embroider with new technical feats the canvas of the old classics. Thus, his Blue Bird was followed by the Winter Bird in Lopukhov's acrobatic *The Ice Maiden*, in which Yermolayev demonstrated his new grand jeté: thrusting his leg forward, he managed in a split second to bend it at an acute

angle and thrust it out again, creating an illusion of untrammeled flight. In this ballet he combined single tours en l'air, landing in fifth position in a deep plié with a cascade of double pirouettes, and introduced the sustained soubresaut, in which he kept his torso curved and his legs parallel to the stage, thrust upward to the level of his shoulders.

Even such minor roles as the Spirit of the Ocean in *The Little Humpbacked Horse* (1926), the Acrobat and the Little God in *The Red Poppy* (1927), and Djamil in *The Limpid Stream* (1927) spurred his imagination, allowing him to deploy his technical exuberance. He never shunned them; they became his experimental laboratory. As the Spirit of the Ocean he depicted his mastery of the elements of wind and water through the combination of big and small pirouettes en tire-bouchon with tours en l'air. In the *Corsaire* Pas d'Esclave he imparted his special quality to jetés en tournant, circling the stage: by reducing the time for taking off and landing he increased the duration of the flight en attitude, with his right arm outstretched to the side and his left above his head.

Yermolayev succeeded in achieving one feat hitherto deemed impossible: he devised the technique of triple cabriole. He was annoyed by the fact that in executing double cabriole his second beat always seemed either slack or very convulsive. His experiments taught him that to enable the feet to beat against each other satisfactorily, one must employ not only the ankles, arched insteps, and totally stretched legs but the hipbones and the pelvic muscles as well. By throwing himself back at a sixty-degree angle, he soared up and stretched his whole body in the air, thereby acquiring the time for his legs to execute three perfect beats.

In 1927 Yermolayev undertook two major classical roles, Basil and Albrecht, which he was to continue dancing for almost twenty-five years. In terms of technique and histrionics his approach to these roles was quite daring for the Russia of the 1920s and 1930s. As an advocate of realistic theatre, he attempted to deepen the psychological projection of these conventional characters by playing Basil as a Figaro type and Albrecht as a Don Juan. Moreover, the Marxist ideas of this period influenced his portrayal of Albrecht as a blasé aristocrat, by implication a scoundrel, though a repentant one at the final curtain. Decades later Yermolayev's black-and-white approach would be totally rejected by Vasiliev, Dolgushin, and Baryshnikov, who tried to vitalize these roles while eschewing social motivations. On the other hand, they all absorbed the technical developments by means of which Yermolayev embellished Basil and Albrecht, transforming the duets with Kitri and Giselle into a form of balletic competition that challenged the traditional supremacy of the ballerina.

In 1930 Yermolayev followed the example of Semyonova and joined the Bolshoi, where from the beginning his name was a byword. In light of the miserable level of male dancing in Moscow, Yermolayev's technique was overwhelming indeed; at that time no one at the Bolshoi could even approximate his miraculous feats. But, as in Semyonova's case, the Bolshoi repertory thwarted his expectations: in Leningrad newfangled drama-ballets had only begun to take root, but in Moscow they were blossoming, nourished by the encouragement of the Kremlin.

In truth, drama-ballets were more congenial to Yermolayev's theatrical instincts than to Semyonova's, but his exuberance was constantly jeopardized by the meager opportunities provided by the Bolshoi repertory. Apart from Siegfried and the Blue Bird, in which Yermolayev made his Moscow debuts in 1931, the Bolshoi could offer him only pedestrian parts in the literal meaning of this word. From 1931 to 1936 Yermolayev danced in only four Bolshoi premieres: Chekrygin's *The Comedians* (1931), Vainonen's *The Flames of Paris* (1933), Moiseyev's *The Three Fat Men*, (1935), and Lopukov's *The Limpid Stream* (1935). He continued his experiments, working on the choreography to the point of total transformation, inventing his own solos and stunts like his fourteen consecutive soubresauts with an axe in his hand in *The Flames of Paris*. But the discrepancy between his dazzling technical maturity and the dramatic shallowness of his farfetched heroes was only underscored by these efforts.

Yermolayev was aware of this, and his despondency grew. Still, he never ceased to experiment, taking a childlike delight in his technical prowess. Elizaveta Gerdt in one of her interviews with me remarked that Yermolayev's situation at the Bolshoi resembled that of a virtuoso pianist forced to play only Tchaikovsky's *The Seasons* or Czerny's Etudes for beginners. Yermolayev's unlimited curiosity and enthusiasm resulted in a serious knee injury in 1937, from which he could never completely recover. After a two-year hiatus he was still unable to regain his former level of technique. The Bolshoi repertory had nothing new for him to dance, and the production of *Spartacus* conceived by Nikolai Volkov and Boris Asafiev specially for him remained unrealized.

And so Yermolayev decided to choreograph for himself. Like Chabukiani's, his choreography seemed to be an extension of technique that no one but he himself could possess or reproduce. Because of the competitive atmosphere at the Bolshoi and the rising star of Leonid Lavrovsky as the great Kremlin-approved Soviet choreographer, Yermolayev was unable to show his creations in Moscow. In 1940, in Byelorussia, he and Fyodor Lopukhov began to mount a ballet called *The Nightingale* (to music of Kroshner) with a plot based on local folklore. In his memoirs Yuri Slonimsky described the choreography as a happy marriage of classical combinations, Lopukhov's acrobatics, and folk dance. But in 1941 the war broke out; the sets and score burned in Minsk, and by 1945 no one, not even Yermolayev himself, could restore the production. Other projects of the 1940s, such as *Golden Rye* and *Toward the Sun*, designed in the monumental style of Eisenstein's *Die Walküre* at the Bolshoi, also came to nought.

After 1946 Yermolayev, as Ulanova's partner, added to his repertory Jean de Brienne and Abdul-Rakhman in *Raymonda*, Tybalt in *Romeo and Juliet*, Yevgeny in *The Bronze Horseman*, the Cavaliere di Ripafrata in *Mirandolina*, and Severyan in *The Stone Flower*. In these roles he displayed his "significant theatricality" rather than his dance artistry. Having said that he was a typical product of the Stanislavsky method, lavishly orchestrating his roles with exaggerated histrionics, one has nothing to add. Today the performances preserved on film simply look grotesque.

In the early 1950s he began to choreograph again. In January 1952, he showed Moscow eight miniatures. Many of them smacked of socialist realism seasoned with political satire, but their artistic value was minimal indeed. His attempts to revitalize old mime roles such as Guirey in *The Fountain of Bakhchisarai* were not particularly successful.

In 1960 Yermolayev became a coach at the Bolshoi. His efforts in this endeavor are hard to overestimate. It was his pedagogical talent that transformed the gifted newcomer Vladimir Vasiliev into a great artist; he fostered Mikhail Lavrovsky, Maris Liepa, Alexander Godunov—all of them bear the Yermolayev stamp. According to Godunov, whom I interviewed about his great teacher, "Yermolayev shared with incredible generosity his enormous balletic knowledge and his personal secrets, regarding all of us as his spiritual sons. He coached us as a choreographer, at times changing designs and patterns that were not his. This resulted in his conflict with the chief choreographer, Yuri Grigorovich."

During his last years Yermolayev became persona non grata at the Bolshoi, employed as little as possible. He felt frustrated and drowned his grief in vodka, despite a serious heart condition. On December 12, 1975, he died of a massive heart attack.

The Slave in the *Corsaire* pas de deux, early 1930s

VAKHTANG CHABUKIANI

VAKHTANG MIKHAILOVICH CHABUKIANI made his Leningrad debut in 1929, three years after Yermolayev, as if receiving from his hand the revolutionary baton of male dancing. He was born on March 12, 1910, in Gruzia, Georgia, on the outskirts of Tbilisi. "Our house stood high on Consideration Mountain," he recalled in his autobiography, *All My Dreams Came True* (1950). "Below gurgled the little Vera River, a tributary of the Kura. I learned to swim in the Vera when I was young. A skinny, frail lad, I loved headlong movement and dizzying dives. . . . My father, a worker, had a difficult time feeding his family. We were starving, and he got a job for me when I was nine, in a workshop, weaving baskets and making toys."

Chabukiani's interest in classical ballet came from out of the blue. In provincial Georgia there existed only an impoverished local opera company (whose creator was Meliton Balanchivadze, the father of George Balanchine). But folklore dance—dancing at weddings and on holidays—flourished, the Georgians being as innately musical and inclined to dancing as the Russians. It happened that the ten-year-old Vakhtang delivered a basket of Christmas decorations that he had made to Maria Perrini, proprietress of Tbilisi's only children's dance studio. "Love for the dance was born in me from my first sight of ballet," Chabukiani recollected in his autobiography. This gradually evolved into a passion that can be compared only to Rudolf Nureyev's.

At Perini's studio, where special emphasis was placed on muscular development, jump technique, and the positioning of the back on which the pirouette depends, Chabukiani studied for more than a year. Then he worked as an extra in the Opera Theatre. The appearance in Tbilisi of Elena Lukom and Boris Shavrov, dancers from Leningrad, opened Chabukiani's eyes to the world of classical ballet. In the fall of 1926 he went to Leningrad to take the entrance examinations for the Choreographic School on Rossi Street.

"Leningrad greeted me with autumn rain," Chabukiani wrote. "I flopped around in my breeches, my coat had been sold, I was terribly cold. . . . They did not take me at the school, where only children under the age of ten were admitted. I had to enroll in evening courses at the school.* It was hard living and studying like that. . . . I went to school at night and worked in the movies during the day, preparing my lessons during breaks. Two years later I was accepted in the regular day division, from which I graduated after passing the examinations for the ten-year middle school."

The Choreographic School (subsequently renamed in honor of Agrippina Vaganova) was at that time the true center of the balletic culture that survived the tsarist era. Even after the postwar exodus of the greatest masters, many peers and students of Petipa—including Vaganova, Alexander Shiriayev, Alexander Monakhov, Vladimir Ponomarev, and Nikolai Soliannikov—remained to carry on the academic tradition. Once ensconced at the school, Chabukiani eagerly set about building up his technique. Mikhail Mikhailov would later recall in his memoirs:

There were some five young enthusiasts, with Chabukiani at their head, who passionately drove themselves almost to the point of exhaustion in perfecting their classical technique, attempting to take virtuosity to incredible lengths. They charged about in all directions, flashing like tops, executing swift chaînés. Without moving a step from the indicated point, the men performed various combinations of the grande pirouette, while the women did fouettés. They sought means of staying longer in the air, sustaining some selected pose or contrived turn. What they devised was later put on stage in daring dances, jewellike in refinement and beauty of perfect form.

*These were instituted in 1923 for talented adolescents of fifteen or sixteen. Feya Balabina and Konstantin Sergeyev were others who started in these courses.

After three years at the school Chabukiani was considered a marvelous dancer, both physically and technically. He was a bit over medium height, with an amazingly well-formed body, elongated and refined. His head was relatively small, his neck thick and powerful. Narrow in the waist and thighs, with thin wrists and ankles and strikingly curved feet, Chabukiani looked like some eternally young deity of the ancient Olympian pantheon. His body was equally expressive on the ground and in the air. His long legs with their moderately developed musculature did not provide him with a large jump, which caused him to be perceived at first as a terre-à-terre dancer with turns that were nothing short of fabulous. Thanks, however, to his good extension and the lightness of his legs in any battement, he gradually learned to extend each leap. Mikhailov recalled:

In performing various jumps Chabukiani had his own secret, being able not only to take off lightly and easily but to hover for a moment in the air. He was particularly effective in movements that began with the throwing up of one leg, such as jeté en avant, jeté entrelacé, saut de basque, and cabriole, especially in arabesque. Here, he would take a very short, springy attack and throw his leg high with the utmost ease, then lift himself into the air to the height of the upper leg and hang suspended in a dynamic pose expressing the proud triumph and joy of flight. In his manège of jetés in the last act of *The Flames of Paris* a resolute sweeping motion of his arm completed each leap. His radically upturned head complemented the strong arching of his back in his jetés and cabrioles. In Solor's whirlwind variation in *La Bayadère*, the devices of takeoff and suspension in the air gave his leaps a forceful sense of flight and great lightness. His jumps from fifth position (entrechat six, soubresaut, sissonne) were less successful; but his fiery rhythm, his drive, the suppleness of his body, and the plasticity of his arms in transitional movements were so expressive that the flaws went almost unnoticed. One part of the variation followed another without visible links—everything was executed in one breath. Even a simple run was so dancelike that it was perceived as one of the combinations in the variation, of a piece with the regular movements. Smoothly springing on slightly bent knees, Chabukiani would throw wide first one leg, then the other, as fluid as a leopard. . . . He would evoke the whirlpools in the sharp bends of a wildly coursing river.

The timing of their careers was an advantage to Yermolayev and Semyonova, but to a great degree the misfortune of Chabukiani, whose artistic potential could be only partially realized in Petipa's ballerina-oriented classical legacy, and the so-called modern repertoire of the 1920s and 1930s. At the beginning of the thirties the daring experiments of Goleizovsky and Lopukhov had been pronounced "bourgeois, decadent tendencies" that had no place in the paradise programmed for the Soviet middle class. Chabukiani suffered from these constraints possibly more than others did, for his balance of technical virtuosity, physical beauty, and artistic projection was exceptional. One must lament the cultural circumstances that hindered his growth, although in this he was not alone. His artistic development, like that of so many Russian male dancers of the period, depended on an effort to modernize Petipa's compositions by rendering them more complex. The original works were referred to with deference, but in the end they were so overlaid with virtuosity that little remained of their creator's intention.

By the time of his graduation in 1929 Chabukiani was perceived as a miraculous phenomenon, a late manifestation of the grandeur of the Imperial ballet. His first-rate technique seemed to require no further development, but his stormy, energetic Georgian temperament ripped apart the framework of the classics' male roles. And so Chabukiani immediately began to compose ballets for himself.

His first attempts were almost grotesque: an eighteen-year-old dancer in a red tunic and wig, carrying a flaming torch, spinning out his fabulous pirouettes on bare feet in his *Dance of Fire*, to music from Rubinstein's opera *Feramors*. In another of his compositions, *The Casting Off of Slavery*, he was a rebellious slave, shedding his stage-prop fetters amid his fellow sufferers, who writhed under "the lash of capitalism" and formed with their backs a living bridge across which ran a ballerina representing "the power of gold." But he made up for these insipid creations with the superb artistry he demonstrated in the mime role of Phoebus in the Perrot-Petipa *Esmeralda* and in his portrayal of an impetuous Bacchant in Petipa's *The Seasons*.

Chabukiani became a star overnight. His first roles tested his potential: the *Swan Lake* pas de trois, the Blue Bird, a cavalier in the Hungarian pas d'action of *Raymonda*, and the Slave in the *Corsaire* pas de deux. The way he portrayed the diffident Slave who dances to amuse an imprisoned lady was quite characteristic of the times and of his approach to classical roles. He supplied the Slave with a social message, deriving him visually from Michelangelo's *Slave*, whose torso is frozen in superhuman efforts to burst his chains. When he performed this number on concert stages, Chabukiani went to such nonsensical lengths as to bind his body with cords from which he attempted to break free. The powerful though terribly farfetched social emphasis led him to a reconsideration of the petrified choreographic canon. Chabukiani was the first to introduce into the variation a traditional character step, the rivoltade (a jump over one's own leg), which he combined with jetés and pirouettes in the final manège of the coda. Male dancers who came after him either did his version or made it even more complex.

The role of the Slave showed that active heroes were Chabukiani's real artistic element. It is not surprising that he remained unresponsive to the dreamy, sluggish Prince Siegfried of the old Petipa-Ivanov *Swan Lake*. In the words of Chabukiani's biographer Vera Krasovskaya:

> Chabukiani's Prince pretended to be melancholy and dreamy in Act I. But when Odette appeared and the famous white adagio began, Chabukiani immediately broke through the imposed limitations of the role. In his very manner of supporting his partner there was a sense of strong will that was in contrast to the elegiac character he had established. In the powerful movement of his arms, as if parting the air around the ballerina, in his decisiveness, even in a certain abruptness with which he stopped her spin after a pirouette, an active quality little suited to the earlier profile of the Prince was apparent. This was especially so in the Prince's variation in the bravura Act III duet. The young dancer seemed disinclined or unable to conceal the fact that his dancing was by nature dynamic and masculine. But for just this reason the Prince's despair became incomprehensible as he set out in search of Odette—naturally this was the aspect of the role that was least successfully handled by Chabukiani. He used time-honored pantomime devices to convey the Prince's confusion: wringing his hands, clasping his heart, grasping his head, rolling his eyes. . . .

Following his debut as Siegfried in March 1930, Chabukiani danced Basil in November of that year and Albrecht in June 1932. These were the two roles in which his

Above: Basil in *Don Quixote*, late 1940s
Left: Basil, with Natalia Dudinskaya as Kitri, late 1940s

OPPOSITE
Top: (left) Solor in *La Bayadère*, 1941; (right) *Diana and Acteon* pas de deux, with Galina Ulanova, 1935
Bottom: Albrecht, with Vera Zignadze as Giselle, mid-1940s

artistic profile was clearly established; all subsequent parts were to a greater or lesser degree variations on his Basil and Albrecht.

In Gorsky's restaging of *Don Quixote* Chabukiani felt relatively unfettered. Discarding Petipa's mimetic approach, Gorsky had composed a refined combination of the kind of classical character dances that had been elaborated by Mikhail Mordkin.

In the 1920s, when Lenin's notion of the people as "the moving force of history" was in vogue, the *españolada* of *Don Quixote*, with its folk heroes and its mob—"the simple people of Spain," as the Soviet press put it—was greeted warmly. By the beginning of the 1930s every major danseur had developed his own version of Basil as the popular hero. Asaf Messerer was a simpleton; Yermolayev, a quick, cunning *pícaro*; Sergeyev, a simple romantic. Chabukiani was, in the words of an anonymous critic, "a potential revolutionary." The concept of the hero as a man of the people became Chabukiani's standard. He actively inspired the corps de ballet, which was armed with Spanish props—cloaks, fans, drums. With Chabukiani "the corps de ballet lost its imperturbability," writes Krasovskaya. "It became a many-headed, animated mob that responded in a lively fashion to the actions of the hero. The tireless, ever-inventive Basil became the center of the mob, whether dancing with castanets in the first act or in the grandes pirouettes of the finale." Chabukiani's dancing, classical and character, seemed to be born of the agitation of the street crowd, of its emotions, of the play of its mood. Following Yermolayev, Chabukiani made both types of dance equal, reinforcing them with mime and, more important, with a springy, aggressive pace—perhaps the most taxing thing in ballet, as difficult as running.

Chabukiani's final duet, which became a model for Bregvadze, Vasiliev, and Baryshnikov, is described by Krasovskaya:

[It] was transformed from a makeweight balletic divertissement into a triumphant fanfare of a finale. It was indeed a dance of victory. When Chabukiani came out before the variation, there was a long pause, which intimated an almost languid foretaste of the dénouement. . . . Chabukiani did not take up the usual pose. He crossed the stage with a springy, headlong stride, then suddenly broke off; or, rather, he tore through the stride with a short jump in place with his hand swept upward. Only then did the waiting orchestra begin to

play, and Chabukiani's dance burst like a waterfall with such dizzying tempo and such decisiveness of timbre that even Minkus's unassuming music seemed to take on new power.

The Basils of Yermolayev and Chabukiani represent a pioneering balletic achievement of the twentieth century in the evolution of highly concentrated dance. Krasovskaya writes:

In this triumphant rush, not only did the movements themselves mean something, but the transitions from one to the other, sometimes almost imperceptible, were at other times underscored by a series of "exclamation points." . . . No empty spaces remained in the dance. The balancés, glissades, faillis, that usually play a subordinate role were here given equal emphasis with the most intricate movements. . . . The frenzied whirl of tours chaînés took in the entire huge space of the stage. The dancer would be in one corner one moment and in another the next, before you had time to catch your breath, then in a third. . . . It seemed that you saw before you not one Chabukiani but four of him at once.

The very same passion and Georgian temperament literally exploded the time-honored interpretation of Albrecht. Chabukiani's approach to the role resembled Yermolayev's in its emphasis on social characteristics; but, strangely enough, Chabukiani's dancing was somehow at odds with this aspect. In Krasovskaya's words, "Chabukiani's Albrecht was too passionate for the bucolic episodes of Act I. Consumed with amorous ardor, he seemed neither respectful of the social prejudices nor indifferent to the sufferings of his beloved. In the Act I waltz, for instance, he had to restrain himself from destroying the image prescribed by Adam's music and the Perrot-Petipa choreography. Nevertheless, his unbridled temperament broke through at times. In the mad scene he depicted Albrecht's despair by means of gestures so expressive and willful that they belied the character's supposed coldness."

In Act II, in Albrecht's encounter with the Wilis, Chabukiani's interpretation was perceived as too dynamic. According to Krasovskaya, he disregarded the traditional opening steps of the variation (glissade, cabriole, coupé, assemblé, entrechat six), usually performed as a unity, an uninterrupted stream of movement. Chabukiani broke the sequence deliberately by pushing violently away from the stage to soar above it abruptly and by executing his beats with vehement emphasis. These beats looked especially daring: the academic rule assumed the incline of the torso at an angle of forty-five degrees against the vertical axis, but Chabukiani threw himself back sixty degrees. In the second part of the variation (tours en l'air, pirouettes, chassés) Chabukiani seemed to extend the two air turns by throwing himself back in swift renversés. His sharp, dashing pirouettes were reinforced by the strong movement of his arms, open above his head.

In the finale, contrary to the canon, he did not spread his hands helplessly or collapse at the feet of Myrtha. Interrupting a chain of pirouettes, he suddenly froze, his hands pressed to his chest, as if, in the words of Krasovskaya, "anticipating his next skirmish with the Wilis."

By the fall of 1933 Chabukiani's repertory already comprised two dozen roles, although, unfortunately, he was miscast in many of them. This murky period, with few clear interludes, lasted until the beginning of the 1940s.

In November 1933 he and the talented ballerina Tatiana Vecheslova arrived in New York for a tour which also took them to Boston, Chicago, Detroit, Los Angeles, and San Francisco. Chabukiani's technique was a revelation to Americans who had no conception of Soviet ballet. After the Carnegie Hall performances in January 1934 the *Daily Mirror* went into raptures over Chabukiani's masculine charm and unheard-of technical exuberance.

Later in 1934 Chabukiani returned to his alma mater, the Kirov. Soviet reality looked utterly drab. The Kirov directorate and its Party supervisors did not actually ignore Chabukiani's phenomenal gift; they simply could not make much use of it. The pedestrian drama-ballets of the day have all (with the exception of *The Fountain of Bakhchisarai*) sunk into oblivion. At best, they provided Chabukiani with a small amount of dancing, as in *The Flames of Paris*, in which he portrayed the role of Jerome, the soldier from Marseille. Jerome was a cardboard social mask, a member of that bustling, importunate throng which took the Tuileries by storm. Asafiev's unimaginative score and the naive, insipid libretto were officially regarded as "an innovative dance foray into revolutionary topics," but had Chabukiani not adorned his variation (which he choreographed himself) with breathtaking double sauts de basque, the role would not be worth mentioning.

During this period Chabukiani also created the static, anemic Vaslav in *The Fountain of Bakhchisarai* and a grotesque cameo in Zakharov's *Lost Illusions*. In *Katerina*, the hapless choreographic debut of Leonid Lavrovsky which had its premiere early in 1936, Chabukiani was obliged to play a serf footman in love with the talented serf actress Katerina. Vasily Vainonen's *Partisans' Days* (to the music of the indefatigable Asafiev, whose productivity was not hindered by his total lack of talent) had Chabukiani impersonating the Georgian revolutionary mountaineer Kirim, apparently conceived as a subtle flattery to Stalin—the premiere was in May 1937, at the height of the great terror.

From 1932 to 1938 Chabukiani danced only two new classical roles: the cameo of Acteon in the Perrot-Petipa *Esmeralda* as revived by Vaganova in April 1935 and the crusader Koloman in the newly "socialized" *Raymonda* in March 1938. As Acteon he displayed his wonderful double saut de basque and pirouettes; but, unfortunately, Vaganova had altered Petipa's refined interlude by eliminating the role of the Satyr, and as a result the whole piece lost its consistency and tension. And in *Raymonda* Chabukiani looked simply grotesque. Vainonen, with his librettist, Yuri Slonimsky, had recast the naïve medieval fairy tale as a social drama, attuned to the fashion of Russia's roaring twenties and no less insane thirties. The Saracen Abdul-Rakhman now epitomized the rebellious, tempestuous Orient, while the crusader Koloman (replacing Petipa's romantic knight, Jean de Brienne) served to illustrate the depravity and perfidy of a feudal lord. Further disfiguring Petipa's choreography, Vainonen, for some mysterious reason, allowed the ferocious Koloman to participate in the elegant variation of the four cavaliers in the Hungarian grand pas.

Frustrated and misemployed, Chabukiani again began to choreograph, although he had no real talent for composition. Both *The Heart of the Hills* (June 1938) and *Laurencia* (March 1939) are virtually forgotten today, although *Laurencia* was danced by Plisetskaya and Shelest during the 1950s. Chabukiani's ballets were, in fact, his own technique expanded into choreography that abounded in imaginative combinations but was far from systematic. And although *The Heart of the Hills* was welcomed by the Soviet press as the first Georgian classical ballet, its value is dubious. Judging by Krasovskaya's meticulous description of the ballet, which she had to praise under the pressure of censorship, Chabukiani repeated himself even in the male variations, which had classical steps supplemented with Georgian male dance movements on pointe and demi-pointe.

In this ballet he reworked the topics of Georgian folklore: a poor hunter, Jarjy, is in love with a princess, Manije, who has been betrothed to an elderly Georgian moneybags; the peasants revolt against Manije's father; she perishes. Structurally it echoed *La Bayadère*, although Chabukiani could not produce choreography to match Petipa's. The music by Andrei Balanchivadze (Balanchine's brother) was full of Georgian folk tunes which served the dancing miserably, although Shostakovich praised its "austerity and noble character."

Laurencia was an adaptation of Lope de Vega's peasant drama *Fuente Ovejuna*, set to the music of Alexander Krein. Chabukiani's choice was motivated by the political climate of the 1930s: the ballet, in a sense, represented a Soviet comment on the Spanish Civil War and the Reconquista period. If Petipa's devices could only be glimpsed in the structure of *The Heart of the Hills*, in *Laurencia* Chabukiani totally relied on the master's established means, as seen, for instance, in *Don Quixote*. Petipa's full-length format, with its balance of pantomime, pas d'action, variations for leading dancers, and character dances, was the perfect vehicle for the transformation of a prose drama into a ballet. Chabukiani employed many of Petipa's motifs: the peasants decorated their cabins with fruit and vine leaves; Laurencia made her entrance astride a donkey; the juxtaposition of the rapacious Commendatore, Laurencia, and her fiancé, Frondoso, echoed that of Gamache, Kitri, and Basil. As in *Don Quixote*, Act I featured a motley Spanish crowd which provided a living backdrop for the presentation of the main characters through their variations. The sumptuous divertissement of Act II, the wedding of Laurencia and Frondoso, reproduced Petipa's alternation of character and classical dances: the flamenco was followed by Jacinta's variation, the jota, and the classical pas de six, accurately fashioned after Petipa's grand pas classique. The finale was at first designed as a pantomime in which the Commendatore kidnaped Laurencia, arousing the indignation of her friends; but following the grand-scale Imperial format, Chabukiani unfolded a fourth act, inconsistent and superfluous, in which the people rose and overthrew the tyrants.

The choreographic structure and vocabulary of *Laurencia* were obviously eclectic, although several passages (Laurencia's variation with sissonnes and pirouettes, Frondoso's Spanish dance with castanets) were inventive. Nevertheless, the Soviet press criticized Chabukiani's choreographic dependency on Petipa and Gorsky, urging him on to more daring experiments, though not making clear what these might be.

Chabukiani's work on *The Heart of the Hills* and *Laurencia* prepared him for the revision of Petipa's *La Bayadère* on which he collaborated with Vladimir Ponomarev. Ever since the premiere in February 1941, this has been considered the standard Soviet version. Chabukiani did not attempt to restore Petipa's fourth act, deleted in 1919 because of the scarcity of stagehands and props in postrevolutionary Russia. His concern was mostly with the nondancing role of Solor and the overall structure of the ballet. He enlarged Legat's adagio for Nikiya and Solor in Act I and included a grand pas in Act II for Solor, Gamzatti, four female soloists, and two male soloists, based on Petipa's pas d'action from the deleted Act IV. The Kingdom of the Shades scene became the last act.

Chabukiani devised a solo for Solor that depicted him as a courageous hunter. According to Vera Krasovskaya's biography of Chabukiani:

> He lingered in a springy, sustained balancé and, softly taking off in assemblé, abruptly moved backward, as a hunter retreats and hides himself in the forest. A series of pirouettes alternating with arabesques escaped from his whirlwind of movements as impetuously and softly as arrows shot from a bow by a powerful arm. There followed a series of triumphant steps circling the stage: Chabukiani would spread himself in the air in jeté en tournant, then suddenly soar up in the distinctive pose of an Indian god—cross-legged, with the arms raised and the fingers touching the shoulders. He would swiftly circle the stage, repeating this pattern several times, and then cut the circle with a series of tours chaînés.

In the coda Chabukiani reproduced Petipa's design—cabrioles, saut de basque and entrechat-six.

IN THE AUTUMN OF 1941 Chabukiani's Leningrad period came to an end: he joined the company affiliated with the Paliashvili Theatre in Tbilisi, where he soon became a chief choreographer. His Georgian period covered thirty years, the most intensive and prolific of his life, although apart from *Othello* (1957, music by Alexei Machavariani), he did not choreograph anything to rival *Laurencia*. Nevertheless, he reorganized the Georgian Ballet School and raised the local standard of classical dancing. Thanks to Chabukiani, one of the most gifted Georgian male dancers, Zurab Kikaleishvili (Iago in his *Othello*), became a considerable artist.

In November 1941 Chabukiani remounted *The Heart of the Hills* and then staged *Giselle* and *Les Sylphides*. His new ballets—*The Tale of Tariel* (1946), *Sinatle* (1947), *Gorda* (1949)—orchestrated the themes of Georgian folklore and the choreographic designs employed in *Laurencia*. Stalin welcomed the flowering of classical dance in his native land and showered on Chabukiani both personal and State awards. In 1957 Chabukiani added to his collection the Lenin Prize, for *Othello*.

However didactic and dated *Othello* might seem today, it was distinguished for its consistency of structure and skillful balance of dance and mime scenes. The choreographic action, commenting on the main episodes of Shakespeare's tragedy, unfolded equally through the imaginative dance duets and the static flashbacks depicting Othello's story, starting from his childhood. The elements of Georgian folk dance that seasoned Chabukiani's classical composition created an atmosphere permeated with Oriental passion and violence. The conflict of Othello and Iago was motivated—quite daringly for puritanical Soviet ballet—by their love-hate relationship, almost sensually colored. As Othello, Chabukiani revealed himself as a great tragedian, although his interpretation of the Moor's drama as a tragedy of faith betrayed remained within the confines of the standard Russian approach to Shakespeare's play.

Othello was Chabukiani's swan song as a great dancer and choreographer. His later ballets—*Demon* (1961), *Bolero* (1962), *Hamlet* (1971), and *Appassionata* (1980)—were variations on his earlier works; but this by no means diminished the value of his unique gift and his particular Romantic flamboyance. His larger-than-life portrayals, his zest and ardor made him seem Nureyev's direct predecessor, the genuine innovator, who was seeking new means of expressivity in male dancing. The specter of Chabukiani's artistry looms over Vasiliev's Basil and Frondoso, and his performance of Solor's variation from *La Bayadère*, preserved on film, became a paradigm for the generations to follow. In 1980 his seventieth birthday was lavishly celebrated in Russia; and recently he has worked as a guest teacher and choreographer abroad, mounting his versions of *La Bayadère* and *Laurencia* in Chile and the Philippines. As Plisetskaya once told me: "Dancing with Chabukiani was like dancing with the god of fire—he gave so much warmth and light that made each role and each ballet he ever touched blaze anew."

Albrecht, 1974

VLADIMIR VASILIEV

MANY BALLET COGNOSCENTI in both Russia and Europe consider Vladimir Vasiliev to be of the same caliber as Nureyev and Baryshnikov, if not greater. In France and Italy, where he performs with his wife, Ekaterina Maximova, far more frequently than at his Bolshoi alma mater, he enjoys a reputation as the greatest Russian dancer since Nijinsky. His Western fame seems all the more legitimate as his career never benefited from the uproar of publicity that has accompanied the leap to freedom of so many Soviet dancers during the last two decades. To defection Vasiliev preferred a strenuous and at times self-destructive artistic struggle in the context of the Bolshoi's stagnant routine, survival among the everlasting hardships of Soviet life. Like so many members of the Russian intelligentsia, Vasiliev is determined to cultivate the heritage of Russian culture on its native soil, to prevent his homeland from deteriorating into a barren wilderness.

In a television film about Vasiliev, the dancer, looking at himself in the mirror, evaluates—half mockingly, half seriously—his own qualifications: his feet are as unprepossessing as his overdeveloped body, which could be taller or better shaped to meet the criteria for a balletic Prince Charming. Nor is his peasant's face suitable to the Romantic cavaliers crowding the realm of Petipa.

Nevertheless, Vasiliev's personality is unique, and his artistic development is truly unparalleled in Soviet ballet. I know of no other Russian dancer who has increased his technique and augmented his projection with such natural ease and audacity as Vasiliev. Moreover, with the years his dancing has acquired an intellectual dimension rarely achieved by Soviet artists. His unprecedented evolution has greatly enhanced his individuality. During the 1960s he established the new standards of male dancing that influenced his entire generation.

In his salad days (1958–1970) Vasiliev's technique was second to none. Fyodor Lopukhov in his essay on Vasiliev singled him out as the only dancer who was technically superior to Chabukiani and Yermolayev:

Vasiliev extends balletic limits because his mastery of both soft and hard pliés makes any step possible for him. He executes double tours en l'air perfectly in either direction; his beats are equally flawless in small and big jumps; his cabrioles are astounding and his double cabrioles put Chabukiani's to shame. His double ronds de jambe in the coda of the last act of *Don Quixote* are unparalleled, invariably arousing a storm in the audience. Usually this movement looks like a dangling of the leg. Vasiliev, however, gives his ronds de jambe an ellipsoid shape, graphically visible through every jump. In seventy-five years of ballet I never saw a dancer able to execute this step so nobly. His double tours en dedans with his leg impeccably held in attitude and his arms rounded at his waist like the knobs of a little samovar became a model to emulate.

During the 1960s Vasiliev produced a real revolution in male dancing by demonstrating his style to the entire pleiad of Bolshoi dancers, from Mikhail Lavrovsky to Alexander Godunov. In Leningrad Valery Panov and Mikhail Baryshnikov followed him extensively. One legendary example of his artistry is his manège in the *Don Quixote* coda: after two jetés en tournant Vasiliev would perform a tour en l'air in attitude followed by a tour en l'air with a rond de jambe. This novel combination, repeated several times en manège, still astounds both the Bolshoi habitués and Western audiences.

V LADIMIR VICTOROVICH VASILIEV was born on April 18, 1940, in Moscow, and studied at the Bolshoi Choreographic School. But his first steps were far from making

clear his unique potential. His graduation performance in 1958 was rather drab and went almost unnoticed. He danced the *Nutcracker* pas de deux with Maximova, and it was she who immediately became the focus of attention: her chiseled legs, soubrette charm, and brio had far more appeal to the public than her squat, slightly uncouth partner.

Vasiliev's first public recognition came at a concert performance just after his graduation in 1958. Garbed in black, with burning eyes and pale face, he played the demi-caractère role of the jealous villain Gianciotto in *Francesca da Rimini*, Alexei Chichinadze's ballet to Tchaikovsky's music. His dramatic impact was so overwhelming that he withstood the competition of the tigerish young Nureyev, who triumphantly danced the *Le Corsaire* pas de deux with the exuberant Alla Sizova. Vasiliev's success seemed to point the direction his career would take: character roles such as Tybalt, Hilarion, and Abdul-Rakhman. It was Galina Ulanova who discerned a natural classical dancer in the fledgling Vasiliev, selecting him as her partner for one of her last performances of *Chopiniana*.

But the character of Fokine's dreaming Poet obviously resisted Vasiliev. His huge, impetuous jumps and the brilliance of his beats seemed at odds with the awkward posing and low-key reverie that he sought to reproduce. In 1974 he danced the same role at the gala of stars in honor of Galina Ulanova. His opinion of his own performance was rather harsh: "It was too mannered. The arms and poses are used inappropriately. It is, generally speaking, hardly my domain."*

His first seasons at the Bolshoi (1958–60) saw Vasiliev cast in accordance with his strongly pronounced Russian physique, as a classical dancer with a potent character strain. He portrayed the inspired stonecutter Danilo in Grigorovich's *The Stone Flower* (1959) and Ivan the Fool in Alexander Radunsky's *The Little Humpbacked Horse* with Maya Plisetskaya as the Tsar Maiden (1960). Both roles were decently choreographed, with a strong flavor of national folk dance that wonderfully matched Vasiliev's good-natured, slightly impish Russian face and his grand-scaled manner of dancing. The ease with which he mastered both the demi-caractère dances in *The Little Humpbacked Horse* and Grigorovich's neoclassical vocabulary, with its cascades of

---

*Vasiliev's statements in this chapter are taken from several interviews I had with him in Moscow in 1974, for a projected book on him that was canceled by my departure from Russia in 1975.

intricate jumps and acrobatic lifts, was truly amazing. Nevertheless, the critics still classified him a demi-caractère rather than a genuinely classical dancer.

In 1960 Vasiliev began to take classes from Alexei Yermolayev. Their meeting was to be a powerful catalyst in Vasiliev's transformation into a great innovator. His revolutionary interpretations—Basil, Frondoso, and Albrecht—were all developed under Yermolayev's supervision. These three parts laid the foundation of a vital new style that influenced everyone who followed him in the part.

To Yermolayev's pedagogical credit, he never imposed upon Vasiliev his 1930s concept of Basil as a product of social determinism. Rather, he helped Vasiliev to revamp the old Bolshoi choreography established by Yuri Kondratov and Gennady Lediakh in the 1950s, essentially rechoreographing the role by investing the standard outline with the most dazzling bravura tricks. Into the final pas de deux, for instance, Vasiliev introduced the unprecedented combination of double saut de basque alternating with a series of jetés, then a grand battement through first position, sauté, and fouetté into attitude. Moreover, his new artistic approach to the part happily equaled his unbelievable virtuosity. Vasiliev transformed Basil, usually seen as a make-believe rake and daredevil, into a living character, a happy variation on Beaumarchais's Figaro, a merry barber whose nature is revealed in both his dancing and his vividly acted mime scenes. Vasiliev's portrayal had such vitality that the disconnected interludes seemed a product of Basil's impulses and no longer appeared arbitrary.

He was the real star of every performance, centering all events around his radiant personality. Like Nureyev in his movie version of *Don Quixote*, Vasiliev's Basil made his first appearance in the barber shop, involved in his business as an ordinary member of the Spanish throng, and he remained an "ordinary" man through his flirtatious duels with Kitri, their hilarious escape, and the ensuing pranks that led to their wedding. Unlike Baryshnikov and Dolgushin, Vasiliev never displayed any irony toward his rather primitive protagonist. On the contrary, with the utmost seriousness he carried on through the mime scenes to tackle the dance sequences with an approach both matter-of-fact and flamboyant. Most remarkable was the spontaneity with which he burst into the intricate combinations, without preparation, and ended them abruptly, as if dancing were a child's game. Thus, he achieved that rare unity of dance and pantomime which results in the evocation of a convincingly real character.

Vasiliev's Frondoso in *Laurencia* was similar to his Basil,

but the old-fashioned choreography could not be extended as easily as that of *Don Quixote*. Nevertheless, he diversified Chabukiani's scheme dramatically: to the bravura and smashing vitality of his predecessor, Vasiliev added the sharpness of a cocky Spanish matador, his vigor and his pride. Still looking like a narrow-waisted adolescent, he dominated the stage by the power of his enormous leaps, energetic turns, and charged poses in his Act II variation, which frequently won him a standing ovation. There was one particularly thrilling detail in his portrayal—the Spanish position of the arms and torso that he introduced into his fiery jetés en tournant.

By 1962 the twenty-two-year-old Vasiliev had partnered all the leading Bolshoi ballerinas—Ulanova, Olga Lepeshinskaya, Plisetskaya, Timofeyeva—winning the taxing competition with them. He was universally acknowledged as an accomplished artist and virtuoso. To confirm his early maturity, in 1964 he overwhelmed Moscow in two major roles, Albrecht and Mejnun in Goleizovsky's *Leili and Mejnun.*

Vasiliev's Albrecht blatantly challenged Soviet tradition and was the forerunner of Baryshnikov's portrayal ten years later. Disregarding the prescribed sociological scheme, Vasiliev emphasized Albrecht's sincere love for Giselle and deepened the psychological dimension of the role. In his interpretation Albrecht's drama stemmed from the conflict between his social position and his inner self; in other words, Vasiliev revealed the human drama of Albrecht's identity. In Act I his open Russian face and large, spontaneous gestures intimated that Albrecht's real character was akin to the simple peasant girl's. By no means did he resemble the standard sullen rake; rather, he appeared to be an immature youth hiding behind the mask of a great lord. He was totally engulfed by the freshness of his first love for Giselle, having forgotten the social differences between them. Giselle's death was an emotional shock that compelled him to reassess his attitudes. The result of his juvenile carelessness forced him to face the problem of choice and his responsibility for the consequences. What Vasiliev demonstrated throughout *Giselle* was the evolution of a young man coming slowly to maturity through an agonizing process of self-examination.

His Act II was especially striking in its dramatic consistency. Rejecting the concept of Albrecht as a Romantic poet, Vasiliev orchestrated the encounter with Giselle the Wili as a vehicle for his expiation. He burst into his duel with the Wilis as if seeking death as an ultimate justification. To reinforce the feeling of frenzy, he choreographed his own variation, inserting dynamic double turns and ri-voltades that would convey Albrecht's mental confusion. His amazing histrionics and ebullient dancing expressed a storm of feelings: bitterness, remorse, self-hatred. In the finale he seemed spiritually transformed, shaken, and infinitely tormented. The Bolshoi had never seen such a profoundly intellectual approach to Albrecht.

It was followed by Mejnun, the role that in my view constituted Vasiliev's greatest achievement at the Bolshoi. Goleizovsky's choreography appealingly combined decorative Oriental poses with outbursts of fiery turns and swift jumps. Goleizovsky seemed to challenge Vasiliev's established reputation as a classical virtuoso: in this ballet he had to be both picturesque and emotionally intense. The role unfolded as a sequence of emotional states, fluctuating from amorous longing to passionate frenzy and insanity. Vasiliev displayed a refined, slightly effeminate plasticity in his Oriental poses and the interplay of his supple arms and torso. Most remarkable was the way he exploded the cantilena of languid movements in circuits of impetuous turns and pirouettes. The mad scene in the desert was imbued with an utterly tragic intensity, as Vasiliev shifted from flamboyant virtuosity to decorative poses in a manner reminiscent of Nijinsky's similar metamorphosis on stage. The unabashed sensuality emanating from the vibrations of his body, whose lines seemed stretched out by the Oriental interplay of his hands and neck, was devastatingly poignant.

Vasiliev's ability to combine feral sensuality and subtle lyricism was revealed in Goleizovsky's *Narcissus*, a miniature set to the music of Tcherepnin (1970). Here the flowing or suddenly breaking graphic movements conveyed the half-human, half-savage aspects of a creature infatuated with his own reflection. *Narcissus* was one of Vasiliev's greatest roles, on a par with his Mejnun. His plastique was saturated with the richness of sensuality, the interplay of shadings, stirring and igniting one's imagination.

B Y 1964 Vasiliev had become a Bolshoi legend. The dean of Russian ballet, Fyodor Lopukhov, pronounced him "an unprecedented phenomenon with whom no one could be compared, including Nijinsky." Perhaps this was exaggerated praise, but in the mid-1960s Vasiliev in fact overwhelmed both Russian and Western audiences with his artistry and prowess. In every role, no matter how small, he invariably displayed the rare union of limitless technique and powerful projection. His range was truly breathtaking, and the gallery of his Bolshoi portrayals was strikingly di-verse: the tragic, oversensual Mejnun; the intellectually intense Albrecht; the epic, stalwart warrior of Jakobson's *Shuraleh*; the frenetic, pagan Pan of the "Walpurgis Night" bacchanale; and the grotesque, crotchety Emperor Paul in the film of the Olga Tarasova–Alexander Lapauri ballet *Lieutenant Kije*. In all of these roles his dancing was inseparably blended with his amazing projection.

Although he has captivated Western audiences since his first tour abroad in 1959, Vasiliev the perfect comedian is still to be discovered in the West. An effervescent sense of humor pervaded his Prince in Zakharov's *Cinderella*, turning a minor, ordinary part into a true gem of wit and exuberance. His entrance was unforgettable: like a zany urchin he flew out of the wings, covering the entire Bolshoi stage with gigantic jetés and plumping down on the throne with a half-mocking, half-majestic mien. Equally hilarious was his tennis player in Tom Schilling's *The Match*: a self-confident, foolish boy infatuated with his partner (Maximova) but diligently concealing his feelings behind a mask of arrogant bravado.

With the appearance of Yuri Grigorovich as chief choreographer at the Bolshoi in 1964, Vasiliev's career took a new direction. This ambitious though unimaginative choreographer (a stage director rather than a ballet designer) made much use of Vasiliev's dance potential and theatricality; but his efforts to subjugate Vasiliev's personality to the needs of his cumbersome drama-ballets (*Spartacus*, *Ivan the Terrible*, *Angara*) were misguided and detrimental to the dancer. Still, the beginning of their collaboration looked promising.

In Grigorovich's *The Nutcracker* (1966) Vasiliev projected so much lyrical power and so intense an identification with the role as to seem inspired, as he said to me, "not so much by Grigorovich's rather blatant and one-dimensional choreography as by Tchaikovsky's music—a symphony of farewell to illusions, saturated with the forebodings that pervade his Sixth Symphony." He seemed to blend all the finest aspects of his earlier portrayals—Mejnun's finesse, Albrecht's vulnerability, Basil's gusto—in his Nutcracker Prince. The ease with which he metamorphosed from ugly mechanical toy into handsome prince was spectacular and breathtaking. He radiated the lyricism of innocence and chaste love; the inspired, visible manifestation of Masha's childish dream. In the Grigorovich repertory the Nutcracker Prince proved Vasiliev's best role.

By 1966 Vasiliev was at the peak of his unique technical brilliance, which was rivaled only by the magic of his persona on the stage. He could display his total maturity and

Left: Romeo, with Ekaterina Maximova as Juliet (Lavrovsky), 1973
Below: Albrecht, mid-1960s
Bottom: (left) Spartacus, 1970s; (right) Romeo, with Maximova as Juliet (Béjart), 1979

OPPOSITE
Top: The Blue Bird in *The Sleeping Beauty*, with Maximova as Princess Florine, 1964
Bottom: (left) The Prince in *The Nutcracker*, with Maximova as Masha, 1966; (right) Ivan
The Fool in *The Little Humpbacked Horse*, with Maya Plisetskaya as The Tsar Maiden,
early 1960s

OPPOSITE
Icarus, 1979

Top: Spartacus, with Natalia Bessmertnova as Phrygia, 1970s
Bottom: Icarus, with Maximova, 1979

control in *Legend of Love* and *Swan Lake*, but, in his words, "after Mejnun, the role of Ferhad lost its appeal for me, while my own concept of Siegfried would have required a total revision of the Bolshoi's *Swan Lake*."

Meanwhile Grigorovich, driven by the spirit of Bolshoi monumentalism, began to work on Vasiliev as a new specimen of dancing superman for his *Spartacus*. What Vasiliev achieved in this redundant, fallacious ballet, so meager in its choreography, was nothing less than a miracle. Although he had to do a dance in chains in the best tradition of Soviet kitsch, the dynamism of his split jetés and the genuine lyricism of his adagio with Phrygia were most eloquent. Without Vasiliev the ballet lost its vitality, revealing its eclectic, one-dimensional structure.

Spartacus brought glory in the form of the Lenin Prize to Vasiliev and his colleagues, but the dancer was fully aware of the narrow confines in which Grigorovich sought to incarcerate him. So, like his predecessor Chabukiani and his teacher Yermolayev, Vasiliev started to explore his own resources as a choreographer.

His first ballet, *Icarus* (1968, music by Sergei Slonimsky), bore more of a resemblance to *Spartacus*'s monumentality than Vasiliev intended. Inexperienced in composition, he saturated his production with so many theatrical and choreographic tricks that it looked heavy and even incoherent. As an artistic advisor, Grigorovich was little help. Vasiliev recalled: "He did not encourage me to set *Cinderella* or *Tyl Eulenspiegel*, which I had in mind in those days. Grigorovich used to tell me: 'First I'll mount them, and then you'll follow.'"

In the early 1970s the difficulties that had been simmering between the rebellious dancer and the autocratic chief choreographer came to a boil. The crisis was brought on by Grigorovich's very awkward production of *Ivan the Terrible*, or, more accurately, by its pronounced ideological apology for tyrannical power. This message aroused the indignation of the Russian intelligentsia, which Vasiliev shared: in a country still recovering from the terror of the Gulag and enduring every day the KGB's persecution of political dissenters, Grigorovich's attitude was perceived as an unconditional surrender to the Soviet regime and a betrayal of the ideal of freedom. Despite Vasiliev's distaste for the role of the awesome Ivan, he performed it (in 1974) just to demonstrate that any tyranny is a perverse bigotry, fed by fear or self-destructiveness. "Besides," he said, "dancing Ivan the Terrible, however campy or kitschy it might seem, stimulated me much more than, for instance,

Grigorovich's second version of *The Sleeping Beauty*, which was simply a waste of time." This harsh opinion was quite justifiable. Although the choreography for Desiré was enlarged with an eye to Vasiliev's virtuosity, his artistic response to the revised *Sleeping Beauty* was rather phlegmatic and formal, so that even his acting lost its customary charm. But his portrayal of Ivan the Terrible, the last role I saw him dance at the Bolshoi, was dramatically convincing, though its didactic values certainly prevailed over aesthetic ones.

Vasiliev's dissent from Grigorovich's policy reached a climax when, as a member of the Bolshoi Art Committee, he openly attacked the choreographer's full-length *Angara*, another specimen of balletic socialist realism. The scandal over *Angara* was the outbreak of a war. Vasiliev organized a small opposition group, subsequently joined by Maya Plisetskaya, another of Grigorovich's fervent adversaries. Their struggle continues even now.

Unlike so many of his great colleagues, Vasiliev's problems with repertory and artistic tyranny have not led to his defection. There are many personal and ideological reasons for this. Paramount among them is the fact that as a deputy of the USSR Supreme Council Vasiliev has enjoyed limitless artistic freedom in terms of his tours abroad and collaboration with Western choreographers.

In the latter he is very selective and even fussy in the arrogant Russian manner. While valuing the diversity of Western styles, he does not feel any affinity with many choreographers, including George Balanchine, Jerome Robbins, and Roland Petit. For all his respect for Balanchine, Vasiliev shares a common Russian attitude to this choreographer as "a cold genius, reveling in the beauty of ice." He is much more attracted to "any individual and imaginative style, tearing the umbilical cord with pure academic forms." Among his favorites are Alvin Ailey, Paul Taylor, and the eccentrically theatrical Maurice Béjart: "However eclectic or tacky Béjart may be, he is thoroughly theatrical. And the way he strews his dance gems in *Le Sacre du printemps* or *Romeo and Juliet*! His audacity will never cease to amaze me." He has collaborated extensively with Béjart: his portrayal of Petrushka in France in 1978 was acclaimed in *L'Express* as "a manifestation of the most refined intellectuality." His Romeo in Béjart's transcription of Berlioz's *Romeo and Juliet* was charged with emotionality and an appealing brooding spirit.

In the summer of 1979 a group of Bolshoi renegades headed by Vasiliev and Plisetskaya startled the audience of

Paris. Instead of the Bolshoi's *Giselle–Swan Lake* routine, they showed three Béjart ballets (*Isadora*, *Leda*, and a pas de deux from *Romeo and Juliet*) and three works by Vasiliev—a second version of *Icarus*, a plotless ballet to Mozart's Symphony No. 40, and *Les Promenades*.

Vasiliev undoubtedly has potential as a choreographer, although his work is still an amalgam of heterogeneous odds and ends, shifting from the monumental style of Soviet drama-ballet to pure dance. It is hard to predict the direction he will take. His inclination toward "pure dance for the sake of dance" seems unlikely to win the approval of the Soviet censors, who demand a definite social message from each choreographer. At the Bolshoi of today, such experimentation seems inconceivable.

Vasiliev's most recent full-length ballet, the 1980 *Macbeth* set to a score by Kirill Molchanov, obviously bears witness to his bent for monumental spectacle cast in the form of drama-ballet. According to letters from Russia, *Macbeth* is noteworthy more as a theatrical experiment than as the expression of a distinctive choreographic style. But the moral message of the ballet has been read in Moscow as a polemic response to Grigorovich's *Ivan the Terrible*. It has been described as follows:

> The Witches pass through the entire ballet as instigators of the action. They are performed by three male dancers on pointe. Clad in greyish yellow rags which hang down like bits of skin, they carry death masks on their backs. They function as witches, or as apparitions of death, or as Erinyes smelling blood. They appear against a drab backdrop behind which the sets change.

The latter are imaginative, though typical of the Bolshoi's grand-scale style: a pair of cumbersome movable constructions, decorated with shields and collapsible platforms, symbolically suggesting the fortresses of the fighting armies or the lateral turrets of Macbeth's castle with its serpentine staircases. As the action proceeds, the sets disappear, leaving visible only a throne in the wilderness, to which Macbeth is tied by the Witches.

The ensemble scenes reveal the Bolshoi hallmark in their sweep and scale. The close combat of two armies, one of which is danced by women and the other by men, is particularly expressive. Meanwhile, the solos and duets betray an overliteral rendering of Shakespeare's metaphors. For instance, the Duncan-Macbeth rivalry is mostly conveyed through Macbeth's gestures of reaching for the crown. Lady Macbeth's monologue has her playing with a dagger. The choreographic transcription of such complex Shakespearean images as "Macbeth hath murdered sleep" is too straightforward: it seems Macbeth has only disturbed Duncan's repose.

At present, the most amazing thing about Vasiliev is that, according to all reports, his technique has not declined, although he has been on the stage for a quarter of a century. Roaring enthusiasm still accompanies each of his frequent appearances in Paris, Rome, Avignon, or Buenos Aires. Even if he soon curtails his dancing career in order to concentrate entirely on choreography, his greatest portrayals will remain in the golden book of Russian classical ballet along with Nijinsky's Petrushka, Mordkin's Mato, and Nureyev's Slave in *Le Corsaire*.

BIBLIOGRAPHY
INDEX

BIBLIOGRAPHY

Austin, Richard. *The Ballerina.* London: Vision Press, 1974.

Barnes, Clive. *Nureyev: Twenty Years in the West.* New York: Putnam, 1982.

Baryshnikov, Mikhail. *Baryshnikov at Work.* New York: Knopf, 1979.

Bourman, Anatole, with D. Lyman. *The Tragedy of Nijinsky.* New York: McGraw-Hill, 1936.

Buckle, Richard. *Nijinsky.* New York: Simon & Schuster, 1972.

———. *Diaghilev.* New York: Atheneum, 1979.

Dandré, Victor. *Anna Pavlova.* London: Cassel and Co., 1932.

Dolin, Anton. *The Sleeping Ballerina: The Story of Olga Spessivtzeva.* London: Muller, 1966.

Fokine, Michel. *Memoirs of a Ballet Master.* Translated by Vitale Fokine. Edited by Anatole Chujoy. Boston: Little, Brown, 1961.

Geva, Tamara. *Split Seconds.* New York: Harper & Row, 1972.

Grigoriev, S. L. *The Diaghilev Ballet, 1909–1929.* Translated and edited by Vera Bowen. London: Constable, 1953.

Guest, Ivor. *The Romantic Ballet in England.* London: Phoenix House, 1954.

———. *The Romantic Ballet in Paris.* London: Dance Books, 1966.

———. *Fanny Elssler.* London: A. and C. Black, 1970.

———. *The Ballet of the Second Empire, 1858–1870.* London: Pitman, 1974.

———. *The Divine Virginia.* New York: Marcel Dekker, 1977.

———, ed. *La Fille mal gardée.* London, 1960.

Karsavina, Tamara. *Theatre Street.* New York: Dutton, 1931.

Kschessinska, Mathilde. *Dancing in St. Petersburg.* New York: Doubleday, 1961.

Kyasht, Lydia. *Romantic Recollections.* Edited by Erica Beale. New York: Brentano, 1929.

Legat, Nicolas. *Ballet Russe.* Translated by Sir Paul Dukes. London: Methuen, 1939.

Lemercier de Neuville, Louis. *Les Figures du temps: Marie Petipa.* Paris, 1861.

Levinson, André. *Marie Taglioni.* Paris: F. Alcan, 1929.

Lifar, Serge. *Serge Diaghilev.* New York: Putnam, 1940.

———. *Carlotta Grisi.* Paris: A. Michel, 1941.

———. *Ma Vie.* Translated by James Holman Mason. London: Hutchinson, 1970.

Makarova, Natalia. *A Dance Autobiography.* Edited by Gennady Smakov. New York: Knopf, 1979.

Malmstad, John. "The Mystery of Iniquity," *Slavic Review*, March 1975.

Massine, Léonide. *My Life in Ballet.* Edited by Phyllis Hartnoll and Robert Rubens. London: Macmillan, 1968.

Migel, Parmenia. *The Ballerinas: From the Court of Louis XIV to Pavlova.* New York: Macmillan, 1972.

Money, Keith. *Anna Pavlova: Her Life and Art.* New York: Knopf, 1982.

Nijinska, Bronislava. *Early Memoirs.* Translated and edited by Irina Nijinska and Jean Rawlinson. New York: Holt, Rinehart and Winston, 1981.

Nijinsky, Romola. *Nijinsky.* New York: Simon & Schuster, 1934.

———. *The Last Years of Nijinsky.* New York: Simon & Schuster, 1952.

Panov, Valery, with George Feifer. *To Dance.* New York: Knopf, 1978.

Percival, John. *Nureyev: Aspects of the Dancer.* New York: Putnam, 1975.

Petipa, Marius. *Meister des klassischen Balletts: Selbstzeugnisse, Dokumente, Errinerungen.* Edited by Eberhard Rebling. Berlin: Henschelverlag, 1975.

Rambert, Marie. *Quicksilver.* London: Macmillan, 1972.

Reiss, Françoise. *Nijinsky.* London: A. and C. Black, 1960.

Roné, Elvira. *Olga Preobrajenskaya: A Portrait.* Translated and introduced by Fernau Hall. New York: Marcel Dekker, 1978.

Schaikevitch, André. *Olga Spessivtzeva: Magicienne envoutée.* Paris: Librairie les Lettres, 1952.

Smakov, Gennady. *Mikhail Baryshnikov: From Russia to the West.* New York: Farrar, Straus and Giroux, 1981.

——— [Georgi Shuvalov, pseud.]. "The Earth and Fate: A Eulogy to Maya Plisetskaya," in *Maya Plisetskaya.* Moscow: Progress Publishing House, 1976.

Sokolova, Lydia. *Dancing for Diaghilev.* Edited by Richard Buckle. London: John Murray, 1960.

Svetlov, Valerian. *Thamar Karsavina.* Translated by H. de Vere Beauclerk and Nadia Evrenov. Edited by Cyril Beaumont. London: C. W. Beaumont, 1922.

Taper, Bernard. *Balanchine.* Rev. ed. New York: Macmillan, 1974.

Vaillat, Léandre. *La Taglioni, ou La Vie d'une danseuse.* Paris: Albin Michel, 1942.

Whitworth, Geoffrey. *The Art of Nijinsky.* London: Chatto, 1913.

SOURCES IN RUSSIAN

Alexei Yermolayev. Moscow, 1974.

Bogdanov-Berezovsky, Valerian. *Galina Sergeyevna Ulanova.* Moscow, 1961.

Borisoglebsky, Mikhail. *A Documentary History of Russian Ballet.* 2 vols. Leningrad, 1938.

Gayevsky, Vadim. *Divertissements.* Moscow, 1981.

Grigorov, Sergei. *The Art of Ballet and Sofia Fedorova.* Moscow, 1914.

Ilycheva, Marina. *Irina Kolpakova.* Leningrad, 1979.

Khudekov, Sergei. *History of Dance.* 4 vols. Petrograd, 1914–18.

Konstantin Sergeyev. Moscow, 1978.

Konstantinova, Marina. *Ekaterina Maximova.* Moscow, 1982.

Krasovskaya, Vera. *Russian Ballet Theatre.* 2 vols. Leningrad, 1958, 1963.

———. *Vakhtang Chabukiani.* Leningrad, 1960.

———. *Anna Pavlova.* Leningrad, 1964.

———. "Natalia Makarova." In *The Leningrad Ballet Today.* Leningrad, 1967.

———. *Russian Ballet in the Early Twentieth Century.* 2 vols. Leningrad, 1971, 1972.

———. *Nijinsky.* Leningrad, 1974.

———. "The Romantic Shades." In *Konstantin Sergeyev,* Moscow, 1978.

Kremshevskaya, Galina. *Natalia Dudinskaya.* Leningrad, 1964.

———. *Agrippina Vaganova.* Leningrad, 1981.

Levinson, André. "Olga Preobrajenskaya," in *Russian Ballet.* St. Petersburg, 1913.

Lidia Ivanova. Leningrad, 1927.

Liepa, Maris. *Yesterday and Today in Ballet.* Moscow, 1982.

Lopukhov, Fyodor. *Sixty Years in Ballet.* Moscow, 1966.

Lvov-Anokhin, Boris. "Nikita Dolgushin." In *Teatre* no. 10 (1964).

———. *Alla Shelest.* Moscow, 1964.

———. *Galina Ulanova.* Moscow, 1970.

———. *Masters of the Bolshoi Ballet.* Moscow, 1976.

Martynova, Olga. *Ekaterina Geltzer.* Moscow, 1965.

Messerer, Asaf. *Dance, Idea, Time.* Moscow, 1979.

Mikhailov, Mikhail. *My Life in Ballet.* Leningrad, 1966.

———. *The Dawn of the Leningrad Ballet.* Leningrad, 1978.

Nosova, Valeria. *Two Ballerinas.* Moscow, 1983.

Plescheyev, Alexander. *Our Ballet.* St. Petersburg, 1899.

———. *What Remained in the Memory.* St. Petersburg, 1914.

———. *In the Shade of the Wings.* Paris, 1936.

———. *Serge Lifar.* Paris, 1938.

Prokhorova, Valentina. *Konstantin Sergeyev.* Leningrad, 1974.

Roslavleva, Natalia. *Maya Plisetskaya.* Moscow, 1968.

Slonimsky, Yuri. *Ballet Masters.* Leningrad, 1937.

———. *The Soviet Ballet.* Leningrad, 1950.

———. *Tchaikovsky and the Balletic Theatre of His Time.* Moscow, 1956.

———. *Giselle.* Leningrad, 1969.

Solodovnikov, Alexander. *Olga Lepeshinskaya.* Moscow, 1983.

Surits, Elizaveta. *Soviet Choreography in the Twenties.* Moscow, 1979.

Svetlov, Valerian. *Olga Preobrajenskaya.* St. Petersburg, 1902.

———. *Terpsichore.* St. Petersburg, 1906.

———. *Contemporary Ballet.* St. Petersburg, 1911.

Tchistiakova, Valeria. "Irina Kolpakova." In *Teatre,* no. 2 (1966).

———. "Mikhail Baryshnikov." In *Teatre,* no. 2 (1966).

———. "Nikita Dolgushin." In *Teatre,* no. 8 (1967).

Techernova, Natalia. *From Geltzer to Ulanova.* Moscow, 1979.

Teliakovsky, Vladimir. *Memoirs.* Leningrad, 1965.

Vazem, Ekaterina. *Notes of a St. Petersburg Bolshoi Theatre Ballerina.* Leningrad, 1937.

Volynsky, Akim. *The Book of Exaltation.* Leningrad, 1925.

UNPUBLISHED SOURCES IN RUSSIAN

Egorova, Lubov. "I Remember." Private collection.

Geltzer, Ekaterina. "Pages of Memory." Private collection.

Ivanov, Lev. "My Recollections." Theatre Museum, Leningrad.

Kchessinsky, Joseph. "Memoirs." Bakhrushinsky Museum, Moscow.

Khudekov, Sergei. "Shadows of the Past." Private collection.

Kuzmin, Mikhail. "Diaries, 1904–34." Central State Archives, Moscow.

Shirayev, Alexander. "The St. Petersburg Ballet." Theatre Museum, Leningrad.

Soliannikov, Nikolai. "Memoirs." Russian Theatre Society Archives (VTO), Leningrad.

Vazem, Ekaterina. "Memoirs." Theatre Museum, Leningrad.

Personal interviews with Mikhail Baryshnikov, Elizaveta Gerdt, Alexander Godunov, Fyodor Lopukhov, Natalia Makarova, Alla Osipenko, Maya Plisetskaya, Yuri Soloviev, Olga Spessivtseva, Elizaveta Timeh, and Vladimir Vasiliev.

INDEX

PHOTO CREDITS

A NOTE ON THE TYPE

The text of this book was set in a film version of Ehrhardt, a typeface receiving its name from the Ehrhardt foundry in Frankfort. The original design of the face was the work of Nicholas Kis, a Hungarian punch cutter known to have worked in Amsterdam from 1680-1689. The modern version of Ehrhardt was cut by The Monotype Corporation of London in 1937.

Composed by Graphic Composition, Inc., Athens, Georgia

Halftones prepared by John Shea, New York, New York

Printed and bound by Halliday Lithographers, West Hanover, Massachusetts

Typography by Joe Marc Freedman